Reformat of Chinese State-Owned Enterprises

What China Can Learn from the Practice of Competitive Neutrality Policy in Australia

Xue Bai

Introduction by Jacques Steenbergen
Foreword by Deborah J. Healey

Concurrences, 2023

106 West 32nd Street, Suite 144 New York, NY, 10001, USA
www.concurrences.com
book@concurrences.com

First Printing, June 2023
978-1-954750-13-5 (Paperback)

Library of Congress Control Number: 2023939048

Cover Design: Yves Buliard, www.yvesbuliard.fr
Book Design and Layout implementation: Nord Compo

Concurrences Books

Tributes

Eleanor M. Fox – Antitrust Ambassador to the World, *2021*

Herbert Hovenkamp – The Dean of American Antitrust Law, *2021*

Frédéric Jenny – Standing Up for Convergence and Relevance in Antitrust, (Vol. I & II), *2019 & 2021*

Albert Foer – A Consumer Voice in the Antitrust Arena, *2020*

Richard Whish – Taking Competition Law Outside the Box, *2020*

Douglas H. Ginsburg – An Antitrust Professor on the Bench (Vol. I & II), *2018 & 2020*

Wang Xiaoye – The Pioneer of Competition Law in China, *A. Emch, W. Ng (eds.), 2019*

Ian S. Forrester – A Scot without Borders (Vol. I & II), *A. Komninos (eds.), 2015*

William E. Kovacic – An Antitrust Tribute (Vol. I & II), *2013 & 2014*

Practical Books

Global Dictionary of Competition Law, *D. Healey, W. Kovacic, P. Trevisan, R. Whish, 2023*

Antitrust in Life Sciences, *M. Cowie, G. Gordon M. Thill-Tayara, 2023*

Antitrust and the Digital Economy, *Y. Katsoulacos (ed.), 2023 (in collaboration with Competition & Regulation European Summer School and Conference)*

State Aid & the Energy Transition, *D. Buschle, L. Hancher, M.-T. Richter-Kuhnert (eds.), 2023 (in collaboration with the Energy Community)*

State Aid & National Enforcement, *J. Derenne, D. Jouve, C. Lemaire, F. Martucci (eds.), 2023*

Competition Law Treatment of Joint Ventures, *B. Bleicher, N. Campbell, A. Hamilton, N. Hukkinen, A. Khan, A. Mordaunt (eds.), 2022 (in collaboration with the IBA)*

Information Exchange & Related Risks, *Z. Marosi, M. Soares (eds.), 2022 (in collaboration with the IBA)*

Rulemaking Authority of the US Federal Trade Commission, *D. Crane (ed.), 2022*

The International Competition Network at Twenty, *D. Anderson & P. Lugard (eds.), 2022*

Competition Case Law Digest – 5th Edition, *F. Jenny, N. Charbit (eds.), 2022*

Competition Inspections in 21 Jurisdictions – A Practitioner's Guide, *N. Jalabert-Doury (ed.), 2022*

Perspectives on Antitrust Compliance, *A. Riley, A. Stephan, A. Tubbs (eds.), 2022 (in collaboration with the ICC)*

Turkish Competition Law, *G. Gürkaynak, 2021*

Competition Law – Climate Change & Environmental Sustainability, *S. Holmes, D. Middelschulte, M. Snoep (eds.), 2021*

Merger Control in Latin America – A Jurisdictional Guide, *P. Burnier da Silveira, P. Sittenfeld (eds.), 2020*

Competition Inspections under EU Law – A Practitioner's Guide, *N. Jalabert-Doury, 2020*

Gun Jumping in Merger Control – A Jurisdictional Guide, *C. Hatton, Y. Comtois, A. Hamilton (eds.), 2019 (in collaboration with the IBA)*

Choice – A New Standard for Competition Analysis? *P. Nihoul (ed.), 2016*

PhD Theses

Abuse of Platform Power, *F. Bostoen, 2023*

Bargaining Power, Competition and Innovation, *M. Guignard, 2023*

Competition & Regulation in Network Industries – Essays in Industrial Organization, *J-M. Zogheib, 2021*

The Role of Media Pluralism in the Enforcement of EU Competition Law, *K. Bania, 2019*

Buyer Power, *I. Herrera Anchustegui, 2017*

General Interest

Women and Antitrust – Voices from the Field (Vol I & II), *E. Kurgonaite & K. Nordlander, 2020*

Conference Proceedings

Antitrust in Emerging and Developing Countries – (Vol I & II), *E. Fox, H. First, 2015 & 2016*

Global Antitrust Law – Current Issues in Antitrust Law and Economics, *D. Ginsburg, J. Wright, (eds.) 2015*

Competition Law on the Global Stage – David Gerber's Global Competition Law in Perspective, *D. Gerber, 2014*

DISCLAIMER

This book is based on my doctoral research at the University of New South Wales (UNSW) Sydney, supervised by Professor Deborah J Healey, Professor Leon E Trakman, Professor Mark Williams and Professor Heng Wang. The dissertation was examined by Professor D. Daniel Sokol and Professor Ioannis Kokkoris. Both of my examiners did me the great honour of writing their testimonials to this book.

The book has been slightly modified so that its "scientific apparatus" is up-to-date as possible.

The author declares that there is no conflict of interest associated with this publication. The opinions expressed in this book are those of the author. The Faculty of Law and Justice of the University of New South Wales (UNSW) neither approves nor disapproves of them. The book won the Concurrences PhD Awards in Law 2022, chaired by Professor Catherine Prieto (University of Paris I Panthéon-Sorbonne the member of French Competition Authority), Professor Sylvaine Poillot-Peruzzetto (University Toulouse I Capitole), Jacques Steenbergen (President, Belgian Competition Authority) and Wouter Wils (Legal Advisor, European Commission).

TABLE OF CONTENTS

INTRODUCTION

Globalisation and the resulting interdependency of socio-economic systems has made our world. But it did and does not benefit to all. Change is moreover especially by the more vulnerable often perceived as a threat. We therefore struggle to find a balance between what it enabled us to achieve, and the opposition and inequality that threatens to split our societies. This is illustrated by recent regulatory initiatives in the EU in respect of the national security aspects of foreign direct investments and the impact of foreign subsidies, by US 'Buy American' policies and aspects of the Inflation Reduction Act, etc. These concerns and the search for an adequate regulatory response are not new. Anti-dumping, anti-subsidy and anti-circumvention rules are key provisions of international trade law, and the US have had an anti-dumping act since 1916. We also tend to forget that China is no newcomer in the world economy. It is said to have had the highest *per capita* income in the world in the 15th century, and to have accounted for one third of the world's GDP as recently as 1820 at a time that the US only accounted for 2%.[1]

In the search for a level playing field', state-owned enterprises have always presented a difficult challenge in market economies: when does the support any enterprise regardless of its ownership structure is entitled to expect from its shareholders becomes an actionable subsidy under international trade law? The wave of privatisations in recent decades has made the issue less pressing in the EU. But it is on the contrary much more complex and sensitive when assessing the transition from a state-planned economy to a market economy. And a serene, effective assessment requires a sufficient knowledge of the relevant policies.

The study by Xue Bai of the different steps in the reform of Chinese state-owned enterprises is therefore most welcome. She analyses not only the successive reforms of the relevant legislation and the political developments they reflect. In order to assess the impact of state-owned enterprises on competitive neutrality in China and the extent to which competition law enforcement can help to achieve it, Xue Bai distinguishes different categories of Chinese state-owned enterprises and examines the different types of advantages they may enjoy in respect of regulation, land user

1 Green, S., *Good value: reflections on morals, money, morality and an uncertain world*, London, Allen Lane, 2009, p. 39 referring to the Economist.

rights and obtaining loans. She also looks at suspected competitive disadvantages that may be caused by a greater role of the Communist Party in their management. The thesis brings a survey of mergers involving state-owned enterprises that have not been cleared by the SAMR or MFCOM, it describes infringement cases decided by the NDRC and SAIC, and the role of the Fair Competition Review System in respect of competitive neutrality. Thus, the study shows that only a sufficiently detailed analysis of what has been achieved can help us to see what is required or mostly likely to create an environment in which state-owned and other enterprises can realise their full potential to contribute to socio-economic development on equivalent terms.

The fact that Xue Bai compares developments in China with the Australian responses aiming at competitive neutrality creates an additional added value, especially for European readers. European competition policy makers follow since many years the contributions to competition law and policy of the Australian Competition and Consumer Commission. But I am afraid that, outside the Commonwealth, we are less familiar with other aspects of Australian law and the way the conclusions of the 1974 *Hilmer Review* and the 2015 *Harper Review* have been implemented. She looks at efficiency and fairness objectives and at the net competitive advantages enjoyed by Australian state-owned enterprises as a result of their government ownership. She describes the development of Australian competition law in the context of the development of a competitive neutrality policy, and the extent to which competitive neutrality issues can be addressed by competition law enforcement. We can therefore also learn from the study's chapters that do not focus on China.

Prof. em. Dr. Jacques STEENBERGEN
Former President, Belgian Competition Authority
Professor Emeritus, KU Leuven

FOREWORD

Competition law and policy at their most basic are about creating a level playing field to enable competition on the merits, with more efficient competitors pricing to take market share from the less efficient. The assumption is that this vigorous market competition results in benefits to the economy and to consumers. Legislation prohibiting identified anti-competitive conduct is crucial to this objective, but other issues may impact the level playing field, including market-distorting regulation and some conduct of government bodies which is not caught by a competition law. Competitive neutrality is the principle that firms should compete on their merits and should not benefit from undue advantages accruing solely due to their government ownership or nationality.

This important book arises from a thesis which was commenced by Dr. Xue Bai when the idea of competitive neutrality was understood but little had been done internationally to introduce it in a systematic fashion across jurisdictions. Australia was a frontrunner when a formal comprehensive system addressing competitive neutrality in respect of government bodies which were competing in markets was implemented in the 1990s following the National Competition Policy Review (the 'Hilmer Review'). The European Union already had provisions on state aid, which were adopted to maintain a level playing field between its member states, and which were relevant to some but not all aspects of competitive neutrality. But many jurisdictions had not really considered the issue. Some were focused instead on the advancement of their state-owned enterprises and the creation of national champions. There was no real consideration, particularly in developing jurisdictions, of competitive neutrality as a positive policy initiative which might improve the efficiency and operations of their SOEs.

Against this background, Xue Bai wrote her important Ph.D. thesis on Reform of Chinese State-Owned Enterprises: What China Can Learn from Practice of Competitive Neutrality Policy in Australia, which is the basis for this book. Dr. Bai addressed the idea of competitive neutrality against the background of the socialist market economy in the People's Republic of China, drawing on the experiences of Australia. The thesis adopts the position that the Anti-Monopoly Law of China (AML), and competition policies within the jurisdiction such as Fair Competition Review, have had limited impact on ensuring a level playing field between

State-Owned Enterprises (SOEs) and non- SOEs in the PRC. Chinese SOEs continue to rely on competitive advantages arising from their government ownership and political connections. This is despite significant developments in the enforcement of the AML, the implementation of competition policy, and significant government pressure on SOEs to be more competitive.

In addressing the question, the book thoroughly investigates the reform of SOEs in China over the last 20 years in a comprehensive and fascinating discussion of the various developments and changes in direction over time. It explores in the context of the PRC the advantages and disadvantages of government ownership and political connections specific to the PRC, which impact the level playing field between businesses, focusing on policy changes and administrative regulations, as well as examples from particular industries.

It applies state capture theory to investigate the shaping of the competitive environment by SOEs. Using a functional approach, it then explores approaches to the issue of competitive neutrality. Detailed comparisons with the Australian approach highlight one jurisdiction's longstanding formal structured approach to competitive neutrality. Comparisons include consideration of the formal complaints systems operating in Australia, using specific examples. This part of the book highlights the strengths and weaknesses of the Australian system and provides some possible lessons for the PRC in developing its own system.

Finally, the thesis considers ways in which a competitive neutrality policy might be introduced to China while continuing to accommodate its distinctive socialist market economy structure. It makes recommendations on what might be appropriate for the PRC.

The importance of Competitive Neutrality has been underlined more recently by the adoption by the OECD in May 2021 of the Recommendation of the Council on Competitive Neutrality. This development was after the submission of the thesis but is noted in the book. The OECD Recommendation recognises the need to address government policies that may distort competition and was conceived to avoid undue regulatory and financial advantage granted to specific enterprises, be they private or state-owned. This OECD approach extends competitive neutrality policy to cover government interventions that alter competitiveness between businesses. The Recommendation thus takes a broader approach to the concept of competitive neutrality than has traditionally been taken in Australia. It is particularly appropriate to the situation in the PRC, where government interventions often apply to private businesses.

Finally, the book also notes the impact of the more recent amendments to the AML itself, which among other things, enshrines the Fair Competition Policy Review into the law. Fair Competition Review Policy in the PRC is a comprehensive system of regulatory review to prevent the introduction of anti-competitive regulations throughout the government.

This is a fascinating thesis and book is essential reading for all scholars and practitioners of competition law and policy in the PRC, and those considering competition law and policy internationally. The Concurrences Award for best thesis in 2021 was recognition of its very high quality. I was fortunate to observe the whole process and to gain significant insights into the PRC system of SOEs and the way in which competitive neutrality might be applied. Of a more general note, the thesis provides extremely useful insights into the possible development and implementation of a competitive neutrality policy in a developing jurisdiction where SOEs have traditionally been prominent. The author is to be wholeheartedly congratulated on the scope of the investigation and the comprehensive analysis contained in the final product.

Deborah J. HEALEY
Professor, UNSW Law and Justice, Sydney

ACKNOWLEDGEMENTS

I am grateful to my PhD supervisors, Professor Deborah J Healey, Professor Leon E Trakman, Professor Mark Williams, and Professor Heng Wang. The lessons I learned from them are hard to put into words. Professor Deborah J Healey, thank you for your insightful guidance and unswerving support during my PhD years and thereafter. Professor Leon E Trakman, thank you for your continuous encouragement during a particularly difficult period in my life. Professor Mark Williams, thank you for taking a chance on me. Professor Heng Wang, thank you for being a source of motivation.

I would like to acknowledge the support from the China International Business & Economic Law (CIBEL) Centre and the University of New South Wales. I would like to give special thanks to my review panel, Professor Bronwen Morgan, Ms Gillian Moon and Associate Professor Weihuan Zhou. My heartfelt gratitude goes to Jenny Jarrett, who welcomed me to the University of New South Wales with a warm heart and assisted me through all stages of my PhD journey. One portion of this book rely on my own previous work. In particular, Chapter 3 contains some material from my co-authored article 'Building A Market Economy Through WTO-Inspired Reform of State-Owned Enterprises in China' (2019) 68(4) *International and Comparative Law Quarterly*, 977, and I have made substantive revisions.

My PhD has witnessed the death of my grandmother, Yilan, my father, Temule, and the birth of my daughter, Fiona. I probably would not have continued without the support of my thoughtful friends. In particular, I would like to thank Jeanette King and Joe King, Megan McElhone, Armin Alimardani, Seiko Yamamoto, Melanie Burton, Sophie Burbidge, Jing Wang, Huiqin Jiang, Shu Zhang, Xie Dan, Xiaomeng Qu, Zhenyu Xiao and Huiyang Li.

My final acknowledgement and deepest gratitude are to my family. To Suzanne and John, thank you for your invaluable support. To my partner, Ewan, and my daughter, Fiona, thank you for being in my life. To my mother, Narisi, thank you for showing me the value of hard-working and unconditional love.

To my father, Temule, my biggest supporter. I know how much you would like to complete the PhD journey with me. I dedicate this book to you.

DEDICATION

In memory of
My beloved father Te Mule
1958–2019

LIST OF FIGURES

LIST OF TABLES

ACRONYMS AND ABBREVIATIONS

ACCC	Australian Competition and Consumer Commission
ACCP	Australian Council for Competition Policy
AGCNCO	Australian Government Competitive Neutrality Complaints Office
AIPA	Australian Industries Preservation Act 1906 (Cth)
AMC	Anti-monopoly Commission
AML	Anti-Monopoly Law of the People's Republic of China
CBIRC	China Banking and Insurance Regulatory Commission
CCA	Competition and Consumer Act 2010 (Cth)
CCNCO	Commonwealth Competitive Neutrality Complaints Office
CCP	Chinese Communist Party
CIRA	Competition and Infrastructure Reform Agreement
Company Law	Company Law of the People's Republic of China
CNPC	China National Petroleum Corporation
COAG	Council of Australian Governments
CPA	Competition Principles Agreement
CSO	Community Service Obligations
CSR	Corporate Social Responsibility
FCRS	Fair Competition Review System
FSDC	Financial Stability and Development Commission
Hilmer Review	Frederick Hilmer and Independent Committee of Inquiry into Competition Policy in Australia, National Competition Policy Review
Harper Review	Ian Harper and others, Competition Policy Review: Final Report (March 2015)

IGA-CPR	Intergovernmental Agreement on Competition and Productivity-Enhancing Reforms
IMF	International Monetary Fund
LURs	Land-Use Rights
MOF	Ministry of Finance
MOFCOM	Ministry of Commerce
NCC	National Competition Council
NDRC	National Development and Reconstruction Commission
NPC	National People's Congress
OECD	Organisation for Economic Cooperation and Development
PBOC	People's Bank of China
PC	Productivity Commission
Property Law	Property Law of the People's Republic of China
SAIC	State Administration for Industry and Commerce
SAMR	State Administration for Market Regulation
SASAC	State-Owned Assets Supervision and Administration Commission
SIE	State-invested Company
SME	Small and Medium-sized Enterprises
SOE	State-Owned Enterprise
SPC	Supreme People's Court
TPA	Trade Practices Act 1974 (Cth)
UNCTAD	United Nations Conference on Trade and Development
USCBC	US-China Business Council
Yangqi	Chinese Central SOEs

CHAPTER 1
INTRODUCTION

1.1 Research Aim and Question

1. This research is an examination of the question of whether China, with a substantial number of state-owned enterprises (SOEs) active in the competitive market, can effectively maintain a level playing field through the existing competition law and policy framework and, if not, what strategies or policies it could adopt in order to address this problem.

2. The book takes the position that the current competition law and policy in China have limited effect in ensuring a level playing field between SOEs and non-SOEs. To be clear, that is not to suggest the existing Chinese competition law – the Anti-Monopoly Law (AML) – and policy framework completely fail to address competition concerns caused by SOEs; on the contrary, there are cases that suggest SOEs, like all other market players, are under the scrutiny of the AML and will continue to be so in the future. Chinese competition policy is developing into a more comprehensive policy, and the newly established Fair Competition Review System (FCRS) potentially addresses some aspects of the competitive neutrality concerns caused by Chinese SOEs, namely the regulatory advantages of SOEs.

3. This book argues that the application of the AML and FCRS cannot address all aspects of competitive neutrality concerns caused by SOEs, which leaves the issue of an uneven playing field between SOEs and non-SOEs unaddressed in China's markets. Given the current reform of SOEs has increased pressure on Chinese SOEs to be more competitive, this book argues that now is a good time for China to reconsider just how level the playing field is between SOEs and non-SOEs. In the absence of a competitively neutral environment, Chinese SOEs can rely on competitive advantages generated by government ownership and political connections to take business from more efficient firms in the market. Markets that

allow less efficient SOEs to survive are unlikely to be competitive and less likely to be economically efficient. Adopting tools to ensure Chinese SOEs compete on the basis of efficiency advantages (rather than those generated by government ownership) will greatly benefit China, a country with a substantial number of SOEs active in competitive markets. The expected benefits to China from having an effectively enforced AML and carefully drafted competitive neutrality policy should be recognised from at least two aspects. Firstly, strong AML enforcement limits anti-competitive conduct of SOEs. Secondly, the introduction of competitive neutrality policy would ensure Chinese SOEs compete on the basis of efficiency (rather than by government ownership and political connections). The improved domestic competition environment brought by the introduction of competitive neutrality policy would pressure Chinese SOEs to be more competitive. Adopting the policy may also help to achieve the goals set by the current SOE reform which urges Chinese SOEs to be 'bigger, stronger and more competitive'[2] because the increased domestic competition could ultimately increase their chances of survival in the international markets. Finally, adopting competitive neutrality policy would provide stronger domestic competition and thus benefit the competitiveness of China as a nation in the long term.

4. This book further argues that competitive neutrality policy is often viewed as one component of a broader competition policy. It is very important because it seeks to ensure a level playing field for competition in which SOEs might enjoy competitive advantages over non-SOEs by virtue of state ownership or control. Australia has had a successful experience in implementing a comprehensive competitive neutrality policy and a well-defined compliance mechanism. Hence, a systematic understanding of Australia's approach is essential to determine the most appropriate way for China to implement a competitive neutrality policy, but only so long as that policy adapts to China's distinctive needs.

5. Irrespective of the outcome of the conclusions drawn from this study, the research will add much-needed knowledge to the understanding of the competition policy field and its component competitive neutrality policy. Importantly, it will pinpoint the advantages and disadvantages that SOEs have as result of government ownership and political connections. The originality of the research is evident from the fact that there is very limited literature on the awareness of the need for a level playing field between SOEs and non-SOEs in China, possibly because competition has not been a high priority in China's socialist market economy.

2 Xi Jinping, '决胜全面建成小康社会 夺取新时代中国特色社会主义伟大胜利 [Secure a Decisive Victory in Building a Moderately Prosperous Society in All Respects and Strive for the Great Success of Socialism with Chinese Characteristics for a New Era]' (Speech delivered at the 19th National Congress of the CPC, 18 October 2017) <http://www.gov.cn/zhuanti/2017-10/27/content_5234876.htm>.

1.2 Outline of Research Methodology

1.2.1 Comparative Analysis Approach

Functional approach

6. The underlying assumption of a functional methodology rests on the idea that 'the legal system of every society faces essentially the same problems and solves these problems by quite different means, though very often with similar results.'[3] The three relational foundations upon which that functional comparison is built are

> the similarity relation between the problems in different societies, the functional relation between each individual problem and the legal institution with which a given legal system responds to it, and the equivalence relation between the institutions in different legal systems.[4]

7. The starting point of the functional approach is to find common or similar problems, often termed factual problems, existing in different legal systems. The factual problem this research focused on asks how rules and institutions protect a level playing field in the market when an SOE is engaging in commercial competition.

8. The functional approach, as a practice-oriented approach, makes it possible to compare rules in different legal systems for two reasons. Firstly, rules and institutions that respond to or are designed to solve the constructed invariant factual problem are deemed to be functionally equivalent despite 'the great difference in their historical development, conceptual structure and style of operation.'[5] Accordingly, rules and institutions in different jurisdictions which respond to the factual problems of this research – that is, protecting a level playing field in the market when SOEs are competing – will be considered as functional equivalents to the competition law and policy framework in China.

9. Secondly, the functional comparative method provides discipline when exploring the rules and institutions that respond to the identified factual problems in different jurisdictions. For example, the regulatory measures adopted by jurisdictions to respond to competitive neutrality issues caused by SOEs may present in various forms but at the same time can be considered as functionally equivalent. For instance, competition law and specific competitive neutrality measures were adopted in Australia to respond to the issue of establishing a level playing field in the Australian market between government-owned

---

3 Konrad Zweigert and Hein Kötz, *An Introduction to Comparative Law* (Tony Weir tr, 3rd edn, OUP 1998) 34.

4 Ralf Michaels, 'The Functional Method of Comparative Law' in Mathias Reimann and Reinhard Zimmerman (eds), *The Oxford Handbook of Comparative Law* (OUP 2006) 339, 373.

5 Zweigert and Kötz (n 2) 39, 45.

businesses and private companies when they compete with each other. In the European Union, the Treaty of Rome[6] was adopted by the European Community in response to the problem of maintaining a level playing field between its member states in the EU market.[7] International organisations, such as the OECD and United Nations Conference on Trade and Development (UNCTAD), have responded to the problem of protecting the level playing field in the context of international markets through competitive neutrality frameworks largely built on the Australian approach.[8] The above example reveals that the constructed factual problem is solved by different means in various jurisdictions.

10. The functional approach is thus useful here insofar as it provides a better understanding of foreign rules and institutions. However, the functional approach does not provide a judgment on whether some alternative solutions are better than others,[9] or whether foreign rules and institutions are suitable for adoption by other jurisdictions.[10] As such, this research is also concerned with suggestions for reform of the current state of competition law and policy framework in China by proposing a variant of competitive neutrality policy suited to China's needs and interests. An evaluation of whether and to what extent competitive neutrality policy, as a foreign policy, can be introduced into the context of China will be essential at the later stage (in Chapter 8) of the analysis.

1.2.2 State Capture Theory

11. Rather than examining how the State interacts with firms, state capture theory[11] investigates 'how firms influence the state' or 'the ways in which

6 Treaty Establishing the European Economic Community, Signed 25 March 1957, art 87 (ex art 92) (Entered into Force 1 January 1958). See also Russell V Miller, *Miller's Australian Competition Law and Policy* (Thomson Reuters 2018) 465.

7 Deborah Healey and Rhonda L Smith, 'Competitive Neutrality in Australia: Opportunity for Policy Development' (2018) 25 CCLJ 223, 226–28.

8 Competitive neutrality has been studied by the OECD and has been consistently developing in its ongoing work. See OECD, 'Regulating Market Activities by the Public Sector' (DAF/COMP(2004)36, February 2005) <http://www.oecd.org/daf/competition/sectors/34305974.pdf>; OECD, 'State Owned Enterprises and the Principle of Competitive Neutrality' (DAF/COMP(2009)37, 20 September 2010) <http://www.oecd.org/daf/competition/46734249.pdf>; Antonio Capobianco and Hans Christiansen, 'Competitive Neutrality and State-Owned Enterprises: Challenges and Policy Options' (OECD Corporate Governance Working Papers No 1, May 2011) <http://dx.doi.org/10.1787/5kg9xfgjdhg6-en>; Matthew Rennie and Fiona Lindsay, 'Competitive Neutrality and State-Owned Enterprises in Australia: Review of Practices and their Relevance for Other Countries' (OECD Corporate Governance Working Papers No 4, 1 August 2011) <http://dx.doi.org/10.1787/5kg54cxkmx36-en>; OECD, 'Competitive Neutrality: National Practices' (2012) <http://www.oecd.org/daf/ca/50250966.pdf>; OECD, 'Competitive Neutrality: A Compendium of OECD Recommendations, Guidelines and Best Practices' (2012) <http://www.oecd.org/daf/ca/50250955.pdf>; OECD, *Competitive Neutrality: Maintaining a Level Playing Field Between Public and Private Business* (30 August 2012) <https://www.oecd.org/competition/competitiveneutralitymaintainingalevelplayingfieldbetweenpublicandprivatebusiness.htm>; OECD, 'Discussion on Competitive Neutrality: Note by the Secretariat' (DAF/COMP(2015)8/FINAL, 13 April 2016) <https://one.oecd.org/document/DAF/COMP(2015)8/FINAL/en/pdf>. For UNCTAD literature, see generally, *Competitive Neutrality and its Application in Selected Developing Countries* (UNCTAD RPP, 2014).

9 Michaels (n 3) 375.

10 ibid 380–81. Michaels, for example, summarised that the functional approach does not help in evaluating functionality and purposes of other rules and institutions.

11 It is worth noting that state capture theory is much discussed in political science literature, management literature, public administration literature, and economics literature. However, the literature on state capture theory is too vast to cite in full. For example, George Stigler in 1971 explained how businesses

firms exert influence on the state.'[12] While there are various ways in which firms interact with the state, state capture theory focuses particularly on two distinct types of interactions whereby firms either *capture* or *influence* the state. Capture here refers to the situation where the firm pays illicit and non-transparent bribes to public officers to shape the formation of the basic rules of game,[13] whereas influence refers to the situation where the firm uses its power (in terms of size, ownership, ties to the state, control over labour, and the economic impact on their local communities) to shape the rules of game.[14] The ultimate result of state capture and state influence is that the firm gains advantages (or rent) generated from the power of the state to intervene in the economy.[15]

12. State capture theory has been applied in China to examine the interaction between Chinese SOEs and the Chinese state. Scholars and commentators have long argued that Chinese SOEs, with their inherited connections to the State (i.e. government regulators and legislatures), can shape the competition environment to their advantage. For example, Zheng Lei, Benjamin Liebman, and Curtis J Milhaupt[16] have investigated whether the shape of legislation and the action of legal institutions (like courts) in China can be explained as the result of state capture by Chinese SOEs. They found

---

sought to influence how the state uses its coercive authority to 'buy' preferential regulation and subsidies. See George J Stigler, 'The Theory of Economic Regulation' (1971) 2(1) Bell Journal of Economics and Management Science 3. The concept of regulatory capture is not used in this research as it is not entirely apt for describing the interactions between SOEs and regulatory bodies. Based on Stigler's 1971 concept of regulatory capture, Joel S Hellman, Geraint Jones and Daniel Kaufmann provide a broader definition of state capture as shaping the formation of the basic rules of the game (i.e. laws, rules, decrees, and regulations) through illicit and non-transparent private payments to public officials. See Joel S Hellman, Geraint Jones and Daniel Kaufmann, '"Seize the State, Seize the Day": State Capture, Corruption, and Influence in Transition' (Policy Research Working Paper WPS2444, World Bank Group 30 September 2000) <http://documents.worldbank.org/curated/en/537461468766474836/Seize-the-state-seize-the-day-state-capture-corruption-and-influence-in-transition>. The World Bank in 2019 discussed the concept of state capture, defining it as the exercise of power by private actors – through control over resources, threat of violence, or other forms of influence – to shape policies or implementation in service of their narrow interests. See Andreas Fiebelkorn, 'State Capture Analysis: How to Quantitatively Analyse the Regulatory Abuse by Business-State Relationships' (Governance Global Practice Discussion Paper No 2, World Bank June 2019) <http://documents1.worldbank.org/curated/en/785311576571172286/pdf/State-Capture-Analysis-How-to-Quantitatively-Analyze-the-Regulatory-Abuse-by-Business-State-Relationships.pdf>. The definition of state capture provided by the Word Bank is, in the present context, most appropriate to illustrate how Chinese SOEs shape the formation of the basic rules of the game in their narrow interest.

12 Joel S Hellman, Geraint Jones and Daniel Kaufmann, 'Seize the State, Seize the Day: State Capture and Influence in Transition Economies' (2003) 31(4) Journal of Comparative Economics 751, 752.

13 ibid 755.According to Hellman, Geraint and Kaufmann, 'capture' is defined as the efforts of a firm to shape the formation of the basic rules of game (i.e. laws, rules, decrees, and regulations) through illicit and non-transparent private payments to public officials; firms do not exert direct power over politicians. Instead collusion between firms and politicians providing preferential treatment creates rents that are then shared. By contrast, 'influence' is defined as a firm's capacity to have an impact on the formation of the basic rules of the game without necessarily involving private payments to public officials; firms wield power over the politician. This power derives from such factors as the firm's size, ownership, ties to the state, control over labour, and the economic impact on their local communities which affects the well-being of potential voters and consequently election outcomes.

14 ibid 761. See also Curtis J Milhaupt and Wentong Zheng, 'Beyond Ownership: State Capitalism and the Chinese Firm' (2015) 103(3) Geo LJ 665, 692.

15 Hellman, Jones and Kaufmann (n 11) 755.

16 Zheng Lei, Benjamin L Liebman and Curtis J Milhaupt, 'SOEs and State Governance: How State-Owned Enterprises Influence China's Legal System' in Benjamin L Liebman and Curtis J Milhaupt (eds), *Regulating the Visible Hand? The Institutional Implications of Chinese State Capitalism* (OUP 2015) 217.

that the close proximity of Chinese SOEs to government regulators (such as lawmaking institutions) and political authorities enables them to exert influence on the legal system of China. As a result of this capture, the legal environment in China is 'fundamentally tilted in favor of SOEs.'[17] Other, related research conducted by Curtis J Milhaupt and Wentong Zheng found that, while both Chinese SOEs and Private-Owned Enterprises can be state-favoured firms by engaging in state capture and in state influence, how these firms interact with state to secure state power-generated advantages are different. For example, Chinese SOEs (often as influential firms) can use their inherited, privileged positions to influence the state, whereas Chinese Private-Owned Enterprises (large, successful private firms) need to bribe and build connections with political authorities to capture the state in China.[18]

13. Employing state capture theory offers insights into the power imbalance between SOEs and non-SOEs when they interact with the state, including whether (and how) Chinese SOEs can exert greater influence to their own advantage by using their 'ties to the state, legacies of previous state ownership and more frequent interactions with public authorities'.[19] Moreover, applying state capture theory in the context of China illustrates that non-SOEs – with limited connection to government and fewer political resources – tend to have less interaction with the Chinese state and thereby have lower influence over the rules of the game. As a result, Chinese SOEs will be treated more favourably than other firms in the market, which leads to competitive neutrality issues in the domestic market.

1.2.3 Interdisciplinary Approach

14. Competition law and policy is interdisciplinary in nature.[20] Thus, to answer a complex question such as whether it is possible for China to adopt a competitive neutrality policy and, if so, what form it should assume, the research represents a convergence of three academic disciplines: economics, politics, and law.

---

17 ibid 222.

18 See generally, Milhaupt and Zheng (n 13) 181–83. For example, Milhaupt and Zheng argue that the Chinese state is highly susceptible to capture because, first, China's huge economy and massive state interventions increase the opportunities for, and payoffs from, capture. The second reason is the lack of procedural checks on the process by which rents are generated and allocated. The legal–regulatory system is particularly vulnerable to political influence and Communist Party directives. Thus, Milhaupt and Zheng argue that firms of all ownership types face a choice: grow and prosper by nestling up to the state and demonstrating the capacity to deliver on key Party-state objectives or seek autonomy from the state and be marginalised.

19 Hellman, Jones and Kaufmann (n 11) 763. This research acknowledges that non-SOEs can be treated more favourably than SOEs, which may lead to competitive neutrality concerns. However, for non-SOEs to be treated more favourably, at least in the Chinese context, they need to engage in state capture (i.e. actively build a connection with the government or Party by hiring retired government officials) as a strategy to achieve this favourable treatment. By contrast, SOEs can achieve favourable treatment from the government simply through their inherited government ownership and privileged political connections, as discussed in detail in Chapter 5.

20 Maher M Dabbah, *International and Comparative Competition Law* (CUP 2010) 49.

15. A basic economic analysis is required in order to understand the vital role that economic theory plays in the formation of competition policy.[21] This will entail, firstly, a brief introduction and explanation of some economic concepts and background essential to understanding the goals underlying competition policy. Secondly, an examination is required into the role of SOEs in the Chinese economy as the insights provided by economic thinking are useful in understanding the rationale for regulating SOEs in the competitive environment and in creating a level playing field. This analysis is important at this time, as the current competition regulation framework in China seems to be struggling to keep up with the development of Chinese SOEs accompanied by current SOE reforms.

16. A political economy analysis will help to provide an understanding of the special role that the Chinese Communist Party (CCP) plays in the market in China. The decision to undertake a political economy analysis is based on the following reasons: first, a political economy approach is essential to understand institutional structures in China, for example, how the government engages in the market and what roles the relevant ministries and regulatory agencies play in a market. Second, this approach is particularly important in China, given the vital role of the CCP in decision making regarding SOEs and the role the Party apparatus has played in coordinating SOEs and industrial policy. For example, as detailed in Section 2.3, the important positions in SOEs, especially central SOEs, are appointed by the Party and subject to the Party's disciplinary roles. Third, it is critical to gain insight into such decision making by analysing the regulations and policies (which albeit tend to be general and sometimes ambiguous in nature) issued by relevant ministries and regulatory agencies.

17. This analysis is especially important in explaining how SOEs are organised and to understand the market advantages or disadvantages granted to SOEs compared to private companies. For example, whether to open a certain market or to allow other enterprises (SOEs or private) to enter the former monopoly (e.g. China Unicom's entry into the telecom field) is decided by administrative departments that are often responsible for related implementation.[22] Moreover, it is crucial to appreciate the influence on markets arising from regulations and industrial policies issued by the relevant ministries and regulatory agencies, such as the State Council, State Administration for Market Regulation (SAMR) and State-Owned Assets Supervision and Administration Commission of the State Council (SASAC). For example, in regard to SASAC – the key regulator of China's central SOEs (*yangqi*) – there was a total of 196 SASAC-controlled SOEs in 2003, with the number dropping to 97 in 2018. Since then, to achieve an efficient management system and

---

21 Barry Rodger and Angus Macculloch, *Competition Law and Policy in the EU and UK* (5th edn, Routledge 2014) 8.

22 Sheng Hong and Qian Pu, *Opening Up China's Markets of Crude Oil and Petroleum Products: Theoretical Research and Reform Solutions* (World Scientific 2015) 143. For example, the former Ministry of Petroleum Industry was abolished and its operating assets taken over by three newly created state-owned petroleum firms, China National Petroleum Corporation (CNPC), Sinopec, and China National Offshore Oil Corporation (CNOOC).

develop 'national champions', SASAC has tried to reduce the number of SOEs through mergers and acquisitions (as detailed in Chapter 6).

18. Competitive neutrality policy, as part of competition policy, involves issues such as state involvement in the marketplace, the impact of SOEs on competition, and how to identify the advantages arising from SOEs participating in competition with private companies. Hence, it is necessary to adopt an inter-disciplinary approach to address this complex issue. Attention will be given to the Constitution of the People's Republic of China (hereafter Constitution) to illustrate the status of SOEs in the Chinese economy, in addition to an examination of the influence of the Law of the People's Republic of China on State-Owned Assets of Enterprises, Company Law and Administrative Law in determining the ownership structure of SOEs. China's competition law, the Anti-Monopoly Law (AML), is directly relevant to the extent that it determines whether the AML covers the anti-competitive behaviour of SOEs.

1.2.4 Research Data Collection

19. Government policy data related to SOE reform, are collected in this book and used to analyse whether and to what extent SOE reform policies have managed to change the close linkage of Chinese SOEs with their government owners and the CCP. The research does not attempt to collect every policy change made by the Chinese government and is cognisant of this limitation when collecting policies. Instead, the data collection methodology will be based on the framework developed by the US-China Business Council (USCBC).[23]

20. China's highest legislative body is the National People's Congress (NPC) and its permanent body is the Standing Committee of the NPC. The State Council can formulate 'administrative regulations, and issue decisions and orders in accordance with the Constitution and other laws.'[24] Administrative regulations and related provisions can also be found in the Legislation Law[25] and the Organic Law of the State Council.[26] Thus, the main legislative foundation for administrative regulations is the Constitution, the Legislation Law and the Organic Law of the State Council. There are also two important administrative regulations governing the procedures of administration regulation, namely the Regulations on Procedures for the Formulation of Administrative Regulations[27] and the Regulations on Procedures for the Formulation of Rules.[28]

---

23 USCBC, 'China 2015 Regulatory Transparency Scorecard' (March 2015) <https://www.uschina.org/sites/default/files/USCBC%202015%20Regulatory%20Transparency%20Scorecard.pdf>.

24 《中华人民共和国宪法》 [Constitution of the People's Republic of China] (11 March 2018) art 89 (Constitution).

25 《中华人民共和国立法法》 [Legislation Law of the People's Republic of China] NPC Order No 3 of the President, 13 March 2023, Chapter III (Legislation Law).

26 《中华人民共和国国务院组织法》 [Organic Law of the State Council of the People's Republic of China] NPC Order No 14 of the Chairman of the Standing Committee, 10 December 1986, art 5.

27 《行政法规制定程序条例》 [Regulations on Procedures for the Formulation of Administrative Regulations] State Council, Decree No 694, 1 May 2018.

28 《规章制定程序条例》 [Regulations on Procedures for the Formulation of Rules] State Council, Decree No 695, 1 May 2018.

21. Thus, based on the law and regulations above, the USCBC compiled the administrative regulations and rules into two categories:

> A 'narrow' interpretation that includes only those documents explicitly labelled as administrative regulations or departmental rules, such as 'provisions' (规定), 'regulations' (条例), and 'measures' (办法); and
>
> A 'broad' interpretation that includes regulations under the 'narrow' interpretation and other documents with a clear regulatory impact, such as 'opinions' (意见), 'notices' (通知), and 'catalogues' (目录).[29]

22. This research adopts the broad category in collecting relevant administrative regulations, departmental rules, regulatory documents, and other relevant information; and its focus, in accordance with the research scope, is largely on the central SOEs. In most cases, policies about reform of central SOEs are published by the Central Government in a timely manner.[30]

23. Thus, this research includes only reform policies issued by provincial or local levels of governments when necessary, due to the large number and fragmented nature of such policies, and on account of the difficulty of verifying such policies in a transparent manner.

24. Ministries and agencies examined include: the supervisor agencies of non-financial SOEs, the SASAC; three competition authorities prior to March 2018, namely the NDRC, MOFCOM, and the SAIC; and the current competition authority, the SAMR.

1.3 Outline of the Book

25. In order to address the research question – whether China, with a substantial number of SOEs active in the competitive market, can effectively maintain a level playing field through the existing competition law and policy framework – the following structure has been employed.

26. Chapter 2 establishes a series of key definitions that are necessary to understand this research. An SOE is defined as an entity that is owned or controlled, directly or indirectly, by the government, which covers SOEs fully owned by the government (purely SOEs) and SOEs controlled by the government

---

29 US-China Business Council (n 22) 4.

30 《国务院国有资产监督管理委员会国有资产监督管理信息公开实施办法》[Implementing Measures of the SASAC of the State Council for the Disclosure of Information on State-Owned Asset Supervision and Administration] Guo Zi Fa [2009] No 18, 5 February 2009.

(the largest shareholder regardless of whether it holds more than or less than 50% of shares). Competition policy is constructed as policies designed to promote competition, including competition legislation and government policies. This chapter also finds that the concept of competitive neutrality is not a homogeneous one. Competitive neutrality used in different disciplines might connote different meanings. For the purposes of this research, competitive neutrality is defined as a principle whereby SOEs (or government-owned businesses), when competing with other market participants (or undertakings) in a national market (rather than international market), should not enjoy competitive advantages or disadvantages solely because of their government ownership. The end of Chapter 2 briefly introduces the essential political context, economic conditions, and governmental system of China to better assist readers unfamiliar with the economic and political environment in which Chinese SOEs operate.

27. Chapter 3 illustrates how different stages of reform to SOEs have transformed traditional SOEs into more market-oriented SOEs. It looks primarily at how each stage of SOE reform has changed the linkages between government owners and SOEs, and the presence of the Party within SOEs. The discussion reveals that the current reform since 2013 seems to be heading in the direction of creating highly commercially-oriented SOEs in the market (rather than causing them to exit the market) without fundamentally changing the government ownership and Party connections within SOEs. The Chinese government has, until very recently, not considered the market impact of the expansion of commercial Chinese SOEs a very high priority.

28. Chapter 4 uses a comparative lens to illustrate that the market impact of commercial SOEs has been studied widely in Australia since the late 1980s. The primary recognition that, in the absence of competitively neutral environment, SOEs can inhibit the competitive process by being exempt from competition law. They can also reduce market efficiency by relying on their government ownership-generated advantages to take business from a more efficient firm in the market. This recognition arguably led the Australian government to seek tools to ensure a level playing field in the Australian market. Two comprehensive tools, the competition law and competitive neutrality policy, were adopted by the Australian government to solve the competitive neutrality concerns caused by SOEs in Australia.

29. Chapter 5 investigates the extent of competitive neutrality concerns caused by SOEs in the Chinese market. The analysis of competitive neutrality advantages (and disadvantages) of Chinese SOEs is largely formed around the parameters of competitive neutrality advantages (and disadvantages) of SOEs identified in Australia. However, the analysis also takes into account how the inherited political connection of SOEs may contribute to competitive neutrality advantages enjoyed by Chinese SOEs and whether this connection, in some circumstances, could limit their ability to compete with non-SOEs.

30. Chapter 6 argues that the competitive neutrality concerns caused by Chinese SOEs identified in Chapter 5 do not necessarily lead to a tilted playing field in China if the anti-competitive conduct of SOEs is successfully scrutinised by the competition law and there are competitive neutrality rules in place to ensure that the competition between SOEs and non-SOEs is based on efficiency (rather than government ownership or political connections). The discussion focuses on two principal mechanisms that can promote competitive neutrality between SOEs and non-SOEs in China, that is, the AML and the FCRS. It concludes that these two mechanisms are currently ill-equipped to effectively address the competitive neutrality concerns caused by Chinese SOEs, leaving the issue of an uneven competitive playing field between SOEs and non-SOEs unaddressed.

31. In order to consider whether China could adopt tools to ensure Chinese SOEs compete on the basis of efficiency, Chapter 7 investigates the operation of competitive neutrality policy in Australia at a procedural level, covering the scope of competitive neutrality policy, the complaint-handling process, and the institutional structures that facilitate the implementation of competitive neutrality policy. The analysis in this chapter is considered useful for Chapter 8, which discusses the possible ways to introduce competitive neutrality policy into the Chinese legal system based on the substantive (Chapter 4) and procedural (Chapter 7) aspects of Australia's competitive neutrality policy.

32. Chapter 8 draws together the analyses in Chapters 2 to 7. It highlights the need for China to adopt measures to safeguard a level playing field between SOEs and non-SOEs. It presents legal reform suggestions in relation to the AML, which are based on the findings in Chapter 6. This chapter further provides specific policy proposals that could accommodate China's distinctive political and economic circumstances when introducing competitive neutrality policy in China.

33. Chapter 9 summarises the overall findings of the research and the proposed recommendations to further address the need for a level playing field between SOEs and non-SOEs in China.

CHAPTER 2

BACKGROUND CONTEXT AND DEFINITIONS

34. This book examines whether China, with a substantial number of SOEs active in the market, can effectively maintain a level playing field through the existing competition law and policy framework. In order to address this question, this chapter provides a series of key definitions and context, and is organised as follows.

35. Section 2.1 clarifies the meaning of SOEs as used in this research. It defines the concept of competition law and competition policy in the context of China, and proposes the use of the term 'competition law and competition policy' throughout to emphasise that competition policy is broader than just competition law.

36. Section 2.2 constructs the concept of competitive neutrality in the context of this research after analysing its various meanings in different contexts. The research argues that the root cause of the lack of competitive neutrality in a domestic market is the participation of SOEs in that market. The Section concludes by explaining why SOEs active in the competitive market should raise competitive neutrality concerns.

37. Section 2.3 seeks to provide the reader unfamiliar with China with the essential political and economic context for understanding the environment in which Chinese SOEs operate. In particular, the influence of the Chinese Communist Party (CCP) over Chinese SOEs and the importance of state sector to Chinese economy will be explained. This Section also outlines the executive arm of government responsible for SOEs and competition enforcement. The aim of Section 2.3 is to set the scene for a more detailed discussion of Chinese SOEs in Chapter 3 and to provide a better understanding of the analysis of competitive neutrality advantages and disadvantages of Chinese SOEs in Chapter 5.

2.1 Key Definitions

2.1.1 The Concept of Chinese SOEs

38. The concept of SOEs is relevant insofar as SOEs are considered market participants and carry on business or commercial activities in that market. The definition of SOEs thus mainly serves as a reference point and a tool to facilitate the analysis of whether the competitive environment between SOEs and non-SOEs is being impaired by government ownership. It is useful, then, to start with a review of the concept of SOEs, with the aim of drawing a boundary between them and privately-owned enterprises, before reviewing the concept of commercial activities carried out by SOEs.

39. The nature of SOEs in the context of China is an evolutionary and multi-faceted concept as almost every round of SOE reform (as noted in Chapter 3) has contributed a new aspect to the concept of SOEs. The term 'SOEs universe'[31] is used to describe SOEs in China by the OECD, which points out that 'China's SOEs vary widely by size, ownership structure, supervision and other characteristics.'[32] Similarly, the term SOE in the context of this research is used to describe a cluster concept which encompasses different corporate forms of SOEs.

40. In the literature on SOEs, different benchmarks are used to draw the boundary between non-SOEs and SOEs. For example, based on the ownership statutes, SOEs are often referred to as enterprises[33] that have more than 50 per cent government ownership while non-SOEs are firms that have less than 50 per cent government ownership. By contrast, based on the degree of control criteria, SOEs refer to enterprises in which government holds either more than 50 per cent of its shares (absolute majority shareholder) or less than 50 per cent of its shares but is still a larger shareholder than others. It is obvious that the classification of SOEs by degree of control is broader in scope than the classification by ownership criteria.

41. Some commentators, like Curtis J Milhaupt and Wentong Zheng, argue that ownership benchmarks and 'degree of control' criteria fail to draw a clear-cut boundary between SOEs and non-SOEs in China.[34] They contend that, based on 'the extent of influence' criteria drawn from state capture theory, enterprises without government interests can be considered as private firms. For example, some private firms in China, like Chinese SOEs, can capture government through 'industrial policies, nationalist sentiment',[35] which renders the boundary of the public or private enterprises discussion less relevant in the

31 OECD, *Economic Surveys: China 2017* (2017) 85.

32 ibid.

33 The term 'enterprise' is used interchangeably with company, firm, and entity.

34 Milhaupt and Zheng (n 13) 676.

35 ibid.

context of China.[36] Classification by the 'extent of influence' does show the difficulty of applying labels of 'private' and 'state' to firms that operate in China.

42. However, the problem of classifying SOEs according to 'extent of influence' criteria is that it may result in an overbroad definition which treats any firm from China as an SOE,[37] and may deflect focus away from the anticompetitive effects flowing from state ownership of an enterprise.

43. For the purposes of this research, the criteria of 'government ownership' and 'degree of government control' are used together to maintain the boundary between non-SOEs and SOEs. An SOE in China is here defined in the given context, as an entity owned or controlled, directly or indirectly, by the government.[38] This definition covers SOEs that are fully owned by government (purely SOEs). It also includes SOEs controlled by the State in which government holds either more than 50 per cent of shares (absolute majority shareholder) or less than 50 per cent but is still a larger shareholder than others.

Operational Form of Chinese SOEs

Unincorporated SOEs

44. Chinese SOEs have both an incorporated and an unincorporated form. SOEs that are established according to the Law of People's Republic of China on Industrial Enterprises Owned by the Whole People (hereafter Industrial Enterprises Law)[39] are often considered as an unincorporated form of SOE. At the end of July 2017, there were 69 central SOEs (*Yangqi*) with their 3,200 subsidiaries (valuated at approximately 13 trillion yuan in assets) remaining as traditional unincorporated SOEs or 'industrial SOEs' (as discussed in detail in Section 3.1.3).[40] This unincorporated type of SOE, however, is diminishing through the current reform process in which unincorporated SOEs are being transformed into incorporated types of SOEs following the Company Law[41] (see Section 3.2.3 for discussion). In specific terms, the SOE

36 For discussion of state capture, see Milhaupt and Zheng (n 13).

37 The term 'China, Inc' is used to describe firms operating in China that are similar either though shared organisations, such as party organisations, or, in the case of state capture, firms that are highly susceptible to being captured by the government and thus should be treated as a single entity, a China, Inc. Several academics have used the term. See, for example, Mark Wu, 'The "China, Inc." Challenge to Global Trade Governance' (2016) 57(2) Harv Intl LJ 261. Angela Huyue Zhang argues that treating a large number of Chinese SOEs as part of the China, Inc may from a competition perspective potentially result in a both over- and under-inclusive outcome: 'The Antitrust Paradox of China, Inc.' (2017) 50 NYU J Intl Law & Pol 159.

38 Government here includes government departments, organisations, institutions, or public institutions.

39 《中华人民共和国全民所有制工业企业法》 [Law of People's Republic of China on Industrial Enterprises Owned by the Whole People] NPC Order No 3 of the President, promulgated 13 April 1988, revised and effective 27 August 2009 (Industrial Enterprises Law).

40 刘青山 [Liu Qingshan], '《攻坚克难 浴火重生——国企国资5年改革掠影》 [Conquer the Challenges, Rise from the Ashes: A Glimpse of the Five Years Reform of State-Owned Enterprises]' (2017) (9) 《国资报告》 [State-Owned Assets Report] 10.

41 《中华人民共和国公司法》 [Company Law of the People's Republic of China] Standing Committee of the NPC Order No 8, promulgated at the 5th Session of the 8th NPC on 29 December 1993; amended 25 December 1999, 28 August 2004, 27 October 2005, and 28 December 2013; effective 1 March 2014, art 64 (Company Law).

reform plan requires traditional unincorporated SOEs at the central group level (*Zhongyang Qiye Jituan Chengmian* in Chinese) to be restructured into two incorporated forms – a wholly state-owned company or an enterprise with diversified shares. This restructuring was subject to approval from either the SASAC or the State Council by the end of 2017. For example, the China National Petroleum Corporation (CNPC) was transformed on 19 December 2017 from a wholly state-owned enterprise established under the Industrial Enterprise Law to a wholly state-owned limited liability company under the Company Law.[42]

Incorporated SOEs

45. The incorporated form of SOEs, according to the Company Law, can be grouped into two types: limited liability companies and shareholding companies (or joint stock companies) in which state ownership is often converted to tradable shares.[43] Incorporated SOEs can be divided into two types.

46. Firstly, the most straightforward type of incorporated SOE is the wholly state-owned limited liability company in which the government is the sole investor. The second type of incorporated SOEs is more complex and referred to as state controlled enterprises. In particular, for a firm to be considered as a state-controlled enterprise, the following three criteria should be satisfied:

> (1) The limited liability or shareholding firms in which the government, individually or collectively, contributes more than 50 per cent of the capital or often holds more than 50 per cent of shares;[44]
>
> (2) the limited liability or shareholding firms in which the government, individually or collectively, contributes less than 50 per cent of the capital, but is the largest shareholder compared to any other single shareholder. It implies that the voting rights of the government shareholder 'are sufficient to exert a material influence on the resolution of shareholders' meetings or general meetings, despite the fact that the shareholder's capital contribution or shares account for less than 50 per cent of the total capital or total share capital';[45]

---

42 SASAC '中国石油集团完成整体改制并更名 [China National Petroleum Corporation completes overall restructure and changes its name]' (Press Release, 21 December 2017) <http://www.sasac.gov.cn/n2588030/n2588924/c8374019/content.html>.

43 For detailed history of corporatising Chinese SOEs, see Wai Ho Yeung, 'Non-Tradable Share Reform in China: Marching Towards the Berle and Means Corporation?' (CLPE Research Paper No 48/2009) <https://core.ac.uk/download/pdf/232618359.pdf>.

44 Nicholas Lardy, 'The Changing Role of the Private Sector in China' in Iris Day and John Simon (eds), *Structural Change in China: Implications for Australia World* (RBA 2016) 37, 38.

45 Company Law (n 38) art 216(2).

> (3) the limited liability of shareholding firms in which the government, individually or collectively, contributes less than 50 per cent of the capital, but has the actual control of the enterprise through investment relations,[46] 'shareholders' agreement, articles of association, board resolution or other agreements or arrangements.'[47]

47. It is worth noting here that this research does not adopt the often-mentioned concept of the State Invested Company (SIE), which is commonly referred to as an enterprise in which the government of China owns shares regardless of the ratio.[48] Generally, SIEs are defined based on the shareholding threshold; thus, SIEs include not only the aforementioned two types of incorporated SOEs but also another type of firm (i.e. state-participating companies) in which Chinese government owns shares but not enough to control it.

48. The determination not to use SIEs in this research is due to the current mixed-ownership reform (as discussed in Section 3.2.4) which provides the Chinese government or Chinese SOEs with the opportunity to become a shareholder in private firms. As a result, SIEs in China will be prevalent and using the term SIE will make it more difficult to distinguish between the state and the private sector. Additionally, it is problematic to assume that a company in which government owns less than 50 percent of the capital or is not the controlling shareholder can necessarily benefit from the government investment, leading to competitive neutrality concerns.

Types of SOEs in China

49. The different types of Chinese SOEs are relevant to the research because they provide a holistic background to the argument that Chinese SOEs are an evolutionary concept, and that almost every round of SOE reform (as noted in Chapter 3) has contributed a new aspect to the concept of Chinese SOEs. Different criteria can be used to classify SOEs into different types. Two are illustrated below.

Industrial SOEs, Financial SOEs and Other Specialised SOEs

50. Based on the principle of supervision, SOEs can be largely divided into two categories. The first is supervised by the Ministry of Finance (MOF) directly or on behalf of the State Council. While this category of SOEs is not the focus here, a brief introduction is provided to better understand the state sector in China. The MOF oversees three groups of SOEs. The first is culture-related SOEs (*Wenhualei Guoyouqiye*) which often operate in media/press, publishing and entertainment industries. The culture-related SOE group is largely

46 ibid art 216(3).

47 《企业国有资产交易监督管理办法》 [Measures for the Supervision and Administration of the Trading of State-Owned Assets of Enterprises] SASAC of the State Council; MOF, Order No 32, 24 June 2016, art 4(4).

48 Huiqin Jiang, 'Does Australia's Foreign Investment Review System Discriminate Against Chinese Government Investors? A Doctrinal, Comparative and Empirical Review' (PhD thesis, UNSW 2017) 80.

supervised by the MOF on behalf of the State Council. For example, China Legal Publishing House, a state-owned publishing company, is affiliated to the Ministry of Justice of the People's Republic of China,[49] but supervised by the MOF. The second group of SOEs overseen by the MOF is the financial related SOEs (*Zhongyang Jinrong Qiye*), which refers to 'the solely state-owned or state-owned holding financial enterprises where the functions of capital contributors are performed by the State Council or its authorized agency [MOF] on behalf of the state'.[50] For example, the MOF listed 23 financial-related SOEs in 2015 including state-owned commercial banks (also noted in Section 5.2.3) and insurance firms.[51] The third group supervised by the MOF are 'SOEs whose financial relations are separately listed by the Ministry of Finance'.[52] For example, the MOF performs the contributor's duties on behalf of the State Council to China Post Group Corporation Limited, a solely state-owned enterprise that provides universal postal services.[53]

51. The second type of SOEs under the supervision of the SASAC are often called industrial SOEs (*Gongyelei Guoyouqiye*). Statistics from the SASAC 2016 Yearbook show that, as of 2015, there were 42,411 SOEs (including 97 central SOEs and their subsidiaries) managed by the SASAC.[54] These firms held an estimated 54.5 trillion yuan in state assets and contributed approximately 1.4 trillion yuan in profit in 2017.[55] There are also provincial direct-controlled, municipal, prefectural and county-level SASACs that supervise the SOEs in their regions (collectively called local SOEs). According to SASAC, as of 2015, there were 82,555 local SOEs under its supervision at local levels.[56]

---

49 Ministry of Justice, 'Affiliated Units' (September 2022) <http://en.moj.gov.cn/2022-08/16/c_384194.htm>.

50 《中央金融企业负责人职务消费管理暂行办法》 [Interim Measures for the Administration of Position-related Consumption of Persons in Charge of Central Financial Enterprises] MOF; Ministry of Supervision and National Auditing Office, Cai Jin [2012] No 125, 10 October 2012 art 2 [Non-effective].

51 For a list of central state-owned financial enterprises published by the MOF, see MOF, '中央金融企业名录 [Central State-Owned Financial Enterprises List]' <http://jrs.mof.gov.cn/jinrongleiqiyeguoyouzichanguanli/201501/t20150123_1183782.html>. In addition, Central Huijin Investment Limited is not a government department like the MOF. It is a wholly run subsidiary of the China Investment Corporation (wholly owned by the MOF), China's sovereign wealth fund. See Wu (n 36) 273–5. The members of Central Huijin's board of directors and board of supervisors are appointed by and are accountable to the State Council. By the end of December 2019, Central Huijin held stakes in the following institutions: China Development Bank, Industrial and Commercial Bank of China Ltd, Agricultural Bank of China Ltd, Bank of China Ltd, China Construction Bank Corporation, China Everbright Group Ltd, China Everbright Bank Corporation Ltd, Hengfeng Bank Co Ltd, China Export & Credit Insurance Corporation, China Reinsurance (Group) Corporation, New China Life Insurance Company Co Ltd, China Jianyin Investment Limited, China Galaxy Financial Holding Co Ltd, Shenwan Hongyuan Group Co Ltd, China International Capital Corporation Ltd, China Securities Co Ltd, Jiantou Zhongxin Asset Management Co Ltd, Guotai Junan Investment Management Co Ltd. See Central Huijin Investment Ltd, 'Company profile' (2009) <http://www.huijin-inv.cn/huijineng/About_Us/index.shtml>.

52 Sheng Hong and Zhao Nong, *China's State-Owned Enterprises: Nature, Performance and Reform* (World Scientific 2012) 44.

53 China Post Group Corporation Ltd, 'About Us' (2020) <http://english.chinapost.com.cn/html1/folder/1408/3920-1.htm>.

54 SASAC《中国国有资产监督管理年鉴》[China's State-Owned Assets Supervision and Administration Yearbook] (中国经济出版社 [China Economic Publishing House] 2016) 689 (SASAC 2016 Yearbook).

55 '国资委举行新闻发布会通报2017年中央企业经济运行情况 [Press Conference on Central SOE Economic Operating Conditions in 2017]' (17 January 2018) <http://www.sasac.gov.cn/n2588025/n2588119/c8494483/content.html>.

56 SASAC 2016 Yearbook (n 53) 689.

Discussion in this research will be limited mostly to SOEs managed by the (central and local) SASAC unless otherwise indicated.

Commercial SOEs and Public welfare SOEs

52. SOEs under the current SOE reforms (2013–present) are in the process of being classified as 'commercial SOEs' and 'public welfare SOEs'.[57] In brief, what sets the two apart is 'the scope of its core business'.[58] Commercial SOEs are defined broadly as SOEs whose core business belongs to: (1) industries and fields of sufficient competition; and (2) major industries and key fields concerning national security or national economic lifeline, or that are responsible for specially assigned missions.[59] Commercial SOEs, as market participants, have been exposed to greater competition and are currently under greater pressure to maximise profits. Table 2.1 shows that profit-related criteria have been required in the performance evaluation of commercial SOEs in China.

Commercial SOEs	
Competitive Commercial SOEs	**Special Commercial SOEs**
SOEs operating in the industries and fields of sufficient competition.	SOEs operating in major industries and key fields concerning national security or national economic lifeline, or SOEs responsible for specially assigned missions.
• General financial indicators (e.g. revenue and profits); • Return on state assets investment; • The market competitiveness of these entities.	• General financial indicators (e.g. revenue and profits); return on state assets investment; and the market competitiveness of these entities. • Non-profit aspects like contributing to national strategy, safeguarding national security, and stabilising national economic growth, developing strategic sectors, and implementing specially assigned tasks.

Table 2.1 Performance evaluation indicator for commercial SOEs.[60]

53. By contrast, public welfare SOEs, as the name suggests, are dedicated to providing public goods and services, and are often located in industries like the postal services, water, electricity, and public transport.

57 《关于国有企业功能界定与分类的指导意见》[Guiding Opinions on the Functional Definition and Classification of State-Owned Enterprises] SASAC of the State Council; MOF; National Development and Reform Commission, Guo Zi Fa Yan Jiu [2015] No 170, 30 December 2015, s 2 (Guiding Opinions on SOEs).

58 ibid.

59 ibid s 1 para 2, s 2(1). Put simply, the term 'commercial SOEs' refers to two types of SOEs. The first type of commercial SOEs are those that compete with non-SOEs in a market. The second type of commercial SOEs are those which do not compete, for example, because they are in industries involved in areas of national security.

60 Table by the author, based on the source: 《国务院国有资产监督管理委员会、财政部关于印发<关于完善中央企业功能分类考核的实施方案>的通知》[Notice of the State-Owned Assets Supervision and Administration Commission of the State Council and the Ministry of Finance on Printing and Distributing the 'Implementation Plan for Improving the Functional Classification and Assessment of Central Enterprises'] Guozifa Zonghe [2016] No 252, 24 August 2016.

54. However, the abovementioned differences between commercial SOEs and public welfare SOEs are constructed based on the industries in which they operate. It is important to bear in mind that both commercial SOEs and public welfare SOEs are SOEs in nature, which means that the enterprise will not solely focus on profitability. Indeed, the SASAC confirms this, stating:

> Commercial SOEs and public welfare SOEs … under a socialist market economy … shall *conscientiously serve national strategies and take the initiative to fulfil social responsibilities*.[61]

55. Thus, both commercial SOEs and public welfare SOEs are required to make profits while at the same time satisfying the demands of a socialist market economy.[62]

The Concept of Commercial Activities of SOEs

56. The notion of 'commercial activities' is relevant in that it delineates the applicability of competition law to SOEs. However, the multiple objectives pursued by SOEs, as noted above, render it difficult to determine whether some of the activities of SOEs are commercial in nature.

57. The concept of commercial activities is based on the notion that commercial and non-commercial activities carried on by SOEs can, at least in theory, be separated. The OECD shares this view. For example, its notion of 'economic activities' refers to 'an activity that involves offering goods or services on a given market and which could, at least in principle, be carried out by a private operator in order to make profits.'[63]

58. The benchmark used to measure whether an activity of government constitutes a commercial activity varies across jurisdictions and presents a different picture when one views it through a different lens. For example, three elements have been used primarily in international trade law to determine whether an activity is commercial.[64] Minwoo Kim has identified these as follows:

> (1) [T]he activities must be carried out for profit-making, not on a cost-recovery or not-for-profit basis; (2) the activities must result in production of a good or supply of a service that will be sold to a consumer in the relevant market in quantities; and (3) the enterprise must be able to determine the price on its own.[65]

61 ibid s 2(4) (emphasis added).

62 ibid.

63 OECD, *Guidelines on Corporate Governance of State-Owned Enterprises* (2015) 16.

64 Kim Minwoo, 'Regulating the Visible Hands: Development of Rules on State-Owned Enterprises in Trade Agreements' (2017) 58(1) Harv Intl LJ 225, 242.

65 ibid, quoting Trans-Pacific Partnership (TPP), 'State-Owned Enterprises and Designated Monopolies', ch 17 <https://ustr.gov/trade-agreements/free-trade-agreements/trans-pacific-partnership/tpp-full-text>.

59. In China, at least from a competition law perspective, the concept of 'undertaking' is used to mark the boundaries of activities that are subject to the AML. For example, an undertaking refers to a natural person, a legal person, and other organisation that engages in manufacturing or selling commodities or providing services.[66] The concept of commercial activity in China is thus based on engaging in manufacturing or selling commodities or providing services. In other words, an SOE that undertakes both commercial and non-commercial activities is, regardless of its type and operational form, defined as an 'undertaking' for the purposes of the AML and thus subject to the AML.

2.1.2 The Concept of Competition Law and Competition Policy

General Discussion of Competition Policy

60. It is important to recognise at the outset that competition policy is much wider than competition legislation.[67] Legislation in the form of the AML is easily identifiable. The concept of competition policy, by contrast, is much broader and more elastic in nature than competition legislation as is suggested in the literature. For example, it is widely recognised that competition policy, in its broadest sense, includes not only statutes governing competition but also 'all other government policies that promote competition in the market.'[68] Competition policy therefore comprises competition legislation. Simply put, competition legislation is the core component of competition policy.

61. Besides competition legislation, competition policy also includes 'government policy to preserve or promote competition among market players and to promote other government policies and processes that enable a competitive environment to develop.'[69] On closer examination, the concept reflects three dimensions:

62. First, competition policy, as an arm of government economic policy, is designed to 'promote competition'. Massimo Motta has defined competition policy based on its objective, characterising it as 'the set of policies and laws which ensure that competition in the marketplace is not restricted in such a way as to

66 《中华人民共和国反垄断法(2022修正)》 [Anti-Monopoly Law of the People's Republic of China (2022 Amendment)] Standing Committee, Order No 116 of the President of the PRC, 1 August 2022, art 15 (AML).

67 Brendan Sweeney, for example, argues that competition law and competition policy are not synonymous: see 'Globalisation of Competition Law and Policy: Some Aspects of the Interface Between Trade and Competition' (2004) 5(2) MJIL 375, 378. In Australia, competition policy encompasses all policy dealing with the extent and nature of competition in the exonomy.See Frederick Hilmer and Independent Committee of Inquiry into Competition Policy in Australia, 'National Competition Policy Review', Australian Government Publishing Service, 25 August 1993) xvi ('*Hilmer Review*').

68 UNCTAD, 'The Importance of Coherence Between Competition Policies and Government Policies' (TD/B/C.I/CLP/9, July 2011) <https://unctad.org/en/Docs/ciclpd9_en.pdf>.

69 UNCTAD, 'The Role of Competition Policy in Promoting Economic Development: The Appropriate Design and Effectiveness of Competition Law and Policy' (TD/RBP/CONF.7/3, November 2010) 3 <http://unctad.org/en/Docs/tdrbpconf7d3_en.pdf>.

reduce economic welfare.'[70] However, using the objective to define competition policy rests on the idea that competition policy serves one objective, namely to increase economic efficiency.[71] A more complicated issue thus emerges when the competition policy is designed to serve multiple objectives. For example, the AML, as the core component of the Chinese competition policy, includes economic and direct goals like 'prohibiting monopoly conduct and protecting competition and consumer welfare'[72] The AML also has non-economic and ultimate goals like 'protecting the public interest'[73] and 'promoting the healthy development of socialist market economy.'[74] When conflicts arise, the enforcement agencies need to decide whether to give priority to economic goals or other non-economic goals in the AML. In its broadest sense, any policy that has an element of 'promoting competition' can be considered as part of competition policy. Under this definition, whether competition policy is designed with one goal or multiple goals is less relevant.

63. Second, competition policy can be used to mediate state intervention through regulations, rules and policy decisions produced by the government.[75] As Stephen Wilks has observed:

> Competition policy can be employed to control private power through market-enforcing measures to curb monopoly, cartels, and the exploitative behavior that they allow. It can also be used to control state power by preventing state monopolization (through nationalization), state-induced cartels, and state intervention and subsidies.[76]

64. In particular, competition policy is often directed at being integrated with other government policy to ensure that regulatory proposals do not have an unjustified impact on competition. In this sense, competition policy can function as a 'co-ordination' tool between other government policies, with the purpose

---

70 Massimo Motta, *Competition Policy Theory and Practice* (CUP 2004) 30.

71 ibid 31.

72 For discussion of the goals of the AML, see Xiaoye Wang and Jessica Su, 'China's Anti-Monopoly Law: Agent of Competition Enhancement or Engine of Industrial Policy?' in Daniel Zimmer (ed), *The Goals of Competition Law* (Edward Elgar 2012) 379; Jessica Su and Xiaoye Wang, 'China the Competition Law System and the Country's Norms' in Eleanor M Fox and MJ Trebilcock (eds), *The Design of Competition Law Institutions: Global Norms, Local Choices* (OUP 2013) 194.

73 Su and Wang (n 71) 212.

74 AML (n 65) art 1.

75 Eleanor M Fox and Deborah Healey have noted that, in extreme cases, state law can be employed to organise private cartels and state-granted monopoly rights blocking entry to essentially competitive markets: 'When the State Harms Competition: The Role for Competition Law' (2014) 79(3) ALJ 769, 769. It is worth noting that competition advocacy (which includes all activities of a competition agency that are intended to promote competition apart from those that involve enforcement of the competition law) can also be employed to mediate state intervention through regulations, rules, and policy decisions produced by the government. For more discussion on competition advocacy, see John Clark, 'Competition Advocacy: Challenges for Developing Countries' (2005) 6(4) OECD J Competition L & Pol <https://doi.org/10.1787/clp-v6-art10-en>.

76 Stephen Wilks, 'Competition Policy' in David Coen, Wyn Grant and Graham K Wilson (eds), *The Oxford Handbook of Business and Government* (OUP 2010) 731, 734.

of developing a 'competitive environment'. It is worth pointing out that competition policy is only an arm of the government's economic policy. There are other policies, like industrial policy, investment policy, trade policy, etc., which are likely to overlap, to be consistent with or even to conflict with the conception and purpose of competition policy. As the OECD has noted:

> Governments play a role in promoting competition through the use of a variety of policies; including economic regulation, trade policy and competition enforcement. As a result, some of the policies may share the same objectives to achieve greater competition; whereas others may promote other objectives. These instruments may not always be in line with competition policy; but are desired for public policy purposes (i.e., industrial policy).[77]

65. This is not to suggest a clear-cut division between competition policy and other forms of government policies. In fact, it must be acknowledged that, in reality, the boundaries between these policies are less obvious and perhaps not wholly distinct. For the purposes of analysis, a narrower definition of the competition policy is preferred as it is largely distinguished from other types of policies by emphasising its purpose to develop a 'competition environment'.

The Concept of Competition Policy in China

66. The unique economic and political context of China has in a way contributed to the formation of a different notion of competition policy, which is still evolving. In particular, the notion of competition policy in China is commonly discussed in conjunction with industrial policy. As the literature suggests, the concept of competition policy in China has three layers. These are discussed below.

First Layer of Competition Policy

67. The first layer of competition policy is the narrowest and defines competition policy as being 'equated with the anti-monopoly law.'[78] Under this definition, competition policy is structured around competition legislation, the AML. The purpose of competition policy is thus to support the enforcement of the substantive provisions in the AML. In practice, a series of AML-implementing policies has been issued by the competition authorities in China over the past 10 years.[79]

---

77 OECD, *State-Owned Enterprises as Global Competitors: A Challenge or an Opportunity?* (2016) 116.

78 Qiong Huang and Renfa Yang, 'A Study on Conflict and Coordination Between Industrial Policy and Competition Policy' in Minli Dai (ed), *Innovative Computing and Information: International Conference, ICCIC 2011, Wuhan, China, September 2011, Proceedings, Part 2* (CCIS 232, Springer 2011) 287.

79 Allan Fels, 'China's Antimonopoly Law 2008: An Overview' (2012) 41(1) Review of Industrial Organization 7, 25.

68. Based on the narrowest definition provided above, competition policy in China should be considered in part as 'a series of AML-implementing policies issued by competition authorities'.[80] For example, the Supreme People's Court (SPC) issued Provisions of the Supreme People's Court on Several Issues Concerning the Application of Law in the Trial of Civil Dispute Cases Arising from Monopolistic Conduct.[81] This provision is considered an integral part of the competition policy system in China as it addresses the substantive scope of the AML.

Second Layer of Competition Policy

69. The second layer is built on the first layer and defines competition policy through its purpose to 'preserve or protect competition.'[82] It implies that competition policy includes not only competition legislation and enforcement related policy but also policies that are designed to protect competition.[83] Recent research developments regarding competition policy in the context of China seem to embrace this type of definition.[84] The development of this second layer of competition policy is very valuable, as it can be considered as a positive step forward, especially in the historical context of favouring government intervention over the market in China. More importantly, it also suggests a different competition culture began to appear domestically following the adoption of the AML since 2008.

70. These changes in the direction of competition policy can be observed historically. One obvious stage in this direction was by 'gradually establishing a fundamental role for *competition policy* in China',[85] founded on regulations issued by the Central Committee of the CCP, along with the State Council

80 In the past 10 years, a series of AML-implementing policies issued by competition authorities has included 12 State Council departmental rules, three regulatory documents, and 10 guideline and guiding opinions. See '新闻办就中国《反垄断法》实施十周年有关情况及展望举行新闻发布会 [Information Office Press Conference on the Progress and Prospect of 10th Anniversary of the Enforcement of the "Anti-Monopoly Law" in China]' (16 November 2018) <http://www.gov.cn/xinwen/2018-11/16/content_5341034.htm#1>.

81 《最高人民法院关于审理因垄断行为引发的民事纠纷案件应用法律若干问题的规定》[Provisions of the Supreme People's Court on Certain Issues Relating to the Application of Law in Hearing Cases Involving Civil Disputes Arising out of Monopolistic Acts] Supreme People's Court, Fa Shi [2012] No 5, 1 June 2012.

82 徐士英 [Xu Shiying], '《中国竞争政策的实施与展望—兼论我国基本经济政策定位》[The Implementation and Prospect of China's Competition Policy – On the Basic Position on China's Economic Policy]' (2017) No 1 经济法论丛 [Economic Law Review] 43, 46.

83 徐士英 [Xu Shiying], 《竞争政策研究—国际比较与中国选择》[Study on Competition Policy: International Comparison and China's Choice] (2013) 法律出版社 [Law Press] 4.

84 For example, Li Qing, the Deputy Director General of the Price Supervision Anti-Monopoly Bureau, defines competition policy as all the policies that protect and promote competition in the market. Competition policy is designed to ensure the function of the competition mechanism and realise the decisive role played by the market in resource allocation. See 李青 [Li Qing], '《中国竞争政策的回顾与展望》[Retrospect and Prospect of China's Competition Policy]' (2018) 7 中国价格监管与反垄断 [Price Supervision and Anti-Monopoly in China] 13.

85 《中共中央、国务院关于推进价格机制改革的若干意见》[Several Opinions of the CPC Central Committee and the State Council on Advancing the Pricing Mechanism Reform] Zhong Fa [2015] No 28, 12 October 2015, s 4 (emphasis added).

in 2015. As noted earlier, industrial policy,[86] as part of economic policy, is often considered to be in tension with competition policy.[87] Despite the ambiguous expression, the emphasis on competition policy is likely to have a profound influence on economic policy in that it could potentially provide an answer to the on-and-off struggles between industrial policy and competition policy that tracks back to the drafting stage of the AML.[88]

71. In addition, the Chinese government's commitment to a stronger competition policy has been reinforced by the newly established FCRS and the recent merger of competition authorities into a single entity, the SAMR.[89] In brief, the FCRS is a competition policy designed to protect competition by addressing restrictions on competition that flows from government regulations, which will be explored in detail in Section 6.3.

Third Layer of Competition Policy

72. The third layer of the concept of competition policy, in its broadest sense, comprises all policies affecting competition in the market.[90] Even industrial policies that create national champions can, under this conception, be understood as a part of competition policy. As one commentator pointed out:

> [W]hether any law or government policy is characterised as part of competition policy is sometimes a matter of perspective. Almost any regulation, if it affects the manner in which business is done, can be characterised as part of competition policy.[91]

73. The conception of competition policy noted above is, however, too broad for the purposes of this research. By contrast, the first layer in the conception of competition policy is too narrow as it fails to illustrate the interaction and sometimes conflict between competition policy and other forms of government policy. This consideration may not be important for a developed

86 Industrial policy is not a clearly defined term, however, in the context of competition, it can be conceptualised as government policies that select the promotion of specific industries or a particular group, like national champions. The UNCTAD defines it as government polices 'applied to sectors or industries in order to advantage them': UNCTAD (n 67) 3–4.

87 Wang Xiaoye and Jessica Su point out that 'the conflict between competition policy and industrial policy has been and will continue to be unavoidable in China'. See Wang and Su (n 71) 393 for more detailed discussion.

88 ibid. The tension over industrial policy and competition policy can also be observed in the context of the AML art 7 and its enforcement. See, D Daniel Sokol, 'Tensions between Antitrust and Industrial Policy' (2015) 22(5) Geo Mason L Rev 1247.

89 《国务院关于在市场体系建设中建立公平竞争审查制度的意见》 [Opinions of the State Council on Establishing a Fair Competition Review System During the Development of Market-oriented Systems] Guo Fa [2016] No 34, 1 June 2016 (Opinions on Establishing FCRS).

90 徐士英 [Xu Shiying] (n 82) 4. As the literature suggests, the concept of competition policy in China is still evolving. While SAMR does not specify the meaning of competition policy, it tended to perceive the concept narrowly, as embracing only the substantial provision of the AML, until 2015 (the first layer of competition policy). Since 2015, competition policy in China has been broadly defined, and embraces a range of other policies (the second layer of competition policy).

91 Sweeney (n 66) 379.

country with a well-established market system, but it is essential in the context of China due to the traditional view of favouring government action over market forces.

74. Therefore, this research adopts the two-layer conception of competition policy noted above, which defines competition policy as those designed to protect competition (or the competitive process). Additionally, the term 'competition law and competition policy' is used deliberately to emphasise that competition policy is broader than just competition law. The competition law and policy 'framework', as it is conceived here, includes the AML, and policies that support the substantive provisions of the AML that are to be enforced. It also includes the policies, entirely or partially, that are designed to promote competition, either by mediating the intervention by regulations, rules, and policy decisions produced by the government, or by addressing market distortions caused by government ownership.

2.2 The Meaning of Competitive Neutrality

75. The concept of competitive neutrality is abstract in nature. In fact, the discussion of what competitive neutrality comprises is still unsettled.[92] Thus, this section reviews the literature on competitive neutrality with the intention of building a functional definition of the concept for the purposes of analysis.

2.2.1 Competitive Neutrality in Domestic Context

76. Firstly, competitive neutrality can be constructed as a relatively narrow concept, which is that 'government businesses should not enjoy any net competitive advantage by virtue of their ownership when competing with other businesses.'[93] A similar but slightly different viewpoint defines competitive neutrality as

> a regulatory framework (i) within which public and private enterprises face the same set of rules and (ii) where no contact with the state brings competitive advantage to any market participant.[94]

77. This narrow definition is often found in domestic contexts, such as in Australia, and is arguably based on the understanding that the root cause of competitive neutrality concerns in a domestic market most often arises from

92 As observed by the OECD, there is no universal definition of competitive neutrality: 'Competitive Neutrality in Competition Policy: Issues Paper by the Secretariat' (DAF/COMP(2015)5, 12 June 2015) 3 <http://www.oecd.org/officialdocuments/publicdisplaydocumentpdf/?cote=DAF/COMP(2015)5&docLanguage=En>.

93 Independent Committee of Inquiry, *National Competition Policy* (AGPS 1993) 305 (*Hilmer Review*).

94 OECD, 'State Owned Enterprises and the Principle of Competitive Neutrality' (DAF/COMP(2009)37, 20 September 2010) 11 <http://www.oecd.org/daf/competition/46734249.pdf>.

the participation of government-owned business in a competitive market. Emblematic of this conception is the *Hilmer Review*, which noted that

> the most systematic distortions appear to arise when government businesses participate in competitive markets. In particular, government businesses were often seen as enjoying a unique set of competitive advantages by virtue of their ownership, including exemption from tax.[95]

78. This relatively narrow concept of competitive neutrality reveals the core concern of competitive neutrality – the distortions of competition caused by one particular type of market participant, SOEs.[96] It is necessary, therefore, to give some consideration to the question of why government-owned businesses, by competing with other companies, may cause competition concerns in the market. The question is discussed in detail in Sections 2.2.3 and 2.2.4.

79. Secondly, a broader definition of competitive neutrality is built on the first definition in that it also focuses on the root cause of competitive neutrality concerns. It first defines competitive neutrality as 'completely undistorted competition between rival companies.'[97] Consequently, competitive neutrality concerns arise when competition is distorted in the marketplace, which can be a local market or even a regional market.

80. However, rather than arguing that the participation of SOEs in the competitive market is the root cause of the competitive neutrality concerns, this approach argues that competitive neutrality concerns are caused by at least six institutional sources, including: entry and exit barriers; special conduct requirements; property rights; ownership policy; governmental taxes and fees, and government aid.[98] Thus, the competitive neutrality concerns are not 'exclusively to the competitive constellation between government-owned and privately owned production entities', but can also appear 'between privately owned entities only or between government-owned entities only', and 'between different markets, like favouring one subregion as a special economic zone over other regions.'[99]

2.2.2 Competitive Neutrality in International Context

81. At the broadest level, competitive neutrality can be observed within transnational discussion in which competitive neutrality is often defined as a legal idea that 'no entity operating in an economic market is subject to undue

95 *Hilmer Review* (n 92) 293.

96 ibid. Government businesses in this research adopted the *Hilmer Review* definition, which included government departments, statutory authorities and other government bodies that provide commercial goods or services to the public, private firms, or other government agencies.

97 Martti Virtanen and Pekka Valkama, 'Competitive Neutrality and Distortion of Competition: A Conceptual View' (2009) 32(3) World Competition 393, 397.

98 ibid 399.

99 ibid 397.

competitive advantages or disadvantages.'[100] The 'economic market' under this definition means 'the international marketplace.'[101] This approach arguably provides an expansive definition of the economic market instead of an abstract one. A few commentators share this viewpoint but provide a slightly different interpretation. For example, Thomas Cheng notes that

> the notion of competitive neutrality need not be confined to the public–private ownership context and can be extended to all sorts of scenario in which there is differential treatment of firms competing in the same market.[102]

82. Another interpretation of this definition is provided by Karl Sauvant and others, which extends the ambit of competitive neutrality beyond ownership by arguing that the root cause of competitive neutrality concerns in the international investment context, entails home country measures.[103] The possible reason for this broad concept, in the international context, is that

> governments typically seek the flexibility to support 'their' multinational enterprises [regardless of being state owned or privately owned] in their quest to be internationally competitive, as they expect that supporting especially national 'OFDI' champions will improve the performance of their own economies.[104]

83. In this sense, the competitive neutrality concerns in the international marketplace are caused by government measures adopted domestically, and the concept of the ownership seems irrelevant in this context.

2.2.3 The Concept of Competitive Neutrality in this Research

84. The three different definitions of competitive neutrality discussed above show that competitive neutrality is not a term with a single definition. The components of competitive neutrality are based on different markets, and the source of competitive neutrality concerns encompasses many viewpoints which emerge on many levels. However, the broadest definition of competitive neutrality (the definition in the international context) is of little relevance to this research as it primarily focuses on the competition distortions in the international or transnational market. Particularly, the competitive neutrality concerns caused by home country measures, though important in international trade

---

100 OECD, 'Maintaining a Level Playing Field' (n 7) 17.

101 OECD, *State-Owned Enterprises as Global Competitors* (n 76) 125.

102 Thomas Cheng, 'Competitive Neutrality from an Asian Perspective' (DAF/COMP/WD(2015)49, 11 June 2015)3<http://www.oecd.org/officialdocuments/publicdisplaydocumentpdf/?cote=DAF/COMP/WD(2015)49&docLanguage=En>.

103 Karl P Sauvant and others, 'Trends in FDI, Home Country Measures and Competitive Neutrality' in Andrea K Bjorklund (ed), *Yearbook on International Investment Law and Policy 2012–2013* (OUP 2014) 3, 91.

104 ibid 94.

and investment contexts, is a sovereignty issue. This research argues that addressing competitive neutrality concerns in the international marketplace will eventually rely on the commitment of participating countries to enforce measures at home (domestically).[105] The second definition comes closer to the scope of enquiry for the purposes of this research, but it proposes a range of elements as the cause of competitive neutrality concerns without clarifying which of these elements is a defining factor.

85. Therefore, it is necessary here to construct a narrower and more precise competitive neutrality concept. The first definition of competitive neutrality in domestic context is thus adopted here. It defines competitive neutrality as a guiding principle that SOEs (or government-owned businesses), when competing with other market participants (or undertakings) in the national market, should not enjoy competitive advantages or disadvantages solely because of their government ownership.

86. This definition has two critical dimensions relevant to this research. First, competitive neutrality under this definition is limited explicitly to the national market context. Second, this definition draws the boundaries of the competitive neutrality concept by reference to the root cause of the competitive neutrality concerns, namely the influence government-owned business or SOEs have upon the competitive market. Adopting this definition allows focus specifically on government ownership as the source of concerns when SOEs competing with other enterprises. Consequently, other factors that may affect the competitive environment between SOEs and other enterprises – for example, the policy to support outward investment – fall outside of the consideration of this research.

87. However, it is worth clarifying that competitive neutrality does not become relevant to the question of whether to diminish the existence of SOEs in the competitive market or the even bigger question of whether SOEs should exist in the first place. Competitive neutrality, here, is secondary to the matter of privatising SOEs or retaining government ownership in enterprises. What is most relevant to competitive neutrality (or the concerns that competitive neutrality policy is specifically designed to address) is when a government-owned enterprise or an SOE is engaging in commercial competition, how a neutral market environment can be established and maintained without changing the innate nature (including the government ownership) of the enterprise.[106]

88. Therefore, it is not the existence of SOEs that causes competitive neutrality concerns but rather the existence of SOEs in the competitive market that gives rise to competitive neutrality concerns. As the OECD has noted: 'Competitive

105 OECD, *State-Owned Enterprises as Global Competitors* (n 76) 68, 126.

106 Rennie and Lindsay (n 7) 14. For example, as discussed in Chapter 4, competitive neutrality policy is designed to ensure that competition between SOEs and non-SOEs is based on efficiency rather than on who can benefit from government ownership and political connections. Whether SOEs should be in the market in the first place is a broader government policy decision and outside the realm of the competitive neutrality policy.

neutrality problems can arise when competition is distorted by the advantages or disadvantages that some government businesses have due to their government ownership.'[107] Accordingly, the question of why the commercial activities of SOEs (or government-owned entities) may be advantaged or disadvantaged because of their government ownership is worth further analysis to more fully understand the concept of competitive neutrality.

2.2.4 Competitive Neutrality Concerns Caused by SOEs

89. This section aims to explain why the commercial activities of SOEs may cause competitive neutrality concerns in the market. Firstly, the use of terms 'competitive neutrality advantages' and 'competitive neutrality disadvantages' in this research may need some qualification. The term 'competitive advantage' is differentiated from the 'competitive neutrality advantage'. Competitive advantage, as defined by Michael Porter, allows firms to succeed when competing with their rivals through either 'the ability to perform the required activities at a collectively lower cost than rivals or to perform some activities in unique ways that create non-price buyer value and support a premium price' (or both).[108] By contrast, 'competitive neutrality advantage' may be understand as a type of competitive advantage, however, 'competitive neutrality advantages' are the result of government ownership, rather than the ability to perform at lower cost or the ability to generate higher revenue.

90. The government ownership-generated competitive advantage is harmful in two respects. First, it sends the signal to firms that, in order to succeed against rivals in the market, they need to pursue government ownership rather than focusing on performing activities more efficiently than their competitors or achieving higher revenue through creating differentiation.[109] Second, government ownership-generated competitive advantage is harmful because it distorts competition between government-owned firms and non-government firms. For example, a government-owned firm, due to its inherent government ownership, enjoys competitive advantages (such as a lower interest rate) which allow it to undercut its more efficient rivals in the competition process and undermine economic efficiency.[110] As noted by the OECD, 'when goods and services are no longer produced by those who can do it most efficiently [this] leads to lower real incomes and sub-optimal use of scare resources'.[111]

107 OECD, 'Regulating Market Activities by the Public Sector' (n 7) 7.

108 Michael E Porter, *On Competition* (HBR Press 2008) 368. See also Michael E Porter, *The Competitive Advantage of Nations* (Free Press 1998) 69.

109 The low-cost firms produce a given output using fewer inputs than competitors require. The differentiated firm achieves higher revenues per unit than competitors. Therefore, competitive advantage of either type translates to higher productivity than that of competitors. See Porter, *The Competitive Advantage of Nations* (n 107) 69.

110 Editorial, 'Competitive Neutrality: At the Crossroads of Reform' (2018) 25 CCLJ 219.

111 OECD, 'Maintaining a Level Playing Field' (n 7) 22.

91. In Australia, the term 'net competitive advantages'[112] is employed by the Australian government to differentiate competitive advantage gained through government ownership from other forms of competitive advantages enjoyed by SOEs resulting, for example, from 'better performance, superior efficiency, better technology or superior management skills.'[113] By contrast, the disadvantages of this form can be termed 'net competitive disadvantages'. The phrase 'undue competitive advantages or disadvantages' is used by the OECD to express a similar intent, that competitive advantages (or disadvantages) obtained in consequence of government ownership is considered 'undue'.[114]

92. The terms 'competitive neutrality advantages' and 'competitive neutrality disadvantages' are thus used for ease of reference in this research. In particular, 'competitive neutrality advantages or disadvantages' is used to characterise the form of the competitive advantages or disadvantages by SOEs resulting from their government ownership. It generally implies that the competitive neutrality advantages or disadvantages granted to SOEs 'are not available' to those rival firms that do not have government ownership (or non-SOE rivals).[115] In addition, the use of competitive neutrality advantages or disadvantages implies that these types of competitive advantages are the result of government ownership, not other forms of competitive advantage (or disadvantage) created by, for example, a more effective use of resources.

93. Second, assessing the competitive neutrality advantages or disadvantages of SOEs will depend largely on the national context as 'the extent of competitive neutrality problems differs between countries because of history, structure and political culture.'[116] Even within one jurisdiction, the process of identifying competitive neutrality advantages or disadvantages of SOEs may be difficult to do with precision or costly for the authority to do with accuracy.[117] For example, the OECD pointed out that '[c]alculating the net competitive edge or hardship borne by an SOE in relation to actual or potential competitors is complex.'[118] Currently, there is no specific technical assessment framework that is tailored to identifying the competitive neutrality advantages or disadvantages of an SOE. This absense of a technical framework renders the further development of competitive neutrality policy uncertain.[119] Acknowledging this difficulty, this research does not attempt to develop a technical framework for assessing competitive neutrality advantages or disadvantages. Instead, it relies

112 *Hilmer Review* (n 92) 297.

113 Capobianco and Christiansen (n 7) 5.

114 OECD, *State-Owned Enterprises as Global Competitors* (n 76) 125.

115 Capobianco and Christiansen (n 7) 6.

116 OECD, 'Regulating Market Activities by the Public Sector' (n 7) 8.

117 The difficulty of assessing net competitive advantages or disadvantages in the context of Australia is recognised in the *Hilmer Review* (n 92) 297.

118 OECD, 'Competitive Neutrality in Competition Policy' (n 91) 7.

119 OECD, 'Scoping Note on Competitive Neutrality as a Long-Term Theme for 2019–2020' (DAF/COMP/WD(2018)5, 23 April 2018) 4. <http://www.oecd.org/officialdocuments/publicdisplaydocumentpdf/?cote=DAF/COMP/WD(2018)5&docLanguage=En>.

on a wide range of research and literature specifically related to determining competitive neutrality advantages or disadvantages of SOEs, to facilitate the analysis of competitive neutrality concerns caused by Chinese SOEs.

Competitive Neutrality Advantages of SOEs

94. The existing literature in the OECD provides a high-level generalised evaluation of a full range of indicators for competitive neutrality concerns. It provides useful guidance for jurisdictions to consider in their specific national contexts on whether to 'implement competitive neutrality policies in practice.'[120] Examples of competitive neutrality advantages that SOEs may have include, but are not limited to, the following:

- no requirement to earn a rate of return, or to pay dividends;
- exemptions from a various national, regional, or local government taxes and charges, and from legislation or regulations that affect the same activity when carried out by a private sector business;
- access to debt at rates below the market rate, and to various publicly resources [like land or nature resources] free of charge, or at the rates below the actual cost of provision;
- the opportunity to cross-subsidise commercial activities from subsidised activities, and the ability to disadvantage competitors because of the dual role in regulating the industry and providing competing commercial services.[121]

95. The above listed competitive neutrality advantages of SOEs may have potentially distortive effects on competition. Take, for example, the perceived competitive neutrality advantages of access to debt at rates below the market rate; SOEs, due to their government ownership status (and sometimes politically privileged positions), are often considered to 'have access to favourable credit rates or enjoy government-provided credit guarantees which reduce their cost of borrowing.'[122] As a consequence, SOEs are able to under-price non-SOEs rivals because the reduced operational costs through cheaper capital when providing commercial goods or services.[123]

96. Debt advantages to SOEs, as noted above, from a competition perspective, tend to be problematic. First, these advantages could provide opportunity for SOEs to undercut competition from their non-SOE rivals in the long run; that is, the cost of providing the same goods or services (hypothetically) by non-SOEs will be higher than SOEs, as the cost of borrowing by non-SOEs

120 OECD, 'Maintaining a Level Playing Field' (n 7) 3.

121 OECD, 'Regulating Market Activities by the Public Sector' (n 7) 33–34.

122 OECD, 'Maintaining a Level Playing Field' (n 7) 93.

123 ibid 92.

is higher than the borrowing costs of SOEs. As a consequence, the price charged by non-SOEs (which needs to reflect costs) will be higher than their SOE competitors. Alternatively, if the price of goods and services charged by non-SOEs is the same as SOEs, it is likely that non-SOEs will make less profit in the long run.

97. Second, the debt advantages to SOEs have the potential to crowd out non-SOE competitors from borrowing at financing institutions such as state banks.[124] A concrete example of non-SOE borrowers being crowded out by SOE borrowers is provided in the context of China at Section 5.2.3. The rise of shadow banking in China also indirectly shows that non-SOEs are being squeezed out of the formal banking sector.

Competitive Neutrality Disadvantages of SOEs

98. Some common competitive neutrality disadvantages of SOEs may include, but are not limited to, the following:

- Accountability and/or reporting requirement which have no equivalent for a private sector business supplying the same goods or services;
- Requirement to pay excessive dividends;
- Restrictions on financial structure and financial management which have no equivalent in the private sector;
- Less flexibility or discretion in managing operations because of the policies and/or practices of public-sector supervisory agencies;
- Requirement to pay higher levels of employer superannuation contributions or remuneration;
- Requirement to provide non-commercial goods or services without compensation.[125]

99. The perceived competitive neutrality disadvantages of SOEs can have potentially distortive effects on competition. As discussed in Chapter 5, while all firms in China are required to include the governance of the Communist Party in their articles of incorporation, the Party Committee in each SOE is required to be involved in the decision-making process of that SOE. Such a requirement may reduce the operational autonomy (especially that of management) of SOEs because it may increase the time and costs for the SOE decision-making process (compared to non-SOEs). Additionally, government involvement in firms provides the opportunity for government to reshape the agenda of the firms (often for reasons aligned to public policy), particularly when government is the controlling shareholder. For example, in response to

124 ibid 93.

125 OECD, 'Regulating Market Activities by the Public Sector' (n 7) 297.

the 2015 equity market meltdown in China, 'SASAC ordered publicly-listed SOEs subsidiaries not to sell shares and to purchase more shares in order to safeguard market stability.'[126]

2.3 Background Context to Understanding SOEs in China

2.3.1 Political Context of China

100. Since the founding of the People's Republic China in 1949, the CCP has been the single ruling party and sits at the top of the political system.[127] The highest leading body, according to the Party's Constitution,[128] is the National Congress of the Communist Party of China (or CPC National Congress), which is held once every five years.[129] President Xi Jinping was selected in 2012 at the 18th CPC National Congress as Party General Secretary, which constitutes one of the most authoritative positions in the Chinese political system.[130] At the most recent CPC National Congress, the 19th CPC National Congress of 18 October 2017, President Xi Jinping outlined in his speech new priorities for China. These included the acceleration of economic reforms to 'ensure … fair and orderly competition, and that business survival is determined by competition' but at the same time, to 'support state capital in becoming stronger, doing better, and growing bigger, and take effective measures to prevent the loss of state assets.'[131] The Central Committee of the CCP carries out these duties of the National Party Congress when the Congress is not in session.[132]

101. The Party's leadership role is not explicitly stated in any of the articles of the Constitution which, at first glance, presents the idea that the State and the Party are formally separate. However, as pointed out by many observers, the Constitution guarantees the leading role of the CCP five times in its Preamble.[133] Fundamentally, China's constitutional structure does not include a comparable division of powers adopted by Western countries. Formally,

126 Daniel H Rosen, Wendy Leutert and Shan Guo, 'Missing Link: Corporate Governance in China's State Sector' (Asia Society November 2018) 13 <https://rhg.com/research/missing-link-corporate-governance-in-chinas-state-sector/>.

127 Arthur R Kroeber, *China's Economy: What Everyone Needs to Know* (OUP 2016) 1–3.

128 《中国共产党章程》 [Constitution of the Communist Party of China] (24 October 2017) ch 2 art 10(3) (CPC Constitution).

129 ibid art 19.

130 Susan V Lawrence and Michael F Martin, 'Understanding China's Political System' (CRS Report for Congress, 31 January 2013) 13 <https://www.everycrsreport.com/files/20130131_R41007_ecf-f2aa5a98d681d66f423fa3afe63b6e8e3faa7.pdf>.

131 Xi Jinping (n 1).

132 CPC Constitution (n 127) art 22.

133 Constitution (n 23) Preamble.

the Constitution outlines the nature of the socialist state, its political structure and the roles of the executive, the legislature, and the courts.[134] However, as Angela Huyue Zhang points out, the 'CCP maintains supreme authority over every apparatus of the country, including the military, legislature, executive, and judiciary.'[135] This view is shared by Mark Williams, who notes that

> the Constitution envisages that the organs of government form part of a single harmonious entity and Western enlightenment notions of a tripartite separation of powers with independence guaranteed to each arm of government are eschewed in favour of a unitary power structure.[136]

102. There is widespread speculation that the CCP is involved in state governance.[137] Barry Naughton accurately points out that

> China's political system is structured around two parallel, overlapping hierarchies: The Communist Party and the government organization, and almost all important individuals have both a party position and a government job.[138]

103. The influence of the CCP in all levels of government and even juridical authorities is pervasive. For example, the President of the Supreme People's Court (SPC), Zhou Qiang, has recently reinforced the impression that the court system in China[139] is not independent from the Party's leadership.[140] Previous research by Yuhua Wang has also established the relationship between the Party and the judiciary, noting that '[e]very court

---

134 Mark Williams, *Competition Policy and Law in China, Hong Kong and Taiwan* (CUP, 2005) 103.

135 Angela Huyue Zhang, 'Bureaucratic Politics and China's Anti-Monopoly Law' (2014) 47(3) Cornell Intl LJ 671, 677.

136 Mark Williams, 'China' in Mark Williams (ed), *The Political Economy of Competition Law in Asia* (Edward Elgar 2013) 88, 93.

137 Mark Williams describes the influence of the CCP as the 'control [of] the system from behind the curtain of the formal institutions of the state': ibid. See also Wendy Ng, *The Political Economy of Competition Law in China* (CUP 2018) 187–91.

138 Barry J Naughton, *The Chinese Economy: Adaptation and Growth* (2nd edn, MIT Press 2018) 102.

139 The highest juridical authority, according to the Constitution, is the Supreme People's Court: Constitution (n 23) art 123. China has adopted a civilian model, which means court proceedings 'are more inquisitorial than adversarial in nature': Yifan Wang, Sarah Biddulph and Andrew Godwin, 'A Brief Introduction to the Chinese Judicial System and Court Hierarchy' (ALC Briefing Paper 6) 8 <https://law.unimelb.edu.au/__data/assets/pdf_file/0004/2380684/ALC-Briefing-Paper-6-Wang,-Biddulph,-Godwin_5.pdf>. In addition, the Supreme People's Court, the Supreme People's Procuratorate, and the State Council are all under the supervision of the NPC. This means that the power of interpreting law resides with the NPC instead of the Court. There are four levels of court built into the current structure of the Chinese judicial system, namely the grassroots, intermediate, higher and Supreme People's Courts. Alongside are special courts that include military, maritime, railway transportation, forestry, agricultural reclamation, and petroleum courts. For more detailed discussion, see Ling Li, 'The Chinese Communist Party and People's Courts: Judicial Dependence in China' (2016) 64(1) AJCL 37; Randall Peerenboom, 'Judicial Independence in China: Common Myths and Unfounded Assumptions' in Randall Peerenboom (ed), *Judicial Independence in China Lessons for Global Rule of Law Promotion* (CUP 2010) 69.

140 Zhou Qiang noted that courts in China are not independent and ultimately answer to the Party leadership. Lucy Hornby, 'China's Top Judge Denounces Idea of Judicial Independence: Civil Rights', *Financial Times* (18 January 2017) 5.

in China has a party committee. In most cases, the president is also the party secretary of the court, and vice presidents are also party committee members.'[141]

104. In relation to SOEs, the important positions in SOEs, SASAC and competition authorities such as the SAMR, are appointed by the Party and subject to the evaluation of the Party. This practice also implies that the Party can discipline its members according to its own 'investigation, detention and disciplinary process.'[142] In particular, the influence of the CCP is obvious when it comes to SOEs (as discussed throughout Chapter 3). For example, commentators often use 'Party-state' to capture the intertwined relationship of the Party and the State when managing SOEs.[143] The current SOE reforms have reinforced this view by noting the unique advantages of SOEs is the Party's leadership, and thus the need to strengthen the Party's position in SOEs.[144] As one commentator remarked: 'In 53 central enterprises, the occupants of top positions, including the board chairman, CEOs, and party secretaries, are appointed and evaluated by the Central Organization Department of the Chinese Communist Party.'[145] Whether these indispensable Party links render SOEs exempt from the scrutiny of competition law is explored in detail in Chapter 6. In addition to appointment influence noted above, the CCP can also discipline its members according to its the Party's disciplinary rules. For example, Zhang Xiwu, former deputy head of the SASAC which oversees the central SOEs, was demoted in 2017 on a Party disciplinary violation charge;[146] Chang Xiaobing, former chairman of China Telecom (a central SOE listed under SASAC of State Council), was sentenced to six years imprisonment and fined 500,000 yuan (US$73,330) over corruption charges in May 2017.[147] What lies beneath the concern about corruption in SOEs is the presumption that so-called 'vested interests' enjoy privileges and profit from the present system.[148]

105. The intertwined relationship of the Party and SOEs also raises competitive neutrality concerns and will be analysed in Chapter 5. Chapter 8 argues further that, for China to effectively level the playing field between SOEs and non-SOEs, the commitment of the Party is essential.

---

141 Yuhua Wang, *Tying the Autocrat's Hands: The Rise of the Rule of Law in China* (CUP 2014) 65.

142 Wu (n 36) 280.

143 For more detailed discussion of the relationship of the Party and the Chinese state, see Li-Wen Lin and Curtis J Milhaupt, 'We are the (National) Champions: Understanding the Mechanisms of State Capitalism in China' (2013) 65(4) Stan L Rev 697; Lei, Liebman and Milhaupt (n 15) 217; Wu (n 36).

144 《国务院办公厅关于进一步完善国有企业法人治理结构的指导意见》 [Guiding Opinions of the General Office of the State Council on Further Improving the Corporate Governance Structure of State-Owned Enterprises] Guo Ban Fa [2017] No 36, 24 April 2017 (Guiding Opinions on Governance).

145 Li-Wen Lin, 'A Network Anatomy of Chinese State-Owned Enterprises' (2017) 16(4) WTR 583, 588.

146 Xiang Bo, 'Former Official Demoted for Disciplinary Violations' *Xinhuanet News* (3 July 2017) <http://news.xinhuanet.com/english/2017-07/03/c_136413333.htm>.

147 'Former China Telecom Boss Chang Xiaobing Sentenced to Six Years for Corruption' *South China Morning Post* (31 May 2017) <http://cdn4.i-scmp.com/tech/enterprises/article/2096382/formerchina-telecom-boss-chang-xiaobing-sentenced-six-years>.

148 Arthur Kroeber, 'Summertime, and the Jailin' is Easy' (Gavekal Dragonomics, 1 September 2014) <http://research.gavekal.com/content.php/10394-China-CEQ-Q3-2014-Summertime-And-The-Jailin-Is-Easy>.

2.3.2 Economic Context of China

106. The ideological legitimacy of the state sector remains at the heart of the Chinese economy. To be exact, this ideology can be traced back to the command economy era. State ownership, before the reforms commencing in 1978, was considered one of the 'most important economic characteristics of communism'[149] and 'other types of ownership were considered as incompatible with state ownership'[150] and should not be developed.[151] The government provided goods and services under the command economy system mainly through SOEs, or more accurately 'state-run enterprises' (*Guoying Qiye* in Chinese). As Wayne Morrison points out, 'by 1978 nearly three-fourths of industrial production was produced by centrally controlled, state-owned enterprises (SOEs), according to centrally planned output targets.'[152]

107. These state-run enterprises were an extension of the government departments, established to implement government mandatory targets with very little autonomy or authority in day-to-day management.[153] By contrast, the non-state sector, particularly the private sector in the national economy, was not recognised until 1988, when an amendment to the Constitution adopted by the National People's Congress stated that the private sector is a 'complement' to the state sector.[154] Take, for example, the restriction of financing to private sectors. In the 1980s, private borrowers were often charged higher interest rates due to the perceived higher credit risks they posed.[155] A significant ideological breakthrough presented by Deng Xiao Ping's 'Southern Tour' in 1992 and the 3rd Plenum of the 14th Party Congress in 1993 laid the foundation for the development of various types of ownership.[156] Since then, a series of reforms that was in line with the 1993 breakthrough pivot were launched and included the reform of SOEs, the tax system, and financial sectors. The reforms extended to the liberalisation of foreign exchange and the creation of a social safety net.[157]

---

149 Wu Jinglian and Ma Guochuan, *Whither China? Restarting the Reform Agenda* (Xiaofeng Hua and Nancy Hearst trs, OUP 2016) 95.

150 ibid.

151 The position of private business was not recognised until 1988 when a constitutional amendment stated that 'the private sector of the economy is a complement to the socialist public economy': Lardy (n 43) 40.

152 Wayne M Morrison, 'China's Economic Rise: History, Trends, Challenges, and Implications for the United States' (CRS Report for Congress, 25 June 2019) 2 <https://fas.org/sgp/crs/row/RL33534.pdf>.

153 Hong and Nong (n 51) 215; Naughton (n 137) 71.

154 《中华人民共和国宪法修正案 (1988年)》 [Amendment to the Constitution of the People's Republic of China 1988] (12 April 1988). In the 1988 amendment to the Constitution, Article 1 added a paragraph which reads: 'The State permits the private sector of the economy to exist and develop within the limits prescribed by law. The private sector is a complement to the socialist public economy. The State protects the lawful rights and interests of the private sector, and exercises guidance, supervision and control over the private sector of the economy.' For more detailed discussion of the rise of the private sector in China, see Lardy (n 43).

155 For more detailed discussion of the financing repression of the private sector in China, see Yasheng Huang, *Capitalism with Chinese Characteristics: Entrepreneurship and the State* (CUP 2008) 155–59.

156 For a more detailed discussion of these ideological changes, see Yingyi Qian and Jinglian Wu, 'China's Transition to a Market Economy: How Far Across the River?' in Nicholas Hope, Dennis Yang and Mu Li (eds), *How Far Across the River? Chinese Policy Reform at the Millennium* (SUP 2003) 31, 36.

157 ibid 42.

108. Simply stated, a variety of reform policies and regulations introduced over the past 40 years since Deng's leadership have managed to change the landscape of the state sector in China. There are some new features of SOEs that have emerged; for instance, internally, SOEs as active market participants are 'subject to greater market discipline, enjoy more autonomy, and are more accountable for their performance.'[158] Internationally, the impact of the changes in SOEs is more obvious. With China's growing integration into international trade and investment after its entry into the WTO in 2001, and industrial policies like Made in China 2025[159] and the Belt and Road Initiative,[160] SOEs are not only competing fiercely with non-state firms in the liberalised sectors of the market in China[161] but also compete with various companies in the global marketplace.[162]

109. Yet, it would be incorrect to assume that the state sector in China is becoming less important. To be sure, the leading position of the state sector has its roots in the Constitution and is still officially regarded as 'the leading force in the national economy'.[163] Official documents still 'describe public ownership – and state ownership in particular – as a long-run feature of the economy that should be "consolidated and developed".'[164] As such, the existence of the state sector in the economy is not only accepted in China, but also expected to play a 'leading' or dominant role in domestic economic development.[165]

2.3.3 Governance Structure in China

National People's Congress of the PRC

110. The current governmental structure of China is important to any discussion of competition neutrality policy. According to the Chinese Constitution, the highest legislative body and organ of State power is the National People's Congress of the PRC, and the Standing Committee of the National People's Congress, which is its

158 Dong Zhang and Owen Freestone, 'China's Unfinished State-Owned Enterprise Reforms' (2013) (2) Economic Roundup 77, 78.

159 Made in China 2025 is a broad industrial policy introduced in May 2015 which seeks to promote the country's competitiveness in the manufacturing sector. See State Council, '"Made in China 2025" Plan Issued' (19 May 2015) <http://english.www.gov.cn/policies/latest_releases/2015/05/19/content_281475110703534.htm>.

160 The Belt and Road Initiative (or sometimes known as One Belt One Road Initiative) is one of President Xi Jinping's most ambitious foreign and economic policies, which aims to strengthen Beijing's economic leadership through a vast program of infrastructure building throughout China's neighbouring regions. See Peter Cai, Understanding China's Belt and Road Initiative (Lowy Institute 22 March 2017) <https://www.lowyinstitute.org/publications/understanding-belt-and-road-initiative>.

161 Zhang (n 36) 190.

162 The growing role of SOEs (not just from China) as global competitors in the world economy was highlighted by the OECD recently. See OECD, *State-Owned Enterprises as Global Competitors* (n 76).

163 Constitution (n 23) art 7.

164 Naughton (n 137) 342, citing 季晓楠 [Ji Xiaonan], 《坚持和完善基本经济制度十论》 [Ten Essays on Adhering to and Improving the Basic Economic System] (社会科学文献出版社 [Social Science Academic Press] 2014).

165 Xi Jinping (n 1).

permanent body.[166] The National People's Congress (NPC) is elected for a term of five years.[167] The current Congress, the 13th NPC, began in March 2018.[168] The NPC undertakes to perform its duties listed in the Article 65 of the Constitution on an annual basis. However, as has been observed by Mark Williams, due to a large number of delegates and the meeting's short time period, 'most legislative activity is undertaken by the Standing Committee or via delegated legislation by the State Council, the executive arm of the central government.'[169]

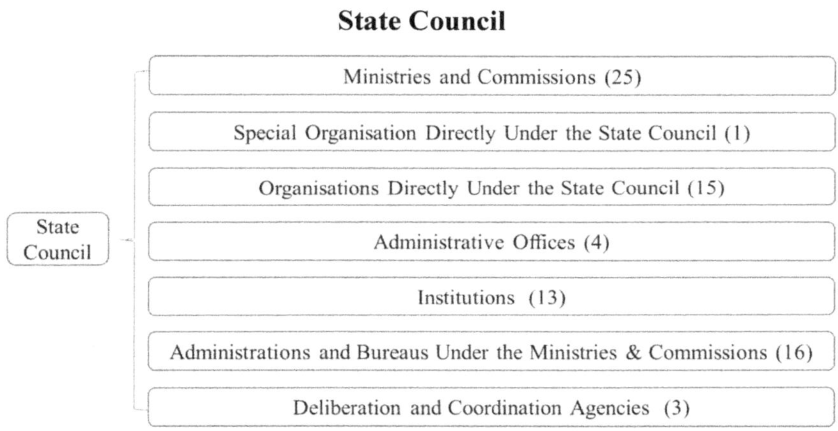

Figure 2.1 The simplified composition of the State Council before 2018 (State Commission Office for Public Sector Reform, scopsr.gov.cn).

111. At the NPC held on 17th March 2018, the 'Plan on Deepening Reform of Party and State Institutions'[170] and the 'State Council Institutional Reform Plan' were unveiled.[171] The reform plan notes that the composition of the State Council has been transformed into 26 ministries and commissions, in addition to the General Office of the State Council.[172] For the purposes of this research, the changes with regard to competition authorities and SASAC will be followed closely, particularly the consolidation of the three competition authorities, NDRC, MOFCOM, and SAIC, into a single authority, termed the State Administration for Market Regulation (SAMR). SAMR is discussed in detail in Chapter 6.

166 Constitution (n 23) art 57.

167 ibid art 60.

168 National People's Congress of the PRC, 'National People's Congress' <http://www.npc.gov.cn/englishnpc/c2846/column2.shtml>.

169 Williams (n 133) 127.

170 《中共中央关于深化党和国家机构改革的决定》 [Decision of the Central Committee of the Communist Party of China on Deepening the Reform of the Party and State Institutions] 28 February 2018 (Decision on Deepening Reform).

171 《国务院机构改革方案》 [The Institutional Reform Plan of the State Council] NPC, 17 March 2018.

172 ibid; 《国务院关于部委管理的国家局设置的通知》 [Notice of the State Council on the Setup of National Bureaus Administrated by Ministries and Commissions] Guo Fa [2018] No 7, 22 March 2018.

SASAC

112. The state ownership agency, SASAC, as a special organisation directly under the State Council, was established in 2003.[173] The legal status of the SASAC presented some degree of uncertainty until the Law of the People's Republic of China on State-Owned Assets of Enterprises (hereafter State-Owned Assets Law) was enacted in 2009.[174] The State-Owned Assets Law formally provides the SASAC is authorised by the government at the corresponding level and acted on behalf of the government to 'perform the duties and responsibilities of the capital contributor of a State-invested enterprise on behalf of the said people's government.'[175] SASAC is thus a special commission of the government, responsible for exercising the State's ownership rights, which makes it the world's largest shareholder.[176] It must be recognised, however, that the responsibility of the SASAC, especially the central SASAC, is far broader than just the exercise of ownership rights in SOEs. For example, SASAC also shoulders some regulatory functions and 'pushes forward the reform and restructuring of state-owned enterprises, advances the establishment of a modern enterprise system in SOEs, improves corporate governance, and propels the strategic adjustment of the layout and structure of the state economy.'[177] The assignment of multiple roles to the SASAC (i.e. regulation and investment roles) and its local branches has increased the likelihood of government intervention in the business activities of SOEs and further blurred the role of government in the management and operation of these entities.[178]

2.4 Conclusion

113. The definition of key terms, such as SOEs, competition policy and competitive neutrality, provides guidance to the following chapters. For example, the comparative study on competitive neutrality policy in Australia (in Chapters 4 and 7) is built on the concept of competitive neutrality noted in this chapter.

---

173 Barry Naughton, 'The Transformation of the State Sector: SASAC, the Market Economy, and the New National Champions' in Barry Naughton and Kellee S Tsai (eds), *State Capitalism, Institutional Adaptation, and the Chinese Miracle* (CUP 2015) 46, 49.

174 The weak legal basis for SASAC was discussed by Mikael Mattlin, who argues SASAC's legal status is established in 2003 by the administrative regulation Interim Regulations on Supervision and Management of State-Owned Assets of Enterprises instead of law: 'Chinese Strategic State-Owned Enterprises and Ownership Control' (2009) 4(6) BICCS Asia Paper 1, 9–10.

175 《中华人民共和国企业国有资产法》 [Law of the People's Republic of China on State-Owned Assets of Enterprises] Standing Committee of the NPC, promulgated 28 October 2008, effective 1 May 2009, art 11 (State-Owned Assets Law).

176 Naughton (n 137) 334. See also Wu (n 36) 271.

177 SASAC, 'What We Do' (17 July 2018) <http://en.sasac.gov.cn/2018/07/17/c_7.htm>.

178 For a detailed discussion of SASAC's multiple roles, see Barry Naughton, 'Top-Down Control: SASAC and the Persistence of State Ownership in China' (China and the World Economy conference paper, 23 June 2006) 1–21 <https://www.nottingham.ac.uk/gep/documents/conferences/2006/june-2006conf/naughton-june2006.pdf>. For a detailed discussion of how the SASAC can be influential on SOEs, see Fei Du, Guliang Tang and S Mark Young, 'Influence Activities and Favoritism in Subjective Performance Evaluation: Evidence from Chinese State-Owned Enterprises' (2012) 87(5) Accounting Review 1555.

114. Additionally, the concept introduced in this chapter provides a foundation for the discussion in Chapters 3 to 8. For example, this chapter recognised that SOEs in China do not operate in a vacuum. The influence of the Party over Chinese SOEs and the importance of state sector to Chinese economy all affect the competition between SOEs and non-SOEs. This context is important for the discussion provided in Chapter 3, which provides a historical study on the ongoing development of Chinese state sector and establishes how each stage of reform has changed the integrated relationship between the Party and SOEs. Moreover, the development of competition policy in China, as has been demonstrated in this chapter, has suggested a better awareness of competition in China. The new role assigned to Chinese competition policy, a fundamental economic policy, suggests a greater readiness for China to develop competitive neutrality policy, as discussed in Chapter 8.

CHAPTER 3

UNDERSTANDING THE REFORM OF SOES IN CHINA

115. A country needs to recognise that the competitive advantages of SOEs generated by government ownership create concerns in the market before it can adopt legal solutions to remedy those concerns. In order to identify the presence of any competitive neutrality concerns caused by Chinese SOEs in the market, it is necessary to understand the nature of SOEs and their close linkages with their government owners and the Chinese Communist Party (CCP). While the political and economic situation of China explored in Chapter 2 provides context for discussion in this chapter, revisiting the history of SOE reform in China provides a useful way of understanding the uniqueness of Chinese SOEs and their market impact.

116. A related purpose of this chapter is to provide a foundation for Chapter 5, which investigates whether government ownership status and Party connections enable Chinese SOEs to enjoy competitive neutrality advantages, or to suffer from any disadvantages. This chapter is also helpful to discussing Chapter 6, which analyses the extent to which Chinese competition law and policy applies to Chinese SOEs. This chapter proceeds as follows:

117. Section 3.1 explains the origins of Chinese SOEs through a historical approach and illustrates how reforms have transformed traditional SOEs into more market-oriented enterprises. It looks primarily at how linkages between government owners and SOEs, and the presence of the Party within SOEs, have changed through reform measures.

118. Section 3.2 outlines the current SOE reform process, which commenced in 2013. It explains the key elements of the current reforms, capturing how these reforms may affect government ownership of SOEs and whether the reforms have increased or decreased the presence of the Party in SOEs. With an increasing number of Chinese SOEs being designed to be profit oriented, a significant question is whether and to what extent these SOEs

benefit (or suffer) from government ownership and their connection to the Party when competing in the market in China.

3.1 Historical Role of SOEs in China (1978–2012)

3.1.1 First Phase of SOE Reform (1978–1986)

119. The first phase of reform (1978–1986), termed 'power decentralisation and profit retention' (*Fangquan Rangli*), commenced in 1978. Before the reform, products in China were mainly produced and delivered by divisions of government or ministries responsible for industrial planning and oversight. Enterprises of this kind were termed 'state-run industrial enterprises' (*Guoying Qiye* in Chinese).[179] Perhaps partly for that reason, the first phase of reform bears some of the characteristics of the planned economy.[180] This stage of reform is characterised by a heavy focus on providing greater economic incentives for workers and managers (or directors) of state-run industrial enterprises. For example, the reform allowed a state-run industrial enterprise to keep profits (by selling surplus products at market price) after it reached the targets planned by the government.[181] The reform also granted government agencies the right to share some of their operational functions with the managers of SOEs on the basis that, in practice, SOE managers may know more about the situation of SOEs than government agencies.

120. However, the proposed reform measures failed to transform the state-run industrial enterprises into market actors, as they were still directly owned and managed by various government administrations.

3.1.2 Second Phase of SOE Reform (1987–1992)

121. In the second phase (1987–1992) of public sector reform, the focus of policy shifted away from 'profit-sharing' to 'separation of ownership and management' (*Liangquan Fenli*). The idea behind this shift was that the first phase of reform was unsatisfactory due to the limited managerial autonomy given to state-run industrial enterprises.[182] Expanding the managerial autonomy of these enterprises was therefore at the centre of this stage of reform and can be observed from legislation and in practice. In particular, the 'contracting responsibility

179 Lei, Liebman and Milhaupt (n 15) 219.

180 The term 'state-run enterprises' (*Guoying Qiye*) was used during this stage of reform, reflecting the character of planned economy.

181 For more detailed discussion, see Jinglian and Guochuan (n 148) 120–34.

182 吴敬琏 [Wu Jinglian], 《当代中国经济改革教程》 [Understanding and Interpreting China's Economic Reform] (2nd edn, 上海远东出版社 [Shanghai Far East Publishers] 2016) 152.

system' (*Chengbaozhi*) was introduced in this phase.[183] *Chengbaozhi* refers to a system where the owner of the state-run industrial enterprises, the government, delegated its managerial power to the manager of the state-run industrial enterprises by signing various contracts for a fixed term.

Industrial Enterprises Owned by the Whole People

122. The contracting responsibility system was implemented and regulated by the Industrial Enterprises Law[184] which was established with the primary purpose of separating ownership from management in state-run enterprises.[185] Article 2 provided that the property of an SOE 'shall be operated and managed by the enterprise ... in line with the principle of the separation of ownership and managerial authority.'[186] The Industrial Enterprises Law introduced a new term, the 'Industrial Enterprise Owned by the Whole People' (*Quanmin Suoyouzhi Gongye Qiye*) or 'industrial SOEs', a substitution for the term 'state-run enterprises'. The difference is that an Industrial SOE does 'make its own managerial decisions, take full responsibility for its profits and losses and practise independent accounting',[187] whereas a state-run enterprise does not.

123. The newly reformed industrial SOEs were prevented from becoming truly competitive in the Chinese market due to governmental administrative control. For example, management decisions on Industrial SOE mergers needed to be approved by relevant government authorities in charge of SOEs at the time.[188] In addition, the internal structure of an Industrial SOE, according to Articles 8–11 of the Industrial Enterprises Law, included: the grassroots organisation of the CCP in the enterprise (the Party Committee, termed *Dangweihui* in Chinese); the Staff and Workers' Representative Congress (*Zhigong Daibiao Dahui*) and the trade union (sometimes called 'labour union', *Gonghui*).[189] As one of the internal organs the industrial SOEs, the Communist Party also played an important role in management decisions, particularly in relation to employment.[190] While industrial SOEs were entitled

183 Hong and Nong (n 51) 10–16.

184 As it was first enacted in 1988 during the initial stage of transition from a planned to a market-oriented economy, it is understandable that the Industrial Enterprises Law inherited features from a planned economy, the most obvious example being that it did not separate wholly SOEs from the hierarchical state bureaucracy. For more detailed discussion, see Barry Naughton, *The Chinese Economy: Transitions and Growth* (MIT Press, 2006) 85–111.

185 Measures proposed by the Industrial Enterprises Law (para 4 art 2) to separate managerial obligations from ownership responsibility of SOEs includes but is not limited to 'contract, leasing or other forms.' However, this provision was repealed in 2009. For a more detailed discussion, see 黄群慧 [Huang Qunhui], 'How "New SOEs" Come of Age: Four Decades of China's SOE Reform' (2018) 13(1) China Economist 58, 64; Yiping Huang, 'State-Owned Enterprises Reform' in Ron Duncan and Yiping Huang (eds), *Reform of State-Owned Enterprises in China: Autonomy, Incentive and Competition* (Asia Pacific Press, 1988) 95, 101–102.

186 Industrial Enterprises Law (n 38) art 2.

187 ibid.

188 ibid art 18.

189 ibid arts 8–11.

190 Huang (n 184) 103.

to retain limited profits, they were not generally held responsible for their losses.[191] As observed by Wu Jinglian:

> The [contract responsibility] system did not turn enterprises into independent entities responsible for their own profits and losses, nor did it realize the separation of government from enterprises or equal competition among enterprises. The system blurred the boundaries of enterprise property rights, exacerbating the conflicts of interest between the contractees and the contractors and making it easier for the contractors to expand their own interests at the expense of those of the contractees.[192]

124. In brief, although the second stage of reform managed to some extent to transform industrial SOEs into market players, the reformed industrial SOEs were by nature still an extension of government and unlikely to operate at arm's length from government.

3.1.3 Third Phase in Establishing Modern Enterprise Reform (1993–2002)

125. The push for a more comprehensive state sector reform commenced in 1993, soon after the ideological breakthrough presented by Deng Xiao Ping's 'Southern Tour', which emphasised 'the need for accelerated economic reform and an experimental, nonideological approach.'[193] The 3rd Plenum of the 14th National Congress of the Communist Party of China was held in 1993,[194] and adopted the Decision on Matters Concerning the Creation of a Socialist Market Economic System.[195] The Decision set out a blueprint for the establishment of a 'Socialist Market Economy' and marked a major turning point in China's transition from a centrally-planned economy to a market-oriented economy.[196]

---

191 Xiaolu Wang, 'China's Macroeconomics in the 40 Years of Reform' in Ross Garnaut, Ligang Song and Cai Fang (eds), *China's 40 Years of Reform and Development 1978–2018* (ANU Press, 2018) 167, 177; Daniel Ho and Angus Young, 'China's Experience in Reforming its State-Owned Enterprises: Something New, Something Old and Something Chinese?' (2013) 2(4) Int J Econ Manag Soc Sci 84, 85.

192 Jinglian and Guochuan (n 148) 70.

193 The 'Southern Tour' of Deng Xiao Ping (*Dengxiaoping Nanxun*) is the start of China's economic liberalisation. See Naughton (n 137) 110.

194 As discussed in Chapter 2, the ruling party in China is the Communist Party of China (CPC). The National Congress of the CPC is held every five years. In the years between the National Congress of the Party, the Central Committee of the Party (one of the highest decision-making bodies of the CPC), is required to meet at least once a year, with each meeting known as a plenum (or plenary session). Plenums usually focus on setting the direction for the country in a specific area, while also approving major personnel decisions. See Lawrence and Martin (n 129).

195 《中共中央关于建立社会主义市场经济体制若干问题的决定》 [Decision of the Central Committee of the Communist Party of China on Matters Concerning the Creation of a Socialist Market Economic System] 3rd Plenum of the 14th Party Congress, 17 November 1993.

196 For a more detailed discussion, see Qian and Wu (n 154); Lee Junyeop, 'State Owned Enterprises in China: Reviewing the Evidence' (OECD Working Group on Privatisation and Corporate Governance of State Owned Assets, 26 January 2009) <http://www.oecd.org/corporate/ca/corporategovernanceofstate-ownedenterprises/42095493.pdf>; Naughton (n 137) 110–11.

126. The third phase of reform aimed to establish modern SOEs. The key tenets of the modern SOEs were: '1) clarification of property rights; 2) clarification of rights and responsibilities; 3) separation of bureaucracy and business, and 4) scientific management.'[197]

Incorporation of Industrial SOEs

127. A dramatic transformation of industrial SOEs happened at this stage of reform. A central part of the reform agenda, from a competition perspective at least, was pulling back government control from industrial SOEs through initiatives of corporatisation and sometimes privatisation.[198] The corporatisation implemented at this stage successfully managed to alter the ownership structure of industrial SOEs into a more market-focused structure while maintaining government ownership. For example:

> More than 90% of state-owned enterprises across the country completed reforms of their corporate and joint-stock systems. Most set up boards of shareholders, directors, managers, and supervisors, plus other organizations, and gradually standardized their corporate governance structures.[199]

128. In addition, government administrations were required to separate ties between administrative functions and their directly managed SOEs[200] by establishing a middle level between the government and the SOEs. For example, internal management structures of corporatised SOEs were established based on the Company Law enacted in 1994,[201] which aligns the interests of managers with government owners by providing incentives for managers of corporatised SOEs to pursue profits and thereby expose SOEs to more competition.[202]

129. Incorporated SOEs were expected to act more like the competitive private firms in the market (despite some degree of government constraints[203]). However, restructuring SOEs at this stage was not without difficulties, particularly in relation to the internal relationships between government shareholders (or government owners) and other organs of incorporated SOEs (such as shareholders, boards of directors, management, the board

197 Decision of the Central Committee (n 194). For more detailed discussion, see 吴敬琏 [Wu Jinglian] (n 181) 158; Junyeop (n 195).

198 Zhang and Freestone (n 157) 80.

199 Angang Hu and others, *The Modernization of China's State Governance* (Springer 2017) 126.

200 Wentong Zheng, 'State Capitalism and the Regulation of Competition in China' in Michael W Dowdle, John Gillespie and Imelda Maher (eds), *Asian Capitalism and the Regulation of Competition: Towards a Regulatory Geography of Global Competition Law* (CUP 2013) 144, 150.

201 Company Law (n 40).

202 Naughton, *The Chinese Economy: Transitions and Growth* (n 183) 315.

203 'Every SOE in China still carries a political rank': Zheng (n 199) 149. For more detailed analysis of government restrains in China, see generally Roselyn Hsueh, *China's Regulatory State: A New Strategy for Globalization* (Cornell University Press, 2011).

of supervisors).[204] For instance, many newly incorporated Chinese SOEs 'either had no boards of directors or had purely nominal boards',[205] which often left the function of the board to be performed by government shareholders (before the establishment of the SASAC) or government-appointed managers (often former industry regulators).[206]

Party Presence in Incorporated SOEs

130. This stage of reform did not diminish the role of the Communist Party Committee (the Party committee) in the newly incorporated SOEs. Under the Company Law, all firms established in China must have a Party committee (or Party organisation) in their operation.[207] At this stage, the activities carried out by SOE Party committees were often linked to ideological–political education of Party members of company employees to ensure the implementation of 'the principles and policies of the Party'.[208] It is worth highlighting that, while Party committees in incorporated SOEs were involved in the personnel recruitment and evaluation process,[209] this function was not formalised in government policy until the next stage of reform (2003–2012). The issues associated with Party involvement in the SOEs will be discussed in depth in the next section.

131. This stage of reform also led to the creation of what is called a hybrid ownership company (termed the 'mixed-ownership company') whereby an incorporated wholly state-owned company could become a hybrid company by selling off some of the shares of the corporation to non-state investors or through a public listing in the stock market.[210] As a result, the hybrid nature of firms made it difficult to draw a clear-cut line between SOEs and non-state firms in China. It also the paved way for the current mixed-ownership reform, which will be discussed in section 3.2.4.

Privatisation of Industrial SOEs

132. The movement towards privatisation of poorly performing industrial SOEs was also carried out as part of this stage of reform, which created

---

204 卢昌崇 [Lu Changchong], '《公司治理机构及新、老三会关系论》[On the Discussion of the Relationship between the New Corporate Governance Organs and the Old Ones]' (1994) 11 经济研究 [Economic Research Journal] 10, 10.

205 Naughton (n 137) 346.

206 For example, Deng Feng not only noted that many boards of Chinese SOEs were deemed to be merely an executive committee of the government shareholder meeting, but also highlighted that the appointment management power enjoyed by the Board of Chinese SOEs were exercised by the government shareholder in reality. See 邓峰 [Deng Feng], '《中国法上董事会的角色、职能及思想渊源: 实证法的考察》[The Role, Function, and Origins of Ideas in the Chinese Corporate Board Legal Institution: From a Positive Perspective]' (2013) 3 中国法学 [China Legal Science].

207 'An organisation of the Communist Party of China (CPC) shall be established in a company to carry out activities of the CPC pursuant to the Constitution of the Communist Party of China. The company shall provide necessary conditions for the activities of the organisation of the CPC': Company Law (n 40) art 19.

208 《中国共产党章程》[Constitution of the Communist Party of China] (2002 version) art 32.

209 For example, as noted in Chapter 2, the board of directors in the incorporated SOEs were often the Party committee member and subject to the evaluation of the Party.

210 Naughton (n 183) 301.

opportunities for non-state firms to enter the market.[211] The phrase 'grasp the big, let go the small' (*Zhuada Fangxiao*) is often used to describe the reform strategy and principles implemented during this phase. It imports a process of reclassification of industrial SOEs based on their business size, and applies differentiated reform measures (like corporatisation or privatisation) accordingly. For example, as large-scale industrial SOEs were often owned by the central government, the reform strategy for this group was focused on corporatisation and listing incorporated SOEs on the stock market, in line with many multinationals.[212] By contrast, small-scale industrial SOEs were largely owned by local Chinese government and the reform strategy was to privatise, either by selling shares to employees or selling to non-state firms.[213] As Curtis J Milhaupt and Wentong Zheng have commented, 'the newly privatised [industrial] SOEs did not become private firms as that term is commonly understood; instead, they became firms with mixed ownership.'[214]

133. The reform at this stage also presented some drawbacks. First, workers in some industrial SOEs that went into bankruptcy (or were privatised) were laid off, sometimes without proper compensation, which led to rising unemployment (*Xiagang*).[215] Second, many industrial SOEs were sold at an undervalued price to their own managers or employees, which led to corruption, cronyism and the loss of state assets.[216] Third, not all industrial SOEs managed to complete the corporatisation or privatisation process required at this stage of reform.[217] As a result, industrial SOEs and incorporated SOEs coexisted in the market of China until 2017 (see Section 3.2 for further discussion).

Concluding Comments

134. While the overall effect of the third phase of state sector reform to the operating forms of SOEs in China was far-reaching, the involvement of the government and the Communist Party in the newly incorporated SOEs was not significantly reduced. Importantly, given the increasing number of incorporated SOEs becoming market actors and competing with private companies in various industries, it is not clear why the question of whether these reformed SOEs might enjoy competitive advantages (or disadvantages)

211 Nicholas R Lardy, *Markets Over Mao: The Rise of Private Business in China* (PIIE 2014) 55–56.

212 Williams, 'China' (n 135).

213 Lardy (n 210) 56.

214 Curtis J Milhaupt and Wentong Zheng, 'Reforming China's State-Owned Enterprises: Institutions, Not Ownership' in Benjamin L Liebman and Curtis J Milhaupt (eds), *Regulating the Visible Hand? The Institutional Implications of Chinese State Capitalism* (OUP 2015) 175, 193.

215 Zhang and Freestone (n 157) 83.

216 Jinglian and Guochuan (n 148) 159.

217 China National Petroleum Corporation (CNPC), an industrial SOE established under the Industrial Enterprise Law, was only corporatised into a wholly state-owned limited liability company under the Company Law on 21 December 2017. See '中国石油集团完成整体改制并更名 [China National Petroleum Corporation Completes its Overall Restructuring and Changes its Name]' (21 December 2017) <http://www.sasac.gov.cn/n2588030/n2588924/c8374019/content.html>.

due to their government ownership and political connections was seldom asked by scholars around this time. One exception was the research conducted in 2003 by Chong-En Bai, David D Li and Yijiang Wang, which offered insights into how non-SOEs were being disadvantaged in the market of China at that time.[218]

3.1.4 Fourth Phase in the Management of State Assets (2003–2012)

135. In contrast to the third stage of reform, the fourth phase of reform (2003–2012) shifted its reform priority from the incorporation and privatisation (restructuring SOEs) to the management and supervision (or protection) of state assets. Therefore, this stage of reform did not dramatically change the operative form of SOEs, but it did increase government and Communist Party involvement in the operation of SOEs.

The Ownership Agency: SASAC

136. SASAC has had a profound effect on the landscape of the state sector in China. Two principal effects particularly relevant to this research are discussed here. First, the creation of SASAC officially sharpened the distinction between central government and local government ownership in SOEs.[219] Importantly, central SASAC, created by the State Council, controls 97 SOEs (*Yangqi*),[220] which are mostly located in the industries deemed as critical to 'national security or the lifeline of the national economy.'[221] By contrast, local SASAC, set up by the government at the corresponding level, control SOEs owned by the local governments (and often sits outside the industries considered as vital to national security or national economy).[222] Second, the multiple roles assigned to SASAC allow it to intervene in the business decisions of SOEs, which in a way leads to the critical question of whether SOEs managed by SASAC (both central and local) are genuinely independent market entities or merely acting on behalf of the government.

---

218 For example, after examining the total fixed investment from 1980 to 2000, the authors argued that in the absence of a level playing field in China, the state sector obtained more funds for fixed investment than the non-state sector, which implies that the non-state sector during that time suffered 'from restricted access to bank credit and financial market': Chong-En Bai, David D Li and Yijiang Wang, 'Thriving on a Tilted Playing Field: China's Non-State Enterprises in the Reform Era' in Nicholas Hope, Dennis Yang and Mu Li (eds), *How Far Across the River? Chinese Policy Reform at the Millennium* (SUP 2003) 97, 114.

219 Naughton (n 177) 3.

220 There were 196 central SOEs listed under the SASAC of State Council in 2003.

221 According to Li Rongrong, the then Chairman of SASAC, the state need to maintain 'absolute control' in seven sectors, namely, military industries, power grids and power generation, the oil and petrochemical sectors, telecommunications, the coal industry, civil aviation, and shipping. The state also needed to maintain 'comparatively strong control' in nine pillar industries, namely equipment manufacturing, automobile manufacturing, electronics and information technology, construction, iron and steel, ferrous metals, chemical products, survey and design, and science and technology. See 任芳 [Ren Fang] and刘兵 [Liu Bing], '国资委：国有经济应保持对七个行业的绝对控制力 [SASAC of State Council: The State Should Keep Absolute Control Over Seven Industries]' *Xinhua News* (18 December 2006) <http://www.gov.cn/jrzg/2006-12/18/content_472256.htm>

222 As noted in Section 2.1.1, not all SOEs are supervised and regulated by SASAC. See also Junyeop (n 195) 8.

Party Presence in Incorporated SOEs

137. The presence of the Communist Party committee in the operation of SOEs was strengthened and formalised during this period of reform. Although the power of appointment and removal of SOE executive teams was entrusted to the SASAC,[223] this power was (and still is) exercised 'in the shadow of the party'.[224] The executive teams of central SOEs[225] were appointed and evaluated by the Central Organisation Department of the Chinese Communist Party (*Zhongzhubu*), sometimes in conjunction with the Party Building Bureau of SASAC.[226] As pointed out by Li-Wen Lin, some appointees to executive positions in central SOEs 'hold ministerial rank equivalent to provincial governors and members of the State Council; others hold the vice-ministerial rank.'[227] As a result, the reforms at this stage formalised the connection between the political party and SOEs, rather than weakening it, as was suggested in the third stage of reform and noted above.

Concluding Comments

138. The involvement of the SASAC and the Party in SOEs frequently attracted attention abroad, and criticism at home, especially after China joined the WTO in 2001. For example, Chinese SOEs, when investing overseas, were often labelled as 'China Inc.' (or 'State Capitalism'[228] or 'Party Capitalism'[229]) and treated in the collective as a single entity controlled by the Chinese government (regardless of whether owned by central or local SASACs).[230]

---

223 State-Owned Assets Law (n 174) art 22.

224 Lin (n 144).

225 The central SOEs' executive teams (*Lingdao Banzi*) often include: chairman of the board, deputy chairman of the board, board members, general manager, deputy general manager, and chief accountant (if the company has a board of directors); general manager, deputy general manager, and chief accountant (if the company does not have board of directors); and secretary of the Party committee (*Dangwei Shuji*), deputy secretary of the Party committee (*Dangwei Fushuji*), the member of the Party committee and secretary of the discipline inspection commission (an anticorruption office, *Jijian Shuji*). See 《中央企业领导班子和领导人员综合考核评价办法 (试行)》 [Provisional Measures on Comprehensive Evaluation of Corporate Leadership Teams and Leaders of Central SOEs (Trial Implementation)] General Office of the CPC Central Committee and SASAC of the State Council, Zhong Zhu Fa [2009] No 17, 2009, s 1(5).

226 《中央企业领导人员管理暂行规定》 [Provisional Rules on Managing Corporate Leaders of Central SOEs] General Office of the CPC Central Committee and General Office of the State Council, 6 November 2009.

227 Lin (n 144) 588; see generally Li-Wen Lin, 'State Ownership and Corporate Governance in China: An Executive Career Approach' [2013](3) Colum Bus L Rev 743.

228 For example, the concern of the cash-rich Chinese state firms, backed by easy credit from state banks and directed by national industry policy, would unfairly grab global market share and cause international market distortions. For more detailed discussion, see Arthur Kroeber, 'Role of the State Sector: Still in Retreat, But Getting Bigger' (2012) 16(4) China Economic Quarterly 17, 17 <http://research.gavekal.com/content.php/7837-DG-CEQ-Q4-2012-Role-Of-The-State-Sector-Still-In-Retreat-But-Getting-Bigger>; Andrew Szamosszegi and Cole Kyle, 'An Analysis of State-Owned Enterprises and State Capitalism in China' (US-China Economic and Security Review Commission 26 October 2011) 5 <https://www.uscc.gov/sites/default/files/Research/10_26_11_CapitalTradeSOEStudy.pdf>; Michael Hirson, 'State Capitalism and the Evolution of "China, Inc.": Key Policy Issues for the United States Testimony Before the U.S.-China Economic and Security Review Commission on "China's Internal and External Challenges"' (2019) <https://www.uscc.gov/sites/default/files/Hirson_USCC%20Testimony_FINAL.pdf>.

229 Hirson (n 227).

230 For general discussion of how the EC assesses whether Chinese SOEs have decision-making power independent of the Chinese state, see Alan Riley, 'Nuking Misconceptions: Hinkley Point, Chinese SOEs and EU Merger Law' (2016) 37(8) ECLR 301–324; Zhang (n 36).

Interestingly, coinciding with the growing number of Chinese SOEs operating abroad, the question of how the expansion of commercial-oriented SOEs might affect the competitive process in the global market was studied widely at this time. For example, in the OECD, the discussion of competitive neutrality concerns caused by SOEs and the possible legal solutions to address these concerns can be traced back to 2004.[231] Robert Hormats, then U.S. Under Secretary of State for Economic Affairs, in 2011 explicitly noted the threat posed by SOEs owned by a foreign government to domestic markets, arguing

> state-owned enterprises, and state-supported enterprises or 'National Champions,' are emerging to become serious global competitors. … And, importantly, there are few accepted international disciplines which effectively ensure a level, competitive playing field between state supported firms and the private sector.[232]

139. While the competitive neutrality concerns caused by SOEs in the global marketplace have been broadly studied, less study has been devoted to how the expansion of Chinese SOEs (with government ownership ties and privileged political positions) may affect the competitive process of the Chinese domestic market. Competition has not been a high priority in the socialist market economy of China. The lack of awareness that competing SOE may undermine market competition may have diminished the focus on competitive neutrality in relation to China (see Chapter 7 for further discussion).[233]

3.2 Making Sense of the Current SOE Reforms (2013–Present)

3.2.1 The General Picture

140. The most recent round of SOE reform was introduced by the 3rd Plenary Session of the 18th Chinese Communist Party Central Committee in November 2013, which aimed to 'deepen economic reform by closely centring around the theme of letting the market play a decisive role in resource allocation.'[234] The extent

231 See n 7 for studies conducted by OECD at this time (2003–2012).

232 Robert D Hormats, 'Ensuring a Sound Basis for Global Competition: Competitive Neutrality' (US State Department, 5 May 2011) <https://2009-2017.state.gov/e/rls/rmk/20092013/2011/163472.htm>.

233 As noted in Chapter 6, the first comprehensive research on the competitive neutrality problems caused by Chinese SOEs in the domestic market of China was conducted by Shiying Xu in 2014. See generally Xu Shiying, 'Competitive Neutrality of SOEs in China' in *Competitive Neutrality and its Application in Selected Developing Countries* (UNCTAD RPP, 2014) 34.

234 《中共中央关于全面深化改革若干重大问题的决定》 [Decision of the Central Committee of the Communist Party of China on Several Major Issues on Comprehensively Deepening Reforms] CPC Central Committee, adopted at the 3rd Plenary Session of the 18th Central Committee of the CPC on 12 November 2013 (CCCPC Reforms Decision).

of the current reform (2013–present), on the available evidence, is broader and more complex than previous rounds of reform. It continues to pursue the goals laid out by the previous SOE reforms,[235] and introduces new goals that link directly to the changing circumstances faced by modern SOEs.[236] In particular, the current reform requirements of 'improving the corporate governance of SOEs' and 'developing mixed-ownership reform' are a continuation of reform initiatives implemented from 1993 to 2002. Similarly, the reform approach of 'improving state asset supervision system' and 'promoting optimised state capital layout through consolidation and reorganisation' used in current reform compares with that used in the fourth phase of reform (2003–2012). What stands out, at least from a competition standpoint, are the reform strategies of 'strengthen and improving the leadership of the Chinese Communist Party in the corporate governance of SOEs', which will be addressed in detail in Section 3.2.3.

141. It is useful to point out that the current reforms are governed by government policies and have adopted a principles-based approach to facilitate the implementation process, often called the '1+N' SOE reform package. The principle framework for the reform (or the '1' in the SOE reform package) was issued in 2015, entitled Guiding Opinions of the Communist Party of China Central Committee and the State Council on Deepening the Reform of State-Owned Enterprises (hereafter Guiding Opinions on Reform).[237] Since its release, there have been at least 110 supportive regulations (the 'N' in the reform package) issued at the central level and at least 837 supportive documents issued at the local level.[238] These regulatory reform policies have served to complicate the current reform, and fragmented reform implementation because of inconsistent interpretation of the Guiding Opinions on Reform at different levels of government and by different responsible authorities.[239]

---

235 ibid. For example, the goals of the current reforms include improving the corporate governance of SOEs and further developing a mixed ownership system. Both goals were first introduced during the third phase of reform (1993–2002). In addition, improving the state asset supervision system, and a more reasonable layout of state capital through consolidation and reorganisation, can be traced back to the fourth phase of reform (2003–2012).

236 ibid. The goals to be achieved from the reform by 2020 also include: developing SOEs with innovation capability and international competitiveness, improving the systems for managing diverse types of state assets and transforming to the state capital-management system, and pushing forward mixed ownership through SOEs classification.

237 《中共中央、国务院关于深化国有企业改革的指导意见》[Guiding Opinions of the Central Committee of the Communist Party of China and the State Council on Deepening the Reform of State-Owned Enterprises] Zhong Fa [2015] No 22, 24 August 2015 (Guiding Opinions on Reform). In general, the Guiding Opinions on Reform comprises eight sections and 30 provisions, which can be further divided into two parts. The first part (the Preface and first section) sets the tone for the overall reform by clarifying the guiding thoughts, the basic principles, and main objectives governing the reforms. Sections 2–7 constitutes the second part, which outlines the six specific elements of the reforms and includes the 'classifying SOEs', 'improving the corporate governance of SOEs', 'transforming to the State capital management system', 'developing mixed ownership', 'preventing the loss of state-owned assets', and 'strengthening the leadership of the Party in SOEs'.

238 刘青山Liu Qingshan (n 39) 11.

239 Paul Hubbard, '"Fragmented Authoritarianism" and State Ownership' (2017) East Asia Forum (23 January 2017) <http://www.eastasiaforum.org/2017/01/23/fragmented-authoritarianism-and-state-ownership/>.

142. Consequently, it is difficult at this early stage to give a definite answer as to whether the current reform has increased or decreased government ties and political connections to Chinese SOEs. A clear understanding of the elements underlying the current SOE reform and its priorities is a vital starting point to answering that question.

3.2.2 Classifying Commercial SOEs and Public Welfare SOEs

143. The current reform requires all Chinese SOEs to be categorised as either commercial SOEs or public welfare SOEs, as detailed in Section 2.1.1.[240] However, it would be incorrect to assume that this classification will solve the troubling issue of conflicting goals (both commercial and non-commercial) of SOEs, as there is no requirement in the relevant policies that SOEs categorised in the commercial group be prohibited from taking on public welfare functions and vice versa.[241] While the classification of SOEs is often viewed as the basis for other reform (such as the mixed-ownership reform), its primary purpose is to apply different evaluation standards on SOEs based on the classification.

144. First, SOEs classified as commercial SOEs typically operate in the competitive market (termed 'general commercial SOEs' for the purposes of this research) and their performance is evaluated based on 'profitability and other familiar financial metrics.'[242] However, there is a subcategory within the commercial SOEs group, termed 'special commercial SOEs', which operates in fields related to national security, or industries of national economic importance, or have their primary task assigned by the state. By contrast, SOEs classified as public welfare SOEs are not involved in the special sectors noted above. They are expected to deliver public goods and services (such as public utilities), sometimes at a regulated price. Thus, the evaluation of their performance must take these functions into account rather than just focusing on financial indicators.

145. Second, mixed-ownership reform is implemented based on the classification of SOEs and is discussed in detail in Section 3.2.4. In brief, for commercial SOEs, whereas general commercial SOEs are allowed to fundamentally change their ownership structures through mixed-ownership reform to the extent that state shareholders are no longer the controlling shareholder group,[243] special commercial SOEs need to 'maintain the position of controlling shareholder'[244] after implementing mixed-ownership reform. For SOEs in the public welfare category, non-state firms can become a participant in the operation but subject to the conditions of the specific enterprises.

240 Guiding Opinions on Reform (n 236) s 2. The implementing regulation for the SOE classification is the Guiding Opinions on SOEs (n 56).

241 The legal base for this classification can be observed in two administrative regulations, namely Guiding Opinions on Reform (n 236) and Guiding Opinions on SOEs (n 56).

242 Nicholas Lardy, *The State Strikes Back: The End of Economic Reform in China?* (PIIE 2019) 94.

243 As discussed in Chapter 2, state controlled SOEs refer to enterprises whose (i) absolute majority shareholder is the state (i.e. the state holds more than 50% of its shares), or (ii) relative majority shareholder is the state (i.e. although the state holds less than 50% of the firm's shares, it is still a larger shareholder than others).

244 Guiding Opinions on SOEs (n 56) s 2(1).

146. In practice, the principle of 'whoever contributes the capital shall be responsible for classification' is used, which means government shareholders need to make the final decision on the classification plan developed by the corresponding SASAC within their region. This decentralised approach, on the one hand, provides flexibility for each level of government to determine its own reform plan based on its interpretation and the real conditions of SOEs under its supervision.[245] On the other hand, differing interpretations of the Guiding Opinions on Reform offered by local authorities have created uncertain or even disjointed SOE reform processes. It has been observed that 'the huge variance in local interpretation and implementation of central government directives creates a greatly fragmented SOE model.'[246]

147. The variance in the classification of SOEs by local SASACs can be observed in practice.[247] According to the data collected to date, the majority of SASAC classifications, by different degrees, are in line with the classification specified in the Guiding Opinions on Reform and Guiding Opinions on SOEs. For example, there are 12 provinces and cities in China categorised SOEs into three groups, namely competitive, functional, and public welfare.[248] SASAC in Shanxi Province goes a step further by listing categorised SOEs on its website.[249] Some classification systems deviate from the Guiding Opinions on Reform by omitting the category of public welfare SOEs. A typical example is the SOE classification offered by the SASAC of Sichuan, which defines all of its SOEs as commercial SOEs and makes no provision for public welfare SOEs.[250]

148. These inconsistent practices suggest that categorisation by itself may not provide clear guidance on whether an SOE is more market-oriented or public policy-oriented, or whether it operates and competes according to market forces.[251]

---

245 It is worth noting that the decentralised approach for SOE reform was also used during the last stage of reform in 2013.

246 Hubbard (n 238).

247 There are currently more than 300 local SASACs at provincial-, prefectural-, county-, and township-levels. See 刘青山 [Liu Qingshan], '《特别策划 下篇：那些已经"消失"的地方国资委 》[Special Focus Sequel: Those Already "Disappeared" Local State-Owned Assets Supervision and Administration Commission]' (2016) (8) 国资报告 [State-Owned Assets Report] 44, 59–73. For the detailed list of provincial SASACs, see SASAC, '地方国资委 [Local SASACs]' (4 January 2016) <http://www.sasac.gov.cn/n2588035/n2641584/index.html>.

248 原诗萌 [Yuan Shimeng], '《共性与差异 地方国企分类改革分析报告》[Similarities and Differences: An Analysis Report on the Classification of Local State-Owned Enterprises]' (2016) (12) 国资报告 [State-Owned Assets Report] 71, 73; 贾尽裴 [Jia Jinpei], '《国有企业分类改革实践与展望》[Practice and Prospect of State-Owned Enterprises Reform]' (CNKI 2018) 76–7 <http://gb.oversea.cnki.net/KCMS/detail/detail.aspx?filename=JJDK201810012&dbcode=CJFD&dbname=CJFD2018>; Guiding Opinions on Reform (n 236) s 2. The implementing regulation for the SOE classification is the Guiding Opinions on SOEs (n 56).

249 《陕西省国资委关于省属企业实施分类管理的意见》[Opinion of the State-Owned Assets Supervision and Administration Commission of the Shanxi Province on the Classification of Provincial-Owned Enterprises] Shanzhengbanfa [2014] No 112, 30 May 2016.

250 《关于印发<关于省属企业功能界定与分类监管的指导意见（试行）>的通知》[Notice on the Printing and Distributing the Guiding Opinions on the Classifications of Provincial SOEs (Trial Implementation)] Sichuan SASAC, Chuan Guoziwei [2016] No 115, 7 June 2016.

251 Weihuan Zhou, Henry Gao and Xue Bai, 'Building a Market Economy Through WTO-Inspired Reform of State-Owned Enterprises in China' (2019) 68(4) ICLQ 977, 984.

3.2.3 Improving the Governance of SOEs

149. As discussed in Section 3.1.3, while corporatisation was introduced as the primary reform strategy in the late 1990s, there are still several industrial SOEs co-existing with the incorporated SOEs in the Chinese market. For example, at the end of July 2017, 69 of the 101 central SOEs (with 3,200 subsidiaries and approximately 13 trillion yuan in assets), remained unincorporated industrial SOEs in China,[252] and efforts continue to further the corporatisation process for the remaining industrial SOEs, especially at the central level. For instance, the State Council in China issued an implementation plan that set the deadline for restructuring all central SOEs into a corporatisation system by the end of 2017.[253] As a result of this reform, over 92 per cent of central SOEs accomplished corporatisation, with provincial-level SOEs reaching 90 per cent since 2018.[254]

150. Since almost all SOEs in China are now incorporated,[255] the current effort is dedicated more to the improvement of the governance structure of SOEs,[256] which is one of the aspects of 'improving the modern enterprise system'[257] required by the current reform. There are several ways to improve the governance of SOEs, according to the Guiding Opinions of the General Office of the State Council on Further Improving the Corporate Governance Structure of State-Owned Enterprises (hereafter Guiding Opinions on Governance),[258] which include: standardising the obligations of the board of shareholders; professionalising the board of directors; increasing operational autonomy; increasing the supervisory role of the board of supervisors; and strengthening the leadership of the Party. Strengthening the leadership of the Party in the governance of SOEs is considered most relevant for the purposes of this research and will be explored further in the section below.

Party Presence in the Incorporated SOEs

151. The presence of the Communist Party committee in the governance of SOEs is described as the 'unique advantage of SOEs' by the current reforms.[259] Consequently, incorporated SOEs are required to reflect this unique advantage

252 刘青山 [Liu Qingshan] (n 39) 10. See also OECD (n 30) 44.

253 Guiding Opinions on Governance (n 143) s 1.3.

254 Li-Wen Lin, 'China's National Champions: Governance Change Through Globalization?' (2017) 11(1) U Pa Asian L Rev 80.

255 '央企公司制改制基本完成 "历史性突破"打开改革新空间 [The Corporatisation Reform of the State-Owned Enterprises is Basically Complete]' (24 April 2019) <http://www.gov.cn/xinwen/2018-04/25/content_5285657.htm>.

256 The OECD noted the current Chinese notion of a modern enterprise system includes separation of business from politics, corporatisation, establishing a board of directors, managing executives by type and level of enterprise, and choosing a remuneration system that fits the country's economic system. See OECD (n 30) 44.

257 The concept of a 'modern enterprise system' has continually evolved since it was introduced in the late-1990s. See the discussion in Section 3.1.3. Five aspects of the modern enterprise system are listed in the Guiding Opinions on Reform, including corporatisation, improving the governance of SOEs, establishing a management framework for executives based on type and level of SOEs, choosing a remuneration system that fits the country's economic system, and improving internal human resource systems: (n 236) s 3.

258 Guiding Opinions on Governance (n 143).

259 ibid s 5(1).

through institutionalising the Party committee in the constitution of SOEs, clarifying the role of the Party committee in relation to other internal management organs within the SOEs, and implementing the 'cross-appointment system' (explained later in this section).

152. In the past, the political power of the Party was displayed in the corporate governance of SOEs in two respects: the personnel management of top executive positions of SOEs,[260] and the institutionalised Party committee inside the corporate governance system of SOEs. For example, the establishment of the Party Committee in SOEs has its legal foundations in both the Chinese Company Law and the Constitution of the Communist Party of China.[261] Additionally, the involvement of the Party in personnel management and evaluations of Chinese SOEs has long been documented by scholars.[262] For example, as Daniel Rosen, Wendy Leutert and Shan Guo note:

> Party committees nominate, approve, and assess senior personnel within the firm, assist selected employees to join the CCP, disseminate political propaganda, and organize study sessions for Party members about central-level policies, key campaigns, and speeches by top leaders like Xi Jinping.[263]

153. What stands out under the current reform is the requirement for the Party committee to participate in the decision-making process of SOEs.[264] For example, the Constitution of the Party notes the role of the Party committee in SOEs as follows:

> The leading Party members groups or Party committees of state-owned enterprises shall play a leadership role, set the right direction, keep in mind the big picture, *ensure the implementation of Party policies and principles, and discuss and decide on major issues of their enterprise in accordance with regulations.*[265]

154. A similar expression can be found in the articles of association of Chinese SOEs. For example, the amended articles of association of Datang International

---

260 The top positions of SOEs including board chairmen, CEOs, and Party secretaries, are appointed and evaluated by the Organisation Department.

261 Company Law (n 40) art 19; CPC Constitution (n 127) art 32.

262 As noted above, Li-Wen Lin points out that the top position of 53 central SOEs are often appointed and evaluated by the Central Organisation Department of the CCP. This appointment practice predates the establishment of SASAC and persists to today. For further discussion, see Lin, 'A Network Anatomy of Chinese State-Owned Enterprises' (n 144); See also Lin, 'China's National Champions: Governance Change Through Globalization?' (n 253).

263 Rosen, Leutert and Guo, 'Missing Link: Corporate Governance in China's State Sector' (n 125).

264 《关于加快推进中央企业党建工作总体要求纳入公司章程有关事项的通知》 [Notice on Matters Regarding Speeding Up and Advancing the Inclusion of Overall Requirements for Central State-Owned Enterprises' Party-Building Work in Articles of Association] Guozi Dangwei Dangjian [2017] No 1, 3 January 2017 (Notice on Central SOEs).

265 CPC Constitution (n 127) art 33 (emphasis added).

Power Generation Co Ltd, a Hong Kong-listed central SOE, included the following clauses:

> Article 10 In accordance with the requirements of the Constitution of the Communist Party of China, an organisation of the Communist Party of China shall be established and play the core leadership role, functioning as the political core of the Company, providing direction, managing the overall situation and ensuring implementation. …
>
> Article 139 (20) The opinions of the Party Committee shall be heard before the board of directors decides on material issues of the Company.[266]

155. The requirement of Party committee participation in the decision-making processes of SOEs has invited ongoing debates on the influence of the Party over SOEs (or whether Chinese SOEs are subject to the Party's control). Barry Naughton, for example, has expressed the view that the requirement that the Communist Party exercise more effective influence over boards of directors seems to be in tension with another requirement of 'building authoritative Boards of Directors … and give the firm more operational autonomy, with the Board as the ultimate authority.[267]

156. However, Xiao Yaqing, the then head of the SASAC of State Council (now the head minister for the Ministry of Industry and Information Technology) does not share this concern.

> Strengthening the leadership of the Party with respect to SOEs, and incorporation of the Party Constitution into SOEs' articles of association, is in line with the Chinese Constitution, because the Constitution provides that the core of leadership should be the Party.[268]

157. It is possible that the requirement for Party committees to discuss 'material issues of firms' (whatever that means) before the board can make a determination, limits the managerial autonomy in SOEs and enables the Party to exercise effective control over the decision-making process of SOEs. It may be too soon to tell at this stage of reform and more empirical evidence will be needed to confirm this point of view.[269]

---

266 Datang International Power Generation Co Ltd 'Proposed Amendments to Articles of Association and Notice of EGM' (30 June 2017) art 10, 139(20) (emphasis added) <https://www1.hkexnews.hk/listedco/listconews/sehk/2017/0630/ltn201706301016.pdf>.

267 Barry Naughton, 'The Current Wave of State Enterprise Reform in China: A Preliminary Appraisal' (2017) 12(2) Asian Economic Policy Review 282, 293–94.

268 '明报：肖亚庆指出上市国企设党委 股东利益更受保护 [Ming Pao: Xiao Yaqing Pointed Out That Set Up Party Commitee at Listed Company Will Increase the Protection of Shareholders Interests]' (23 October 2017) <http://www.sasac.gov.cn/n2588025/n2588139/c8089518/content.html>.

269 Rosen, Leutert and Guo (n 262) 30–31.

Cross-Appointment System

158. Another way of increasing Party involvement in SOEs is the 'cross-appointment system' (*Shuangxiang Jiaoliu*),[270] which refers to the practice of the senior member of an SOE holding concurrent Party committee posts.[271] The 'cross-appointment system', according to Jiang Daxing, is designed to blend the members of the Party committee into the internal management organ of SOEs.[272] In particular, under the 'cross-appointment system', the chairman of the board should also serve as the secretary of the Party committee of the SOE; the general manager should also serve as the deputy secretary of the Party committee of the SOE; and 'other senior executives and board personnel are encouraged to overlap with members of the Party committee in the SOE.'[273] As Wendy Leutert notes: 'By the end of Xi's first term in 2017, the percentage of China's core central state-owned enterprises led by leaders serving simultaneously as board chairman and Party secretary topped 90%.'[274]

159. Therefore, it is safe to say that the current reform further increases the presence of the Party in the state sector. On the one hand, the current reform tightened the connection between the Party and Chinese SOEs, which may augment the politically privileged position of SOEs. On the other hand, from a pure competition perspective, requiring Party committee discussion before a board decision may disadvantage SOEs as it may undermine their ability to govern efficiently. The issue of how the linkage between the Party and SOEs may cause competitive neutrality problems in China's market will be analysed further in Chapter 5.

3.2.4 Balancing Mixed Ownership Reform with State Assets Protection

160. The mixed ownership of SOEs is aptly described as 'an important manifestation of the basic economic regime of China'.[275] In practice, mixed ownership means that non-state firms can hold shares in SOEs and vice versa. There are various ways for SOEs to achieve mixed ownership, for example, 'restructuring, IPO, introducing strategic investors, converting part of the state-owned shares into preferred shares or employee share ownership.'[276]

---

270 SASAC, Notice on Central SOEs (n 263).

271 Cross appointment system (*Shuanxiang Jiaoliu*) is also translated as 'two-way entry, overlapping position holding' by Wendy Leutert. According to Leutert, it is common for central SOE executives to hold two of these positions simultaneously under the requirement of 'two-way entry, overlapping position holding': Wendy Leutert, 'The Political Mobility of China's Central State-Owned Enterprise Leaders' (2018) 233 The China Quarterly 1, 5.

272 蒋大兴 [Jiang Daxing], '《走向"政治性公司法"——党组织如何参与公司治理》 [Political Company Law: How Party Organisation Participates in Corporate Governance]' (2017) 23(3) Journal of Central South University (Social Science) 27.

273 The cross-appointment system is mentioned in the Guiding Opinions on Governance (n 143) s 2(5).

274 Wendy Leutert, 'Firm Control: Governing the State-Owned Economy Under Xi Jinping' (2018/1–2) China Perspectives 27.

275 CCCPC Reforms Decision (n 233).

276 OECD (n 30) 87.

However, as the case of Yunan Baiyao Holdings, China Unicom and Jiangxi Salt (detailed below) revealed, the injection of capital into SOEs (rather than selling the existing equity in SOEs) is the most commonly used method to achieve mixed ownership.[277]

161. Mixed ownership SOEs, as noted in Section 3.1.3, is not new and can be traced back to the late 1990s. On the one hand, mixed-ownership reform can incorporate non-state interests in the governance of SOEs by introducing additional checks and balances in the applicable board, thereby improving transparency in the decision-making of SOEs.[278] As explained by the OECD, a 'private owner may not be able to prevent the expropriation of wealth from minority shareholders and tunnelling, but at a minimum can enhance transparency.'[279] On the other hand, mixed ownership, from a pure competition perspective, may do little to weaken the linkage between SOEs and their government owners. As observed by Curitis J Milhaupt and Wentong Zheng, conducting mixed-ownership reform in China 'will not, in reality, yield significant changes in how SOEs are positioned in relation to the state.'[280]

162. In light of the above observations, it may be useful to conduct case analyses to discover whether the linkage between SOEs and government owners has changed as the result of the mixed-ownership reforms. With this aim in mind, the analysis in the next section is based on the ownership structure of the firm after implementation of the mixed-ownership reform, including: 100 per cent privately owned firms; firms with minority government ownership; firms with majority government ownership; and 100 per cent state-owned firms.

100% Privately Owned Firms

163. Hypothetically speaking, implementing mixed-ownership reform could lead to privatisation insofar as government could sell all its shares to non-SOEs. Firms of that kind would not be 'mixed ownership' firms, but will be briefly discussed here to give context to the meaning of wholly state-owned enterprises. Again, in theory, privatisation could bring about a dramatic reduction of the linkages between government and firms (and reduced competitive neutrality problems caused by SOEs). But due to the ideological sensitivities associated with privatisation in the context of the socialist market economy (coupled with the requirement to 'prevent the loss of state assets'), and due

277 This viewpoint is shared by Chen Long, the Chinese economist at Gavekal Dragonomics, who used the case of Jiangxi Salt to illustrate that the mixed ownership reform of Jiangxi Salt was a capital injection rather than an asset sale. For more detailed discussion, David Keohane, 'SOE You Think You Can Reform? Mixed-Ownership Edition', *Financial Times* (28 September 2015) <https://ftalphaville.ft.com/2015/09/28/2140985/soe-you-think-you-can-reform-mixed-ownership-edition/>.

278 OECD (n 30) 36.

279 ibid 87.

280 Curtis J Milhaupt and Wentong Zheng, 'Why Mixed-Ownership Reforms Cannot Fix China's State Sector' (Paulson Policy Memorandum, January 2016) 2 <http://www.paulsoninstitute.org/wp-content/uploads/2017/01/PPM_SOE-Ownership_Milhaupt-and-Zheng_English_R.pdf>.

to the launch of China's anti-corruption campaign since 2012[281], Chinese government officials may be unwilling to pursue privatisation for the fear of making mistakes. In particular, for government officers in China, the decision to sell all shares in an SOE to non-state investors carries the risk of being accused of devaluating state assets, or engaging in corruption and underhanded transactions. It is thus reasonable to believe that privatisation is not feasible in the foreseeable future of SOE reform.

Minority Government Ownership

164. The government can become a minority shareholder by conducting mixed-ownership reform, permitting non-state firms (including private investors and foreign investors) to hold a majority of shares in a given SOE and thus gain effective control of the SOE. As discussed in Section 3.2.2, only general commercial SOEs can adopt the mixed-ownership structure above.[282] The mixed-ownership reform implemented by the provincial SOE, Yunnan Baiyao Holdings, serves as a good example and will be discussed directly below to show how the ownership structure and the corporate governance of Yunnan Baiyao Holdings changed after the mixed-ownership reforms.

Yunnan Baiyao Holdings Case

165. The SASAC of the Province of Yunnan (hereafter Yunnan SASAC) initially held 100 per cent of the shares in Yunnan Baiyao Holdings, a profitable provincial SOE which manufactures and sells traditional Chinese medicine (TCM), pharmaceutical medicine raw materials, and preparations, personal care products, and native herbs.[283] In 2016, as a response to the mixed-ownership reform, the Yunnan SASAC introduced strategic investors to Yunnan Baiyao Holdings. In particular, Yunnan SASAC approved a private investor, the New Huadu Industrial Group, for the first time in 2016. Yunnan SASAC diluted its shareholding to 50 per cent and the New Huadu Industrial Group obtained 50 per cent.[284] In 2017, Yunnan SASAC, and the New Huadu Industrial Group, further diluted their shareholdings by allowing another private investor, Yuyue Technology Development Co Ltd, to inject capital into Yunnan Baiyao

281 The current anti-corruption campaign is launched soon after the 18th National People's Congress, which selected Xi Jinping (now PRC President) as the new Party leader and Chair of the CCP Central Military Commission. Since 2012, more than 1.5 million Chinese government officials have been found guilty of some corruption-related charge, including some of the Party's most senior leaders. For more detail about the anti-corruption campaign, see Yuen Yuen Ang, *China's Gilded Age: The Paradox of Economic Boom and Vast Corruption* (CUP 2020) 65.

282 For example, a 100 per cent state-owned enterprise could either sell out its government shares to non-SOEs or absorb private capital to dilute its government shares (to the extent the government becomes a minority shareholder).

283 'Yunnan Baiyao Group', *Forbes* (Company Profile, 12 May 2020) <https://www.forbes.com/companies/yunnan-baiyao-group/#71deea1a7287>.

284 Yunnan Baiyao Group, 《云南白药集团股份有限公司2016年年度报告》 [Yunnan Baiyao Group Co Ltd Annual Report 2016] (2016) <http://www.yunnanbaiyao.com.cn/upload/files/1704/%E4%BA%91%E5%8D%97%E7%99%BD%E8%8D%AF%EF%BC%9A2016%E5%B9%B4%E5%B9%B4%E5%BA%A6%E6%8A%A5%E5%91%8A.PDF> (Yunnan Baiyao 2016).

Holdings.[285] Taken together, these two transactions transformed Yunnan Baiyao Holdings from a wholly government-owned SOE into a state minority-owned company. Yunnan SASAC is now a minority shareholder with only 45 per cent of the shares in Yunnan Baiyao Holdings (see Figure 3.1).

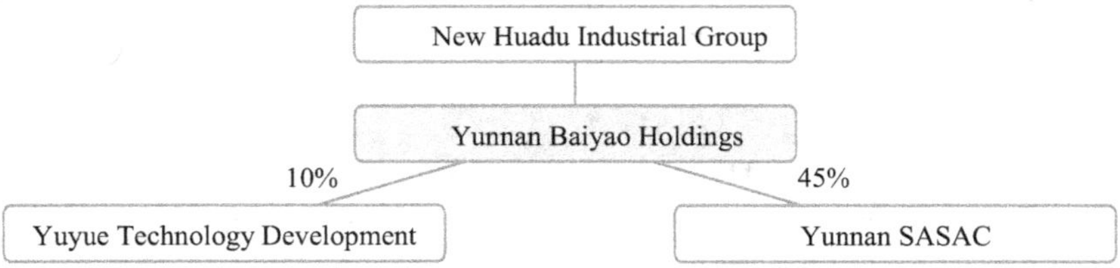

Figure 3.1 Shareholding structure of Yunnan Baiyao Holdings after the mixed-ownership reform.

166. The case study reveals a number of interesting points. First, while Yunnan SASAC did not provide information on whether Yunnan Baiyao Holdings was classified as a commercial SOE or public welfare SOE, the outcome of two private investors together hold the majority proportion of shares (55 per cent). Yunnan Baiyao Holdings suggests that it belongs to the commercial SOEs group, or more precisely a general commercial SOE that is expected to be competitive in the market. Second, the link between government and Yunnan Baiyao Holdings was weakened (though not completely removed) by the establishment of a standard board of directors and the addition of new board members from the private investors. The composition of the board of directors in Yunnan Baiyao Holdings was changed to include five directors, with two members from the New Huadu Industrial Group, one from the Yuyue Technology Development Co Ltd and two from the Yunnan SASAC.[286] Third, the linkage between the Party and Yunnan Baiyao Holdings may have weakened as the executive team of Yunnan Baiyao Holdings[287] no longer enjoys administrative ranking equivalent to that of provincial governors.[288]

Majority Government Ownership

167. The government can become (or remain) a majority shareholder after implementing mixed-ownership reform, which implies that non-SOEs interest will exist as the minority shareholders in SOEs. SOEs that are categorised in

285 Yunnan Baiyao Group, 《云南白药集团股份有限公司 2017 年半年度报告摘要》 [Yunnan Baiyao Group Co Ltd First Half-Year 2017 Report Summary] (2017) <http://www.yunnanbaiyao.com.cn/upload/files/1708/%E4%BA%91%E5%8D%97%E7%99%BD%E8%8D%AF%EF%BC%9A2017%E5%B9%B4%E5%8D%8A%E5%B9%B4%E5%BA%A6%E6%8A%A5%E5%91%8A%E6%91%98%E8%A6%81.PDF> (Yunnan Baiyao 2017).

286 Yunnan Baiyao Group ‘《关于控股股东完成工商变更登记的公告》[Announcement on Changing the Controlling Shareholders of Business Registration]’ (28 June 2017) <http://pdf.dfcfw.com/pdf/H2_AN201706280674602279_1.pdf>.

287 李自良 [Li Ziliang] and 吉哲鹏 [Ji Zhepeng], ‘《老字号云南白药的创新路：“均衡股权”探索混改路径》 [Traditional Brand Yunnan Baiyao’s Innovation: Exploring “Balanced Equity” for Mixed-Ownership Reform]’ 新华网 [Xinhuanet News] (31 January 2019) <http://www.xinhuanet.com/local/2019-01/31/c_1124067844.htm>.

288 《关于王明辉等三名同志免职的通知》[Notice to Remove the Government Positions of Wang Huiming] Government of Yunnan Province, Yunzhengren [2017] No 22, 22 April 2017.

the special commercial SOEs group are more likely to achieve this mixed-ownership outcome because the government is required to be a controlling shareholder for these SOEs, according to Opinions of the State Council on the Development of Mixed Ownership Economy by State-Owned Enterprises issued by the State Council.[289] The mixed-ownership reform implemented by one of the central SOEs, China Unicom (also known as China United Network Communications Group Co Ltd), has been selected to show whether the connection between the government (and the Party) and China Unicom has changed after the mixed-ownership reform.

China Unicom's Mixed Ownership Reform Case

168. China Unicom is one of 97 central-owned SOEs (*Yangqi*) under the supervision of the SASAC of State Council. China Unicom was selected as one of six candidates for a pilot program in mixed-ownership reform by the National Development and Reform Commission (NDRC) in 2016.[290] Before the mixed-ownership reform, China Unicom held 62.74 per cent of the shares in its subsidiary company, China United Network Communications Limited listed in Shanghai (Unicom A-Share Company), while public shareholders held around 37.25 per cent[291] (see Figure 3.2).

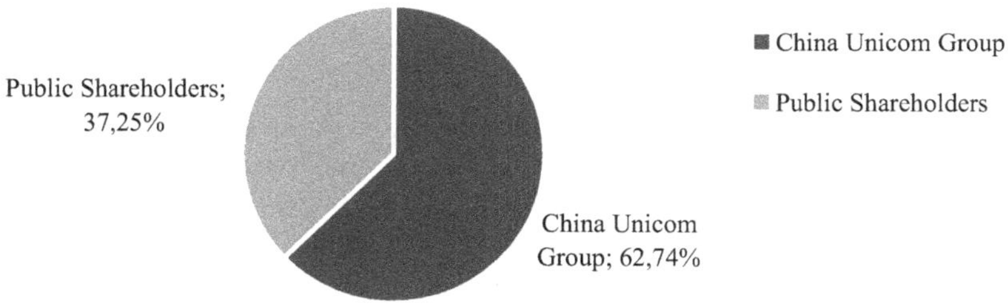

Figure 3.2 Shareholding structure of Unicom A-Share company before the mixed-ownership reform (as of 13 April 2017).[292]

169. In August 2017, in line with the current reform, Unicom A-Share Company announced its mixed-ownership reform plan.[293] To diversify equity and shareholding, the mixed ownership plan of China Unicom was designed

289 《国务院关于国有企业发展混合所有制经济的意见》[Opinions of the State Council on the Development of Mixed Ownership Economy by State-Owned Enterprises] Guo Fa [2015] No 54, 23 September 2015, s 2(4).

290 '《以混合所有制改革试点作为深化国企改革的突破口　实现完善治理强化激励突出主业提高效率的改革试点目标——国家发展改革委召开国有企业混合所有制改革试点专题会》[Pilot Programs of Mixed-Ownership Reform of SOEs]' (Press Conference, National Development and Reform Commission, 28 September 2016) <https://www.ndrc.gov.cn/xwdt/xwfb/201609/t20160930_955188.html>.

291 China Unicom, *Annual Report of China Unicom* (Hong Kong) Ltd (2016) 20 <https://www.chinaunicom.com.hk/en/ir/reports/2016_20f.pdf> (China Unicom 2016).

292 ibid. The 0.01% shares of Unicom A-Share Company are held by two other promoters.

293 For an official announcement of the reform, '中国联通关于混合所有制改革有关情况的专项公告 [The Special Announcement by China Unicom Regarding Proposal of Mixed Ownership Reform]', China United Network Communications Ltd (20 August 2017) <http://static.cninfo.com.cn/finalpage/2017-08-21/1203829685.PDF>.

to introduce strategic investors (or new investors) to inject capital into the company. As a result, the shares held by China Unicom were diluted from 62.74 per cent to 36.67 per cent,[294] with the result that China Unicom lost its majority share position but retained its position of controlling shareholder. In fact, 35.19 per cent of the shares of the company were now in the hands of new investors (both from state and non-state sectors).[295] Taking a close look at the new investors, the most prominent is state-owned China Life, which holds 10.22% of the shares on issue in Unicom-A Share. Another state investor is China Structural Reform Fund Co Ltd, which has a 6.11 per cent shareholding[296] (see Figure 3.3).

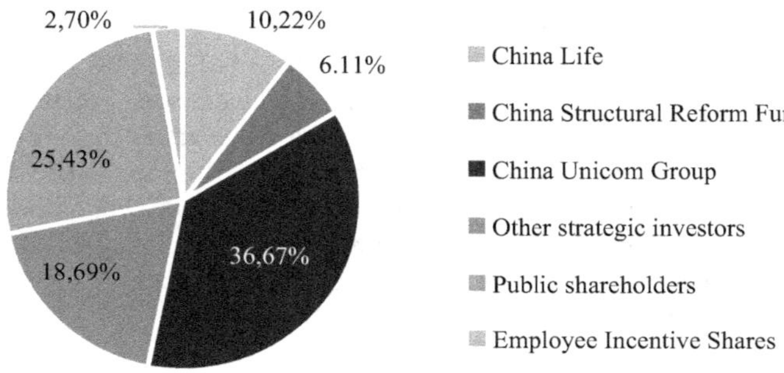

Figure 3.3 Shareholding structure of Unicom A-Share Company after the mixed-ownership reform in 2017.[297]

170. Two things are revealed by the Unicom case. First, the connection between government and Unicom A-Share Company was not weakened by the mixed-ownership reform, despite efforts to introduce new investors. For example, the diversified group of government shareholders (China Life [10.22 per cent], China Structural Reform Fund Co Ltd [6.11 per cent] and China Unicom [36.67 per cent]) still hold over 53 per cent of Unicom A-Share Company. That means the controlling shareholders in the Unicom A-Share Company are still the government.

171. Second, the connection between the Party and the newly reformed Unicom A-Share Company is weakened because the corporate governance of the Unicom A-Share Company improved after mixed ownership reform. For example, five directors from the new investors (like China Life Insurance

294 ibid 3.

295 ibid. Perhaps the most eye-catching investors are private technology companies, including Tencent (5.18%), Baidu (3.30%), JD.com (2.36%), Alibaba (2.04%), Suning Commerce Group (1.88%), and Kuang-Chi Group (1.88%).

296 China Structural Reform Fund Co Ltd, established on September 22, 2016, is a state-owned and invested private fund with the aims of provide fund or direct investment to facilitate mixed-ownership reform and restructuring of central and local government-controlled enterprises. For more information, see China Structural Reform Fund Co Ltd 'Company Profile' (2017) <http://www.cctfund.cn/index.php?c=content&a=list&catid=39#page1>.

297 Source: '中国联通关于混合所有制改革有关情况的专项公告 [The special announcement by China Unicom regarding proposal of mixed ownership reform]' (n 292).

Company, Tencent, Baidu, JD.com and Alibaba[298]) are being added to the Board of directors of the Unicom A-share Company. While the majority of the Board of directors is still drawn from SOEs, the newly assembled board benefits from directors from private sectors as these people could enhance the transparency of the decision making of the China Unicom A-Share Company.

100% Government Ownership

172. The government can still own 100 per cent of the shares in SOEs after mixed-ownership reform. As the case with the firm with zero per cent government ownership mentioned at the beginning of this section shows, a firm that is 100 per cent owned by government is not a mixed-ownership firm. While the connection between government and the reformed SOEs remains the same, the mixed reform provides a new meaning to the wholly state-owned enterprise in China. A relevant example, the Jiangxi Salt Company, is discussed here to help to illustrate that claim.

Jiangxi Salt Company Case

173. The SASAC of the Province of Jiangxi (hereafter Jiangxi SASAC) initially held 100 per cent of shares in the Jiangxi Salt company, which has 'a legal monopoly in China's salt market.'[299] As a way to push forward mixed-ownership reform, Jiangxi SASAC announced that it would introduce strategic investors (or new investors) into the company.[300] Consequently, four new investors became the shareholders of Jiangxi Salt by investing capital into the company. However, as observed by one commentator, 'none of the new investors in Jiangxi Salt actually came from the private sector.'[301] For example, Cinda Asset Management Co was 83 per cent owned by the Ministry of Finance.[302] The other three strategic investors were local SOEs under the supervision of corresponding level SASACs. As a result, the Jiangxi Salt company remains a wholly state-owned firm but with a diversified group of government shareholders. Therefore, a wholly state-owned enterprise in China will in the future more likely be an enterprise owned by a diversified group of government shareholders rather than just one government shareholder, as was formerly the case.

Concluding Comments

174. Although many optimists interpret mixed-ownership reform as a transitional step towards privatisation of SOEs, the requirement that government maintain the position of the controlling shareholder in 'Special SOEs'

298 '中国联合网络通信股份有限公司第五届董事会第十四次会议决议公告' [Announcement on the 5th Meeting of the Board of Directors, No 14 Conference Resolutions of China United Network Communications Limited] 3 <http://static.cninfo.com.cn/finalpage/2018-01-24/1204357843.PDF>

299 US-China Economic and Security Review Commission, *2016 Annual Report to Congress* (2016), 97 <https://www.uscc.gov/Annual_Reports/2016-annual-report-congress>.

300 Keohane (n 276).

301 ibid.

302 US-China Economic and Security Review Commission (n 298).

constitutes a hurdle to achieve the goal of privatisation. Also, whether the connection between hybrid SOEs and their government owners (and the Party) is strengthened or weakened is currently uncertain. On the one hand, implementing mixed-ownership reform could dilute government control over hybrid SOEs by introducing additional shareholders, as the Yunnan Baiyao case suggests. On the other hand, mixed ownership offers little change in the connection between government and hybrid SOEs, as the China Unicom case reveals.[303]

175. A more troubling issue, as pointed out by scholars, is that the mixed-ownership reform has the potential to extend rather than reduce current state sectors in China because SOEs are also encouraged to invest in competitive private firms under the mixed-ownership requirements.[304] For example, Barry Naughton warns 'the reform may actually encourage the extension of SOEs into competitive markets where they do not currently have a presence … [by] encouraging state capital to expand its investment in, and control of, private firms.'[305]

176. Nevertheless, a growing number of hybrid SOEs in the market of China should be expected in the near future. From a competition standpoint, the question of whether these hybrid SOEs are competing with private firms on a level playing field in China's market becomes significant and will be explored in Chapter 5.

3.2.5 Upgrading State Asset Supervision System

177. The current reform calls for upgrading the current state asset management system to one that can make more efficient use of state capital.[306] Measures to achieve this goal include: transforming the function of state assets regulatory bodies (i.e. SASAC and its local branches); establishing state capital investment companies (SCICs) and state capital operation companies (SCOCs), or collectively state capital investment and operation companies (SCIOs), to improve the investment of state capital in the market. In practice, SASAC

303 The China Unicom case revealed that the connection between the government and Unicom A-Share Company was not weakened by the mixed-ownership reform because the controlling shareholders in the Unicom A-Share Company are still the government. A similar view is shared by Milhaupt and Zheng (n 279).

304 As noted at the beginning of Section 3.2.4, mixed ownership means that non-state firms can hold shares in SOEs and vice versa. For example, the appearance of SOEs in the modern services and technologies sectors is being observed by commentator Andrew Batson, 'The State of the State Sector' (Gavekal Dragonomics 2017) 9. See also Lardy (n 241) 92.

305 Barry Naughton, 'Restructuring and Reform: China 2016' in Iris Day and John Simon (eds), *Structural Change in China: Implications for Australia and the World* (RBA Annual Conference Volume 2016) 55, 69 <www.rba.gov.au/publications/confs/2016/pdf/rba-conference-volume-2016-naughton.pdf>.

306 《国务院关于改革和完善国有资产管理体制的若干意见》[Several Opinions of the State Council on Reforming and Improving the State-Owned Asset Management System] Guo Fa [2015] No 63, 25 October 2015 (Several Opinions on Reforming); 《国务院关于印发改革国有资本授权经营体制方案的通知》[Notice of the State Council on Printing and Distribution of the Plan for Reforming the System of Authorised Operation of the State-Owned Capital] Guo Fa [2019] No 9, 19 April 2019 (Notice of the Plan for Reforming).

is expected to authorise some of its ownership rights to the SCIOs,[307] which are established to specialise in the management of state assets in the market.

178. In particular, SCIOs are expected to function as state asset managers, which implies that the investment of state assets by SCIOs should be based on commercial and market principles.[308] Yet, it would be incorrect to presume that SCIOs are likely to operate as pure commercial investment companies (like the Central Huijin Investment Company under the current system[309]) as their investments are also required to service national strategies and national industrial policies.[310] In this sense, the role of SCIOs in the state asset management system is more like a state policy or development fund rather than a wealth fund, as observed by Barry Naughton.[311]

179. SCIOs are essentially subordinates of central or local SASACs. In practice, the goals pursued by SCICs and SCOCs are slightly different.[312] Particularly, SCICs focus more on national strategy and industrial policies, whereas SCOCs focus on 'enhancing returns and operational efficiency of state capital.'[313] The progress of establishing SCICs and SCOCs are tangible at both the central and local levels. For example, two pilot SCOCs, China Chengtong Holdings Group Ltd and China Reform Holdings Group Ltd, set up at least four funds, managing about RMB (renminbi) 950 billion in capital.[314] The China Structural Reform Fund (CSRF), the country's largest state-owned private equity fund (worth RMB 350 billion[315]), was initiated by China Chengtong Holdings and nine other SOEs,[316] with the main aim of using state capital to 'provide state-owned enterprises [SOEs] support in development, industrial consolidation, professional reorganization, capacity adjustment and international merger and acquisitions by establishing sub-funds as well as direct investment.'[317] The involvement of CSRF in the China Unicom case (noted in Section 3.2.4) is a

307 《国务院国资委关于印发<国务院国资委授权放权清单(2019年版)>的通知》 [Notice on Issuing the List of Powers Granted and Delegated by the SASAC of the State Council (2019 Edition)] Guo Zi Fa Gai Ge (2019) No 52, 3 June 2019.

308 Guiding Opinions on Reform (n 236).

309 For more detail, see n 50; See also Wu (n 36) 273–75.

310 Several Opinions on Reforming (n 305) s 3(7).

311 Naughton (n 266) 291.

312 ibid 291–92.

313 《国务院关于推进国有资本投资、运营公司改革试点的实施意见》 [Implementation Opinions of the State Council on Promoting the Pilot Reform of State-Owned Capital Investment and Operation Companies] Guo Fa [2018] No 23, 14 July 2018, s 2(1).

314 张锐 [Zhang Rui], '《国有资本投资运营公司将在改革中获更多赋能》 [More Power Will Be Given to State-Owned Capital Investment or Operation Companies During the Reform]' 证券时报网 [Securities Times] (8 March 2018) <http://www.stcn.com/2018/0308/14011770.shtml>.

315 Zheng Chengqiong, 'China Establishes SOE Structural Adjustment Fund' (27 September 2016) <https://www.scio.gov.cn/32618/Document/1492508/1492508.htm>

316 For the list of nine SOE investors, see China Structural Reform Fund (n 294).

317 ibid. See also the interview of CSRF President Zhu Bixin who noted that 'the fund [CSRF] has invested in a number of SOEs already, including China Metallurgical Group Corp, Air China Ltd and Power Construction Corp of China Ltd … In the future, the CSRF will augment investment in high-tech and high-end equipment industry … actively implementing the Made in China 2025 strategy and improving the degree of internationalization of central SOEs': '经济日报：结构调整基金成国企改革重要推手 [Economic Daily: The China Structural Reform Fund Becomes Important Promoter of State-Owned Enterprise Reform]' (21 September 2017) <http://www.sasac.gov.cn/n2588025/n2588139/c7895224/content.html>

good example of how CSRF can support the reform of SOEs in the context of China. At a local level, Chongqing has made impressive progress setting up SCICs and SCOCs schemes.[318] For example, Chongqing Yufu Group, as one of the three SCOCs in Chongqing, is mainly responsible for investing state capital in finance and strategic emerging industries.[319] Chongqing Mechanical and Electrical Group, as one of the three SCICs in Chongqing, has a mandate to invest in high-end computerised machine industries and industries noted in Made in China 2025.[320]

180. It is perhaps too early at this stage to evaluate whether the operation of SCICs and SCOCs will have a positive or negative impact on the playing field in the Chinese market. While the SCICs and SCOCs are established to serve 'national strategy' rather than raising funds for SOEs per se, companies that operate in sectors deemed as important to 'national security key aspects of the national economy' are often SOEs. Consequently, the chance of SOEs receiving funds from SCICs and SCOCs will be much higher than non-SOEs. On the one hand, SCIOs may invest in SOEs and require them to earn commercial rates of return like comparable businesses. Practices of this kind are consistent with the competitive neutrality policy. On the other hand, if SCIOs simply inject a large amount of state capital into SOEs due to their government ownership (without requiring a commercial rate of return),[321] the establishment of SCIOs may create a high risk of subsiding Chinese SOEs, and thereby aggravate competitive neutrality concerns caused by Chinese SOEs (which will be discussed in Chapter 5).

3.3 Conclusion

181. China has been reforming its state sector since 1978, alongside the wider move towards a more market-orientated economy. The operating form of the Chinese SOE is dynamic in the sense that it has come in many different forms, at different stages of its reform journey. However, the reforms have done little to change the dominance of the Party in SOEs. As discussed in Section 3.1, at the beginning of the reform program in 1978, the operating form of SOEs was mostly 'state-run industrial enterprises' (*Guoying Qiye*),

318 Chongqing SASAC has incorporated three provincial-level municipality SOEs into SCOC. In particular, Chongqing Water Group, as one of the SCOCs in Chongqing, is responsible for investing into water-related, wastage, environmental industries etc; Chongqing Land Group is investing in public service industries like education. Chongqing Chemical and Pharmaceutical Group is responsible for investing in biomedical, polymeric materials industries.

319 Government of Chongqiong《关于重庆渝富控股集团深化国有资本运营公司改革试点方案的批复》[Reply to the Pilot Plan Proposed by the Chongqing Yufu Holding Group on Deepening Reform of State-Owned Capital Operation Companies] Yufu [2020] No 12, 19 March 2020.

320 庄冠蓉 [Zhuang Guanrong], '重庆国企改革：抓住管资本"牛鼻子 [Chongqing's Reform of SOEs: Regulating Capital by "Capturing the Nose"]' (中国经济时报 [China Economic Times] 15 August 2016) A07.

321 Sometimes with the purpose of structural adjustment, supporting strategic new enterprises, or preserving the environment.

which were not only owned by the State but also managed by the government in terms of production plans.[322] The state-run industrial enterprises were not market actors as they functioned more like a government department rather than commercial enterprises.

182. The 1987–1992 reforms changed the operation of state-run industrial enterprises into industrial SOEs ('Industrial enterprise owned by whole people', *Quanmin Suoyouzhi Gongye Qiye*), which involved a separate legal entity controlled by government-appointed directors or managers (without shareholders).[323] While the industrial SOEs can be considered to have been market-oriented actors insofar as they had some managerial autonomy,[324] they were unable to compete with non-state firms due to price controls and production plans assigned directly by the Chinese government.[325]

183. The reform of the 1993–2002 period fundamentally altered the operational form of SOEs and introduced market discipline. For example, some industrial SOEs were incorporated into either limited liability companies (LLC) or companies limited by shares (CLS), with all (or a majority of) shares owned by the Chinese government, as explained in Section 3.1.3,[326] whereas others (often small-scale industrial SOEs) were privatised. As a result of this stage of reform, an increasing number of incorporated SOEs as well as industrial SOEs began to participate in the competitive market in China.

184. While the fourth phase of reform (2003–2012) did not dramatically change the operating forms of SOEs, nor the presence of the Party in SOEs, it did increase the involvement of government in the operation of SOEs, resulting in more Chinese SOEs going abroad.[327] Interestingly, with the growing number of competitive SOEs in the market, the question of whether the then newly incorporated SOEs might enjoy competitive advantages due to their government ownership and linkages with the Party was seldom asked by scholars inside China. By contrast, at that time, the question of how the expansion of commercial-oriented SOEs in general may affect the competitive process was widely studied at the international level, resulting in the competitive neutrality principle being adopted in bilateral or multinational investment treaties.

---

322 Naughton (n 183) 92; Shiying (n 232) 35.

323 Hong and Nong (n 51) 317.

324 Naughton (n 183) 118.

325 Zhang Jun, 'China's Price Liberalisation and Market Reform: A Historical Perspective' in Ross Garnaut, Ligang Song and Cai Fang (eds), *China's 40 Years of Reform and Development: 1978–2018* (ANU Press 2018) 215, 292.

326 For example, Nicolas Lardy noted that 'over 10,000 traditional state-owned industrial enterprises, about a fifth of the total, were corporatized as early as 1999': Lardy (n 210) 56.

327 For example, the 'Going Out' strategy (*Zouchuqu*) under the 10th Five Year Plan (2001–2005) was implemented by the Chinese central government with the aim to encourage more Chinese firms (mainly SOEs) to expand their business aboard. For more detailed information about this strategy, see '更好地实施"走出去"战略 [Better Implement the "Going Out" Strategy]' (General Office of the State Council, 15 March 2006) <http://www.gov.cn/node_11140/2006-03/15/content_227686.htm>.

185. While the current reform of the state sector has been implemented since 2013, the reform impact on the operation of Chinese SOEs (generally) and their capacity to compete in the Chinese market is far from clear. However, by analysing the reform measures implemented to date, the following trends can be observed. First, more Chinese SOEs are expected to be competitive in various markets due to the classification and evaluation standards introduced in the current reform. Second, the organisational form of industrial SOEs is diminishing because of the current reform requirement of corporatisation. As a result, incorporated SOEs will be the main operational form of Chinese SOEs. Additionally, while efforts to improve the corporate governance of Chinese SOEs aim to improve their internal structure, the close linkage between the Party and SOEs has been strengthened, and the institutionalised Party committee in SOEs is being viewed as the 'unique advantage of SOEs'. Fourth, how the mixed-ownership reform may affect the connection between SOEs, and their government owners is currently unclear. On the one hand, implementing mixed-ownership reform to SOEs (especially those in the general commercial SOEs group) can dilute government control over SOEs and can introduce additional shareholders to increase decision-making transparency. On the other hand, implementing mixed-ownership reform of SOEs in the special commercial SOEs group provides little change to the current connection between SOEs and their government owners because of the requirement that government should remain the controlling shareholder. Finally, while it is difficult to assess how the level playing field between SOEs and non-SOEs will be affected by the operation of SCICs and SCOCs, there is a risk of subsidising Chinese SOEs if there is no requirement of earning commercial rates of return for the investment provided by the SCICs and SCOCs.

186. Overall, the current reform seems to be heading in the direction of creating highly commercially-oriented SOEs in the market (rather than causing them to exit the market), without fundamentally changing the government ownership and Party connections within SOEs. Given that the market presence of SOEs is increasing, the question of whether competitive SOEs are benefitting (or suffering) from their government ownership and their connection with the Party when competing in China's markets is significant and will be further studied in Chapter 5. Whether the existing legal tools in China – the current competition law and competition policy – are well equipped to deal with the competitive neutrality concerns caused by SOEs (discussed in Chapter 5) will be explored in Chapter 6.

CHAPTER 4

A COMPARATIVE ANALYSIS OF AUSTRALIA'S RESPONSES TO THE COMPETITIVE NEUTRALITY PROBLEMS CAUSED BY SOES

187. In competitive markets, SOEs may have competitive advantages (or disadvantages) as a result of government ownership. Market analysis is essential for identifying the competitive neutrality advantages and disadvantages of SOEs.[328] The regulatory means (or policy solutions) adopted by national governments are therefore tailored to remove the specific competitive advantages (or disadvantages) of SOEs in order to maintain a neutral market environment. While legal and policy means adopted in various jurisdictions are different in form, they are considered in this research to be functionally equivalent[329] as the various legal means are all employed to solve the same (or constant) problem – namely, the lack of competitive neutrality. Consequently, comparative research on the various regulatory and policy means utilised to solve the problem is considered 'an important tool in seeing universalities in what may look like differences'[330] and a useful method to find a desirable model for China (further discussed in Chapter 8).

188. International organisations like the OECD and UNCTAD,[331] as noted in Chapter 2, have since 2004 been conducting extensive comparative research on competitive neutrality concerns caused by SOEs in different jurisdictions.

328 For terminological convenience, 'government businesses' is used interchangeably with SOEs (implying the public ownership of entities) to differentiate from non-government-owned or non-state-owned entities. The 'government businesses' in this research adopts the *Hilmer Review* definition, which includes government departments, statutory authorities, and other government bodies that provide commercial goods or services to the public, private firms, or other government agencies. See *Hilmer Review* (n 92) 293.

329 See Section 1.3.1 for an explanation of the idea of functional equivalence used in this research.

330 Michaels (n 3).

331 For discussion of national practice in the OECD literature since 2003, see generally n 7. For UNCTAD literature, see generally n 232.

One crucial insight provided by comparative research is that the regulatory framework employed in Australia to address those concerns is considered to be the most complete globally,[332] and recommendations are largely built on Australia's framework.[333]

189. This chapter is organised as follows: Sections 4.1 and 4.2 are dedicated to showing, from an observer's viewpoint, how the Australian government identified the competitive neutrality concerns caused by SOEs in its domestic market. The process of identifying competitive neutrality advantages or disadvantages of SOEs in Australia may be relevant to its domestic market but can provide insights (as discussed in Chapter 5) when analysing the perceived competitive neutrality advantages or disadvantages of SOEs in the context of China.

190. Section 4.3 aims to provide a better understanding of why the Australian government decided to address the identified competitive neutrality concerns of SOEs in its market. Sections 4.4 and 4.5 discuss the legal and policy solutions adopted by the government of Australia and how the two principal mechanisms, the competition law and competitive neutrality policy, address the identified (in Section 4.2) competitive neutrality concerns caused by SOEs in the context of Australia. The chapter also attempts to provide a foundation for the propositions put forward in Chapter 7, namely the operation of competitive neutrality policy in practice and the construction of its key institutions in Australia.

4.1 Introduction

191. Competitive neutrality concerns arising from SOEs were recognised in Australia and New Zealand[334] in the 1980s as governments started exposing their SOEs to competition.[335] In particular, the movement towards market-oriented reform,[336] adopted in Australia at the time,[337] transformed traditional

---

332 OECD, 'Maintaining a Level Playing Field' (n 7) 107.

333 For example, the concept of competitive neutrality in the OECD is built on Australia's definition and has been consistently developing. For more discussion of the meaning of competitive neutrality, see Section 2.2.

334 The discussion of the competitive neutrality principle can be traced back to the 1980s as part of SOE reform in New Zealand. For more details of competitive neutrality in New Zealand, see Michael Taggart, *Corporatisation, Privatisation and Public Law* (Legal Research Foundation, UoA 1990) 12.

335 Gary Sturgess, *A Fair Field and No Favours: Competitive Neutrality in UK Public Service Markets* (Confederation of British Industry 2006) 28. Paul Gretton, 'National Economic Reform in a Federal System: The Case of the Australian National Competition Policy and Related Reforms' in Stephen Howes and M Govinda Rao (eds), *Federal Reform Strategies: Lessons from Asia and Australia* (OUP 2013) 34, 41–46.

336 Reform measures such as commercialisation, privatisation, or corporatisation were used at this stage.

337 For more detailed information regarding Australia's microeconomic reform in the 1980s, see Peter J Forsyth, 'Microeconomic Policies and Structural Change', *The Australian Economy in the 1990s* (RBA 2000) 235.

SOEs[338] largely shielded from competition into more profit-oriented SOEs that competed with private companies in various industries. Simply put, the direct influence of the market-oriented reform is evident in the increasing participation of government businesses in both traditional (or monopolistic)[339] and private-sector markets.[340]

192. Consequently, the question of how the expansion of commercial SOEs may affect the competitive process has been asked and studied widely in Australia since the late 1980s. For example, the risk associated with the competitive SOEs in the market was initially examined at the state level in Australia.[341] An excerpt provided by the New South Wales government in 1988 first pointed out the special advantages and disadvantages of its government trading enterprises[342] (GTEs) in NSW may include:

> The cost of debt ... the availability of equality capital for GTEs and the pressure on GTEs to achieve a return on equity capital in line with the riskiness of the assets employed; the capital structure of GTEs; GTEs' tax statues; the cost of inputs provided by other GTEs and the labour market regulations applying to GTEs.[343]

193. It then directly linked GTEs in NSW to the inefficient use of resources, noting that

> if a GTE ... enjoys special advantages or suffers special disadvantages by virtue of its ownership, the resources controlled by the GTE will be influenced by its ownership status ... diverting resources from more efficient competitors or more highly-valued end uses.[344]

194. SOEs (or government-owned businesses), as market participants that operate in a competitive environment, were also found not to be subject to market disciplines such as competition law. For example, as pointed out by then

338 Government business before the market-oriented reform in the 1980s existed as a form of government department within government bureaucracies (without separate legal entities) or statutory authorities (with separate legal entities but subject to government appointed boards). For detailed discussion of the historical evolution of government businesses in Australia, see John Quiggin, 'Governance of Public Corporations: Profits and the Public Benefit' in Michael J Whincop (ed), *From Bureaucracy to Business Enterprise: Legal and Policy Issues in the Transformation of Government Services* (Ashgate 2003) 27, 28–29; Deborah Healey, 'Australian Experience with Competition Law: The State as a Market Actor' in Thomas Cheng, Ioannis Lianos and D Daniel Sokol (eds), *Competition and the State* (SUP 2014) 205, 207.

339 *Hilmer Review* (n 92) 298.

340 OECD, 'Roundtable on Competitive Neutrality in Competition Enforcement: Note by Australia' (DAF/COMP/WD(2015)19, 29 May 2015) 2 <http://www.oecd.org/officialdocuments/publicdisplaydocumentpdf/?cote=DAF/COMP/WD(2015)19&docLanguage=En> (Roundtable CN Australia).

341 Bronwen Morgan, Sophia Bai and Jyotsana Bhasker, 'Competitive Neutrality and the Challenge of Social Enterprise' (2018) 25(3) CCLJ 249, 250.

342 The term 'government trading enterprise' (GTE) is used to describe business units engaged in trading activities, including the provision of goods and services to other parts of the public sector. See New South Wales Steering Committee on Government Trading Enterprises, *A Policy Framework for Improving the Performance of Government Trading Enterprises: A Report* (NSW Government 1988) 1.

343 ibid 18.

344 ibid.

Prime Minister Bob Hawke in 1991, 'some Commonwealth enterprises, State public sector businesses'[345] were excluded from the coverage of the competition law (then TPA).

195. The above findings suggested that further studies were needed to better understand the impact of recent commercial-oriented government businesses on market competition in Australia as a whole (rather than fractional studies at the state and territory level[346]). An independent inquiry into national competition law and policy, headed by the then Dean of the Australian Graduate School of Management at the University of New South Wales, Professor Frederick Hilmer, was commissioned in October 1992.[347] One of the aims of the Hilmer Committee was to provide a broader, national-level study on how to maintain a level playing field in the Australian market. One year later, the Committee's report (now known as the *Hilmer Review* or *Hilmer Report*, after the chair of the committee) was released.[348]

4.2 Recognition of Competitive Neutrality Concerns of SOEs in Australia

4.2.1 Inadequate Coverage of Competition Legislation

196. As noted above, some SOEs were outside the reach of competition law, which constituted the first competitive neutrality concern caused by SOEs in the Australia context. To get a clear picture of the scope of the competition legislation (the Trade Practices Act 1974 [Cth]), the *Hilmer Review* first provided an overview of all the existing exemptions in the competition law.[349] The principle behind this evaluation process, as noted by the *Hilmer Review*, was that 'any exemptions from the application of competitive conduct rules should only be justified on the showing of a clear public interest.'[350] The overall examination touched on a number of exemptions relating to SOEs which are important to the research and will be discussed below. In general, the *Hilmer Review* found that some

345 Commonwealth of Australia, *Parliamentary Debates*, House of Representatives, 12 March 1991, 1761 (Bob Hawke, Prime Minister).

346 Six states in Australia includes Queensland (Qld), New South Wales (NSW), Victoria (Vic), Tasmania (Tas), South Australia (SA) and Western Australia (WA), and two territories, the Australian Capital Territory (ACT) and Northern Territory (NT), which are largely self-governing. See *OECD Reviews of Regulatory Reform: Australia 2010 Towards a Seamless National Economy* (OECD 2010) 68.

347 Bronwen Morgan, *Social Citizenship in the Shadow of Competition: The Bureaucratic Politics of Regulatory Justification* (Ashgate 2003) 66; Frederick G Hilmer, 'The Bases and Impact of Competition Policy' (1995) 25(1) Economic Analysis and Policy 19, 19.

348 *Hilmer Review* (n 92); Rennie and Lindsay (n 7) 7.

349 *Hilmer Review* (n 92) 89–122.

350 ibid 87–88.

exemptions of SOEs enacted years earlier were still justified on the public interest ground, whereas others had lost their justification over time and may need to be changed or repealed.

197. Firstly, the evaluation of the *Hilmer Review* showed that the *ex-ante* authorisation process under the competition law can exempt firms (regardless of their ownership) from the application of competition law.[351] SOEs (at both Commonwealth and state/territory levels), as market players, were no exception. For example, an evaluation of public interests on the one hand and anti-competitive effects of conduct on the other must be conducted by an independent body (currently the ACCC and, on appeal, the Australian Competition Tribunal) before granting immunity to bodies including SOEs. Immunity of this kind, according to the *Hilmer Review*, was appropriate and justified on public interest grounds.

198. Secondly, the federal nature of Australia's system means that state and territory governments could enact state- and territory-based laws and regulations, permitting exemptions for certain conduct of firms from the reach of competition law. In other words, all firms (regardless of ownership) could be granted exemptions under state and territory laws and regulations through specific authorisation. However, some state and territory SOEs in particular had often benefited from this kind of exemption.[352] For example, as stated by Deborah Healey: 'The Australian States and Territories often made laws and regulations favouring their own industries and undertakings, and the Commonwealth could not control this.'[353] In addition, exemptions legislated by state and territory statutes or regulations did not have an expiration date, which meant they would effectively remain in place once enacted even when circumstances changed. As a result, the *Hilmer Review* argued that exemptions of this kind risked favouring particular interests (and may undermine overall public interest) and should be changed or repealed.

199. Thirdly, the *Hilmer Review* found that state and territory SOEs (not Commonwealth SOEs) were often entitled to Crown immunity (also known as the doctrine of Crown immunity[354]), which exempted them from the coverage of competition law.[355] Crown immunity is built on the presumption that

---

351 See for example, ACCC, 'Guidelines for Authorisation of Conduct (Non-Merger)' (5 March 2019) <https://www.accc.gov.au/system/files/Guidelines%20for%20Authorisation%20of%20conduct%20%28non-merger%29.pdf>; ACCC, 'Merger Authorisation Guidelines' (24 October 2018) <https://www.accc.gov.au/system/files/Merger%20Authorisation%20Guidelines%20-%20October%202018.pdf>.

352 *Hilmer Review* (n 92) 10–13. See also Healey (n 337) 220. For example, Deborah Healey pointed out that 'conduct specifically authorized by commonwealth, state, or territory statute or regulation was not traditionally subject to the Act [Trade Practices Act 1974].'

353 Deborah Healey, 'Australia' in Mark Williams (ed), *The Political Economy of Competition Law in Asia* (Edward Elgar 2013) 344, 352. See also Healey (n 337) 209.

354 The term 'Crown', according to Robertson Wright, refers to the relevant executive governments (including their instrumentalities etc). Accordingly, the Crown in right of the Northern Territory, for example, can mean the Northern Territory government. See Robertson Wright, 'The Future of Derivative Crown Immunity: With a Competition Law Perspective' (2007) 14(3) CCLJ 240, 240–41.

355 *Hilmer Review* (n 92) 116–20.

no statute binds the activities of the executive government (its instrumentalities, agents and employees[356]) unless it is expressly named in the statute, or there is a necessary implication that it should be bound.[357] As Deborah Healey and Jack Coles comment:

> Before Hilmer reported, the High Court in *Bropho v Western Australia* found that the Aboriginal Heritage Act 1972 (WA) would bind the Crown in the absence of express words or necessary implication where the provisions of the legislation, including by reference to its subject matter, purpose and policy (when construed in the context of permissible extrinsic aids) disclosed an intention to bind the Crown.[358]

200. The *Hilmer Review* found that, under the TPA, only the 'business activities' of the Crown in the right of the Commonwealth and its instrumentalities were subject to competition law at the time.[359] However, in determining whether the activities of the Crown could be described as 'carrying on business,' a close assessment by way of a case-by-case basis by the Court was required.[360] On the other hand, the Crown in the right of the states and the Crown in the right of territories were found by the Courts to be outside of the reach of competition law due to 'the absence of express words or a necessary implication' that they should be covered.[361] As a consequence, the Crown in the right of the Commonwealth was covered by competition law at the time, whereas the Crown in the right of the states and territories were left outside. The *Hilmer Review* concluded that there was little justification for this outcome. Moreover, Crown immunity in fact permitted an ownership-based exemption from competition law which could not be justified on the public interest ground.

201. Lastly, some unincorporated state SOEs (not Commonwealth or territory SOEs) may be exempt from the competition law due to constitutional constraints.[362] As discussed in the previous section, Australia is a federation made up of states and territories, with a separate Commonwealth government[363] superimposed

356 Robertson Wright, 'Derivative Governmental Immunity: Lessons from Baxter and the Trade Practices Act' (2008) 16 CCLJ 114, 115.

357 Stephen G Corones, *Competition Law in Australia* (6th edn, Thomson Reuters 2014) 241. See also Anthony Gray, 'Options for the Doctrine of Crown Immunity in 21st Century Australia' (2009) 16(4) AJ Admin L 200.

358 Deborah Healey and Jack Coles, 'From "Carries on Business" to "In Trade or Commerce": Efficiency in Government or Semantic Endeavour?' (2018) 26 CCLJ 47, 51.

359 *Hilmer Review* (n 92) 116.

360 A detailed discussion of jurisprudence on the meaning of 'carries on a business' in the Australian context is set out in Healey and Coles (n 357), 54–64.

361 ibid 51; for a brief historical overview of Crown Immunity in Australia, see Healey (n 337) 211–19.

362 ibid 212–13. State SOEs would generally be caught under the 1974 TPA as they would constitute 'corporations' in the constitutional sense if they were incorporated and carrying on business.

363 In this research, the Commonwealth government of Australia is also referred to as the Australia federal government. The term federal regulation is used interchangeably with Commonwealth regulation.

over the individual governments in each state and territory.[364] Under Australia's federal constitutional structure, certain powers[365] are specifically conferred on the Commonwealth government by each of the states[366] and the states exercise residual power.[367] The competition law, as Commonwealth legislation, must have its basis in the legislative powers of Commonwealth Parliament in the Australian Constitution. The legislative powers relied upon to found competition law were the powers to make law with respect to 'foreign and trading or financial corporations formed within the limits of the Commonwealth'[368] and to 'interstate or overseas trade or commerce.'[369] At that time, the *Hilmer Review* found that, due to the constitutional constraint, the application of competition law was affected by the legal form of business (some unincorporated businesses such as professional partnerships or farmers escaped coverage of the competition law[370]) and the character of the transactions (e.g. the intra-state trading activities of the Commonwealth, states, or territories were outside the coverage of competition laws).[371]

4.2.2 Competitive Neutrality Advantages of SOEs

202. The second competitive neutrality concern caused by SOEs in the Australian market is the 'net competitive advantages' enjoyed by SOEs due to government ownership. A brief word on terms is useful here. Instead of using the term 'competitive neutrality advantages' (as explained in the section 2.3.3), the *Hilmer Review* adopted the term 'net competitive advantages' to describe the type of competitive advantages enjoyed by SOEs as a result of their government ownership. The term implies the 'net competitive advantages' are differentiated from other forms of competitive advantages created by SOEs through 'differences in size, assets, skills, experience and culture.'[372] It is understandable that the government, as a shareholder, has an incentive to maximise its financial interest in its commercial enterprise. However, the government as a regulator oversees the commercial activities of an enterprise. The multiple roles played by the government may, from a competitive neutrality viewpoint, cause concern in that the government may favour SOEs over other competitors by, for example, shielding SOEs from competition.

203. It is appropriate to point out at the outset that identifying net competitive advantages of SOEs with precision may be challenging in practice. In fact, this difficulty is expressly acknowledged in the *Hilmer Review*, which notes: 'In any

364 Rennie and Lindsay (n 7) 5.
365 Australian Constitution s 51.
366 Rennie and Lindsay (n 7) 5.
367 Healey Deborah, *Australian Trade Practices Law* (2nd edn, CCH Australia 1993) 7–22.
368 Healey (n 337) 209, quoting Australian Constitution s 51(xx).
369 ibid 209, quoting *Australian Constitution* s 51(i).
370 *Hilmer Review* (n 92) 133.
371 ibid 115–16.
372 ibid 293.

particular case, it may be difficult to determine the extent of the net competitive advantage or disadvantage with precision.'[373] A similar view is shared by Deborah Healey, who argues that competitive neutrality advantages of SOEs may 'manifest in number of ways. Distortions by advantaged government business enterprises may be direct and clear-cut or more subtle.'[374]

204. Unfortunately, the analytical framework used by the *Hilmer Review* to assess and identify net competitive advantages (or disadvantages) associated with SOEs is not specified. Instead, a list of competitive advantages enjoyed by SOEs by virtue of their government ownership is provided by the *Hilmer Review*, including

> immunity from various taxes and charges; immunity from various regulatory requirements; explicit or implicit government guarantees on debts; concessional interest rates on loans; not being required to account for depreciation expenses; not being required to achieve a commercial rate of return on assets; and effective immunity from bankruptcy. In some cases a government business will also operate in both monopoly and competitive markets, presenting opportunities for cross-subsidisation.[375]

205. The list above is not exhaustive and other unidentified net advantages (and disadvantages) may vary across SOEs and be more difficult to identify.[376] However, the most common or widespread net competitive advantages of SOEs in the context of Australia can be summarised into four, as follows:

- exemptions from various taxes
- access to borrowings at concessional interest rates
- exemptions from complying with regulatory arrangements imposed on private sector competitors, and
- other benefits associated with not having to achieve a commercial rate of return on assets.[377]

206. Besides those identified above, other net competitive advantages enjoyed by the SOEs are more 'difficult to identify and correct'[378] and will rely on individual consideration of the facts by the governments.[379]

---

373 ibid 297.

374 Deborah Healey, 'Competitive Neutrality: The Concept' in *Competitive Neutrality and its Application in Selected Developing Countries* (UNCTAD RPP, 2014) 12, 12.

375 *Hilmer Review* (n 92) 296–97.

376 Commonwealth of Australia, Commonwealth Competitive Neutrality Policy Statement (June 1996) 15–16 <https://treasury.gov.au/sites/default/files/2019-03/cnps.pdf> (Commonwealth CN Policy Statement).

377 ibid 6.

378 ibid.

379 Deborah Healey, 'Competitive Neutrality: Addressing Government Advantage in Australian Markets' in Josef Drexl and Vicente Bagnoli (eds), *State-Initiated Restraints of Competition* (Edward Elgar 2015) 3, 17.

207. The above noted competitive neutrality advantages enjoyed by SOEs potentially impact competition. In particular, these government ownership-generated advantages can give SOEs significant competitive advantages over their rivals. For example, SOEs can benefit from government ownership through low-cost borrowing as lending to government is often perceived as low risk. This low cost of borrowing will enable SOEs to price below more efficient or equally efficient rivals and take business from competitors. Allowing a less efficient SOE to take business away from a more efficient competitor, simply because advantages are generated from its government ownership (rather than merit), is problematic from a competition perspective as it indicates that resources are not being used efficiently (allocation efficiency is further discussed in Section 4.3.1).

4.2.3 Competitive Neutrality Disadvantages of SOEs Identified in the Hilmer Review

208. The *Hilmer Review* notes that the competitiveness of SOEs may be impaired by the competitive disadvantages resulting from their government ownership status. A list of examples of the potential net competitive disadvantages associated with SOEs in the context of Australia is provided by the *Hilmer Review* which includes:

> greater accountability obligations; requirement to provide community service obligations; reduced managerial autonomy; requirements to comply with various government policies on wages, employment and industrial relations; and higher superannuation costs.[380]

209. The listed net disadvantages, such as the greater level of reporting to either portfolio ministers or other agencies (which only apply to SOEs)[381] or higher public sector superannuation standards,[382] may increase the costs of SOEs, thus placing them in a disadvantaged position compared to their private rivals. Additionally, due to the nature of SOEs, community service obligations (also known as public service obligations) are often entrusted to them and may also have implications for the cost of SOEs. Issues involving community service obligations are more complicated and will be considered further in Chapter 7.

210. Compared to frequently exposed competitive neutrality advantages of SOEs, there is relatively limited published information on their competitive neutrality

380 *Hilmer Review* (n 92) 297.

381 Commonwealth of Australia, *Australian Government Competitive Neutrality Guidelines for Managers* (February 2004) 40 <https://storage.googleapis.com/converlens-au/treasury/p/prj20bc99942a7a416b-9dc2a/public_assets/2004%2520Competitive%2520Neutrality%2520Guidelines%2520for%2520-Managers%2520AGCN_guide_v4.pdf> (*CN Guidelines for Managers*).

382 For a more detailed list of potential advantages and disadvantages of SOEs, see National Competition Council, 'Considering the Public Interest Under the National Competition Policy' (November 1996) 11 <http://ncp.ncc.gov.au/docs/PIRePu-001.pdf>.

disadvantages. For example, at the time of writing, no complaints concerning the competitive disadvantages of SOEs had been reported in Australia. This low level of exposure might suggest that Australian governments are permitted to solve the competitive disadvantages of SOEs internally[383] rather than rely on the more transparent external complaint-handling process.

4.3 Rationale for Solving the Competitive Neutrality Concerns of SOEs in Australia

211. To understand why Australia decided to address the competitive neutrality concerns caused by SOEs, it is first helpful to analyse the potential purpose(s) or intent(s) of competitive neutrality policy. As noted above, competitive neutrality concerns caused by SOEs are accompanied by the market reforms of the late 1980s. Before this time, the impact of commercial-oriented government bodies in the market was less developed, particularly as they barely participated in the competitive process. The need to 'find some mechanism to deal with "competitive neutrality" concerns'[384] was not recognised until the *Hilmer Review*.

4.3.1 Efficiency Objective

212. In the absence of a competitively neutral environment, possible inefficiencies in the allocation of resources by SOEs that enjoyed competitive neutrality advantages is frequently viewed as one potential rationale for the design of competitive neutrality policy in Australia.[385] For example, the correlation between efficiency and competition is acknowledged by the *Hilmer Review*:

> Competition offers the promise of lower prices and improved choice for consumers and *greater efficiency*, higher economic growth and increased employment opportunities for the economy as a whole.[386]

213. Economic efficiency, as an economic term, generally comprises three aspects: technical or productive efficiency, allocative efficiency, and dynamic

383 For example, government policy permits any claim for a competitive disadvantage to be used to offset competitive advantages, so that competitive neutrality adjustments (and any associated competitive neutrality payments) reflect only the net competitive neutrality advantage: *CN Guidelines for Managers* (n 380) 39.

384 *Hilmer Review* (n 92) xxxiv.

385 Council of Australian Governments, Competition Principles Agreement, 11 April 1995 (as amended to 13 April 2007) cl 3(1) (CPA); Commonwealth CN Policy Statement (n 375); *CN Guidelines for Managers* (n 380).

386 *Hilmer Review* (n 92) 1 (emphasis added).

efficiency.[387] In particular, allocative efficiency (or resource efficiency) occurs 'where resources used to produce a set of goods or services are allocated to their highest valued use (i.e. those that provide the greatest benefit relative to costs).'[388] In essence, firms in the market environment are rivals. Competition between them can therefore increase allocative efficiency as 'firms that can use their particular resource more productively can afford to bid those resources away from firms that cannot achieve the same level of returns.'[389]

214. Without measures to safeguard a level playing field in the market, the competitive pressure faced by SOEs in particular are likely to be reduced. The price of an SOE competitor thus may not necessarily reflect its 'actual production costs or other business costs borne by their private-sector competitors'[390] because of its competitive neutrality advantages.[391] For example, an SOE competitor can convert its ownership-generated competitive advantages (like cheaper interest rates on loans) into lower production costs, and therefore may be able to lower the market price for goods or services it produces. Accordingly, the SOE competitor can not only lower the market price of goods or services,[392] it can also take business away from its (actual and potential) rivals.[393] Under this scenario, the reason for the SOE competitor to produce lower-priced goods or services is not because it can produce the resource more efficiently than its rivals, but because its government ownership has generated competitive advantages (or competitive neutrality advantages).[394] This outcome leads to an inefficient allocation of resources (or allocative inefficiency) because a less efficient government business is able to rely on net competitive advantage to take business from a more efficient firm.[395] As a result, goods and services are not allocated to the consumers who value it most[396] and society's resources are not being put to their best use.[397]

---

387 According to definitions provided by the *Hilmer Review* (n 92) 4 (emphasis added): 'Technical or productive efficiency … is achieved where individual firms produce the goods and services that they offer to consumers at *least cost*. … Dynamic efficiency reflects the need for industries to make timely changes to technology and products in response to changes in consumer tastes and in productive opportunities.'

388 ibid.

389 ibid.

390 Commonwealth of Australia, *Australian Government National Competition Policy Report: 2005–07* (2007) 46 <https://treasury.gov.au/sites/default/files/2019-03/NCP_Report_2005_07.pdf>.

391 ibid. For example, the pricing decisions of SOEs may not fully reflect actual production costs or other business costs borne by their private sector competitors.

392 ibid.

393 ibid. SOE competitors can also use its underpriced goods or services to build an effective barrier to the entry of potential competitors.

394 Put simply, this SOE competitor is being rewarded for its competitive neutrality advantages rather than its more efficient use of resources.

395 *Hilmer Review* (n 92) 297.

396 Maximum allocative efficiency is attained when the cost of resources used in production is equal to the consumer's willingness to pay. That is, allocative efficiency is maximised when market price is equal to marginal cost. Barak Y Orbach, 'The Antitrust Consumer Welfare Paradox' (2011) 7(1) JCL & E 133, 141.

397 *Hilmer Review* (n 92) 297.

215. Overall, competitive neutrality concerns caused by SOEs to some extent inhibit the competitive process and may lead to 'sub-optimal use of scarce resource' (relative to a baseline scenario).[398] This recognition led Australian governments to commit to ensuring there is a level playing field in the market by rectifying the identified competitive neutrality advantages or disadvantages of SOEs (as noted in Sections 4.2.2 and 4.2.3).[399] The elements contained in the competitive neutrality commitment are therefore influenced by the specifics of the competitive neutrality advantages or disadvantages being addressed, which will be detailed in Section 4.5 below.

4.3.2 Fairness Objective?

216. Compared to efficiency, concerns about the unfairness or inequity caused by the competitive neutrality advantages of SOEs are less frequently mentioned in Australia.[400] Interestingly, the potential unfairness to private rivals when competing with commercial SOEs was noted by the *Hilmer Review*:

> From an equity perspective, the disadvantaged firm may feel justifiably aggrieved in this situation, particularly if its owners consider they are, in effect, subsidising their rival through their tax contributions.[401]

217. Based on those words alone, one might suggest that the competitive neutrality measures are enacted to protect competitors, particularly the private firms, in order to ensure that competition between private firms and SOEs is fair.[402] For example, Stephen King, from an economist's perspective, argues that '[c]ompetitive neutrality under NCP seems to be justified as much on the basis of fairness as on economic efficiency.'[403] Competitive neutrality, according to King,

> requires that the GBEs not be favoured by their government ownership. This makes economic sense in some circumstances … for example, favoured tax treatment … In other circumstances, competitive neutrality makes little sense. For example, GBEs can often borrow funds at a relatively low cost. This reflects their government ownership. Lending money to governments in

398 OECD, 'Maintaining a Level Playing Field' (n 7) 19.

399 National Competition Council, *Competitive Neutrality Reform: Issues in Implementing Clause 3 of the Competition Principles Agreement* (January 1997) <http://ncp.ncc.gov.au/docs/PICo-001.pdf> 7.

400 For example, the *Hilmer Review* mentions that competitive neutrality advantages enjoyed by SOEs can 'also give rise to legitimate equity concerns': (n 92) 305. This research argues that fairness should not be considered as an objective of a competitive neutrality policy.

401 ibid 297.

402 For more discussion of fairness, see Section 6.3.1.

403 Stephen P King, 'The Economics of National Competition Policy' in Christopher Arup and David Wishart (eds), *Competition Policy with Legal Form: Reviewing Australian and Overseas Experience* (Federation Press 2002) 6, 17.

> Australia had a low risk and this is reflected in a low interest rate. Under competitive neutrality, however, a GBE ... must act as if it faces the same borrowing costs as a more risky private firm ... this application of competitive neutrality will artificially and inefficiently raise GBE costs.[404]

218. The discussion of whether competitive neutrality policy is designed on the fairness ground is, in essence, the question of whether competition policy is designed to 'protect competitors' or 'competitive process.' In Australia, the prevailing thought for the design of competition policy is reinforced by the more recent *Harper Review*, which noted:

> The CCA [the Competition and Consumer Act] (and competition policy more generally) is not designed to support a particular number of participants in a market or to protect individual competitors; instead, it is designed to prevent competitors' behaviour from damaging the competitive process to the detriment of consumers.[405]

219. The core aim of competition policy in the Australian context is to protect the competitive process.[406] As a result, the underlying rationale for competitive neutrality policy, as a distinct competition policy element in Australia, should not be interpreted as protecting a particular competitor (private competitor) against commercial conduct of SOEs. In particular, removing government ownership-generated advantages enjoyed by SOEs will likely improve the competitive environment for private rivals and may help to achieve fairness. However, achieving fairness or equity is a significant side benefit rather than a core objective of competitive neutrality policy.

4.4 Regulating SOEs Under the Competition Law

220. Some competitive neutrality concerns can be remedied through the universal application of competition law to all firms (regardless of their ownership status).[407] However, as observed by the *Hilmer Review* (as discussed in

---

404 ibid 17–18.

405 Ian Harper and others, *Competition Policy Review: Final Report* (March 2015) 307 <https://treasury.gov.au/publication/p2015-cpr-final-report> (Harper Review).

406 Although in the process of protecting competition (or the competitive process), protection to competitors (implicitly or directly) might be provided to ensure there are (actual and potential) competitors in the market. However, this view is highly controversial, at least in Australia, insofar as it may conflict with the core objective that competition policy pursues. For more detailed discussion about goals of competition legislation, see Eleanor M Fox, 'Against Goals' (2013) 81(5) Fordham L Rev 2157.

407 As pointed out by Deborah Healey, the 'most basic step in levelling the playing field for competition between government bodies and private companies is the application of the competition law to government businesses.' See Deborah Healey, 'Competitive Neutrality and the Role of Competition Authorities: a Glance at Experiences in Europe and Asia-Pacific' in Paulo Burnier Da Silveira and William Evan Kovacic (eds), *Global Competition Enforcement: New Players, New Challenges* (Wolters Kluwer 2019) 187, 189.

section 4.2.1), there were deficiencies and some reluctance to apply competition legislation to SOEs at that time.[408] Particularly given Australia's federal system of government, it is difficult for the Commonwealth government to apply legislation to state and territories in respect of their SOEs (as the interests of state and territory governments will be directly affected by this application). As pointed out by Russell Miller, the decision to apply competition law universally in Australia at that time involved 'either a constitutional amendment or a State referral of power'.[409]

221. Recommendations for extending the competition law to include SOEs at all levels were made by the *Hilmer Review* wherein the process of achieving this goal involved amending the competition law to apply to previously exempted state and territory SOEs and refining the application of Crown immunity so that it could narrow the scope of ownership-based exemptions. A brief sketch of the legislative history of competition law in Australia is provided in the section immediately below for the reader who may not be familiar with the context.

4.4.1 Brief History of Competition Legislation in Australia

222. The Australian Industries Preservation Act 1906 (Cth) (AIPA) marked Australia's first statutory foray into the field of competition law[410] and was largely modelled on the Sherman Antitrust Act in the United States.[411] However, the AIPA was held to be unconstitutional by the High Court.[412] As a result of the failure of the AIPA, the Trade Practices Act 1965 (Cth) was introduced.[413] The 1965 Act was also invalidated on constitutional grounds[414] and replaced by the Restrictive Trade Practices Act 1971 (Cth).[415] The constitutional validity of the 1971 Act was never subjected to a constitutional challenge because it was of much more limited application.[416] Despite their limitations, both the 1965 and 1971 Acts raised awareness about the extent

---

408 For example, the importance of universal application of competition law to all business activities, whether public sector or private sector, corporate or otherwise, was noted by the Swanson Committee in the 1970s. However, the slow implementations process reflects the resistance to universal coverage of competition law in Australia. Trade Practices Act Review Committee, 'Report to The Minister for Business and Consumer Affairs' (1976), 84 <https://www.australiancompetitionlaw.org/reports/pdf/swanson1976.pdf> (Swanson Report)

409 Russell V Miller (n 5) 129.

410 Simon Peart, 'Australia and New Zealand: Their Competition Law Systems and the Countries' Norms' in Eleanor M Fox and MJ Trebilcock (eds), *The Design of Competition Law Institutions: Global Norms, Local Choices* (OUP 2013) 49, 49.

411 Allan Fels, 'Australia: A Regulator's Perspective' in Mark Williams (ed), *The Political Economy of Competition Law in Asia* (Edward Elgar 2013) 379; Russell V Miller (n 5) 11; Rhonda L Smith and Arlen Duke, 'Agreements and Competition Law in Australia' (2014) 54(22) CCLJ 54.

412 David Merrett, Stephen Corones and David Round, 'The Introduction of Competition Policy in Australia: The Role of Ron Bannerman' (2007) 47(2) AEHR 178, 179.

413 Smith and Duke (n 410) 57. See also Kerrie Round and Martin P Shanahan, *From Protection to Competition: The Politics of Trade Practices Reform in Australia* (Federation Press 2015) 33–39.

414 For more detailed cases relating to the 1965 TPA, see Swanson Report (n 407) 7–9.

415 Arlen Duke, *Corones' Competition Law in Australia* (7th edn, Thomson Reuters 2019) 174.

416 Smith and Duke (n 410) 58. Round and Shanahan (n 412) 183–84.

of anti-competitive practices in Australia in the industrial sector and their effects, laying the foundation for the 1974 Trade Practices Act.[417]

223. The Trade Practices Act 1974 (Cth) (TPA), which constitutes the principal source of Australian competition law, came into force in October 1974 and superseded the 1971 Act.[418] Although significantly amended, the central provisions of the TPA remain in force today.[419] In 2011, the name of the TPA was changed to the Competition and Consumer Act 2010 (Cth) (CCA).[420] This change of name, however, did not alter the substance or the numbering of any of the competition law provisions.[421]

4.4.2 Amending the Constitutional Limitations

224. The *Hilmer Review*, as explained in Section 4.2.1, observed that constitutional restraints present a hurdle for the universal application of competition law.[422] To achieve universal coverage, the *Hilmer Review* proposed that an agreement (the Conduct Code Agreement 1995) between the Commonwealth, state and territory governments be implemented to extend the coverage of competition legislation (TPA) to include incorporated enterprises and SOEs that were 'within the jurisdiction of the states'[423] In particular, the Commonwealth government agreed to introduce a legislative amendment to the competition law (TPA) by inserting the Competition Code (Part XIA) to ensure it applied to unincorporated enterprises and SOEs at all levels.[424] All states and territories agreed to enact complementary legislation[425] to give effect to the Competition Code as part of their own law.[426] As a result of the Conduct Code Agreement 1995, SOEs created by the state laws are now under the coverage of competition law.

4.4.3 Statutory Exemptions

225. As discussed in the 4.2.1, state and territory laws and regulations could make certain anti-competitive conduct (including of SOEs) lawful by specifically

---

417 OECD, *OECD Reviews of Regulatory Reform: Competition Policy in Australia* (2010) 12 <http://www.oecd.org/gov/regulatory-policy/44529918.pdf>.

418 Duke (n 414) 175. See also Philip H Clarke, *Competition Law and Policy: Cases and Materials* (3rd edn, OUP 2011) 11.

419 Peart (n 409).

420 Russell V Miller (n 5) 58.

421 Duke (n 414) 175.

422 *Hilmer Review* (n 92) 114.

423 Gretton (n 334) 46.

424 Productivity Commission, *Review of National Competition Policy Reforms* (Inquiry Report No 33, 28 February 2005) 13 <http://www.pc.gov.au/inquiries/completed/national-competition-policy/report/ncp.pdf> (*Productivity Commission Review 2005*).

425 For example, Competition Policy Reform (New South Wales) Act 1995 (NSW) was enacted by NSW to give effect to the extended coverage of competition law in its jurisdiction. See Competition Policy Reform (New South Wales) Act 1995 No 8 pt 2.

426 Russell V Miller (n 5) 54; Gretton (n 334) 45.

authorising it in legislation.[427] The *Hilmer Review* found that exemptions of this kind were prevalent and had the potential to fragment the universal application of competition law.[428] Additionally, states and territory governments could be captured and grant exemptions that favoured specific interests rather than public interest as a whole. For example, state and territory SOEs could use their link with their government owners to seek exemptions provided by the state and territory statutes or regulations (albeit less likely in the context of Australia compared to China).[429] After considering the *Hilmer Review*, the government decided to retain the statutory exemptions[430] but tightened the states and territories' ability to grant statutory exemptions in order to increase the certainty of competition law.[431] For example, the statutory exemptions are now designed as a time-limited exemption, which means any exemption provided by statute is only effective for a fixed period of time (two years).[432] In addition, the exemption authorised by the state/territory statute[433] may be overridden[434] if the state or territory cannot demonstrate that 'the community benefits outweigh the costs, and ... the restriction of competition cannot be avoided.'[435]

4.4.4 Refining the Application of Crown Immunity

226. Due to the existence of Crown immunity, as explained in Section 4.2.1, competition law (TPA) failed to bind the Crown at all levels in Australia (or at least silence it when it comes to the Crown in light of the states and territories) when they were engaging in business.[436] Crown immunity enacted under specific laws with the intent of benefitting special interests thus presented a particular problem for the uniformity of competition law at the time of the *Hilmer Review* and could be remedied only by amending the legislation itself. The *Hilmer Review* recommended removing Crown immunity at all levels from the competition law 'in so far as the Crown in question carries on a business or engages in commercial activities in competition (actual or potential) with other businesses.'[437] The Competition Policy Reform Act 1995 (Cth) amended the TPA following the recommendations in the *Hilmer Review*. As part of this process, the competition law (CCA) now

427 OECD (n 339) 9.

428 *Hilmer Review* (n 92) 108.

429 See Chapter 1 on state capture theory.

430 *Hilmer Review* (n 92) 121.

431 'Section 51 in Part IV sets out a process by which governments (the Australian government and state and territory governments) may, by legislation, authorise conduct (other than mergers) that would otherwise contravene Part IV': *Harper Review* (n 404) 278. See also Healey (n 337) 220.

432 Competition and Consumer Act 2010 (Cth) s 51(1C)(c), (e) (CCA).

433 ibid s 51(1)(b)-(e).

434 Russell V Miller (n 5) 54.

435 Corones (n 356) 261.

436 *Hilmer Review* (n 92) 116; Healey and Coles (n 357) 48.

437 *Hilmer Review* (n 92) 121–22.

applies uniformly to Crown in right of Commonwealth, states and territories (and local governments) 'in so far as it carries on a business.'[438]

227. The existence of Crown immunity in the competition legislation has been limited in scope (by section 2C[439] and case law[440]) but is still considered as undesirable by many scholars. Nick Seddon, for example, consistently argues that the procurement activities of governments in Australia are not bound by the CCA due to Crown immunity.[441] A similar comment is shared by Justice John Griffiths who notes that 'the Crown may undertake a commercial transaction including the delivery of infrastructure projects or the heavy demands of health and education systems, but will not technically carry on a business, and so the shield of Crown immunity continued to apply.'[442] In response to the growing concerns, the *Harper Review* in 2015 expressed the view that a broader scope of government activities (including procurement) should be subject to the competition law in Australia.[443] In particular:

> Through its commercial transactions entered into with market participants, the Crown (whether in right of the Commonwealth or the States and Territories, including local government) has the potential to harm competition. The Panel considers that the NCP reforms should be carried a step further and that the Crown should

---

438 CCA (n 431):

s 2A Application of Act to Commonwealth and Commonwealth authorities

(1) Subject to this section, this Act (other than Part X) binds the Crown in right of the Commonwealth in so far as the Crown in right of the Commonwealth carries on a business, either directly or by an authority of the Commonwealth.

(2) Subject to the succeeding provisions of this section, this Act applies as if –

(a) the Commonwealth, in so far as it carries on a business otherwise than by an authority of the Commonwealth; and

(b) each authority of the Commonwealth (whether or not acting as an agent of the Crown in right of the Commonwealth) in so far as it carries on a business;

were a corporation.

(3) Nothing in this Act makes the Crown in right of the Commonwealth liable to be prosecuted for an offence.

s 2B Application of Act to States and Territories

(1) Part IV, and the other provisions of this Act so far as they relate to Part IV, bind the Crown in right of each of the States, of the Northern Territory and of the Australian Capital Territory, so far as the Crown carries on a business, either directly or by an authority of the State or Territory. …

s 2BA Application of Part IV to local government bodies

(1) Part IV applies in relation to a local government body only to the extent that it carries on a business, either directly or by an incorporated company in which it has a controlling interest.

439 CCA (n 431). For example, 2C of the CCA listed the situation when the Crown could be exempt from the application of the CCA.

440 A detailed discussion of jurisprudence on the meaning of carries on a business in Australia context is set out in Healey and Coles (n 357); Justice John Griffiths, 'Application of the Australian Consumer Law to Government Commercial Activities' (Paper delivered at Commercial Law and Government Conference, NSW State Library, 16 September 2016) <https://www.fedcourt.gov.au/digital-law-library/judges-speeches/justice-griffiths/griffiths-j-20160916>.

441 Nick Seddon, 'Holes in Hilmer Re-visited: Government Exemption from Australian Competition and Consumer Law' (Pt 4) (2012) 20 AJCCL 239.

442 Griffiths (n 439).

443 *Harper Review* (n 404) 278–82.

be subject to the competition laws insofar as it undertakes activity in *trade or commerce*.[444]

228. It is clear from the discussion above, under the *Harper Review* recommendation, the coverage of the CCA would be extended from the Crown that 'carries a business' to the Crown that 'undertakes activity in trade or commerce'.[445] Unfortunately, this recommendation was not adopted by the government, which concluded that further consultation with the states and territories was needed regarding 'the implications of extending the CCA to apply to government activities in trade or commerce.'[446]

229. The implication of the proposed change in terms of Crown immunity is currently uncertain. On the one hand, in assessing the proposed extension of the CCA, Deborah Healey and Jack Coles argue that it may further complicate the way in which the CCA applies to the Crown in general, by noting that 'how the construction would differ from determining when the government carries on a business' is not clear.[447] Some state governments also questioned the applicability of the CCA to broader government activities.[448] However, the amendment suggested by the *Harper Review* would not actually broaden the ambit of the existing provisions.[449] On the other hand, the extension of the breadth of the CCA to cover more government activities reflects the political acceptance of 'expos[ing] government activities to greater market disciplines' and the seriousness of commitment to the value of competition in the Australian context.[450]

4.5 Formation of Competitive Neutrality Policy

230. The role of universally applied competition legislation is undoubtedly indispensable, particularly in the sense that it provides the juridical foundation to regulate the commercial-oriented conduct of SOEs in the market, and general competition enforcement measures are applicable to SOEs. For instance, mergers between SOEs will be treated in the same manner as a merger between private firms under the *CCA*. Subsequently, several cases

444 ibid 282 (emphasis added).

445 ibid.

446 Commonwealth of Australia, *Australian Government Response to the Competition Policy Review* (2015) 20 <https://treasury.gov.au/sites/default/files/2019-03/Govt_response_CPR.pdf> (*Response to Harper Review*).

447 Healey and Coles (n 357) 49. A similar view is shared by Griffiths (n 439): 'there is little reason to believe that the concept of "in trade or commerce" is more certain and predictable than is the case with the concept of "carrying on a business".'

448 For example, the Queensland government questioned the application of competition law to procurement and other government activities and stated that it does not support the recommendation of the *Harper Review* regarding Recommendation 14: *Harper Review* (n 404) 280.

449 Healey and Coles (n 357) 77–81.

450 *Harper Review* (n 404) 278.

involving the application of the *CCA* to SOEs in Australia have been heard.[451] However, the competition law alone (as amended) is likely to be inadequate to address all the competitive neutrality issues because competition law has limited jurisdiction.[452] For example, as pointed by Deborah Healey and Rhonda L Smith,

> competitive neutrality is an issue of policy, not law, because even where competition law expressly applies to such entities [SOEs], these 'advantages' do not generally relate to issues or behaviours within the ambit of competition law itself.[453]

231. While competition law can effectively remedy the anti-competitive conduct of SOEs within its scope, it can only address those competitive neutrality concerns that qualify as breaches of competition law. Some of the competitive neutrality concerns, such as cheaper debt rates or certain tax exemptions, may not qualify as breaches of competition and cannot be addressed by the enforcement of competition law.[454] Moreover, the *ex-post* nature of competition enforcement means competition law can only rectify (or remedy) the competitive neutrality concerns caused by SOEs after they occurred and can do very little to prevent the competitive neutrality issues occurring in the first place.[455]

232. The *Hilmer Review* concluded that, instead of allowing the competitive neutrality issues to persist in the Australia market, a principles-based policy mechanism was necessary to work in conjunction with competition law to provide a forward-looking solution to competitive neutrality issues. An *ex-ante* competition policy, which principally obliges a proactive responsibility for government to prevent its SOEs from being advantaged by its ownership, was thus recommended. It remains the present competitive neutrality policy position and has wider implications for the enforcement frameworks discussed in Chapter 7.

4.5.1 Brief Overview of National Competition Policy Framework

233. Competitive neutrality policy in Australia is often viewed as part of broad-ranging competition policy reform (rather than as a single stand-alone competition policy). It seems useful here to have the overview of the structure

451 For example, *NT Power Generation Pty Ltd v Power and Water Authority* (2004) 219 CLR 90.

452 Capobianco and Christiansen (n 7) 15. For example, the authors pointed out that while subjecting government business activities to the provisions of competition was important, it would not address all concerns about the cost advantages and pricing policies of government business.

453 Healey and Smith (n 6) 224.

454 According to Deborah Healey, competition laws only attack prohibited anticompetitive behaviour, and many of the advantages of government bodies are outside their scope. See Healey (n 7) 5.

455 *Hilmer Review* (n 92) 296.

of National Competition Policy (NCP) in mind before going into the detailed discussion of competitive neutrality policy.

234. In general, the recommendation in the *Hilmer Review* focused on three main elements: the competition legislation, the additional competition policy elements that went beyond the legislation, and the administrative institutions to assist implementing the recommended changes.[456] Drawing on the blueprint laid down by the *Hilmer Review*, competition policy reforms, in the form of the NCP, were committed to an agreement and signed by all Australian governments.[457] In Figure 4.1, the NCP was implemented by three intergovernmental agreements. The first component of the NCP reform is the Conduct Code Agreement, which obligated governments to apply the competition law (then TPA) to all business activity in Australia regardless of ownership or corporate status.[458] The second component of the NCP reform is the Competition Principles Agreement (CPA) which was designed to implement competitive neutrality policy, price oversight of government businesses, structural reform of public monopolies, legislative review, and third-party infrastructure access.[459] The Agreement to Implement the National Competition Policy and Related Reforms, as the third component of the NCP reform, provided for payments from the Commonwealth[460] to the states and territories for satisfactory progress in implementing their reform commitments.[461]

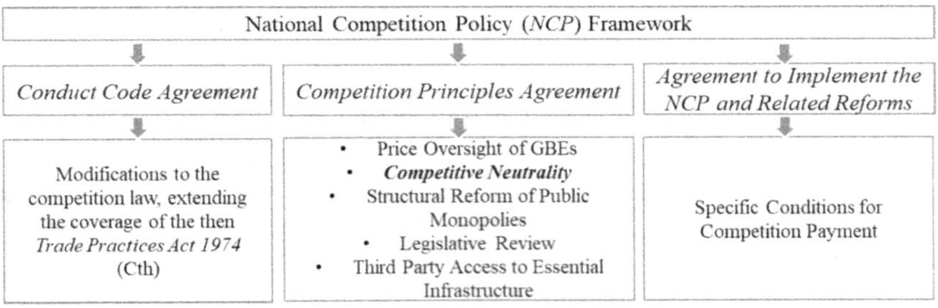

Figure 4.1 National Competition Policy Framework.[462]

456 ibid. See also Stephen P King, 'National Competition Policy' (1997) 73(222) Economic Record 270, 270.

457 All Australian governments here include federal, six state, two territory, and local governments.

458 OECD (n 416) 5–8.

459 King, 'National Competition Policy' (n 455) 271.

460 In the context of this research, the Commonwealth government of Australia is also referred to as the Australia federal government or federal government. The term federal is used interchangeably with Commonwealth.

461 OECD (n 345) 158.

462 Source: Council of Australian Governments, *Conduct Code Agreement*, 11 April 1995; CPA (n 384); Council of Australian Governments, Agreement to Implement the National Competition Policy and Related Reforms, 11 April 1995.

4.5.2 Contractual Competitive Neutrality Commitments

235. Competitive neutrality policy was officially constructed in the provisions of the CPA:

> The objective of competitive neutrality policy is the elimination of resource allocation distortions arising out of the public ownership of entities engaged in significant business activities: Government businesses should not enjoy any net competitive advantage simply as a result of their public-sector ownership. These principles only apply to the business activities of publicly owned entities, not to the non-business, non-profit activities of these entities.[463]

236. Competitive neutrality commitments in Australia are by nature contractual because they are agreed to and signed off by governments (the owners of SOEs). The implementation of competitive neutrality commitments in the Australian context has relied heavily on the political agreement (willingness) of governments at all levels (as discussed in detail in Chapter 7).

237. In complying with their competitive neutrality commitments, governments (as owners) are required to level the playing field of competition by neutralising the advantages (and disadvantages) arising from government ownership of those SOEs. As noted at the beginning of this section, competitive neutrality policy distinguishes itself from the application of competition law. Firstly, the consequences of violating competitive neutrality obligations are different from the violation of competition legislation. For example, the threat of legal sanctions (both civil and criminal) is the crucial part of competition law to deter undesirable conduct, but the threat of legal sanctions is absent for the violation of competitive neutrality policy. As noted by Deborah Healey and Rhoda L Smith, at least in the context of Australia, '[n]o provision was made for penalties for noncompliance with competitive neutrality policy.'[464] The liability for breach of competitive neutrality commitments was negotiated by all governments in the agreement and was monetary in nature.

238. Secondly, compliance with competitive neutrality commitments is more flexible and largely relies on bureaucratic processes adopted by governments. For example, government can not only 'set its own agenda'[465] but can also exercise its discretion to make a decision to not apply competitive neutrality obligations to its SOEs if they can demonstrate that the benefit of implementing competitive neutrality policy does not outweigh the cost.[466] To some extent, government authorities have a responsibility to conduct a

463 CPA (n 384) cl 3(1).

464 Healey and Smith (n 6) 230.

465 ibid 229.

466 CPA (n 384) cl 3(6); *Productivity Commission Review 2005* (n 423) 129.

public interest test (or public benefit test) in researching such a determination. The issue associated with government discretion when conducting a public interest test for the implementation of competitive neutrality policy is discussed in Chapter 7.

239. By contrast, the enforcement of competition law is undertaken by the competition authority in the Courts. Enforcement activities are less flexible and confined to specific enforcement procedures and administrative guidelines. A public interest test is permitted in some circumstances under the administrative permissions granted by the competition law, but is conducted by the competition regulator, the ACCC (or on review by the Australian Competition Tribunal), under a specific authorisation process and subject to high transparency standards.[467]

240. Additionally, under the competitive neutrality policy, the need for a remedy for government non-compliance with its competitive neutrality commitments is fulfilled by the complaint-handling bodies (or sometimes the department of government), rather than the ACCC. Simply put, complaint-handling bodies, staffed by experts, can respond to a specific competitive neutrality complaint and provide advice tailored to solve the non-compliance of such policy.[468] However, a government that is under investigation is 'not obliged to accept this advice',[469] which gives rise to concerns over the effectiveness of the complaint-handling procedures under the competitive neutrality policy. The issues in relation to competitive neutrality complaint-handling are discussed in detail in Chapter 7.

4.5.3 Elements of Competitive Neutrality Commitments

241. Governments and their SOEs are committed to neutralising the advantages (and disadvantages) arising from government ownership. Regulatory means adopted by the government and its SOEs to achieve the aim of levelling the playing field are considered to be the key elements in fulfilling competitive neutrality commitments. For the purpose of this research, the regulatory means adopted by the Australian government fit into two broad categories: firstly, the regulatory means required under the CPA (which can directly remove those identified net competitive advantages and disadvantages of SOEs) include tax neutrality, debt neutrality, regulatory neutrality, and commercial rate of return requirements.[470] Secondly, the regulatory measures implemented by the government that can indirectly neutralise the advantages (and disadvantages) arising from the government ownership, which include corporatisation, privatisation, and commercialisation of SOEs, mainly fall outside of the scope of this research.

---

467 CCA (n 431) s 88.

468 OECD (n 339) 4.

469 ibid.

470 CPA (n 384) cls 3(4)–(5).

Taxation Neutrality Commitment

242. As explained in Section 4.2.2, SOEs in Australia were perceived to enjoy tax immunity or favourable tax treatment resulting from their government ownership status. The requirement of taxation neutrality reflects the policy choice to subject all firms (no matter what ownership) to a similar tax burden in similar circumstances.[471] Neutrality in terms of taxation is noted in Clause 3(4) of the CPA, which reads:

> (b) the Parties will impose on the Government business enterprise … (i) full Commonwealth, State and Territory taxes or tax equivalent systems.

243. Tax neutrality requirements may be satisfied in three ways, according to the *Australian Competitive Neutrality Guidelines* (2004). Firstly, by simply removing the existing exemptions of SOEs (or favourable terms) from the taxation regulations, SOEs are required to pay actual tax and will be subject to the same tax burden as its competitors.[472] Alternatively, the government can continue to provide tax exemptions to SOEs, but need to have a 'taxation equivalence regime (TER)' in place to ensure that SOEs are not unduly advantaged.[473] TER was introduced following the recommendation of the *Hilmer Review* and was designed to make SOEs pay tax-equivalent payments calculated according to the current taxation legislation to the Official Public Account (OPA) or the state governments.[474] As a result of TER the tax payment of SOEs is closely mirrored with, or at least applied similarly to, their private rivals.[475] Taxation neutrality adjustments (TNA), as the third way to satisfy the tax neutrality requirement, are utilised by governments and their SOEs 'when determining a pricing strategy'.[476] The TNA and TES share similar objectives to neutralise the tax advantages of SOEs and to require SOEs to calculate tax liability in a manner comparable to their competitors; however, they have their obvious differences. According to Andrew Deitz, the TNA is just a notional tax adjustment (it does not require actual payment to either the OPA or state governments), whereas the TES requires actual payment.[477]

244. Potential benefits of the tax neutrality commitment include increased public transparency of an SOE's taxation and, perhaps more importantly, enabling

---

471 OECD (n 339) 3.

472 *CN Guidelines for Managers* (n 380) 18.

473 ibid.

474 OECD, 'Maintaining a Level Playing Field' (n 7) 80.

475 Josephine Doueihi, 'The Effectiveness of the National Tax Equivalent Regime (NTER) in Encouraging Competitive Neutrality' (PhD thesis, Curtin University 2019) 54 <https://espace.curtin.edu.au/bitstream/handle/20.500.11937/75706/Doueihi%20J.%202019.pdf?sequence=1&isAllowed=y>.

476 *CN Guidelines for Managers* (n 380) 19.

477 Andrew Deitz, 'Competitive Neutrality in Australia' (Presentation to the OECD 11th Global Forum on Competition: Session III – OECD Project on State Owned Enterprises and Competitive Neutrality, 17 February 2012) <https://www.oecd.org/competition/globalforum/49771663.pdf>.

an additional monitoring process to ensure compliance (by the complaint-handling body). For example, a recent investigation by the complaint-handling body, the AGCNCO (AGCNCO), looked at the accounting processes of an SOE, Australian Hearing (an Australian government body that sits within the portfolio of the Department of Human Services). The investigation confirmed that Australian Hearing complied with competitive neutrality commitments by having a tax-equivalent system in place to ensure that there were no advantages relative to its competitors as a result of its government ownership.[478]

Debt Neutrality Commitment

245. Government ownership status in SOEs, as explained in Section 4.2.2, implicitly or explicitly results in lower default risk which may translate into a lower cost of borrowing. Debt neutrality commitments under the CPA require that SOEs pay a debt guarantee fee (notionally or actually) to offset their cost advantages as a consequence of government ownership.[479] The design of the debt guarantee fee is similar to the design of the tax neutrality adjustment mentioned above, which is to 'subject SOEs to borrowing costs similar to those faced by private sector businesses'[480] under similar circumstances. Debt neutrality requirements may be satisfied by paying a debt neutrality adjustment, which is monetary in nature and is the difference between the actual cost of borrowing (cost of debt) of an SOE and the cost of borrowing for a private firm under a similar circumstance (benchmark cost of debt).[481] Under the debt neutrality requirement, SOEs must factor in debt neutrality adjustments to their borrowing if they benefit from debt advantages due to their public ownership in their financial statements.[482]

246. Having debt neutrality in place brings benefits such as a better understanding of the actual cost of borrowing by SOEs and a more competitive environment between SOEs and private rivals. Regular monitoring by the complaint-handling body would also be enabled through debt neutrality commitment.

478 AGCNCO, *Australian Hearing* (Investigation No 16, 23 May 2018) <https://www.pc.gov.au/competitive-neutrality/investigations/australian-hearing/australian-hearing.pdf>.

479 CPA (n 384) cl 3(4)(b)(ii).

480 OECD (n 339) 3.

481 For detailed information on how the Australian government calculates benchmark cost of debt, see *CN Guidelines for Managers* (n 380) 21–27. For example, competitive neutrality policy requires debt neutrality provisions to be applied when monies are borrowed through two channels, namely the Australian Government Budget or raised in the market at a rate of interest, which reflects the risk of the Australian Government and not that of individual businesses. Accordingly, SOE can have two types of debt based on the source of debt, budget debt and market debt. In general, budget debt (that borrowed from the Department of Finance and Administration) will not require any debt neutrality adjustments, as the appropriate CN adjustments will already be incorporated into the cost of debt. For market debt, the manager of the SOEs is required to assess whether SOEs are borrowing funds at a lower rate than their competitors as a result of public ownership. If the answer is yes, the manager of SOEs must pay or notionally include a debt neutrality charge. The amount of any debt neutrality charge must be factored into pricing.

482 ibid 23.

For example, 16 competitive neutrality complaints have been investigated by the AGCNCO. Among them, four cases involved an assessment of whether SOEs complied with the debt neutrality requirement.[483]

Regulatory Neutrality Commitment

247. Governments in Australia are required by the CPA to subject their SOEs to the regulations to which private firms are normally subject in the same situation.[484] The design of regulatory neutrality reflects the desire to equalise the regulatory difference between SOEs and private firms. Regulatory advantages of SOEs may take various forms such as: exemptions from local planning, building, and environmental laws; exemptions from the prudential requirement; preferred treatment by other agencies; or amended reporting and/or licensing requirements.[485] Being exempted from the coverage of competition law due to its government ownership status, as discussed in Section 4.4, can be considered as a regulatory advantage enjoyed by SOEs in the context of Australia.

248. Neutrality in terms of regulation can be satisfied in two ways in practice. Firstly, amending legislation and regulation (e.g. amendment of competition law) to directly remove the exemption that applies only to SOEs as a consequence of their government ownership status could satisfy the requirement of regulatory neutrality. The difficulty and cost (in terms of both time and money) of identifying such an exemption and amending the legislation accordingly should not be underestimated. As a short-term alternative way to satisfy regulatory neutrality requirements, SOEs could make a regulatory adjustment (notional or actual) that reflects its regulatory benefits, which are calculated on a case-by-case basis.[486]

249. Like debt neutrality noted above, regulatory neutrality commitments empower the complaint-handling body to provide an *ex-post* means to address regulatory advantages of SOEs. The AGCNCO has investigated four cases related to breach of regulatory neutrality commitments.[487]

---

483 *Australian Hearing* (n 477); CCNCO, *Docimage Business Services* (Investigation No 9, 20 December 2001) <https://www.pc.gov.au/inquiries/completed/docimage/report9.pdf>; AGCNCO, *NBN Co* (Investigation No 14, 8 December 2011) <https://www.pc.gov.au/inquiries/completed/nbnco/report14-nbnco.pdf>; AGCNCO, *PETNET Australia* (Investigation No 15, 4 April 2012) <https://www.pc.gov.au/inquiries/completed/petnet/report15-petnet.pdf>.

484 CPA (n 384) cl 3(4)(b)(iii).

485 *CN Guidelines for Managers* (n 380) 27.

486 OECD (n 339) 4.

487 CCNCO, *Australian Institute of Sport Swim School* (Investigation No 2, 3 November 1999) <https://www.pc.gov.au/competitive-neutrality/investigations/ais-swim-school/report2.pdf>; CCNCO, *Customs Treatment of Australian Post* (Investigation No 5, 7 July 2000) <https://www.pc.gov.au/inquiries/completed/customs-australia-post/report5.pdf>; CCNCO, *ARRB Transport Research Limited* (Investigation No 6, 14 September 2001) <https://www.pc.gov.au/competitive-neutrality/investigations/arrb-transport-research/report6.pdf>; CCNCO, *Meteorological Services to Aviation* (Investigation No 7, 20 December 2001) <https://www.pc.gov.au/inquiries/completed/aviation-meterological-services/report7.pdf>; CCNCO, *Sydney and Camden Airports* (Investigation No 8, 20 December 2001) <https://www.pc.gov.au/inquiries/completed/sydney-camden-airports/report8.pdf>; *Docimage Business Services* (n 482); *Australian Hearing* (n 477).

Commercial Rate of Return Commitment

250. Although not specifically mentioned in the CPA, the commercial rate of return (RoR) requirement was agreed to by all jurisdictions in the Competition and Infrastructure Reform Agreement (CIRA) in 2006.[488] The commercial RoR requirement is perceived as one element of competitive neutrality policy in Australia. For example, according to the Commonwealth Competitive Neutrality Policy Statement (hereafter Commonwealth CN Policy Statement):

> All commonwealth organisations identified as engaging in significant business activities will be required to earn commercial returns at least sufficient to justify the long-term retention of assets in the business and to pay commercial dividends (i.e. equivalent to the average for their industry) to the Budget from those returns.[489]

251. The need for SOEs to earn a commercial RoR on assets is explained by the Commonwealth Competitive Neutrality Complaints Office (CCNCO; now the Australian Government Competitive Neutrality Complaints Office, AGCNCO), which points out that an SOE 'is often able to undercharge for its goods and services ... if over a reasonable period of time, its revenue does not cover all its costs.'[490] Put simply, SOEs can undercut rivals by undercharging as a consequence of not being required to earn commercial RoR. Under the commercial RoR commitment, SOEs are required by government owners to make an RoR on its assets equivalent to that expected of their private rival in the same industry (relevant peers)[491] but are also required to pay commercial dividends from those returns to their government owner.[492] Additionally, the governing boards of SOEs are responsible for the assessment of the performance of SOEs to ensure that the RoR target has been met and to publish an annual report.[493]

252. Guidelines regarding the analytical methods that are used in setting and calculating the RoR of SOEs was developed by the CCNCO[494] and the *Australian Competitive Neutrality Guidelines*. A more detailed guideline on the issue of RoR, particularly the period in which start-up SOEs should earn a commercial RoR, was recommended by the recent *Harper Review* (as discussed below) and supported by the government.[495] Consequently, the

488 'The Parties agree to enhance the application of competitive neutrality principles to government business enterprises engaged in significant business activities in competition with the private sector: (a) That the enterprise has clear commercial objectives': Council of Australian Governments, Competition and Infrastructure Reform Agreement (February 2016) cl 6.1 (CIRA).

489 Commonwealth CN Policy Statement (n 375) 17.

490 CCNCO, 'Rate of Return Issues' (Research Paper, December 1998) vii <https://www.pc.gov.au/research/supporting/rate-of-return/cnror.pdf>.

491 OECD (n 339) 4.

492 Russell V Miller (n 5) 467.

493 CIRA (n 487) cls 6.1(d), (g), (i).

494 CCNCO (n 489).

495 *Response to Harper Review* (n 445) 15.

review of the Commonwealth CN Policy Statement was conducted by the Treasury, with a special focus on issues like how to 'define the "longer-term" for the purposes of earning a commercial rate of return.'[496] As at the time of writing, the outcome of this review is still pending.

4.5.4 Competitive Neutrality Policy Developments Since the Hilmer Review

Competition and Infrastructure Reform Agreement

253. With the primary aim of 'enhance[ing] the application of competitive neutrality principles to government business enterprises engaged in significant business activities in competition with private sector',[497] the Competition and Infrastructure Reform Agreement (CIRA) was agreed by all jurisdictions in Australia in 2006. Building on the competitive neutrality policy in the CPA, the scope of the CIRA is narrower as it focused only on SOEs that undertake significant business activities and face competition (rather than other government agencies engaged in significant business activities).[498] Under the CIRA, the government made an additional 11 commitments of competitive neutrality, which include:

> clear commercial objectives for SOEs; specified and reported non-commercial objectives of SOEs; prohibit SOEs to exercise regulatory or planning approval functions in markets where they compete with private firms; responsibility of the governing boards of SOEs and the accountability against published performance measures; based on the needed skills to appoint the board; the management autonomy of SOEs; clarified and published dividend policy for SOEs; transparency in terms of competitive neutrality payment to government and any payment to the government shareholder; periodic reporting obligation of SOEs on both commercial and non-commercial performance; publishing government direction to SOEs; and publish any derogations from competitive neutrality commitment through authorization of legislation.[499]

254. Additional monitoring tasks were assigned to the Heads of Treasuries under the CIRA. An ongoing monitoring report, the Competitive Neutrality Matrix report, is published by Heads of Treasuries on a yearly basis to

496 Treasury, 'Review of the Commonwealth Government's Competitive Neutrality Policy: Consultation Paper' (March 2017) 12 <https://storage.googleapis.com/converlens-au/treasury/p/prj20bc99942a7a416b-9dc2a/public_assets/CN%2520Review%2520Consultation%2520Paper.pdf> (CN Review 2017)

497 CIRA (n 487) cl 6.1.

498 Australian Government, *2015–16 Heads of Treasuries Competitive Neutrality Matrix* (February 2017) 4 <http://web.archive.org/web/20210309132758/https://www.federalfinancialrelations.gov.au/content/performance_reporting/CNMR_2015-16.pdf>.

499 CIRA (n 487) cls 6.1(a)–(k).

assess compliance of competitive neutrality commitments (in both CPA and CIRA) in each jurisdiction.[500] Up to the time of writing, there had been 11 Competitive Neutrality Matrix reports published.[501]

255. Thus, since 2006, compliance with competitive neutrality commitments, in the context of Australia, is not only overseen by the complaint-handling body in an *ex-post* manner but also regularly supervised by Head of Treasuries in each jurisdiction.

Harper Review

256. Competitive neutrality policy was further advanced by the recent independent 'root and branch' review of Australia's competition law and policy, the Competition Policy Review (the *Harper Review*), chaired by Professor Ian Harper.[502] The *Harper Review* was released on 31 March 2015[503] and was considered as the most comprehensive report since the *Hilmer Review*.[504] Part 3 of the *Harper Review* is dedicated to the discussion of competition policy and the analysis of competitive neutrality.[505] Generally, the *Harper Review* supported the existing position of competitive neutrality policy but recommended improvements.[506]

257. The *Harper Review* concluded there was a need for all governments to recommit to competition policy by updating their existing competitive neutrality policy documents. As mentioned above, the Treasury has been conducting a review of the Commonwealth government's competitive neutrality policy since March 2017.[507] Specific matters to be taken into account when conducting the review, as clarified in the *Harper Review*, include:

- the coverage of the competitive neutrality policy, which touches on issues of policy application during start-up stages of government businesses and the threshold tests for identifying significant business activities;
- the effectiveness of the competitive neutrality complaint-handling processes; and,

500 Australian Government (n 497) 4.

501 The competitive neutrality matrix reports for 2017-18, 2016-17, 2015-16, 2014-15, 2013-14, 2012-13, 2011-12, 2010-11, 2009-10, September 2009, January 2008 are publicly available at the Council on Federal Financial Relations website <http://web.archive.org/web/20210309094211/https:/www.federal-financialrelations.gov.au/content/performance_reporting.aspx>.

502 OECD (n 339).

503 *Harper Review* (n 404).

504 Healey (n 378) 36.

505 *Harper Review* (n 404) 255–68.

506 OECD (n 339).

507 Treasury has established a Competitive Neutrality (CN) Review Secretariat to review the Commonwealth's competitive neutrality policy, in consultation with the Department of Finance, see CN Review 2017 (n 495).

- compliance reporting for competitive neutrality by SOEs (i.e. to incorporate a periodic report into government businesses' annual reports[508]).[509]

258. The scope of competitive neutrality policy and the design of compliant-handing processes are a more controversial issue and will be analysed in Chapter 7. The recommendation concerning the compliance reporting of competitive neutrality by SOEs will be briefly discussed here.

259. To ensure greater ongoing compliance with the competitive neutrality policy in the absence of competition payments, the *Harper Review* suggested that SOEs should self-document their compliance with competitive neutrality policy in their annual report.[510] The rationale for this self-documentation requirement is that it can increase the transparency of the compliance while also 'instilling a culture within government businesses of complying with competitive neutrality policy.'[511] However, this recommendation is not free from debate. On the one hand, the self-reporting requirement may in fact impose a burden that binds only SOEs,[512] and may even be deemed as placing them at a competitively disadvantaged position (as the burden of compliance is absent for its private counterparts). Additionally, this self-reporting requirement may, to some extent, duplicate the current compliance reporting requirement. For example, when conducting tendering, the *Australian Competitive Neutrality Guidelines* required that '[a]ll agencies conducting a tendering process must include a requirement for public sector bidders to declare that their tenders are compliant with CN principles.'[513] On the other hand, as argued by the Productivity Commission, the self-reporting requirement 'would both aid in the assessment of compliance and also provide some transparency to private-sector competitors that the business is operating in line with government policy.'[514] In 2015, the government announced that it endorsed the recommendations of the *Harper Review* in terms of competitive neutrality reporting but noted that further discussion may be required.[515]

Intergovernmental Agreement on Competition and Productivity-Enhancing Reforms

260. Building upon the commitments in the CPA (1995) and CIRA (2006), the commitment to competitive neutrality was reaffirmed as one of the eight competition principles in the 2016 Intergovernmental Agreement on

508 ibid 51.

509 *Harper Review* (n 404) 50.

510 ibid 268.

511 ibid 262.

512 ibid 262. The South Australian government suggests that such reporting duplicates current arrangements and would add to the administrative burden of states.

513 *CN Guidelines for Managers* (n 380) 43.

514 Productivity Commission, 'Submission to the Competition Policy Review' (June 2014) 34 <https://www.pc.gov.au/research/supporting/competition-policy-review/competition-policy-review-submission.pdf>.

515 *Response to Harper Review* (n 445) 17.

Competition and Productivity-Enhancing Reforms (IGA-CPR).[516] Although the IGA-CPR is viewed as 'a successor to' the CPA,[517] it was not agreed by all heads of governments in Australia, which means that the coverage of IGA-CPR is limited.[518] All the signing parties agreed to recommit to competitive neutrality and to be guided by competition principles, including:

> Government business activities that compete with private providers, whether for-profit or not-for-profit, should comply with competitive neutrality principles to ensure they do not enjoy a net competitive advantage simply as a result of government ownership.[519]

261. Under the IGA-CPR, a review of current competitive neutrality policies is required and aims to provide a better understanding of issues involving: the coverage of competitive neutrality (including the definition of 'significant business activities' and application of competitive neutrality to new SOEs during the start-up stage); the compliance with competitive neutrality commitment through compliance reporting by SOEs; and the appropriateness of competitive neutrality complaint processes.[520] However, the IGA-CPR was not agreed by all heads of governments, which means that the competitive neutrality commitments under IGA-CPR apply only to the governments who signed the agreement. For those governments who did not sign the IGA-CPR, such as Queensland, Victoria, South Australia, the competitive neutrality commitments under the CPA and CIRA still apply.

4.6 Conclusion

262. The primary recognition that SOEs can not only inhibit the competitive process by being exempt from competition law but also reduce allocative efficiency by relying on their government ownership-generated advantages to take business from a more efficient firm in the market, has led the Australian government to seek regulatory tools to solve the competitive neutrality concerns caused by SOEs. In particular, the analysis in this chapter has highlighted how two comprehensive tools, the competition law and competitive neutrality policy, are used by the government to provide a level playing field between SOEs and non-SOEs.

---

516 Council of Australian Governments, Intergovernmental Agreement on Competition and Productivity: Enhancing Reforms (9 December 2016) <https://www.coag.gov.au/sites/default/files/agreements/IGA-productivity-reforms.pdf> (IGA-CPR).

517 National Competition Council, 'Corporate Plan 2018–19' (August 2018), 6 <http://ncc.gov.au/images/uploads/Corporate_Plan_2018-19,_August_2018_(PDF,_734_KB).pdf>.

518 At the time of writing, Qld, Vic, and SA had not signed the IGA-CPR.

519 IGA-CPR (n 515) 9(f) 10–11.

520 ibid.

263. Particularly, the Australian experience with competition law reform shows that to achieve the universal application of competition law to all firms (regardless of their ownership status), it is essential to ensure that any kind of exemptions from the application of competition law are carefully evaluated and justified on the public interest ground. However, as the analysis in Section 4.4 revealed, the universal application of competition law in Australia is a relatively recent phenomenon and was primarily achieved after the *Hilmer Review* in the 1990s. Before this time, some SOEs were able to benefit by exemptions effected decades ago (like Crown immunity) to escape the scrutiny of all laws including competition law, whereas private firms could not. The legitimacy of these exemptions in competition law was thus questioned by the *Hilmer Review*, resulting in a re-evaluation of all the exemptions in the competition law based on public interest grounds. As a result of several rounds of reform, the current application of the Competition and Consumer Act 2010 (Cth) to SOEs is comprehensive and subject to very limited exceptions.

264. The experience in Australia further shows, as discussed in Section 4.5, that while competition law can effectively remedy the anti-competitive conduct of SOEs within its scope, it can only address competitive neutrality concerns qualifying as breaches of competition law. Some of the competitive neutrality concerns, such as cheaper debt rates or certain tax exemptions, may not qualify as breaches of competition law and cannot be addressed by the enforcement of competition law. A principles-based policy mechanism, the competitive neutrality policy, was introduced, working in conjunction with competition law to provide a forward-looking solution to competitive neutrality issues. Competitive neutrality policy principally obliges governments to prevent SOEs from being advantaged or disadvantaged by government ownership. The means adopted by the Australian government to fulfil their competitive neutrality commitments, as explained in Section 4.5.3, include tax neutrality, debt neutrality, regulatory neutrality as well as the commercial rate of return. While the substantive aspects of Australia's competitive neutrality policy have remained mostly unchanged since 1995, the policy has been further refined by the CIRA in 2006, the *Harper Review* in 2015, and the Intergovernmental Agreement on Competition and Productivity-Enhancing Reforms (IGA-CPR) in 2016, making the competitive neutrality policy in Australia the most complete globally.

CHAPTER 5

PRELIMINARY ANALYSIS OF COMPETITIVE NEUTRALITY CONCERNS IN CHINA

> The most effective way to set goals is to begin with the perceived problems and to develop legal tools specifically designed to solve them.
>
> David J Gerber[521]

265. As the comparative study in Chapter 4 revealed, in the absence of a competitively neutral environment, SOEs enjoy government ownership-generated competitive neutrality advantages (or suffer from competitive neutrality disadvantages) when competing with private firms, causing competitive neutrality concerns (distortions of the competition landscape) within the market. In addressing this observation, this chapter investigates whether there is a competitively neutral environment when Chinese SOEs compete in various markets in China.

266. By analysing whether Chinese SOEs are being advantaged or disadvantaged by their government-ownership status, this chapter aims to show the extent of competitive neutrality concerns caused by SOEs in the market of China. The examination of competitive neutrality advantages (and disadvantages) of Chinese SOEs is largely formed around the parameters of competitive neutrality advantages (and disadvantages) of SOEs in Australia (the focus of Chapter 4). The rationale for this arrangement is that the competitive neutrality advantages enjoyed by SOEs based on their government ownership may present some similarity despite the obvious differences in legal environments.

---

521 David J Gerber, 'Asia and Global Competition Law Convergence' in Michael W Dowdle, John Gillespie and Imelda Maher (eds), *Asian Capitalism and the Regulation of Competition: Towards a Regulatory Geography of Global Competition Law* (CUP 2013) 36, 45.

267. However, the evaluation of competitive neutrality advantages (and disadvantages) of Chinese SOEs will be less meaningful if one fails to consider the proximity of Chinese SOEs to the political authorities, as the discussion in Chapter 3 revealed. Therefore, rather than focusing only on the government ownership-generated competitive neutrality advantages or disadvantages of SOEs (as in the Australian context), this research also evaluates whether the inherited political connection of SOEs, deemed as the unique characteristic of Chinese SOEs, can impact how the government treats Chinese SOEs in practice.

268. The chapter proceeds as follows. Section 5.1 reviews how the existing literature deals with the competitive neutrality concerns caused by Chinese SOEs, especially the method used by scholars when identifying the competitive advantages (and disadvantages) enjoyed by Chinese SOEs as the result of government ownership. The aim of this section is to propose a suitable analytical method to identify the competitive neutrality concerns caused Chinese SOEs due to their government ownership status and political position. The rationale for using this approach as a benchmark for further evaluation will be explained at the end of this section.

269. After setting the analytical framework Sections 5.2 and 5.3 proceed to investigate the competitive neutrality advantages and disadvantages of Chinese SOEs.

5.1 Literature on Competitive Neutrality Concerns caused by Chinese SOEs

5.1.1 Overview of the Findings

270. The review of Chinese literature on competitive neutrality revealed three features. First, the notion of competitive neutrality is relatively new in the context of China and most of the discussion is explicitly concerned with competitive neutrality policy that has been developed in the context of international trading and investment rather than from a competition standpoint. For example, some Chinese researchers[522] warn that the adoption of competitive neutrality in multinational trade and investment agreements will

522 For the discussion of competitive neutrality from an international trade and investment perspective, see 屠新泉 [Tu Xinquan], 徐林鹏 [Xu Linpeng] and 杨幸幸 [Yang Xingxing], '《国有企业相关国际规则的新发展及中国对策》[New Development of International Rules Concerning State-Owned Enterprises and Its Impacts on China]' (2015) 2 亚太经济 [Asia- Pacific Economic Review] 45; 赵学清 [Zhao Xueqing] and 温寒 [Wen Han], '《欧美竞争中立政策对我国国有企业影响研究》[The Influence of the Competitive Neutrality Policy on China's State-Owned Enterprises]' (2013) 31(1) 河北法学 [Heibei Law Science] 33; 黄志瑾 [Huang Zhijin], '《国际造法过程中的竞争中立规则——兼论中国的对策》[Competitive Neutrality in the Law-Making Process: A New Challenge for China]' (2013) 3 国际商务研究 [International Business Studies] 54.

impose significant challenges on Chinese SOEs.[523] Second, the discussion on competitive neutrality is often confined to the different interpretations of the term rather than the reason contributed to the different interpretations of competitive neutrality in the first place. For example, a comparative study of the meaning of competitive neutrality in the domestic context, the international organisations context, and in the context of regional trade agreements (RTAs) or free trade agreements (FTAs) was conducted by Ying Pinguang.[524] It is notable that, when providing descriptions of competitive neutrality, almost all the authors reference the experiences that Australia has had in implementing its competitive neutrality policy. However, as discussed in Chapter 2, competitive neutrality is used in different disciplines to mean different things. For example, the root cause of the competitive neutrality concerns in the international investment area may be more concerned with home country measures (HCM) rather than government ownership.[525]

271. Third, the discussion of competitive neutrality policy in Chinese literature shows that competitive neutrality is largely accepted and welcomed by the academic community, despite the challenges it poses to Chinese SOEs in general. Most of the authors consider introducing competitive neutrality policy in the context of China as an opportunity to assist the reform of Chinese SOEs so they can become more efficient by putting more competitive pressures on them. Encouragingly, the recent government attitude and policy suggest a greater readiness for China to develop competitive neutrality policy. For example, Li Keqiang in the *Government Work Report* of 2019 announced:

> We will follow the *principle of competitive neutrality*, so that when it comes to access to factors of production, market access and licenses, business operations, government procurement, public biddings, and so on, enterprises under all forms of ownership will be treated on an equal footing'[526]

---

523 For example, Dong Yan and Zhang Lin considered the potential impacts of the competitive neutrality principle to Chinese SOEs in the context of the Trans-Pacific Partnership Agreement (TPP). They concluded that the competitive neutrality principle embodied in the TPP would create challenges to the functioning of Chinese SOEs, to the economic model of SOEs, and to the current management structure of SOEs in China. 东艳 [Dong Yan] and 张琳 [Zhang Lin], '《美国区域贸易投资协定框架下的竞争中立原则分析》 [An Analysis of the Competitive Neutrality Principle in the Framework of U.S. Regional Trade and Investment Agreements]' (2014) (6) 当代亚太 [Journal of Contemporary Asia-Pacific Studies] 117.

524 Pin-guang Ying, 'Competitive Neutrality and SOEs Reform: Recent Development and China's Practice' (Paper delivered to ARTNeT conference 'Trade in the Asian Country: Delivering on the promise of economic prosperity') 11 <http://www.unescap.org/sites/default/files/Competitive%20Neutrality%20and%20SOEs%20Reform%20Recent%20Development%20and%20China's%20Practice.pdf>. For example, authors Zhao Xueqing, Wenhan, Ying Pinguang, Dong Yan, and Zhang Lin all offer comparisons of the definition of competitive neutrality in Australia, OECD, and EU.

525 See the discussion in Section 2.2.

526 Li Keqiang, 'Report on the Work of the Government' (2nd Session of the 13th National People's Congress of the PRC, 5 March 2019) (emphasis added) <http://english.www.gov.cn/premier/speeches/2019/03/16/content_281476565265580.htm>.

272. The principle of competitive neutrality is mentioned in Guiding Opinions on Promoting the Healthy Development of Small and Medium-Sized Enterprises, the official government document issued by the General Office of the Communist Party of China Central Committee and the General Office of the State Council in 2019:

> according to the *principle of competitive neutrality*, to create a fair and convenient business environment, to stimulate the development of the small and medium-sized enterprises [SMEs].[527]

273. Similarly, People's Bank of China Governor Yi Gang, one of the top Chinese government officials, has stated that it is worth considering the applicability of the competitive neutrality principle to Chinese SOEs.[528]

274. However, there are a few commentators, often from an international trade and investment perspective, who do not share this positive view. They believe that the design of competitive neutrality policy is to discipline Chinese SOEs in particular and will set obstacles for SOEs to invest abroad.[529] For example, Tang Jing cautions against the application of the competitive neutrality principle in the international investment treaty environment, arguing it may ignore the transitional nature of the Chinese market and derogate the non-commercial objectives carried out by SOEs.[530] A broadly similar point has been made by Peng Huagang, the former deputy head of the SASAC, who stated during an interview in 2018 that 'we promote the principle of "ownership neutrality", but against rules that discriminate SOEs in the international rule-making process.'[531]

275. Discussion within the competitive neutrality policy literature also revealed two gaps. First, most authors have automatically classified Chinese firms into two categories, SOEs and non-SOEs, when discussing competitive neutrality problems. However, they fail to provide an explanation of what benchmark is used for this categorisation of SOEs and non-SOEs in China. Second, due to the pervasiveness of the state sector in China, a majority

527 《关于促进中小企业健康发展的指导意见》 [Guiding Opinions on Promoting the Healthy Development of Small and Medium-Sized Enterprises] General Office of CPC Central Committee and General Office of the State Council, 4 July 2019, s 1 (Guiding Opinions on SMEs).

528 Yi Gang's speech seems the first time Chinese officials take a clear stand publicly on competitive neutrality policy and its application to Chinese SOEs. See Editorial, How China Can Achieve 'Competitive Neutrality', *Caixin* (23 October 2018) <https://www.caixinglobal.com/2018-10-23/editorial-how-china-can-achieve-competitive-neutrality-101338043.html>

529 For example, 王婷 [Wang Ting], '《竞争中立: 国际贸易与投资规则的新焦点》 [Competitive Neutrality: The New Focus in the International Trade and Investment Regime]' [2012] (9) 国际经济合作 [World Economy and Trade] 75.

530 汤婧 [Tang Jing], '《"竞争中立"规则: 国有企业的新挑战》 [Rule of "Competitive Neutrality": A New Challenge for State-Owned Enterprises]' (2014) (3) 国际经济合作 [Journal of International Economic Cooperation] 46.

531 Peng Huagang, '《国新办举行2018年前三季度央企经济运行情况发布会》 [The State Council Information Office Held a Press Conference on the Economic Performance of Central SOEs in the First Three Quarters of 2018]' (15 October 2018) <http://www.scio.gov.cn/xwfbh/xwbfbh/wqfbh/37601/39092/index.htm>.

of authors used representative groups of SOEs to investigate competitive neutrality concerns.[532] For example, Thomas Cheng[533] used Chinese central petroleum SOEs as a representative group to identify 'how the state-owned oil giants have been unfairly assisted by the government.'[534] A similar approach was taken by Xu Shiying, who selected the central SOEs operating in the cement industry as a case study to demonstrate competitive neutrality advantages or disadvantages in relation to individual SOEs.[535] However, the reason these SOEs in a selected industry are representative is largely missing from the literature.

276. This research attempts to address the gaps identified in the literature by, first, using the criteria of 'government ownership' and 'degree of government control' to draw the line between SOEs and non-SOEs (as discussed in Section 2.1) and, second, using state capture theory (as noted in Chapter 1) as an analytical method to diagnose the competitive neutrality advantages or disadvantages of political Chinese SOEs (SOEs that enjoy political rankings).

Political SOEs

277. For the purposes of this research political SOEs were selected as the main SOE group in order to investigate the extent of competitive neutrality advantages. Although having a Communist Party committee in SOEs is the 'unique advantage of SOEs', not all Chinese SOEs enjoy political ranking. Based on the top executives' political (or bureaucratic) rank, Chinese SOEs can be grouped into political SOEs and non-political SOEs. For example, the central SOEs under the SASAC are currently ranked either at the vice-ministerial level (*Fubuji*, equivalent to provincial governors) or department-level (*Zhengtingji*).[536] Some of the SOEs at the local level can also be considered political SOEs[537] if one of their board members is currently an 'employee or a member of political organizations, like the national government, local government, the national parliament, local parliament, the National Party Congress, local Party congress, and the People's Liberation Army (PLA).'[538]

---

532 Arguably, the analytical approach used in the literature to discover how Chinese SOEs breach the competitive neutrality principle is an exploratory, qualitative one.

533 See generally, Cheng (n 101).

534 ibid 6.

535 Xu Shiying (n 232).

536 Wendy Leutert, 'Challenges Ahead in China's Reform of State-Owned Enterprises' (2016) (21) Asia Policy 83, 87. Wendy Leutert, (n 270).

537 For example, before the mixed ownership reform, Wang Minghui, then president of Yunnan Baiyao Group Co Ltd, enjoyed provincial governor-equivalent treatment.

538 Based on the observations of Yuhua Wang, almost 90 per cent of listed firms in China are considered as politically connected if 'one of its board members is formerly or currently an employee or a member of these [political] organizations': Yuhua Wang, 'Beyond Local Protectionism: China's State–Business Relations in the Last Two Decades' (2016) 226 The China Quarterly 319, 320.

278. In the assessment of competitive neutrality concerns caused by Chinese SOEs, the politically privileged SOEs were selected as its primary focus as the political strength of SOEs (often along with government ownership) may aggravate the competitive neutrality concerns, especially in the one-party political system of China.

5.1.2 Review of the Literature on Competitive Neutrality Concerns caused by Chinese SOEs

279. There is a relatively small body of literature concerned with competitive neutrality policy in a domestic setting. By far the most relevant research has been conducted by Xu Shiying.[539] The competitive neutrality advantages or disadvantages enjoyed by Chinese SOEs in the context of China formed the central focus of Xu Shiying's research which found that, compared with non-SOEs, the competitive neutrality advantages enjoyed by Chinese SOEs include: 'government subsidies; credit finance; personal relationships with the government; policy support; land-use rental; mineral resource rental; and enterprise income tax.'[540] By contrast, the competitive neutrality disadvantages suffered by Chinese SOEs, according to Xu Shiying, include: 'broader corporate social responsibility; public welfare-oriented functions; and inefficiency of corporate governance.'[541] On the basis of these findings, Xu Shiying has gone one step further by selecting SOEs located in the petroleum and cement industries as case studies to demonstrate how, for example, the petroleum SOEs (compared to private oil enterprises) enjoyed regulatory advantages, advantages of human networks, land advantages, and other advantages from government subsidies.[542]

280. Ying Pinguang compared the meaning of competitive neutrality in different contexts and observed that, despite the common wording of competitive neutrality, interpretation and ways to achieve competitive neutrality may vary depending on the domestic setting.[543] For example, Ying argues that the '30-years history of China's SOEs reform were … in line with the requirements of competitive neutrality', which operate 'to the greatest extent to ensure fair competition among market players.'[544] This view is shared by the former Secretary-General of SASAC, Peng Huagang, who in a 2018 interview said:

> after 40 years of reform and opening up … reformed SOEs in general are 'independent market players' in the sense that they are engaged in autonomous operations, make profits and assume

539 See generally, Xu Shiying (n 232).

540 ibid 50–53.

541 ibid 53–54.

542 ibid 65–73.

543 Ying (n 523) 11.

544 ibid 18.

> losses independently, bear risk on their own and pursue self-development. Therefore, SOEs are no different from other enterprises ... This is consistent with the principle of 'competitive neutrality'.[545]

281. In terms of whether China is ready for introducing competitive neutrality policy into its legal system, both Ying Pinguang and Xu Shishing shared the view that it may be too early for China to accept the concept of competitive neutrality, noting: '[i]n majority's opinion, the SOEs (sic) are still the basis for China's economy, and also an important means for China to participate in international competition.'[546] By contrast, scholars such as Hu Gairong are more optimistic.[547] Hu emphasises the benefits for China to adopt competitive neutrality in three perspectives: the development of the non-state sector, the improvement of the performances of Chinese SOEs, and the increasing delivery of public service. In addition, Hu suggests a workable competitive neutrality policy for China should at least contain the following elements: the scope of competitive neutrality should be confined to the state-controlled enterprise (rather than state invested enterprise) at both central and local levels; the competitive neutrality policy should be limited to industries that are fully-controlled by the state-owned economy; the further separation should be drawn between government regulatory and ownership functions; rules be developed to prevent cross-subsidies, to strengthen the transparency around the operation of SOEs; and the scope of exemptions from the application of competitive neutrality policy should be limited.

282. The research conducted by Bu Lingqiang appears to be related to the study of Hu Gairong as they both favour the establishing of a comprehensive competitive neutrality regime in China.[548] However, Bu stresses that the design of competitive neutrality policy for China must be considered with caution for the following three reasons. Firstly, the design of competitive neutrality policy needs to find its legal base in Article 15 of the Constitution.[549] In particular, Bu argues that 'socialist market economy' connotes the meaning of 'let the market play a decisive role in resource allocation' and 'enact market rules that are fair', which are the essential content of competitive neutrality rules.[550] However, the legal basis for competitive neutrality policy could potentially

545 Huagang (n 530).

546 Xu Shiying (n 232) 18 and Ying (n 523) 11.

547 胡改蓉 [Hu Gairong], '《竞争中立对我国国有企业的影响及法制应对》 [The Impact of Competitive Neutrality on China's State-Owned Enterprises and Legal Response]' (2014) 6 法律科学 (西北政法大学学报) [Science of Law (Journal of Northwest University of Political Science and Law)] 165.

548 卜令强 [Bu Lingqiang], '《竞争中立规则与中国国有企业改革初论》 [A Preliminary Appraisal on Competition Neutrality Rules and the Reform of China's State-Owned Enterprises]' (2017)(2) 经济法论丛 [Economic Law Review] 95.

549 Constitution (n 23).

550 This point is shared by scholar Ding Maozhong, who argues that to let the market play a decisive role in allocating resources, competitive neutrality policy should be introduced. 丁茂中 [Ding Maozhong], '《我国竞争中立政策的引入和实施》 [On China's Adoption of Competitive Neutrality Policy]' (2015) 9 法学 [Law Science] 107.

conflict with the other provisions in the Constitution, especially in the aim to reserve a range of essential activities to SOEs (Articles 6 and 7).[551] Bu argues the design of competitive neutrality rules in China needs to reflect the balance between these potential conflicts rather than denying the possibility of introducing competitive neutrality due to the conflicts.

283. Secondly, the design of competitive neutrality policy needs to find the incentive for local government to implement competitive neutrality rules to local SOEs. Bu points out that, due to the decentralised feature of governance in China, local governments often rely on local SOEs to generate revenue and to deliver public services. Consequently, local governments often provide support for their SOEs in return for encouraging SOEs to undertake more public service activities, which in a way creates an uneven playing field in the market. Bu argues that implementing competitive neutrality rules to local SOEs, on the one hand, will need assistance from local governments to neutralise the advantages that local SOEs have enjoyed. On the other hand, it is understandable that local government in China will resist the implementation of such policy because most of the advantages enjoyed by local SOEs are provided by the local government itself. Bu thus suggests the implementation experiences from Australia are worth considering in designing competitive neutrality rules for China, especially when tackling the issue of lack of incentives for compliance by local governments. Finally, the design of competitive neutrality policy needs to consider the potential conflict between competition policy and industrial policy in the context of China. To increase the acceptability of competitive neutrality policy, Bu argues, the exemption rules under the competitive neutrality policy could be utilised to allow some flexibility for the industrial policy.

284. Based on these three reasons, Bu suggests the following structure may be suitable for the application of competitive neutrality regime in China. The scope of the competitive neutrality rules should be designed to adapt to the current classification of SOEs. Particularly, the competitive neutrality rules should apply first to the competitive commercial SOEs, then gradually expand to SOEs in the regulated sector. The Free Trade Zones[552] in China, Bu argues, should be used as a transitional step for competitive neutrality policy to limit uncertainty in the marketplace.[553] The content of competitive neutrality policy, Bu argues, should include: a review agenda that is designed to identify the

551 Constitution (n 23) arts 6–7.

552 In March 2017, the State Council approved seven new free-trade zones (FTZs), taking the total number in China to 11. See '《新增7个自贸区和深化上海自贸区改革开放方案政策解读》 [Policy Briefing on Seven New Free Trade Zones and Plans for Deepening Reform of the Shanghai Free Trade Zone]' (State Council Information Office, 1 April 2017) <http://www.scio.gov.cn/34473/34515/Document/1546919/1546919.htm>.

553 However, other researchers such as Ma Qijia and Fan Fuqiang disagree with this suggestion, arguing the scope for competitive neutrality should be limited to central SOEs instead of local and small and medium-sized SOEs. See 马其家 [Ma Qijia] and 樊富强 [Fan Fuqiang], '《论国际竞争中立规则适用范围的扩张》 [On the Extended Scope of International Competitive Neutrality Rules]' (2017) (6) 法律适用(司法案例) [Journal of Law Application (Judicial Case)] 88, 91.

competitive neutrality problems caused by Chinese SOEs; a legislative review programme to identify the regulation that accords differential treatment to enterprises without justification; a set of administrative rules that provide acceptance for the implementation of competitive neutrality at all levels of government; and a complaints mechanism for competitive neutrality policy.

285. The competitive neutrality policy framework suggested by Bu contains all the necessary elements in the competitive neutrality framework in Australia, as discussed in Chapter 4. However, by quoting the finding of Xu Shiying,[554] Bu emphasises that the competitive disadvantages suffered by the Chinese SOEs should be given appropriate consideration in the content of competitive neutrality policy in China.

5.2 Suspected Competitive Neutrality Advantages of Chinese SOEs

5.2.1 Competitive Advantages of Chinese SOEs in Relation to Regulation

286. To evaluate whether Chinese SOEs are able to use their 'unique characteristics' (the government ownership status and the close proximity to the political authorities) to shape the competitive environment in China, this section examines whether SOEs can influence the enactment and enforcement of the legislation to their advantage.[555] The role Chinese SOEs played in the two distinctive but related legislative processes – the legislation drafting stage and the legislation application stage – will be analysed separately in the section below.

The Influence of SOEs in the Law-Making Process

287. The enactment of legislation in China often involves three steps, 'drafting, approval and promulgation.'[556] However, as pointed out by Bruce Owen, Su Sun and Wentong Zheng, '[m]ost of the bargaining among various interests affected by the proposed bills is done in the drafting or pre-drafting stage.'[557] The legislative power (as noted in Section 2.1.3) is exercised by the National People's Congress (NPC) and its Standing Committee. Generally, the legislative process in China has less transparency, so it is hard to know the exact

554 Xu Shiying (n 232) 53–54.

555 ibid 51. See also general discussion in Lei, Liebman and Milhaupt (n 15) 203.

556 Bruce M Owen, Su Sun and Wentong Zheng, 'Antitrust in China: The Problem of Incentive Compatibility' (2005) 1(1) JCL & E 123, 135.

557 ibid.

reasons that shape the outcome of the legislation. Nevertheless, by analysing the parties who participated in the legislative process and their relationship with SOEs, the close ties between Chinese SOEs and members of the NPC and its Standing Committee allow SOEs to become a more powerful lobby group (with respect to the non-SOEs group) and to exert a greater influence over the formational of legislation than private firms.

288. Firstly, the senior executives of politically privileged SOEs provide political connections to government regulators.[558] For example, seven executives of central SOEs also serve as representatives on the 13th NPC (which commenced on 5 March 2018), while 43 executives serve as representatives on the 13th National Committee of the Chinese People's Political Consultative Conference (CPPCC).[559] These political connections between the executives of SOEs and legislative bodies thus form an 'alignment of interest',[560] encouraging the legislators to cater to the interests of SOEs in the drafting stage of legislation. For example, the top leaders of SOEs can act as an in-house lobby group to influence the legislative outcome either to correlate with the benefits of SOEs or to weaken the outcome that disadvantages SOEs.[561] A familiar example is the involvement of the sectoral regulatory agencies during the draft stage of the AML, which is explained in the case study below.

The Influence of SOEs in the Making of the AML

289. The making of the AML goes back as far as the 1980s, soon after China's transition to a market economy, and through at least ten drafts before the 29th Meeting of the Standing Committee of the 10th NPC on 30 August 2007, approved and promulgated on 1 August 2008.[562]

290. It is commonly accepted by competition law scholars that the AML should be applied universally throughout the economy to create a level playing field for all firms regardless of ownership.[563] However, the proximity of Chinese SOEs to the participants of the drafting process – especially the sectoral regulatory authorities (who regulate SOEs in their sector) and local governments (who often own SOEs)[564] – enabled SOEs to try to persuade the

558 For more information about the political career path of SOEs, see Xiaping Cao and others, 'Political Promotion, CEO Incentives, and the Relationship Between Pay and Performance' (2018) 65(7) Management Science 2947; Leutert (n 270).

559 For the full list of people, see '十三届全国两会代表委员中的50名央企老总 [50 SOE CEOs in the 13th National Congress]' 新浪财经 [Finance Sina] (12 Feburary 2018) <http://finance.sina.com.cn/china/2018-02-13/doc-ifyrmfmc2232055.shtml>.

560 Ng (n 136) 218.

561 Sheng Hong, Zhao Nong and Yang Junfeng, *Administrative Monopoly in China: Causes, Behaviors and Termination* (World Scientific 2015) 178. See also Leutert (n 535) 87.

562 AML (n 65).

563 Healey (n 406). See also 王晓晔 [Wang Xiaoye], '《我国<反垄断法>修订的几点思考>》 [Some Reflections on the Amendment of Anti-Monopoly Law in China]' (2020) 2 法学评论 [Law Review] 11, 12.

564 Ng (n 136) 366.

legislators not to adopt universal coverage of the AML and to shield them from its application.[565] Mark Williams noted that '[b]oth the Ministries of Railways and Aviation proposed that as railways and airports were natural monopolies they should be exempted from the scope of the proposed [AML] law.'[566] Exempting regulated industries from the application of the AML is obviously in the interests of Chinese SOEs because the majority of SOEs at the time of drafting were operating in the regulated sectors. Exempting regulated sectors from the AML also means that some commercial activities of SOEs in these sectors would have been sheltered from the competition rules.

291. It is not entirely clear what induced the legislator to decide to shift away from universal coverage of the AML towards a more compromised result that accommodating the interests of SOEs by inserting Article 8. This research argues that the built-in advantages of SOEs contributed to this legislative outcome. For example, Article 8 is expressed as follows:

> The state protects the lawful business activities of undertakings in industries controlled by the state-owned economy and vital to the national economy and national security, as well as in industries subject to exclusive operation and sales according to the law. The state shall supervise, adjust and control such undertaking and the prices of their goods or services in order to protect the interests of consumers and to promote technological progress.
>
> The undertaking specified in the preceding paragraph, shall operate in good faith and in accordance with the law, and in strict self-discipline, shall subject themselves to public supervision, and shall not use their exclusive or controlling positions to harm consumer welfare.[567]

292. Article 8 (before the revision of the AML in 2020, Article 7) has long been criticised by scholars on grounds that it lacks clarity as there are at least three different interpretations of this Article. As a result, it is difficult to determine whether certain types of SOEs are covered by the AML and unclear, too, whether some SOEs may qualify for an exemption. The different interpretations of Article 8 and how these affect the application of the AML will be discussed in Chapter 6. In terms of regulatory agencies, the AML is silent on the sensitive relationship between the anti-monopoly enforcement agencies and the relevant sectoral regulators.[568] This silence reflects the conflict of

565 Huang Yong, 'Pursuing the Second Best: The History, Momentum, and Remaining Issues of China's Anti-Monopoly Law' (2008) 75(1) Antitrust LJ 117. For example, Huang Yong, who participated in the drafting of the AML, noted that during its drafting, an immunity clause was once added which completely insulated these sectors from the reach of the AML.

566 Williams (n 133).

567 AML (n 65) art 8.

568 H Stephen Harris Jr and others, *Anti-Monopoly Law and Practice in China* (OUP 2016) 26.

industry and public interest when regulating SOEs and implicitly suggests that political compromise with SOEs took place in the AML legislative process.

293. Additionally, the political personnel pathway (also known as revolving door policyhe[569]) between political SOEs and government regulators further increased the lobbying power of SOEs to influence the legislative outcome compared to non-SOEs. Notably, the frequent rotation over the years of government regulators and executives of SOEs has built up necessary personal connections (*Guanxi* in Chinese) between SOEs and government regulators.[570] Such personal connections, on the one hand, undermine the independence of government regulators, which makes them susceptible to the influence of SOEs while, on the other hand, the advantages of this personal connection of SOEs may incentivise government regulators to favour legislative outcomes that benefit SOEs, as many government regulators have assumed executive positions in SOEs in transitioning to retirement.[571]

294. However, it worth pointing out that the personal ties are not unique to Chinese SOEs. Non-SOEs in China are also motivated to actively build connections with government agencies at all levels to 'profit [from] opportunities located in the state's bureaucracy'.[572] Non-SOEs need to devote time and money to cultivate these types of connections at a cost (i.e. buying favours), whereas the political connection and personal ties enjoyed by SOEs are inherent in nature, with zero or low cost. For example, despite reforms aimed to separate regulatory functions from the corporate activities of SOEs,[573] the personnel exchanges between SOEs and regulatory agencies (or government officials) are still prevalent in China.[574] In practice, the top managers of SOEs may have worked in sectoral regulatory agencies or governments departments before their positions in SOEs.[575] Shang Bing,

569 The revolving door in this book refers to the system in which top managers of SOEs can be transferred or appointed to government official positions and vice versa. For a more detailed discussion about the rotation of government officials and SOEs management, see Li-Wen Lin, 'Balancing Closure and Openness: The Challenge of Leadership Reform in China's State-Owned Enterprises' in Benjamin L Liebman and Curtis J Milhaupt (eds), *Regulating the Visible Hand? The Institutional Implications of Chinese State Capitalism* (OUP 2015) 133. See also Lin (n 144). However, China is not distinct in application of the revolving door, other jurisdictions face similar problems. See general Wentong Zheng, 'The Revolving Door' (2015) 90(3) Notre Dame L Rev, 1262.

570 As pointed out by Deborah Healey, the informal interpersonal networks and relationships are an important part of the legal system and operate alongside the law and legal institutions: Healey, 'A Comparative Look at the Competition Law Control of State-Owned Enterprises and Government in China' in Josef Drexl and others (eds), *More Common Ground for International Competition Law?* (Edward Elgar 2011) 122, 126. See also Fan Jijian, 'The Value of Political Connections in China: Government Officials on the Board of Directors' (2016) SSRN Electronic Journal.

571 Lin (n 144); Leutert (n 144) 7.

572 Wang (n 537) 320, quoting David L Wank, *Commodifying Communism: Business, Trust, and Politics in a Chinese City* (CUP 1999) 4.

573 For more information on reform aimed to separate regulatory function from corporate SOEs, see Section 3.1.3. See also State-Owned Assets Law (n 174) art 11.

574 The trend of interchanging executives of SOEs and provincial governors was observed in 2017: see Cheng Li and Lucy Xu, 'The Rise of State-Owned Enterprise Executives in China's Provincial Leadership' (China-US Focus, 21 Feburary 2017) <https://www.chinausfocus.com/political-social-development/the-rise-of-state-owned-enterprise-executives-in-chinas-provincial-leadership>; Lin (n 568) 141.

575 Hong, Nong and Junfeng (n 560) 178.

for example, served as a vice-minister at China's Ministry of Industry and Information Technology before becoming an executive director and chairman of one of the central SOEs, China Mobile Communications Group until 2019.[576] Similarly, Ma Guoqiang, who served as chairman and Party secretary of a central SOE (China Baowu Steel Group Corporation Ltd), was appointed as the Hubei Provincial Party deputy secretary and secretary of Wuhan Municipal Party Committee from 2018 to 2020.[577]

295. Finally, the proximity of Chinese SOEs to government regulators and political authorities, according to Xu Shiying, may provide opportunities for SOEs 'to communicate with government' and thus can access information often not available to the less connected non-SOE competitors.[578] It is, however, difficult to provide tangible or quantifiable evidence of how and to what extent these personal connections can bring beneficial information to SOEs due to the very nature of the relationship and an understandable lack of disclosure.

The Influence of SOEs in the Law Enforcement Stage

296. How Chinese SOEs could use their government ownership and privileged political positions to influence the application stage of legislation will be explored in greater detail in Chapter 8. In brief, the proximity of Chinese SOEs to regulatory and political authorities could shape the enforcement of regulatory measures to favour SOEs over non-SOEs.

297. A large and growing body of literature has investigated how law enforcement is biased towards Chinese SOEs. For example, a study conducted by Sarah Eaton and Genia Kostka found that the enforcement of environmental regulations in China are subject to the influence of central SOEs under the SASAC. The study also found that central SOEs under the SASAC are often protected from environmental enforcements,[579] despite being the source of many serious pollution incidents across China. The study posits that the privileged political position and government ownership of central SOEs, among other reasons, are the major contributing factors to a more lenient enforcement of environmental regulation in relation to SOEs. The authors contend further that the environmental authorities, especially local ones, may

---

576 Gerry Shih, 'China Mobile Names MIIT Vice Minister Shang Bing New Chairman', *Reuters* (24 August 2015) <https://www.reuters.com/article/china-mobile-managementchanges/china-mobile-names-miit-vice-minister-shang-bing-new-chairman-idUSB9N10E00U20150824>.

577 刘娜 [Liu Na], '马国强任武汉市委书记（图/简历） [Ma Guoqiang Appointed Secretary of Wuhan Municipal Party Committee (Photo/Resume)]' 新华网 [Xinhuanet News] (20 July 2018) <http://www.xinhuanet.com/politics/2018-07/20/c_1123156034.htm>.

578 Xu Shiying (n 232) 51. The discussion provided by the OECD also pointed that 'SOEs may also be perceived to have access to data and information which are not available to their private competitors or only available to a limited extent.' However, it fails to link the personal relationship between SOEs and government officials with SOEs' privileged access to information. See Biau C and others, *Governments as Competitors in the Global Marketplace: Options for Ensuring a Level Playing Field* (E15Initiative, ICTSD and WEF 2016) 28 <http://e15initiative.org/wp-content/uploads/2015/09/E15-Investment-OECD-FINAL.pdf>.

579 Sarah Eaton and Genia Kostka, 'Central Protectionism in China: The "Central SOE Problem" in Environmental Governance' (2017) 231 The China Quarterly 685.

have insufficient authority to regulate central SOEs with 'high administrative rank, economic clout and *guanxi* 关系 ties to political elites.'[580] In another recent innovative study, Yuhua Wang indicates that juridical outcomes in the context of China are also subject to the influence of SOEs.[581]

298. Inspired by the research of Eaton and Kostka, this study attempts to examine the effect of government ownership and the political influence of SOEs on the AML enforcement process in Chapter 6. In particular, it argues that the ability of political SOEs to influence enforcement processes is increasing. That increase is also perceived as a concern on grounds that the current structural reform of SOEs (noted in Section 3.2.3) has aggravated the linkage between Party and SOEs interests.[582]

Section Conclusion

299. As accurately summarised by the OECD, '[p]roximity of SOEs to policy-makers puts them at an unfair advantage than private sector counterparts to exert influence on the policy-making process in favour of their business operations.'[583] The inbuilt advantages of SOEs, especially political SOEs, provide them with greater opportunities to shape the legal environment to their own advantage. Implicitly, the inbuilt privileged political position and government ownership of SOEs can accommodate their interests in the rule-making process, affording them the opportunity to lobby for beneficial provisions with zero or low cost. In contrast, non-SOEs often need to seek or cultivate political influence, like hiring or lobbying people with government working experience at high costs and expended effort.

300. SOEs can also use their inbuilt advantages to influence the regulatory enforcement process. Evidence in the literature suggests that high-ranking central SOEs may be shielded from the enforcement of environmental regulations. Further research on how SOEs use their built-in advantages to influence the application of the AML is explored in Chapter 8.

301. Taken together, the government ownership and the politically privileged position conferred on Chinese SOEs suggests that they may be 'subject to a lighter regulatory approach than similar enterprises undertaking the same type of activities.'[584] As a result, the regulatory environment may undermine the ability of non-SOEs to compete with SOEs, and to accentuate concerns that the regulatory landscape in China favours SOEs

580 ibid 700–01.

581 Yuhua Wang, 'Relative Capture: Quasi-Experimental Evidence From the Chinese Judiciary' (2018) 21(8) Comparative Political Studies 1012.

582 Jennifer Hughes, 'Communist Party Control Written into Law at China's Big Companies', *Financial Times* (15 August 2017) 1; Naughton (n 266) 292.

583 OECD, 'Maintaining a Level Playing Field' (n 7) 84.

584 ibid.

over non-SOEs. From a competition perspective, this general regulatory favouritism shown to SOEs in the legal environment poses risks of breaching the competitive neutrality principle of equal treatment in law and regulation.[585]

5.2.2 Competitive Advantages in Relation to Land

302. The land-related regulations issued by government authorities, as observed by the OECD, 'often serve valuable social purposes' but at the same time may have the potential to 'create the most severe competition problems.'[586] The competitive advantages of SOEs in free- or below-market-price use of land resources are directly related to their regulatory advantages if such advantages are caused by the regulatory differences between SOEs and non-SOEs.[587] However, the land-related regulations in China are very sensitive and complex by nature and will therefore be discussed separately from the competitive advantages in relation to regulations noted in Section 5.2.1.

China's Land Situation Overview

303. At the outset, it is essential to point out that private ownership of land does not exist in China,[588] as Article 10 of the Constitution states: 'Land in the cities is owned by the State. Land in the rural and suburban areas is owned by collectives'.[589] The land resources allocation in China is primarily subject to the oversight of government authorities at various levels. Prior to 1986, SOEs were treated as part of the government department or its subordinate (*Li Shu Yu*) government branch who could use land free of charge, while non-SOEs and individuals could not use land because they 'did not possess land-use rights.'[590] In 1988, however, China's Constitution was officially amended to separate the right to use land (or land-use rights, hereafter LURs) from the land ownership itself. The amendment also clarified that LURs (as a property interest[591]) could

585 According to the state capture theory noted in Section 1.2.2, non-SOEs (who often do not have government ownership and personal connections) will actively seek to cultivate connections with the state to secure relief from regulations.

586 OECD, 'Land Use Restrictions as Barriers to Entry' (2010) 10(3) OECD J Competition L & Pol 7, 10.

587 OECD, 'Maintaining a Level Playing Field' (n 7) 84.

588 Zhenhuan Tuan, 'Land Use Rights in China' (2004) 3 Cornell Real Estate Review 73–78.

589 Constitution (n 23).

590 US Department of Commerce, 'China's Status as a Non-Market Economy' (26 October 2017) 95 <https://enforcement.trade.gov/download/prc-nme-status/prc-nme-review-final-103017.pdf>; Shouying Liu, 'The Structure of and Changes to China's Land System' in Ross Garnaut, Ligang Song and Cai Fang (eds), *China's 40 Years of Reform and Development: 1978–2018* (ANU Press, 2018) 427, 430; Ross Garnaut, Ligang Song and Yang Yao, 'Impact and Significance of State-Owned Enterprise Restructuring in China' (2006) 55 The China Journal 35, 52.

591 The legal basis of land use is the Property Law of China, which defines the land-use right as 'a usufructuary right, namely the right to the property owned by others.' For more general discussion of the nature of the land-use rights in China, see Mo Zhang, 'From Public to Private: The Newly Enacted Chinese Property Law and the Protection of Property Rights in China' (2008) 5(2) Berkeley Bus LJ 317.

be traded in the market.[592] Particularly, LURs are further grouped as urban LURs and rural LURs and regulated separately under different legal frameworks.[593] Typically, whereas only urban LURs may be transferred in the market, the rural LURs (largely agricultural land) need to be converted into urban LURs by government authorities before being traded in the market place.[594]

304. The land market in China is structured in two tiers as primary and secondary land markets. Figure 5.1 provides a general picture to help understand the Chinese land market situation. In particular, the primary land market (*Tudi Yiji Shichang,* the blue coloured area in the chart) refers to the market in which only government authorities have power to transfer LURs to land users.[595] The supply of LURs in the primary market is therefore wholly monopolised by the government.[596] The secondary land market (*Tudi Erji Shichang,* the orange coloured area) arises after the primary market, in which land users can exchange their LURs based on market measures.[597] However, it is worth bearing in mind that the ownership of the land will always belong to the state, and that which can be traded in the market is the LURs.

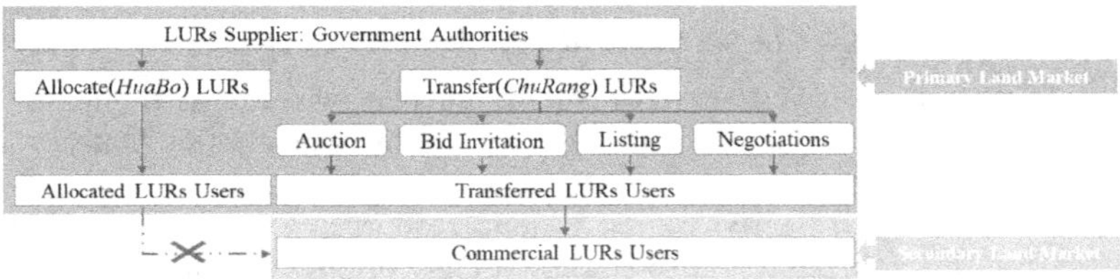

Figure 5.1 Urban Land Market in China.[598]

---

592 Although land-use rights were first trialled in special economic zones in Shenzhen in 1987, the 1988 Amendment to the Constitution officially recognised the land-use rights by deleting the paragraph in Article 10 which stated: 'No organisation or individual may appropriate, buy, sell or lease land or otherwise engage in the transfer of land by unlawful means' and revised to read: 'No organisation or individual may appropriate, buy, sell or otherwise engage in the transfer of land by unlawful means. The right to the use of land may be transferred according to law': Amendment to the Constitution 1988 (n 153).

593 This separation is according to land ownership, which is urban land (that owned by the state) and rural land (which is under the collective landownership and contracted to village households). For a detailed discussion of rural land system in China, see Liu (n 589). See also Meg Elizabeth Rithmire, 'Land Institutions and Chinese Political Economy: Institutional Complementarities and Macroeconomic Management' (2017) 45(1) Politics and Society 123, 128.

594 For discussion of land-related policy reform history, see World Bank; Development Research Center of the State Council, *China 2030: Building a Modern, Harmonious, and Creative Society* (World Bank 2013) 129–30.

595 Richard Hu, 'China's Paradoxical Reforms on Land and Real Estate Property Markets' (2013) 8(3) Global Built Environment Review 11, 18.

596 According to Li Zhang and Xianxiang Xu, government controls land supply by setting the annual construction land quotas: 'Land Policy and Urbanization in the People's Republic of China' (ADBI Working Paper Series No 614, November 2016) 7 <https://www.adb.org/publications/land-policy-and-urbanization-prc>.

597 Richard Hu, 'Understanding Chinese Real Estate: The Property Boom in Perspective' in John Garrick (ed), *Law and Policy for China's Market Socialism* (Routledge 2012) 87; Liu (n 589) 440; Ting Xu, *The Revival of Private Property and Its Limits in Post-Mao China* (Wildy, Simmonds & Hill 2014) 120.

598 Chart drawn by the author, based on the source: Meg E Rithmire, *Land Bargains and Chinese Capitalism: The Politics of Property Rights Under Reform* (CUP 2015) 8.

Acquiring Urban LURs in the Primary Land Market

305. In the primary land market, as shown in Figure 5.1, land authorities can either 'allocate' (*HuaBo*) or 'transfer' (*ChuRang*[599]) LURs to land users.

Allocations (Hua Bo)

306. Allocation of LURs refers to the administrative process by which government authorities transfer LURs to land users.[600] Given that the allocation of land is administrative in nature, the land users (who receive the allocated LURs) are not required to pay market rates[601] and do not have rights to trade allocated LURs in the secondary market.[602] The underlying rationale for the government to allocate LURs is associated with public-welfare and security purposes. For example, according to the Directory of Allocated Land, allocated LURs should be used for the purposes of:

307. state organs or military purposes … urban infrastructure or public utilities … projects of energy, communications or water conservancy, etc. which are selectively supported by the state … and other purposes as provided by laws or administrative rules and regulations.[603]

308. On closer examination of the purposes above, firms with public welfare functions are often SOEs, as explained in Section 3.2.2. Accordingly, compared to non-SOEs, Chinese SOEs are more likely to receive the allocated LURs.[604] The process for land allocation is generally less transparent (compared to the transfer process) and subject to the discretion of government authorities to determine which entities are eligible to receive allocated LURs. It is not surprising that SOEs may have opportunities to use their government and political connections to influence the land authorities to allocate LURs to them (at low cost) and use those LURs for commercial purposes. Legitimate concerns about uneven playing fields between SOEs and non-SOEs in the land allocation process may arise and further contribute to the uneven competition landscape because the operational cost of SOEs compared with non-SOE competitors is likely to be lower due to the way LURs are allocated.

---

599 *Chu Rang* also can be translated as 'assignments 'or 'granting'.

600 《中华人民共和国物权法》 [Property Law of the People's Republic of China] NPC, Order No 62, 1 October 2007, art 137 (Property Law); Xu (n 596) 119.

601 Allocated land users need to pay an 'allocation price' (now called compensatory fee for the use of state-owned land) in exchange of LURs, but this allocation price is substantially lower than transfer fees. The cost of the allocation price is calculated based on three parts: the expropriation cost (*Zhengdi Fei*), the stipulated land fees (*Tudi Guifei*), and the allocation fee set by government. For more information, see Samuel PS Ho and George CS Lin, 'Emerging Land Markets in Rural and Urban China: Policies and Practices' (2003) 175 The China Quarterly 681, 688.

602 Hu (n 594) 14.

603 《划拨用地目录》 [Directory of Allocated Land] Ministry of Land and Resources, Order No 9, 22 October 2001.

604 While land allocation is often not very transparent, research conducted by the EC found that some official documents in China favour land allocation to SOEs. See European Commission, 'On Significant Distortions in the Economy of the People's Republic of China for the Purposes of Trade Defence Investigations' (SWD [2017] 483 final/2, 20 December 2017) 207 <https://trade.ec.europa.eu/doclib/docs/2017/december/tradoc_156474.pdf>.

309. Fortunately, the issue of misuse of allocated LURs is being recognised by the Chinese government. As a response, a policy was issued in 2016[605] with the aim of narrowing the proportion of allocated land in China. It noted that 'SOEs holding allocated LURs should now convert to paid LURs if the land-use purpose no longer falls within the statutory scope of allocated land after the reform.'[606] Whether this policy issued has a real impact on the government's preferential allocation of LURs needs further empirical research.

Transferring (Chu Rang)

310. Government authorities transferring LURs to commercial land users in exchange for payment is often called *ChuRang* in Chinese.[607] Based on the land-use purpose, the transferred LURs are subject to a specific term.[608] The transfer fee for LURs is charged by land authorities and often needs to be paid upfront by the commercial land user. In principle, transferring LURs by land authorities is a commercial (rather than administrative) activity, and the transfer fee, in theory, should reflect the market value of LURs.[609] To ensure the transfer fee reflects the market value, the relevant regulation explicitly requires that transferred LURs to be acquired through market means, such as an auction (*Paimai*), bid invitation (*Zhaobiao*), or listing (*Guapai*).[610] Negotiations (*Xieyi*) between land authorities and commercial land users (both SOEs and non-SOEs) are allowed under the current regulation, however, the price of LURs should not be lower than the lowest price stipulated in accordance with the regulations of the state.[611]

Crowding Out of Non-SOEs in the Primary Market

311. As Figure 5.2 shows SOEs, as commercial land users, are in competition with other land users (both SOEs and non-SOEs) over the commercial LURs in the transfer process.

---

605 《关于扩大国有土地有偿使用范围的意见》 [Opinions on Expanding the Scope of Payable Use of State-Owned Land] Guo Tu Zi Gui [2016] No 20, 31 December 2016, s 2(2).

606 ibid. According to the regulation, if the land-use purpose still fits the scope of allocated land, the newly reformed SOEs have the option to either keep the allocated land-use rights (without paying fees but transfer of land-use rights are restricted in the market) or convert the allocated land-use rights into the paid-use rights by paying certain fees (granting fees or rent) to government authorities.

607 *Chu Rang* is sometimes translated as 'conveyance' or 'granting' in the literature.

608 The State Council in China stipulates the maximum term of land use. 《中华人民共和国城市房地产管理法》 [Urban Real Estate Administration Law of the People's Republic of China] Standing Committee of the NPC, Order No 72, 30 August 2007, art 14.

609 Hu (n 594) 17.

610 《招标拍卖挂牌出让国有建设用地使用权规定》 [Provisions on Transfer of the Right to Use State-Owned Construction Land Through Tendering, Auction and Listing] Ministry of Land and Resources (dissolved), Order No 39, 1 November 2007 (MLR Provisions).

611 Urban Real Estate Administration Law (n 607) art 13.

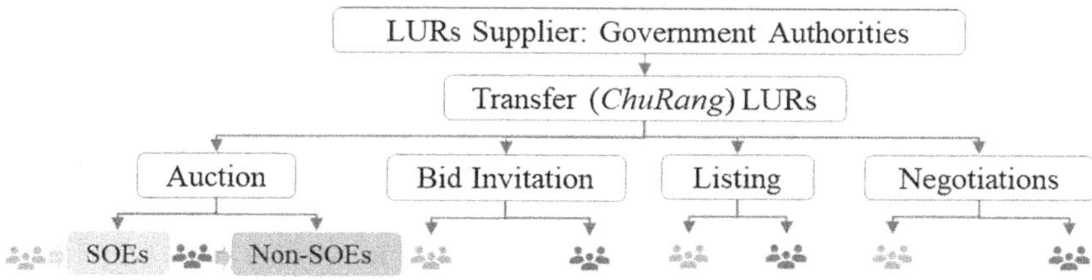

Figure 5.2 Urban LURs transferring process.

312. However, when the land department, especially local land authorities, are LURs sellers, there are concerns that SOEs may use their government and political connections to negotiate a cheaper transfer fee; this is especially so when the LURs are negotiated between SOEs and land authorities.[612] However, even if LURs are transferred through the more transparent auction process, SOEs can still use their advantages in the banking sector and their information advantage to trade in land at higher prices than their non-SOEs rivals can afford.[613] As a result, non-SOE competitors that have neither advantages arising from government ownership nor comparable access as SOEs to the banking market are squeezed out of land acquisition markets by their SOE rivals.

Lower Land Price from Government Authorities to Obtain LURs

313. An empirical study found that in China's primary land market, when local government is the sole seller, 'firms connected to local governments receive an average of 15 per cent discount over similar transactions with other local governments with whom they have no connection.'[614] By contrast, the political connection seems less likely to translate to a discounted price in secondary land markets as the seller of LURs are commercial land users (rather than government authorities). A similar study also argues that firms with political connection to government are better at securing price discounts in the primary land market.[615]

314. As a result, the discounted price for transfer of LURs to political SOEs in the primary land market can translate to lower operational costs to SOEs compared with the cost to non-SOE competitors. This raises concerns about an uneven playing field between SOEs and non-SOEs in the land market.

---

612 For example, a 2017 USCBC survey listed 'lower land costs' as one of top ten benefits that SOE competitors receive when competing with non-SOEs. See USCBC, '2017 US-China Business Council Member Survey' (6 December 2017) 3 <https://www.uschina.org/sites/default/files/2017_uscbc_member_survey.pdf>.

613 Long Wang and Yang Yang, 'Political Connections in the Land Market: Evidence from China's State-Owned Enterprises' (2018 August) SSRN Electronic Journal.

614 Ting Chen and others, 'Political Connections and Rent-Seeking: Evidence from China's Land Market' (14 June 2015) <https://editorialexpress.com/cgi-bin/conference/download.cgi?db_name=NEUDC2015&paper_id=355>.

615 Ting Chen and James Kai-sing Kung, 'Busting the "Princelings": The Campaign Against Corruption in China's Primary Land Market' (2019) 134(1) The Quarterly Journal of Economics 185, 185.

Higher Land Price to Obtain LURs

315. SOEs can use their built-in advantages to secure preferential treatment in the banking sector such as lower interest rates or better access to loans from state-controlled banks (see the discussion in Section 5.2.3). This preferential position of SOEs in the banking sector may be leveraged into other markets when the activities of SOEs expand. For example, SOEs can leverage their preferential position in the bank sector to acquire more LURs in the land market by having more financial resources to outbid their non-SOE competitors. The inbuilt government ownership and political ties of SOEs may therefore crowd out more efficient competitors in the land market.

316. The study also reinforced the assumption that the advantages of Chinese SOEs have enabled them to access more financial resources from banks than their non-SOE rivals.[616] As a result, this favourable access of SOEs in the banking sector enables them to 'bid up land prices to acquire valuable and quality land' in land auctions,[617] which ultimately 'crowd[s] out opportunities for other players to acquire quality land parcels.'[618] The evidence to support this view can be grouped into two types. First, scholars compared price differences among various types of land bidders by measuring a 'dataset of 325,064 [land] transactions from 2000 to 2016 in 2,300 counties in China.'[619] They found that 'SOEs[620] paid 9.7% (in the matched sample) to 11.9% (in the full sample) more than their non-SOE counterparts for land parcels in auctions.'[621] Second, scholars identified the possible reasons for the price gap between land purchased by SOEs and non-SOEs through the linkage between the four trillion yuan stimulus program introduced during the financial crises in 2008 and the price premiums paid by SOEs during the corresponding time. The authors concluded that 'the injected capital increased the price premiums SOEs paid in land auctions after 2008',[622] while injected capital seems to have had less effect on non-SOEs during the same period.

317. A similar study reached a comparable conclusion that Chinese SOEs can leverage their advantageous capital positions to obtain land-use rights in the secondary land market.[623] SOEs can do so by raising the price in public bidding processes or by leveraging their bargaining power with local

---

616 Wang and Yang (n 612).

617 ibid 22.

618 ibid 27.

619 ibid 1.

620 ibid 12. The study focuses on two types of SOEs, the first being wholly state-owned enterprises of which the state is sole owner; the second type has many other shareholders involved, including private individuals, but the state retains dominant control.

621 ibid 3, 10.

622 ibid 26.

623 Deng Feng, 'Indigenous Evolution of SOE Regulation' in Benjamin L Liebman and Curtis J Milhaupt (eds), *Regulating the Visible Hand? The Institutional Implications of Chinese State Capitalism* (OUP 2016) 3.

governments to obtain LURs through private interest exchanges.[624] As a result, some SOEs are, as Deng Feng points out, labelled as 'land kings', contributing to the inflation in urban land-use rights price in China. The observations offered by other scholars are consistent with the general discussions above. For example, Curtis J Milhaupt and Wentong Zheng, from an institutional perspective, point out that the Chinese government has taken measures to rein in fast-rising housing prices by requiring that 'seventy-eight central SOEs whose main business was not real estate withdraw from the real estate sector.'[625]

Acquiring LURs in the Primary Land Market

318. SOEs, like all the other types of land users, can obtain LURs through allocation or transfers in the primary land market. However, for historical reasons, three other methods are occasionally used by SOEs to acquire LURs. (See the orange-coloured area in Figure 5.3 for SOE acquisition of LURs in the primary land market.)

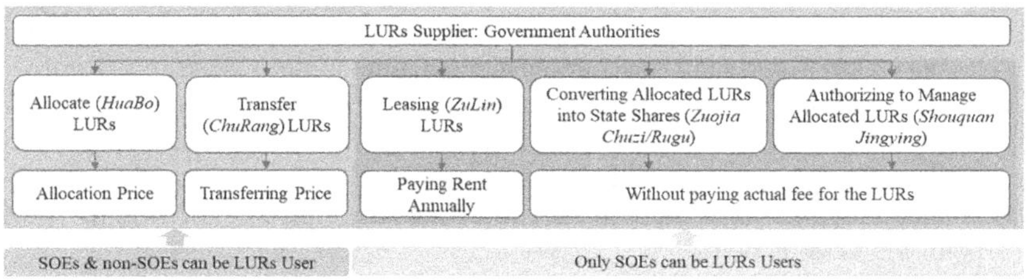

Figure 5.3 Five methods for SOEs to acquire LURs in the primary land market.

319. Before the reform of the 1980s, SOEs were treated as government bodies and used the land for free (also noted in Section 3.1.1). In the reform of the 1990s, a large number of SOEs were requested to incorporate into limited liability companies and shareholding companies (or joint-stock companies).[626] The free land used by pre-reformed SOEs in the process of corporatisation created major obstacles to reform at that time.[627] In particular, pre-reformed SOEs needed to pay high transfer fees to land authorities to convert the allocated LURs into transferred LURs before conducting corporatisation required by the reform policy. However, during the Asian financial crisis in the late 1990s, pre-reformed SOEs were experiencing financial difficulties and did not have capital to pay transfer fees to land authorities.[628]

---

624 ibid 21.

625 Milhaupt and Zheng (n 213) 192.

626 See the discussion of operational forms of SOEs in China in Section 3.1.

627 Carl B Cheng, 'Land' in Michael J Moser and Fu Yu (eds), *Doing Business In China* (Juris 2014) vol III-1.13 [c] Quasi-Granted land use rights.

628 ibid.

320. To address land disposal problems, governments have issued a few relevant policies to help fully incorporated SOEs acquire the transferred LURs without paying large transfer fees to land authorities. In particular, incorporated SOEs can lease (*ZuLin*) LURs from the land department (at a small fee); incorporated SOEs can also convert allocated LURs into state shares of the company (*Zhujia Chuzi/Rugu*); and some incorporated SOEs are being authorised by land authorities to manage the allocated LURs (*Shouquan Jingying*).[629] The three methods (indicated by the orange-coloured area of Figure 5.3) were specially designed to help with SOE reform in the 1990s, but remain influential and grandfathered into the current reform of SOEs which started in 2013. For example, in the corporatisation process, wholly state-owned industrial enterprises at the central level (or, as often termed, group-level SOEs[630]) can convert initially allocated LURs into shares in the corporation or can be authorised to manage LURs subject to the approval of government (provincial level or above).[631]

321. Nevertheless, converting allocated LURs into state shares of SOEs (*Zhujia Chuzi/Rugu*) and authorising SOEs to manage the allocated LURs (*Shouquan Jingying*) have been criticised on different grounds.[632] One criticism is that land authorities may lack a sound legal foundation necessary to transfer the allocated LURs to SOEs because the underpinning documents are only two administrative regulations rather than laws.[633] This research supports this criticism and further argues that both LURs converting and authorising methods may have the potential to create favourable conditions for SOEs in the land market.

322. Entrusting SOEs to manage LURs directly will skew the competitive landscape in their favour. Under the authorisation model, the entrusted SOEs have two concurrent roles as users and managers of LURs.[634] As a manager of LURs, entrusted SOEs (often parent SOEs) can collect rent (or granting fees) of LURs

---

629 《国有企业改革中划拨土地使用权管理暂行规定》 [Interim Provisions on the Allocated Land-Use Rights Transferred in the State-Owned Enterprises Reform] National Land Resource Management Bureau, Order No 8, 1 March 1998, which now repealed by 《自然资源部关于第一批废止和修改的部门规章的决定》 [Decision of the Ministry of Natural Resources on the First Group of Repealed and Amended Departmental Rules] (Ministry of Natural Resources Order No 5, 24 July 2019) (Interim Provisions); 《国土资源部关于加强土地资产管理促进国有企业改革和发展的若干意见》 [Several Opinions of the Ministry of Land and Resources on Strengthening Land Asset Management and Promoting the Reform and Development of State-Owned Enterprises] Ministry of Land and Resources (dissolved), Guo Tu Zi Fa [1999] No 433, 25 November 1999 (MLR Opinions).

630 See Section 5.2.3.

631 《国务院办公厅关于印发中央企业公司制改制工作实施方案的通知》 [Notice of the General Office of the State Council on Printing and Distributing the Implementing Plan for Corporate-style Restructuring of Central Enterprises] Guo Ban Fa [2017] No 69, 18 July 2017, s 3(1).

632 雷爱先 [Lei Aixian], '《关于国有土地使用权授权经营问题的探讨》 [A Discussion on the Issue of the Authorization Management of the State-Owned Land-Use Rights]' (2001) (1) 中国土地科学 [China Land Science] 22. See also 雷爱先 [Lei Aixian], '《国有企业改制土地资产处置政策略论》 [A Brief Discussion on the Disposal of Land Assets in the SOEs Reform]' (2006) (11) 中国地产市场 [China Real Estate Market] 70.

633 *Interim Provisions* (n 628) art 4; *MLR Opinions* (n 628).

634 Like the case of CNPC and PetroChina discussed here, CNPC can not only use LURs by itself but can also, as a manager of LURs, directly profit from lease or grant the authorised LURs to their subsidiaries.

from its subsidies, which in theory should belong to the land authorities.[635] In practice, however, the rent generated from LURs is collected by entrusted SOEs as 'legal incomes'.[636] For example, China National Petroleum Corporation (CNPC)[637] was selected by the (now dissolved) Ministry of Land and Resources to manage LURs authorised to them.[638] On 10 March 2000, the CNPC and its subsidiary, PetroChina Company Ltd, signed a Land Use Rights Leasing Contract and agreed that 'CNPC has leased … approximately 1,145 million square metres … to the Company [PetroChina] for a term of 50 years at an annual fee of RMB 2 billion. … The total rent [collected by the CNPC] … at the expiration of the 10-year term ... [can] be adjusted.'[639] Subsequently, the Land Use Rights Leasing Contract was amended four times since 2000, respectively in 2011, 2014, 2017 and 2021.[640] The leased land obtained by PetroChina is currently approximately 1,142 million square metres, and the annual rental paid by PetroChina is approximately RMB5,673 million (exclusive of taxes).[641] This is problematic as the profits from the allocated LURs is equivalent to a subsidy to SOEs. The subsidiary of an entrusted SOE like PetroChina can also benefit from this authorising model because it allows inter-group transfers of LURs between parent SOEs (authorised SOEs) and their subsidiaries.[642] By contrast, non-SOE competitors need to get approval and go through an administrative procedure to obtain LURs in the primary land market, which inevitably raises the transaction costs. As a result, this research argues that the practice of authorising LURs for SOEs to manage allows the subsidiaries of authorised SOEs to price more efficiently than their non-SOE rivals simply because those subsidiaries can obtain LURs easily and at a lower cost.[643]

---

635 Entrusted SOEs could only transfer or lease their authorities' LURs to their subsidiaries without going through government approval. Entrusted SOEs can transfer or lease their authorities' LURs to third-party firms, but need to get approval from land authorities and pay fees to convert their LURs into transferred LURs.

636 Hong and Nong (n 51) 53.

637 As a petroleum and petrochemical conglomerate, CNPC is a state-authorised investment corporation and state-owned enterprise. CNPC is the controlling shareholder of PetroChina Co Ltd. For more detailed information about the three amendments of the Land Use Rights Leasing Contract, see *PetroChina Company Limited: 2017 Annual Report, 48-9* <https://www.annualreports.com/HostedData/AnnualReportArchive/p/NYSE_PTR_2017.pdf>. For information on the latest Land Use Rights Leasing Contract and Supplemental Agreement, see *PetroChina Company Limited: 2021 Annual Report*, 52 <http://www.petrochina.com.cn/ptr/ndbg/202204/e459eded7f9246fe8009622174a765a5/files/47b58253c2504b4cb45f3c170394dfe7.pdf> (*PetroChina 2021 Annual Report*).

638 《关于中国石油化工集团公司股份制改造土地估价结果确认和土地使用权处置的复函》[Reply to the Disposal of Land Use Rights and the Result of the Land Evaluation Regarding the Joint-Stock Reform of China Petrochemical Corporation] Ministry of Land and Resources, Guotuzi Han [2000] No 261, 18 April 2000.

639 *PetroChina 2017 Annual Report* (n 636) 48. Land Use Rights Leasing Agreement (22 August 2003) <https://www.sec.gov/Archives/edgar/data/1123658/000134100407001222/china_ex4-16.txt>.

640 *PetroChina 2021 Annual Report* (n 636) 52.

641 ibid.

642 In particular, the land-use right enjoyed by authorised SOEs is limited in terms of transfer conditions. For instance, government approval is needed for the land authorised to SOEs to be transferable to firms that not related to the authorised SOEs. That is, the state-owned land authorised to SOEs is only transferable between an authorised SOE and its subsidiary.

643 For instance, the LURs leasing contract is negotiated between a parent company and its subsidiary, which gives rise to the concern of whether and to what extent the negotiated rent price reflects market rate even if the relevant regulation requires that the rent shall be not less than the reserve price. See also 《国土资源部关于印发<规范国有土地租赁若干意见>的通知》 [Notice of the Ministry of Land and Resources on Issuing the Opinions on Regulating the Lease of State-Owned Land] Ministry of Land and Resources (dissolved), Guo Tu Zi Fa [1999] No 222, 27 July 1999.

323. The decision to convert LURs into shares of SOEs (*Zhujia Chuzi/Rugu*) also has potential implications for levelling the playing field between authorised SOEs and their rivals, depending on the transparency and accountability in converting those shares. Under the converting model above, government authorities treat allocated LURs as a capital contribution to SOEs. Although only a limited number of SOEs are eligible to convert allocated LURs into corporate shares,[644] local land authorities may have a broader discretion to determine whether and under what conditions to convert allocated LURs into share of SOEs in practice. Given the extent of their potential gains, SOEs may have the incentive to influence or even bribe relevant government officials to convert allocated LURs into shares of enterprises.

Section Conclusion

324. In the primary land market, there are generally two ways for land users (both SOEs and non-SOEs) to obtain LURs from land authorities, through allocation and transfer. The analysis in this section shows that when land authorities transfer LURs in the primary land market, SOEs can use their built-in advantage to either negotiate a cheaper price from land authorities or to leverage their favourable position (generated by their inherent advantages) in the banking sectors to outbid their competitors in obtaining LURs from land authorities. As a result, in the absence of further governmental reform directed at levelling the playing field in the land market, non-SOE competitors (that have neither government ownership status nor privileged political positions) are being increasingly squeezed out by SOE rivals in the land acquisition process, which is competitively undesirable and will harm consumer interest in the long term.

325. In addition, for historical reasons, SOEs have three more channels (not available to non-SOEs) to acquire LURs in the primary market – namely leasing, converting allocated LURs into shares of enterprise, and authorising selected SOEs to manage LURs. These three methods, while providing practical solutions for land disposal in the context of the reform, also provide SOEs with preferential access to LURs.

5.2.3 Competitive Advantages of Chinese SOEs in Relation to Obtaining Loans

326. SOEs, like all other market players, can obtain debt from various channels such as 'commercial banks (state-owned or private), capital markets,

644 According to the regulation, SOEs that operate in 'natural monopoly sectors, or sectors that provide important public products and services, important backbone enterprises in pillar industries and high-tech industries' can convert allocated LURs into shares of company: *MLR Opinions* (n 628) s 2(2).

government-owned credit institutions, or from local funds.'[645] The main channel for Chinese SOEs to seek financial resource in the context of China is from the bank-dominated financial system. This research therefore gives particular attention to the commercial banking sector and examines how the government ownership and the political privileges of SOEs (together termed as built-in advantage of SOEs) are manifested in bank lending practices in China.

327. This section argues that bank lending practice in China is influenced by SOEs in two distinct forms. Firstly, the built-in advantage of SOEs may have an impact on the access to the loans provided by Chinese banks, resulting in preferential access to bank loans or credit from the banks compared to its competitors.[646] Secondly, the built-in advantage of SOEs may influence the lending interests rate (or merely borrowing cost) which may result in their receiving concessional rates in practice. These two distinct forms are discussed in this part.

China's Banking Sector Overview

328. Before evaluating the bank lending practices towards SOEs in specific areas, it is useful to first provide a general picture of the Chinese banking sectors. China's financial system, as has been pointed out, 'is particularly hard to analyze because it is highly opaque and evolving rapidly.'[647] However, what remains the same is that the Chinese banking sector dominates the allocation of financial resources. Statistics from the 2017 annual report of the People's Bank of China (PBOC)[648] indicate that RMB-denominated bank loans represented 60.3 per cent of total social financing (TSF, which is a broad indicator of the total amount of funds obtained from non-financial enterprises and individuals[649]) compared to 9.4 per cent of corporate bonds and 2.9 per cent of non-financial corporate domestic equity financing. Thus, this research will focus mainly on the banking sector in China to evaluate the perceived advantages of Chinese SOEs in relation to bank loans.

329. Central to the banking sector in China is perhaps its two categories of banks: the five large commercial banks, the 12 joint-stock commercial banks. As Figure 5.4 reveals, these two types of banks controlled over 56 per cent of the total banking assets at the end of 2016.

645 OECD, 'Competitive Neutrality: National Practices' (n 7) 68.

646 For example, the joint OECD-China National Bureau of Statistics empirical study in 2005 indicated that non-SOEs' access to credit is more limited than that of SOEs: OECD, *Economic Surveys: China 2005* (2005/13, September 2005) 142 <http://homepage.ntu.edu.tw/~lbh/ref/OECD/42.pdf>.

647 Douglas J Elliott and Kai Yan, *The Chinese Financial System: An Introduction and Overview* (China Center Series No 6, July 2013) 3.

648 PBOC, *The People's Bank of China Annual Report 2019* (2019) 129 <http://www.pbc.gov.cn/en/3688110/3688259/3689032/3709448/3984236/4188833/2021020518200911862.pdf> *(PBOC Annual Report 2019)*.

649 For a detailed explanation of total social financing (TSF), see Elliott and Yan (n 646) 9.

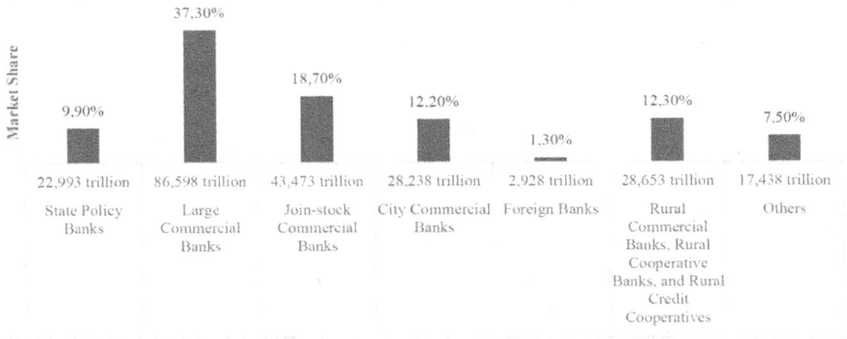

Figure 5.4 Market share of banks in China by category at the end of 2016.[650]

330. Government (mostly central government departments) involvement in the three types of banks noted above is based on the ownership indicator. In particular, the five largest commercial banks (often referred to as the 'Big Five') are the dominant players across China's banking sector. For example, Figure 5.5 reveals the controlling shareholders of the five large commercial banks are all state entities. Therefore, the key market players in the commercial banking sector are all are state-owned commercial banks.

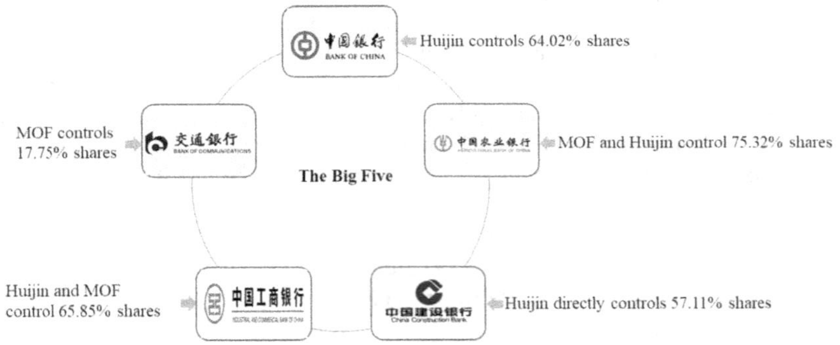

Figure 5.5 Present of state ownership in the Big Five at the end of 2021.[651]

331. As of 2021, government involvement as a percentage of shares in the Big Five banks was as follows:

- Bank of China (Central Huijin Investment Ltd, the wholly state-owned investment company, controlled over 64.02 per cent);[652]

650 Based on data from the 2017 annual report of China Banking Regulatory Commission (now known as the China Banking and Insurance Regulatory Commission), the calculation is provided by the author and the asset is valued in yuan. The category named 'Others' in the figure 5.4 includes: Non-bank financial institutions (3.4%); Urban credit co-operatives banks (0%); New type rural financial institutions; and post savings banks (4.1%).

651 Figure composed by the author, based on the 2021 annual report of each bank.

652 Bank of China, *Bank of China Limited 2021 Annual Report* (2022) 132 <https://pic.bankofchina.com/bocappd/report/202203/P020220329577864326448.pdf>.

- Agricultural Bank of China (MOF and Huijin controlled 75.32 per cent);[653]
- China Construction Bank (Huijin controlled over 57.11 per cent);[654]
- Industrial and Commercial Bank of China (MOF and Huijin controlled over 65.85 per cent);[655] and
- Bank of Communications (MOF controlled over 17.75 per cent).[656]

332. China's 12 joint-stock commercial banks are also considered state-owned (or at least state-controlled) banks based on the government ownership metric.[657] For example, China CITIC Bank (formerly known as CITIC Industrial Bank) is one of the dozen joint-stock commercial banks in which different state-owned legal entities held over 73 per cent shares together in 2017.[658] Finally, the three-state policy banks,[659] which are designed to fund state-led development projects,[660] are solely owned by the Chinese government and the board of supervisors are appointed by the State Council.[661]

Access to Bank Loans from State-Owned Banks by SOEs

333. When state-dominated banks are the key supplier of formal bank loans, the question of whether SOEs can use their built-in advantages in securing more bank loans has drawn scholarly attention over the past two decades.[662] One approach used to address this question is to compare the share of bank lending

653 Agricultural Bank of China Ltd, *Build a Beautiful China: 2021 Annual Report* (2022) 102 <www.abchina.com/en/investor-relations/performance-reports/annual-reports/202204/P020220427580795705015.pdf> (*AgBank 2021 Annual Report*).

654 China Construction Bank Corporation, *Annual Report 2021: New finance be with every family* (2021) 152 <http://www.ccb.com/en/investorv3/annualreports/20220429_1651233438.html> (*CCB Annual Report 2021*).

655 Industrial and Commercial Bank of China Ltd, *Annual Report 2021* (2021) 92 <https://v.icbc.com.cn/userfiles/Resources/ICBCLTD/download/2022/2021AnnualReport20220427.pdf> (*ICBC Annual Report 2021*).

656 Bank of Communications Co Ltd, *2021 Annual Report* (2012) 76 <https://www.bankcomm.com/BankCommSite/shtml/jyjr/en/2600223/2600236/2600243/2642441.shtml?channelId=2600236> (*BoCom Annual Report 2021*).

657 The 12 joint-stock banks include: China Everbright Bank; China Guangfa Bank; China CITIC Bank; Industrial Bank; China Bohai Bank; Shanghai Pudong Development Bank; China Merchants Bank; Huaxia Bank; China Zheshang Bank; Hengfeng Bank, Ping An Bank and China Minsheng Bank. In total, the 12 joint-stock banks held roughly 18.7% of total banking assets at the end of 2016.

658 CITIC Industrial Bank, *2017 Annual Report* (2017) 113 <http://iis.quamnet.com/media/IRAnnouncement/998/EN_US/003128598-0.PDF> (*CITIC Annual Report 2017*).

659 Three state policy banks are the Agricultural Development Bank of China, the Export-Import Bank of China (EXIM), and the China Development Bank.

660 Elliott and Yan (n 646) 57.

661 《国有重点金融机构监事会暂行条例》 [Interim Regulations on the Board of Supervisors of Important State-Owned Financial Institutions] State Council, Decree No 282, 15 March 2000, Art 3.

662 In China, bank lending to private firms only started in 1997. For further information, see Wenli Cheng and Yongzheng Wu, 'Bank Finance for Private Firms in China: Does Political Capital Still Pay off?' (Discussion Paper, December 2015) <https://www.monash.edu/business/economics/research/publications/publications2/0716bankfinancechengwu.pdf>. For the evolution of the banking system in China, see Gregory C Chow, *China's Economic Transformation* (3rd edn, John Wiley & Sons 2015) 233–51.

between SOEs and non-SOEs to illustrate that SOEs in China have better access to bank loans.[663] For example, Nicolas Lardy, in his recent research, observed that SOEs could secure a far higher percentage of bank loan finance than non-SOEs.[664] He commented that 'the share of bank loans to nonfinancial corporations that went to private firms fell from 57 per cent in 2013 to only 19 per cent by 2015, while the share that went to SOEs almost doubled over the same period – from 35 per cent to 69 per cent.'[665] Similar research[666] presented complementary evidence that shows SOEs have better access to bank loans. For example, by examining the economic stimulus packages implemented by the Chinese government in 2008,[667] the research found that the expansion in the supply of bank loans has resulted in more loans being allocated to SOEs than non-SOEs through bank lending, regardless of their profitability or creditworthiness.[668]

334. To explain why SOEs could receive more bank loans from state banks, the linkage between the lending activities of banks and the built-in advantages of SOEs has been studied in the literature. For example, research conducted by Robert Cull, Wei Li, Bo Sun, and Lixin Colin Xu established a positive link between political SOEs and access to bank loans. In particular, the research found that firms with government ownership and political connections (notably through the appointment of CEOs) have better access to loans compared to firms without linkage to government ownership and government connections (non-government-appointed CEOs). The study also confirmed that firms without links to government ownership or political connections tend to face tighter financial constraints in obtaining loans from formal financial institutions in China.[669] More empirical evidence is presented in different research to support the same finding: Chinese private firms are unfavourably treated in accessing bank loans and face the highest degree of financial

663 For example, Matthew Bunny compared bank lending conditions faced by SOEs and private firms in China. The author concluded that, by comparing implied interest rates constructed from the financial statements of listed companies in China, the rate for private firms remain higher than those for state firms, which is consistent with the commonly cited view that state firms receive loans on better terms. See Matthew Bunny, 'Private Sector Financial Conditions in China' (17 September 2020) 93–94 <https://www.rba.gov.au/publications/bulletin/2020/sep/pdf/private-sector-financial-conditions-in-china.pdf>.

664 Nicholas Lardy, 'Private Sector Development' in Ross Garnaut, Ligang Song and Cai Fang (eds), *China's 40 Years of Reform and Development 1978–2018* (ANU Press 2018) 329–44.

665 ibid 339.

666 Qigui Liu, Xiaofei Pan and Gary Gang Tian, 'To What Extent Did the Economic Stimulus Package Influence Bank Lending and Corporate Investment Decisions? Evidence from China' (2018) 86 Journal of Banking and Finance 177.

667 In 2008, the State Council announced an approximately RMB 4 trillion economic stimulus package to stabilise the impact of the global financial crisis (GFC): Che Yuming and Zhang Xudong, '《我国财政和货币政策同时调整 4万亿资金力撬内需》 [Fiscal and Monetary Policies Are Simultaneously Adjusted by 4 Trillion Yuan to Leverage Domestic Demand]' *China News* (19 November 2008) <http://www.gov.cn/jrzg/2008-11/10/content_1143810.htm>.

668 Liu, Pan and Tian (n 665) 178. For similar research on the impact of Chinese economic stimulus on bank lending, see Lin William Cong and others, 'Credit Allocation Under Economic Stimulus: Evidence from China' (2019) 32(9) Review of Financial Studies 3412.

669 Robert Cull and others, 'Government Connections and Financial Constraints: Evidence From a Large Representative Sample of Chinese Firms' (2015) 32 Journal of Corporate Finance 271.

constraints, whereas SOEs and foreign firms (often with foreign financing channels) were less financially constrained, based on firm-level data between 1998 and 2005.[670]

335. The indirect evidence of the growth of shadow banking in China[671] is also frequently used in the literature to support the finding that Chinese SOEs enjoy preferential access to loans from the banking sector. As Shen Wei comments: 'State-owned enterprises can borrow money from (state-owned) banks whereas private businesses are often left to fend for themselves in an informal market of moneylending'.[672] Shen Wei noted that 'SMEs [small and medium-sized enterprises] and farmers have been severely marginalised by the state banking system.'[673] For example, 'in 2011, only 19% of bank lending went to small business'.[674] SMEs and farmers, according to Shen Wei, 'have no option but to turn to these informal lending firms ... [while] large SOEs are able to obtain over 75% of loans from state-owned commercial banks at a 7.2% interest rate, compared with the one-year benchmark interest rate of 6.56%.'[675] The linkage between private firms having less access to loans in the formal banking sectors and the rise of informal financial markets in China has also been studied by Yunlin Lu and others. In their research, the authors explain that 'the Chinese banks are primarily interested in lending money to SOEs ... [thus] only a limited amount of capital from the banks was lent to private enterprises'.[676] As a result, some private firms (often SMEs) unable to rely on the formal banking sector to obtain sufficient capital resources, seek external financing. Therefore, the authors argue that SOEs' preferential access to bank loans has contributed to the rapid growth of shadow banking in China.[677]

336. The selective literature mentioned above is by no means exhaustive. However, the selective nature of the literature should not detract from the conclusion that Chinese SOEs enjoy preferential access to the available capital provided by the Chinese state-owned banks. As a result, non-SOEs are being marginalised and have difficulty obtaining loans from formal channels 'due to increasing borrowing costs.'[678] Non-SOEs thus increasingly rely on the shadow banking

670 Sandra Poncet, Walter Steingress and Hylke Vandenbussche, 'Financial Constraints in China: Firm-Level Evidence' (2010) 21 China Economic Review, 411.

671 Broadly, informal financing, in contrast to formal financing, is not regulated by financial regulatory authorities. The term 'shadow banking' in the context of this Thesis refers to financial markets and institutions that perform credit, maturity, or liquidity outside the formal banking system. For more detailed discussion on the definition of shadow banking, see Zoltan Pozsar and others, 'Shadow Banking' (Staff Report No 458, NY Federal Reserve Bank February 2012) 4–7 <https://www.newyorkfed.org/medialibrary/media/research/staff_reports/sr458.pdf>.

672 Wei Shen, *Shadow Banking in China: Risk, Regulation and Policy* (Edward Elgar 2016) 241.

673 ibid 230.

674 ibid.

675 Wei Shen, 'Market-Based Regulatory Responses to Private Lending in China: Beyond a Law and Society Paradigm' (2017) 4(1) AsianJLS 59, 61.

676 Yunlin Lua and others, 'Shadow Banking and Firm Financing in China' (2015) 36 Intl Rev of Economics and Finance 40, 47.

677 ibid.

678 Shen (n 671) 87.

system and thereby contribute to the growth of shadow banking in China. Borrowing from informal channels also increases the borrowing costs of non-SOEs as the interest rate in informal lending could be potentially five or even six times higher than the Chinese central bank's benchmark lending rate.[679]

337. Fortunately, some of the issues discussed above have been acknowledged by a newly established regulator, the Financial Stability and Development Commission (FSDC). For example, a meeting of the FSDC held in October 2018, identified that banks should provide more loans to small private firms.[680] The message of 'lending more to smaller and private firms', according to Thomas Gatley, implies 'lending less to SOEs.'[681] This shift reflects that the FSDC has indirectly taken measures to redress 'the bank system's history of lending mainly to state-owned enterprises.'[682] Another positive indicator is the policy issued in August 2018,[683] which dedicated one section to urging Chinese banks to increase credit to SMEs, farmers, and private firms, and indirectly pull back the shadow banking system in China.[684] Whether these more recent and evolving regulatory measures, along with bank lending policies, can effectively address the long-standing preferential treatment of SOEs by state-dominated banks remains unclear at this stage. However, it is essential to acknowledge such measures are being implemented by the Chinese government and are a step in the right direction.

SOEs' Lending Interest Rates

338. Besides easier access to bank loans, Chinese SOEs are perceived to receive favourable interest rates over their bank loans because of implicit guarantees from the government. For example, the International Monetary Fund (IMF) stated that '[i]mplicit guarantees have biased credit to SOEs by lowering the cost of capital and shielding SOEs from defaults.'[685]

---

679 In general, the interest rate charged by informal lenders, like private lending, is often contract-based and thus hard to quantify in relation to the one-year benchmark interest rate. However, since 2015, the Supreme Court has noted that where the interest rate agreed upon by the borrower and the lender exceeds the annual interest rate of 36%, the agreed interest on the excessive part shall be null and void.

680 '刘鹤主持国务院金融稳定发展委员会专题会议 [Liu He presides over the special meeting of the State Council Financial Stability and Development Committee]' (国务院 [State Council], 20 October 2018) <http://www.gov.cn/guowuyuan/2018-10/21/content_5333237.htm>.

681 Thomas Gatley, 'More Loans for the Private Sector' (Gavekal Dragonomics 18 October 2018) 1.

682 ibid.

683 'Economic Watch: China's Monetary Policy Unchanged Despite Reserve Requirement Cut' *Xinhua News* (19 April 2018) <http://www.xinhuanet.com/english/2018-04/19/c_137121802.htm>; 《中国银保监会办公厅关于进一步做好信贷工作提升服务实体经济质效的通知》 [General Office of the China Banking and Insurance Regulatory Commission on Further Doing a Good Job in Credit Work: Notice to Improve the Quality and Efficiency of Serving the Real Economy] China Banking Regulatory Commission Release No 76, Prudential Regulation Bureau, 17 August 2017 <http://www.cbrc.gov.cn/chinese/newShouDoc/78EB4C12EEF94CCBABF28E8D807388F9.html> s 2.

684 Barry Naughton, 'Economic Policy Under Trade War Conditions: Can China Move Beyond Tit for Tat?' (2018) (57) China Leadership Monitor; Thomas Gatley, 'Softening Up on SOE Deleveraging' (Gavekal Dragonomics 9 August 2018).

685 IMF, 'People's Republic of China: Selected Issues' (IMF Country Report No 19/274, 23 August 2019) 40 <https://www.imf.org/en/Publications/CR/Issues/2019/08/15/Peoples-Republic-of-China-Selected-Issues-48593>.

339. In order to examine the interest rates given to SOEs, it is useful to understand that interest rates in China are undergoing market-oriented transformation and deregulation. For example, the regulated interest rates on deposit rates and loan rates have been lifted by the Chinese government since 2015, and a 'corridor interest rate' approach (which sets a floor and a ceiling boundary on interest rates) is being introduced to guide key money market rates.[686] However, the rate corridor approach seems to have had limited impact on primary lending and deposit rates charged by banks as that interest rate is currently still being followed by the PBOC through the benchmark lending and deposit rates.[687] As observed by Zheng Liu, Pengfei Wang and Zhiwei Xu, the corridor interest rates approach 'has permitted banks to offer a range of deposit and lending rates within a relatively narrow band, and it has adjusted the bands occasionally.'[688]

340. The perception that Chinese SOEs enjoy discounted interest rates from state-bank loans over non-SOEs is also often subject to anti-subsidy investigations under the WTO regime on a case-by-case basis.[689] The European Commission, in a recent countervailing duty investigation,[690] concluded that the hot-rolled, flat steel products from Chinese companies (which are partially or fully state-owned companies) are benefitting from preferential lending both from state-owned banks and other financial institutions.[691] However, investigations have revealed the difficulty of assessing whether and to what extent loan interest rates of SOEs are subsidised (sometimes termed 'interest subsidy') as loan interest rate data is rarely measured according to the types of borrowers in China and subject to different maturity.

341. There is nevertheless growing empirical evidence in the literature that demonstrates Chinese SOEs enjoy preferential or below-market interest rates from state banks compared to non-SOEs. For example, the OECD interpreted the

686 OECD (n 30) 22; Yiping Huang and Xun Wang, '"Strong on Quantity, Weak on Quality': China's Financial Reform Between 1978 and 2018' in Ross Garnaut, Ligang Song and Cai Fang (eds), *China's 40 Years of Reform and Development: 1978–2018* (ANU Press 2018) 291, 295; Güneş Kamber and MS Mohanty, 'Do Interest Rates Play a Major Role In Monetary Policy Transmission In China?' (Bank for International Settlements Working Paper No 714, April 2018) 5–6 <https://www.bis.org/publ/work714.pdf>.

687 The benchmark interest rates are reference rates published by the PBOC and often used by the financial institutions as a basis for determining individual lending rates.

688 Zheng Liu, Pengfei Wang and Zhiwei Xu, 'Interest-Rate Liberalization and Capital Misallocations' (Working Paper 2017–15, SF Federal Reserve Bank, January 2020) 1 <https://doi.org/10.24148/wp2017-15>.

689 See generally US Department of Commerce, 'Review of China's Financial System for Countervailing Duty (CVD) Benchmarking Purposes' (Memorandum, 21 July 2017).

690 Countervailing duty (CVD) laws are designed to provide relief to domestic industries that have been materially injured or are threatened with material injury by imported goods subsidised by a foreign government or other public entity. See Ming Du, 'China's State Capitalism and World Trade Law' (2014) 63(2) ICLQ 409, 430.

691 For instance, Commission Implementing Regulation (EU) 2017/969 of 8 June 2017 imposing definitive countervailing duties on imports of certain hot-rolled flat products of iron, non-alloy or other alloy steel originating in the People's Republic of China and amending Commission Implementing Regulation (EU) 2017/649 imposing a definitive anti-dumping duty on imports of certain hot-rolled flat products of iron, non-alloy or other alloy steel originating in the People's Republic of China (OJL 146/32) s 3.4 paras 83–344.

trend of growing lending below the benchmark rate in China[692] as implicit evidence that 'lending to SOEs and other public entities that carry implicit government guarantees' are increasing.'[693] More recent research conducted by Hong Yu, using average monthly prime lending rates in China to calculate, found that the average interest rates for short-term loans (of less than a year) was 5.4 per cent in 2010. By contrast, the average interest rate for short-term loans borrowed by the two central SOEs (China Petrochemical Corp and China National Offshore Oil Corp) were about half of the average interest rate at 2.7 per cent and 3.4 per cent respectively in 2010.[694] The IMF, using different measurements to calculate loan interest rates of listed SOEs, also found that 'the lending costs of listed SOEs are about 40–50 basis points below the benchmark lending rate … and are about two to three notches above those of comparable private firms.'[695]

342. Research by Cheng Sun, Jiangmin Xu and Yinuo Zhang also found that, compared to non-SOE borrowers, SOE borrowers on average obtained '40.6% more credit … at 0.282 per cent lower spread … and 16% longer duration [in borrowing contracts]' before the anti-corruption movement in 2013.[696] However, from the perspective of lending institutions (i.e. banks), the authors argue that the lending decisions of commercial banks make sense in favour of Chinese SOEs. According to the research, the government ownership status of SOEs provides 'advantages in obtaining government contracts and licences, which would generate profit and cash flow correspondingly.'[697] The political connection of SOEs to government can also help SOEs to 'have easier access to capital markets … which also helps to secure their cash flow position.'[698] Hence, it is rational for lending institutions to favour SOEs over non-SOEs in the lending practice.

343. Additionally, corruption concerns are always associated with transactions with SOEs because 'in order to fulfil their political agendas or their promise after briberies, the government officials may directly ask banks or loan officers to issue loans to specific SOEs to exchange for political favors.'[699] Fortunately, the anti-corruption movement launched in 2013 will have an impact on the advantages of SOEs in obtaining bank loans while having limited impact on non-SOE borrowers – a view supported by the statistics. For example, due to the anti-corruption movement, the borrowing advantage of SOEs diminished between 2013 and 2016, and resulted in shrinking 'the inequality between two

692 ibid.

693 OECD (n 30) 22.

694 Hong Yu, 'The Ascendency of State-Owned Enterprises in China: Development, Controversy and Problems' (2014) 23(85) Journal of Contemporary China 161, 176–77.

695 IMF, 'The People's Republic of China: Selected Issues' (IMF Country Report No. 16/271, August 2016) <https://www.imf.org/external/pubs/ft/scr/2016/cr16271.pdf>.

696 Cheng Cai Sun, Jiangmin Xu and Yinuo Zhang, 'Anti-corruption and Bank Lending' (March 2018) <http://pubdocs.worldbank.org/en/277631528721196341/SXZ-Anticorruption0415.pdf>.

697 ibid 1.

698 ibid.

699 ibid.

types of ownership'.[700] Correspondingly, the lending environment for non-SOEs is improving, so they can now receive more borrowing contracts with larger credit amounts, lower interest rates, and longer loan durations from banks.[701]

344. The research above reveals a tendency that Chinese banks are providing more loans and favourable interest rates to SOEs than to non-SOEs in China. Such favourable loans and interest rates translate into lower-cost finance for SOEs. However, due to data limitations, the analyses presented in the literature above offers only a glimpse of the lending conditions enjoyed by SOEs. To accurately capture the extent to which SOEs can borrow money at preferential interest rates, more commercial lending data and information based on the types of borrowers will be needed.

Section Conclusion

345. This section has provided a general picture of lending practices in the commercial banking sector towards SOEs and non-SOEs in terms of accessing bank loans and loan interest rates. There is limited data available to identify the full spectrum of inbuilt advantages that Chinese SOEs enjoy across the banking sector and how they impact on bank lending practice, including how they disadvantage non-SOEs. However, based on available information, the evidence overwhelmingly suggests that, compared to non-SOEs, Chinese SOEs have benefited from bank loan access and loan interest rates because of their government ownership. The literature also shows that the privileged position of SOEs over bank loan access is more evident than the advantages over loan interest rates that banks provided to them.

346. These competitive neutrality advantages enjoyed by Chinese SOEs in the banking section has had a distortive effect on market competition. For example, SOEs can channel their privileged position across the bank sector to other markets. As discussed in Section 5.2.2, SOEs can use their financial advantage to obtain more LURs by outbidding non-SOE competitors in the commercial land market.

5.3 Suspected Competitive Neutrality Disadvantages of Chinese SOEs

347. While the discussion above has largely focused on the potential for Chinese SOEs to leverage their government ownership and political connections for their competitive advantages, the government ownership and political connections can in some circumstances limit the ability of Chinese SOEs to compete with non-SOEs.

700 ibid 42.

701 ibid.

5.3.1 Role of the Party Committee in SOEs

348. As discussed in Chapter 3, all Chinese firms must include the governance of the Communist Party in their articles of incorporation, and include rules that facilitate the activities of the Party committee (such as promoting ideology) in accordance with Article 32 of the Constitution of the Communist Party of China.[702] However, the requirement of establishing Party committees, while mandatory for SOEs, seems more relaxed among non-SOEs.[703] In 2017, SOEs were required to amend their constitutions to institutionalise the functions of the Party committee based on the Constitution of the Communist Party of China.[704] As a result, all 97 central SOEs had incorporated provisions on the Party committee into their articles of association by the end of 2017.[705] Over 30 HK-listed SOEs had established Party committees through amendments of articles of association.[706]

349. While both SOEs and non-SOEs established the Party committee in their articles of association, the function of the Party committee in SOEs will be significantly different from the role of the Party committee in non-SOEs.[707] As explained in Section 3.2.3, the involvement of the Party committee in the decision-making process of SOEs is more intensive than non-SOEs. In SOEs, 'material issues' (whatever that means[708]) are required to be discussed by the Party committee before the SOE Board, and the Party committee members and board members of SOEs are overlapping.

350. From a competitive neutrality perspective, the involvement of the Party committee in the governance of SOEs is a double-edged sword. On the one hand, institutionalising the Party committee may aggravate the political advantage of SOEs and may reinforce the competitive neutrality advantages in relation to regulation, land, or loans. (See the discussion in Sections 5.1 and 5.2.) On the other hand, the required role of the Party committee may reduce the operational autonomy (especially that of management) of SOEs, which can be considered a competitive neutrality disadvantage compared to non-SOEs. For example, as Lucy Hornby has observed, '[p]urely business decisions that once might have been handled by division managers within an SOE are getting routed through the party hierarchy instead, leading to frustrating

---

702 CPC Constitution (n 127) art 32.

703 Jiang Daxing (n 271) 32.

704 Notice on Central SOEs (n 263); CPC Constitution (n 127) art 32.

705 '《强根铸魂抓党建 踏石留印见实效——国务院国资委党委推进中央企业党建工作纪实》[Enhancing the Party Building to Strengthen the Roots: The State-Owned Assets Supervision and Administration Commission of the State Council to Promote the Party building in Central State-Owned Enterprises]' (10 October 2017) <http://www.sasac.gov.cn/n2588030/n2588919/c7979758/content.html>.

706 Hughes (n 581); Naughton (n 266) 292.

707 However, for hybrid (or mixed ownership) SOEs (as noted in Section 3.2.4), how to establish the leadership of the Party committee in the article of association of mixed ownership corporations is still unclear.

708 Jiang Daxing (n 271). According to Jiang Daxing, the authority of the Party over SOEs' governance should be reflected not only in deciding political matters but also in providing opinions and suggestions, as well as in deciding commercial matters that may have higher commercial risks.

delays at the operational level.'[709] In particular, if the discussion of material issues by the Party committee is required before an SOE board can make a decision, the governing efficiency of SOEs may potentially be reduced due to the time and way in which costs are increased compared to non-SOEs.

351. By comparison, although non-SOEs in China (including foreign firms) should also be including the Party organisation in their corporate governance (based on Article 19 of the Company Law), it does not require the Party organisation to participate in the decision-making process of the company. Thus, non-SOEs have more flexibility than SOEs to set up the role of the Party in its articles of association.

352. A relevant question is whether the influence of the Party committee on major economic decisions, such as competitive or other commercial strategies, might render all Chinese SOEs being treated as a single entity controlled by the Party, especially when they engage in cross-border transactions. There are cases in the merger context that indicate that Chinese SOEs are being treated as the personification of a monolithic 'China Inc.'[710] See, for example, the decision of the Commission of the European Communities (European Commission) on Electricité de France SA (EDF) and China General Nuclear Power Corporation (CGN) in 2016,[711] which treats all SOEs in the energy sector as a single entity despite being owned by different levels of government.[712]

5.3.2 Non-Commercial Obligations of SOEs

353. Non-commercial obligations (sometimes referred to as non-commercial service obligations, universal service obligations, community service obligations, or public service obligations) are defined as 'requirements to provide a service of a given quality at a "reasonable" price for consumers.'[713] In contrast to commercial obligations (the maximisation of profits and shareholder value), non-commercial obligations 'are those benefitting the general public within the SOE's own jurisdiction.'[714] For example, non-commercial obligations (termed community service obligations or CSOs in Australia) are defined as:

> when a government specifically requires a public enterprise to carry out activities relating to outputs or inputs which it would not elect to do on a commercial basis, and which the government

709 Lucy Hornby, 'Communist Party Asserts Control over China Inc', *Financial Times* (3 October 2017).

710 For general discussion of how the European Commission assesses whether Chinese SOEs have the power of decision making independent of the Chinese state, see Riley (n 229); Zhang (n 36).

711 Commission Decision No. M.7850 (EDF / CGN / NNB) 10 March 2016 <https://ec.europa.eu/competition/mergers/cases/decisions/m7850_429_3.pdf>.

712 Zhang (n 36). For more detailed discussion of the case, see Angela Huyue Zhang, *Chinese Antitrust Exceptionalism: How The Rise of China Challenges Global Regulation* (2021 OUP), Chapter 4.

713 OECD, 'Non-Commercial Services Obligations and Liberalisation' (2006) 7(1) OECD J Competition L & Pol 83, 86.

714 OECD (n 62) 15.

> does not require other businesses in the public or private sectors to generally undertake, or which it would only do commercially at higher prices.[715]

354. SOEs (and sometimes non-SOEs) are directed to carry non-commercial or non-profit activities (alongside their commercial activities) to meet social policy objectives.[716] For example, in China (as noted in Section 6.2.2), even competitive SOEs are required to '*conscientiously serve national strategies and take the initiative to fulfil social responsibilities.*'[717]

355. When SOEs have the dual goals of carrying out commercial activities and delivering public policy objectives, the issue of compensation and transparency arises.[718] For example, it has been long recognised in Australia's practice that the way government funds CSOs could have distortionary effects on resource allocation in the market (see detailed discussion in Chapter 7).[719] Particularly, funding CSOs through internal cross-subsidisation could aggravate the competitive neutrality advantages (or disadvantages) enjoyed by SOEs.[720] Internal cross-subsidisation of CSOs can cause spillover effects by forcing one group of consumers to absorb the costs of delivering CSOs.[721] To ensure that public funds are not used to carry out commercially oriented activities, Australian governments require that SOEs separate their commercial account from non-commercial accounts (to increase transparency)[722] and that CSOs are clearly identified and funded so that prices reflect full cost attribution.[723]

356. In China, SOEs are not required to separate the accounts between non-commercial obligations and commercial activities,[724] and cross-subsidisation

---

715 Australia Industry Commission, 'Community Service Obligations: Policies and Practices of Australian Governments' (February 1997) 7 <https://www.pc.gov.au/research/supporting/community-service-obligation-policy/cso.pdf>.

716 OECD, 'Ownership and Governance of State-Owned Enterprises: A Compendium of National Practices' (2018) 49 <https://www.oecd.org/corporate/ca/Ownership-and-Governance-of-State-Owned-Enterprises-A-Compendium-of-National-Practices.pdf>.

717 *Guiding Opinions on SOEs* (n 56) s 2(4) (emphasis added).

718 See generally Hans Christiansen, 'Balancing Commercial and Non-Commercial Priorities of State-Owned Enterprises' (Corporate Governance Working Papers No 6, OECD 2013) <https://www.oecd.org/corporate/OECDCorporateGovernanceWorkingPaper6.pdf>.

719 CSOs could be funded in different ways. For example, acceptance of a lower rate of return to the government to compensate for expenses incurred in providing the CSO; levies on industry; cross-subsidy between different users; and direct funding form the budget to the service provider. For more detail see Standing Committee on Financial Institutions and Public Administration (Commonwealth), House of Representatives *Cultivating Competition: Report of the Inquiry into Aspects of the National Competition Policy Reform Package* (Committee Report, June 1997) 33 (Standing Committee Report).

720 Andrew Trembath, 'Competitive Neutrality: Scope for Enhancement' (NCC Discussion Paper, June 2002) 31 <http://ncp.ncc.gov.au/docs/PIReCn-001.pdf>.

721 ibid. For example, a public transport entity may have been required to provide concessional fares for students and pensioners without receiving any government funds. This necessitated the entity effectively cross subsidising the concessional fares from within its own business; other passengers were carrying the burden of the subsidies.

722 OECD (n 715).

723 Capobianco and Christiansen (n 7).

724 There is no practice for separating the accounts of commercial and non-commercial activities in China. OECD (n 715) 48.

from profit-making to loss-making non-commercial activities are generally permitted.[725] From a competition perspective, low transparency and lack of data on how non-commercial obligations are carried out by SOEs introduces the risk of competitive neutrality issues in the market because there are no measures in place to ensure that public funds are not used for the commercial activities of SOEs.

Higher Corporate Social Responsibility of SOEs

357. Corporate social responsibility (CSR), as an example of a public service obligation, is referred to as establishing a set of principles that entities (both SOEs and non-SOEs) are encouraged to follow in the marketplace in China. These principles include, but are not limited to:

> abiding by the law and regulations and conduct business honestly; improving the sustainable profitability; providing high quantity goods and high-level services [to consumers]; improving resource efficiency and protecting the environment; promoting innovation and technological development; guaranteeing production safety; protecting employee rights; and proactively participating in public welfare [i.e. involved in community development, charity, donations, and participating in public welfare projects like education, culture and health].[726]

358. While all firms in China are encouraged to carry out CSR activities voluntarily, Chinese SOEs are required by regulation to maintain higher disclosure standards. For example, central SOEs (*Yang Qi*) are required by regulation[727] to integrate CSR into their articles of association and mandated to publish their CSR reports on an annual basis. Sinopec, for example, has been annually publishing its *Corporate Social Responsibility Report* since 2006.[728] Additionally, a steering committee for CSR under the SASAC was established in 2012, which is mainly responsible for guiding and monitoring the central SOEs to engage in CSR practices and report on CSR activities.[729]

359. On the one hand, expecting SOEs to deliver CSR-related tasks is valuable, especially in the context of China as the CSR activities are often related

---

725 ibid 49. The public service obligations of the Chinese companies may be compensated through derogations from other obligations.

726 '《关于印发<关于中央企业履行社会责任的指导意见>的通知》 [Notice on Issuing the "Guiding Opinions on the Performance of Social Responsibilities of Central Enterprises"]' SASAC (国资发研究[2008]1号 [Development Research [2008] No 1], 29 December 2007) <http://www.sasac.gov.cn/n2588030/n2588939/c4297490/content.html>.

727 ibid.

728 Sinopec, 'Company reports and publications' <http://www.sinopecgroup.com/group/en/companyprofile/Companyreportsandpublications>.

729 '关于成立国资委中央企业社会责任指导委员会的通知 [Notice on the Establishment of the Central Corporate Social Responsibility Steering Committee of the SASAC]' (国资厅发研究〔2012〕49号 [SASAC (2012) No 49]) <http://www.sasac.gov.cn/n2588030/n2588939/c4297362/content.html>.

to the government's social policy objectives.[730] For example, central SOEs contributed to the ongoing poverty relief campaign by investing approximately RMB30 billion into the central government's poverty alleviation fund as of 2019.[731] On the other hand, requiring SOEs to deliver CSR-related tasks alongside their commercial activities means SOEs may have to put maximising profits as a secondary objective.[732] To motivate SOEs to deliver CSR, the government often compensates SOEs for their CSR activities.[733] An obvious question arising from the competitive neutrality viewpoint is how to compensate SOEs for fulfilling certain non-commercial related activities without distorting the level playing field with non-SOE competitors.[734]

5.4 Conclusion

360. The state sector in China has undergone significant change since the first phase of reform in the late 1970s. However, pushing SOEs to participate in the competitive market of China is associated with many problems. The lack of a level playing field between SOEs and non-SOEs is an example of this. While it is important to provide a comprehensive picture of the competitive neutrality advantages enjoyed and disadvantages suffered by Chinese SOEs, it is beyond the scope of this research to provide an exhaustive assessment of all the potential competitive neutrality concerns caused by Chinese SOEs as a result of government ownership and political connections. For example, the favourable tax treatment of Chinese SOEs and issues of not being required to earn a commercial rate of return are not included in the discussion of this chapter and remains an important area in which competitive neutrality research needs to be further addressed.

361. Nevertheless, the findings presented in this chapter indicate the lack of a level playing field between SOEs and non-SOEs in various markets of China. Particularly, Section 5.2.1 showed that the proximity of SOEs to Chinese legislators may enable SOEs to exert a greater influence than their private counterparts over the formation of legislation. Section 5.2.2 found that, in the land market of China, Chinese SOEs, due to government ownership and political connections, are benefitting from the preferential access to LURs.

730 Wei Yu and Ying Zheng, 'Government stakeholder and CSR reports: Evidence from China' (2017) 19(2) China Accounting and Finance Review 91.

731 '募资300亿 投资170亿 撬动1700亿 央企扶贫基金全力决战脱贫攻坚 [To Assist Poverty Alleviation, 30 Billion Fund-Raised, 17 Billion Invested, 170 Billion Leveraged by Central SOEs]' (17 October 2019) <http://www.sasac.gov.cn/n2588030/n2588939/c12367152/content.html>.

732 Li-Wen Lin, 'Corporate Social Responsibility in China: Window Dressing or Structural Change?' (2010) 28(1) BJIL 64, 64.

733 Almost all jurisdictions compensate firms (regardless of ownership) that deliver public service obligations. See OECD, 'Competitive Neutrality: National Practices' (n 7) 51.

734 For example, as identified by the OECD, one of the most challenging issues for competitive neutrality arises where SOEs operating in a competitive environment are required to carry out non-commercial activities in the public interest. See OECD, 'Maintaining a Level Playing Field' (n 7) 24.

Section 5.2.3 revealed that, in the banking sector, Chinese SOEs are benefitting from more favourable lending conditions (i.e. access to loans and lending rates) than their non-SOE rivals. Meanwhile, Chinese SOEs are also found to suffer from competitive disadvantages (compared to non-SOEs) resulting from their government ownership and political position. Examples include less discretion in managing operations because of Party committee involvement (Section 5.3.1) and higher discloser standards of corporate social responsibility imposed by government regulations (Section 5.3.2).

362. The recent reform decision by China's government to encourage more Chinese SOEs to compete in the marketplace, as discussed in Chapter 3, is likely to deepen the issue of lack of a level playing field between SOEs and non-SOEs in the future. This issue will have a significant impact on the competitive landscape. From a competition perspective, the main issue to be confronted in the short term is the crowding out of non-SOEs in the market (as noted in Section 5.2.2). In the long term, allowing less efficient SOEs to take business away from a more efficient competitor, simply because advantages generated from its government ownership (rather than its own merits), is likely to reduce economic efficiency.

CHAPTER 6

A CRITICAL EVALUATION OF CHINA'S RESPONSE TO THE LACK OF COMPETITIVE NEUTRALITY IN THE MARKET

363. As the experience in Australia shows, the presence of SOEs in the market does not necessarily cause competitive neutrality issues if the anti-competitive conduct of SOEs is successfully scrutinised by the competition law and there are competitive neutrality rules in place to maintain a level playing field between SOEs and non-SOEs in the market. For example, while subjecting SOEs to the same competition rules as non-SOEs is important to promote competitive neutrality in the market, it cannot eliminate all the identified competitive neutrality concerns caused by SOEs (as explained in the discussion of the *Hilmer Review* in Chapter 4). To solve the problem of a lack of competitive neutrality in the market, other government policies, in particular a competitive neutrality policy aimed at improving the competitive environment between SOEs and non-SOEs, need to co-exist with the application of competition law.

364. Building on the experience observed in Australia, this chapter focuses on two principal mechanisms that can promote competitive neutrality between SOEs and non-SOEs in China: The Anti-Monopoly Law (AML) and the Fair Competition Review System (FCRS). The analysis in this chapter is important as it forms the basis of the recommendations presented in Chapter 8, which focus on how the AML can be reformed to more effectively address competitive neutrality issues caused by SOEs, and what approach China can adopt to introduce a competitive neutrality policy to create a level playing field vis-à-vis the presence of SOEs in the market. The chapter proceeds as follows:

365. The first part of this chapter explains how the AML regulates Chinese SOEs and identifies any ownership-based exemptions that exist in the content of AML. Section 6.2 evaluates whether the current competition agency in China

is sufficiently equipped to handle newly reformed Chinese SOEs and the problem of lack of competitive neutrality accompanying them. Section 6.3 assesses the current competition policies that can promote competitive neutrality between SOEs and non-SOEs in China. Section 6.3 argues that there are no specific rules in China functionally equivalent to Australia's competitive neutrality policy which specifies that SOEs should not enjoy any competitive advantages simply as a result of government ownership. While the FCRS can potentially reduce the regulatory advantages of SOEs, as will be shown below, the FCRS is not specifically designed to address other issues in relation to competitive neutrality and SOEs. For example, the competitive advantages of Chinese SOEs in obtaining loans falls outside of the FCRS. Section 6.4 concludes with the proposition that the current application of the AML and the implementation of FCRS have limited impact on competitive neutrality concerns caused by SOEs, as identified in Chapter 5. Chapter 8 provides recommendations to address the competition neutrality issues caused by the presence of Chinese SOEs in the domestic market.

6.1 Regulating Chinese SOEs Under the AML

6.1.1 General Picture of the AML

366. China, as noted in Chapter 5, adopted competition legislation in the form of the AML in 2007, effective from 1 August 2008, and amended in 2022.[735] The AML has transplanted the provisions on 'prohibitions on anti-competitive agreements, abuse of dominance, and anti-competitive mergers [which] are in language that is similar to that of most OECD countries.'[736] And, as Wentong Zheng observed, 'the AML can be said to be largely a legal transplant shaped in the mold of Western antitrust laws.'[737]

367. The coverage of the AML includes the competition restraints from private firms as well as the government bodies (i.e. administrative monopoly)[738] and SOEs.[739] As a general matter, the application of the AML is irrelevant to the type of ownership, the form of enterprises, or the sector in which the firm

735 AML (n 65).

736 Fels (n 78) 12–13.

737 Wentong Zheng, 'Transplanting Antitrust in China: Economic Transition, Market Structure, and State Control' (2010) 32(2) U Pa J Intl L 643, 648.

738 Prohibition of government activities often termed as 'administrative monopolies' (*Xingzheng Longduan*) and regulated in ch V of the AML. More discussion on administrative monopoly in China can be found in AML (n 65) s 6.3.4.

739 For example, AML (n 65) art 15 para one states: 'For the purposes of this Law, undertakings include natural persons, legal persons, and organisations without legal personality that engage in production or operation of products or the provision of services.' Thus, an SOE constitutes a legal person and is subject to the coverage of the AML.

operates.[740] Particularly, SOEs, like all the other firms, are defined as 'undertakings' (or sometimes translated as business operators) under Article 15 and subject to the AML. However, the number of exemptions[741] available to SOEs in the AML (as discussed in Section 6.1.2) and the current competition enforcement actions towards SOEs (as discussed in Section 6.2) have raised important questions as to whether Chinese SOEs are enjoying favourable regulatory treatment in the application of the AML.

6.1.2 Exemptions to SOEs in the AML

368. As discussed in Section 4.2.1, the exemptions regime contained in Australia's competition law is relatively small and largely established based on the principle that 'any exemptions from the application of competitive conduct rules should only be justified on the showing of clear public interest'.[742] In contrast to Australia's exemption regime, the exemptions system in the AML lacks a detailed legal guidance and the boundaries of every exemption are determined by the competition authority in practice.[743] This section focuses on the exemptions applicable (or potentially applicable) to Chinese SOEs under the AML and explores whether the AML has ownership-based exemptions.

Does Article 8 exempt SOEs?

369. The ambiguous language of Article 8 of the AML (previously known as Article 7) has contributed to the intense debate in relation to the intent of this provision and in particular its linkage to Chinese SOEs.[744] Article 8 reads:

> In industries that implicate national economic vitality and national security, which are controlled by state-owned enterprises, and in industries in which monopolies are granted by law, the State shall protect the lawful business activities of those enterprises, supervise and control their conduct and prices for the products and services pursuant to law, protect the interests of consumers, and promote the technological progress.

---

740 One exception is the agricultural sector. For example, AML (n 65) art 69 provides a statutory exclusion for alliances or other concerted practices among agricultural producers.

741 According to R Shyam Khemani, the term exemption means 'being excused or free from some obligation to which others are subject'. By contrast, exception refers 'to be excluded from or not conforming to a general class, principle, rule, etc.' In this research, the term exemption is used. See R Shyam Khemani, 'Application of Competition Law: Exemptions and Exceptions' (UNCTAD/DITC/CLP/Misc.25, 2002).

742 *Hilmer Review* (n 92) 87–88.

743 Wang Xianlin, 'Some Key Issues Concerning Further Development of China's Anti-Monopoly Law' in Tembinkosi Bonakele, Eleanor M Fox and Liberty Mncube (eds), *Competition Policy for the New Era: Insights from the BRICS Countries* (OUP 2018) 219, 224.

744 Eleanor Fox and Deborah Healey, 'Competition Law and the State: Volume 1: Summary of Answers to Questionnaire' (UNCTAD/DITC/CLP/2015/3, 2015) 5 <https://unctad.org/en/PublicationsLibrary/ditcclp2015d3_en.pdf>.

> The undertakings in the industries specified in the preceding paragraph shall conduct their business according to law, act in good faith, observe strict self-discipline, subject themselves to the supervision from the public, and shall not use their controlling position or exclusive position to harm consumer welfare.[745]

370. Scholars often argue that the language of this provision is intentionally drafted ambiguously, allowing flexibility for competition enforcement agencies to interpret it in practice when dealing with SOEs. As explained in Section 6.2.1, the AML was until March 2018 enforced by three different government authorities in China. Each enforcement authority had power to interpret Article 8, opening the way for conflicting interpretations.[746] The vague wording of Article 8 may be read to allow different treatments to SOEs operating in certain industries, which only adds to the suspicions that the AML treats SOEs more favourably than other firms. Three different interpretations in relation to Article 8 and its implications to the coverage of the AML will be discussed below.[747]

371. The first interpretation of Article 8 is that it provides complete exemptions for certain sectors, which are often dominated by Chinese SOEs. For example, Mark Williams argues that this particular Article 'shelter[s] dominant state enterprises from antitrust scrutiny', leaving the status quo of SOEs unchallenged.[748] Similar views are shared by the US Chamber of Commerce[749] and the US-China Business Council (USCBC).[750] Both bodies argue that, while Article 8 only exempts national economic or security related industrials from the enforcement of the AML, companies in these exempted industrials are dominated by Chinese SOEs.

---

745 AML (n 65) art 7.

746 Fortunately, Article 7 has never been applied in AML enforcement and the establishment of SAMR in 2018 (as noted in Section 5.2.1) resolved this issue. Healey (n 569) 130; Xiaoye Wang, Jessica Su and Wei Han, *Competition Law in China* (3rd edn, Wolters Kluwer 2018) 39; Fox and Healey (n 74); Ping Lin and Yue Qiao 'Understanding the Economic Factors that Have Affected China's Anti-monopoly Law' in Michal S Gal and others (eds), *The Economic Characteristics of Developing Jurisdictions: Their Implications for Competition Law* (Edward Elgar 2015), 114, 146. This research argues that the reason that Article 7 has never been applied in AML enforcement is because there is not sufficient guidance on how to interpret this article in practice.

747 Fels (n 78) 15.

748 Mark Williams, 'Foreign Investment in China: Will the Anti-Monopoly Law Be a Barrier or a Facilitator?' (2009) 45(1) Tex Intl LJ 127, 134-5. Similar opinion is expressed by Eleanor M Fox, who argues that 'exemption of the state monopolies in strategic sectors could drive a huge hole in China's efforts to help the market work': 'An Anti-Monopoly Law for China: Scaling the Walls of Government Restraints' (2008) 75(1) ALJ 173, 176.

749 US Chamber of Commerce, 'Competing Interests in China's Competition Law Enforcement: China's Anti-monopoly Law Application and the Role of Industrial Policy' (9 September 2014) 15–16 <https://www.uschamber.com/report/competing-interests-chinas-competition-law-enforcement-chinas-anti-monopoly-law-application>.

750 USCBC, 'US-China Business Council Comments on Antimonopoly Law Amendment Questionnaire' (18 December 2015) <https://www.uschina.org/advocacy/regulatory-comments-on-china/uscbc-comments-antimonopoly-law-amendment-questionnaire>.

372. The second interpretation of Article 8 is that it constitutes the expression of the state action defence,[751] which creates exemption for the authorised anti-competitive conduct of firms. For example, an SOE may be authorised or required by legislation to act in an anti-competitive manner, thus avoiding liability for breaching the AML. Some scholars argue that the reading of the 'undertakings in the industries [vital to the national economy and national security] ... shall conduct their business according to law' in Article 8 permits other legislation to create exemption in the AML by authorising anti-competitive conduct in its provisions.[752] For example, the wording of 'conduct their business according to law' could mean conduct business according to 'any other law (i.e. sector-specific laws) rather than the AML'. Under this scenario, if the anti-competitive conduct of an SOE is authorised by other legislations (or considered legitimate under other laws), it then can be exempted from the application of the AML.[753]

373. However, the wording of 'according to the law' could also be interpreted 'according to both the AML and other legislations'. If this is the case, then Article 8 does not constitute the expression of the state action defence. This research argues the wording of 'according to law' in Article 8 should be interpreted as according to both AML and other laws, so it will not permit other legislation to create a blanket AML exemption. However, the interpretation noted above relies on the general premise of conduct that complies with 'other laws' will not breach the AML. This assumption is problematic because conflicts between legislation happen in practice, and the enforcement authority will need to seek to resolve such conflicts of legal norms.[754] (The issue of conflicts between legislation is further discussed in the section below.)

374. The third interpretation of Article 8 is that it does not establish a definitive AML exemption for SOEs and is one with which this research is in accord. For example, Wendy Ng argues that while Article 8 acknowledges the dominant position of SOEs in certain industries, it does not necessary

---

751 State action defence can be found in US and EU competition rules. For example, the EU state action doctrine has been developed to solve a conflict between two bodies of regulation, EU competition rules and an individual state's anti-competitive legislation. By contrast, the US state action doctrine, in the antitrust law context, has been applied to rein in the scope of antitrust statutes and to preserve the state sovereignty (as opposed to federal governance). For more comparative analysis on the state action doctrine in the EU and US, see Albert Sánchez Graells, *Public Procurement and the EU Competition Rules* (2nd edn, Hart Publishing 2011) 177–79; Eleanor M Fox, 'State Action in Comparative Context: What if Parker V Brown Were Italian?' in Barry E Hawk (ed), *International Antitrust Law & Policy: Fordham Corporate Law 2003* (Juris 2004) 463.

752 Wentong Zheng, 'Competition law in China' in John Duns, Arlen Duke and Brendan J Sweeney (eds), *Comparative Competition Law* (Edward Elgar 2015) 433, 449.

753 Fels (n 78) 15. 'Sectoral law' has been used throughout this research to indicate sector-specific legislation. For example, compared to the AML, the *Energy Law of the People's Republic of China (Draft)* is considered a sector-specific law because it only applies to energy exploitation and utilisation within the territory and other sea areas under the jurisdiction of the PRC.

754 OECD, 'OECD Reviews of Regulatory Reform: China 2009: Defining the Boundary Between the Market and the State' (2009) 144 <http://dx.doi.org/10.1787/9789264059429-en>. For example, Chinese SOEs often operate in a specific sector such as military industries, power grids and power generation, the oil and petrochemical sectors, telecommunications, the coal industry, civil aviation, and shipping. These SOEs are subject to sector-specific law and regulated by sector regulators.

mean that their conduct will be exempted from the application of the AML.[755] Similarly, Deborah Healey and Eleanor M Fox point out that the enforcement experience of the AML over recent decades contradicts the argument that Article 8 provides blanket exemptions to SOEs in certain industries.[756] This research agrees that, as the limited number of AML cases involving Chinese SOEs can hardly match the significant number of SOEs in China's market, Article 8 should not be interpreted as SOEs being entirely immune from AML investigations.

Do Sectoral Laws Exempt SOEs?

375. Whether sectoral laws or regulations exempt SOEs from the application of the AML is an essential question in the context of China because many SOEs operate in regulated sectors and are subject to sectoral laws and regulations.[757] For analytical purposes, sectoral laws and sectoral regulation are considered separately.

Lex Specialis Principle

376. As pointed out by the OECD, 'claims of inconsistency between different legal norms might be resolved by reference to their hierarchy.'[758] Challenges arise in determining whether the sectoral-based law (with competition components) can prevail over the AML. Many academics hold the view that this issue is to be worked out through AML enforcement practice.[759]

377. However, that sectoral laws operate at the same level of hierarchy as the AML may override the AML. According to Article 92 of the Legislation Law:

> With regard to laws, administrative regulations, local regulations, autonomous regulations, separate regulations or rules, if they are formulated by one and same organ and *if there is inconsistency between special provisions and general provisions, the special provisions shall prevail;* if there is inconsistency between the new provisions and the old provisions, the new provisions shall prevail.[760]

---

755 Wendy Ng, 'The Influence of Socialist Principles on the Legal Regulation of Markets in China' in Hualing Fu and others (eds), *Socialist Law in Socialist East Asia* (CUP 2018) 351, 361–62.

756 Deborah Healey and Eleanor M Fox, 'State Restraints in China: A Different Case?' in Adrian Emch and Wendy Ng (eds), *Wang Xiaoye Liber Amicorum: The Pioneer of Competition Law in China* (Concurrences 2019) 187, 194. Similar opinion is expressed by Ping Lin and Yue Qiao (n 745) 138–39.

757 For example, Angela Huyue Zhang argues that 'SOEs that operated in regulated sectors are either legal monopolies and/or natural monopolies. These sectors … including energy, aviation, telecoms, banking, railway, and shipping. … [are] controlled by the central government and are granted exclusive privilege roles, thus shielding them from competition from private investors.' Angela Huyue Zhang, 'Antitrust Regulation of Chinese State-Owned Enterprises' in Benjamin . Liebman and Curtis J Milhaupt (eds), *Regulating the Visible Hand? The Institutional Implications of Chinese State Capitalism* (OUP 2015) 85, 91–92.

758 OECD (n 753) 144.

759 Harris and others (n 567) 26.

760 Legislation Law (n 24).

378. In short, the Chinese Legislation Law follows the principle of *lex specialis*[761] when dealing with conflicts of legal norms at the same level of heirarchy.[762] The principle of *lex specialis* is built on the presumption that 'a legislator, in regulating a specific case, wants to carve out an exception from the general rules existing for a set of matters.'[763] In the context of this research, the AML is perceived to be the general rule that applies in all Chinese markets while sector law may apply more specifically to one sector. When there is conflict between the AML and sectoral law in the same level of the hierarchy (formulated by the same organ as the AML, the Standing Committee of the NPC), the sector-specific law could be conceptualised as *lex specialis* and override the AML.[764]

379. A theoretical example is provided here. If the conduct of an SOE is required by the sector-based legislation but violates the AML, there exists a conflict between sector-based legislation and the AML.[765] In this situation, more specific legislation – the sector-based legislation – will take precedence over the AML based on the principle of *lex specialis*. Consequently, the anti-competitive conduct of the SOE is exempted from the application of the AML. However, the problem with sectoral legislation exemption in the AML extend even further. Particularly, it raises the important issue of whether Chinese SOEs could use their linkage with their sector regulators to seek AML exemptions provided by sectoral legislation. As Wendy Ng has pointed out:

> Some sector-specific laws that are administered by industry regulators contain competition-related provisions; hence, they have incentives to protect their regulatory turf from encroachment by the AML. Similarly, SOEs prefer to be subject to sector-specific laws, regulations and supervision, as those arrangements are generally regarded as being favourable to their interests.[766]

380. The discussion of the statutory exemptions in Australia (Section 4.4) has demonstrated that there exists a real risk that sectoral regulators can be captured by SOEs and sweeping exemptions in sectoral legislations favouring those SOEs. To protect against a sectoral regulator being captured by SOEs and enacting sectoral legislation that favours the special interest of SOEs, the recommendations presented in Chapter 8 call for better disclosure when granting exemptions based on the sectoral legislation.

---

761 Based on the principle of *lex specialis*, when there is conflict between two legal norms (at the same level of the hierarchy) that regulate the same subject matter, the special rules take priority over general rules.

762 Zhu Shaoming, *Chinese Conflicts of Laws: A Restatement and Legisprudence Proposal* (Wildy, Simmonds & Hill 2018) 50.

763 Ralf Michaels and Joost Pauwelyn, 'Conflict of Norms or Conflict of Laws? Different Techniques in the Fragmentation of Public International Law' (2012) 22 Duke J Comp & Intl L 349, 354–55.

764 Legislation Law (n 24) art 92.

765 However, it is worth noting that sectoral regulation does not necessarily contravene the AML. Even if it does, it will be very difficult to identify with the certainty of whether a sectoral regulation contains provisions that contradict the AML in practice.

766 Ng (n 754) 363.

Do Sectoral Regulations Exempt SOEs?

381. To understand whether complying with sectoral regulations can exempt Chinese SOEs from the AML, it is important to first understand the hierarchical relationships between the AML and sector-specific regulations. There are generally three kinds of legal norms in the Chinese legislative system (as noted in Section 1.2.4). In brief, the Constitution has the highest legal effect in the hierarchy and prevails over laws and regulations.[767] The legal effect of the AML, as a law adopted by the highest legislative body – the NPC and its Standing Committee – is above that of 'administrative regulations, local regulations, and rules.'[768] In other words, the hierarchy of the AML may be at the same level as the sectoral legislation but is certainly higher than sectoral regulations. This means that the AML can override the application of sectoral regulations.[769]

382. In the case of *China Ocean Shipping Tally Shenzhen (China Ocean) and China United Tally (Shenzhen) (China United),* the competition authority, SAMR, rejected the defence that the price-fixing behaviours of the two companies were guided by the government sectoral regulations issued by the Ministry of Transport and that the AML should not apply.[770] The SAMR held that just because the government policy recommended price or intervened in relation to price, it did not mean that China Ocean and China United should not compete with each other independently.[771] As a result, the SAMR ruled that the joint price increase by two competing companies constituted price-fixing and should be prosecuted under the AML. This ruling of the SAMR further confirmed the precedent that the AML prevails over sectoral regulations circumstantially.

Does Industrial Policy Exempt SOEs?

383. Industrial policy in its narrowest sense can be considered as sectoral policy, as Chapter 2 discussed. Due to the inherent difference between SOEs and non-SOEs, Chinese SOEs often shoulder the responsibility of providing universal services or carrying development strategies such as industrial policy (as noted in Section 5.3). Many scholars have questioned whether the requirement of implementing national industry policy, like Made in China 2025, could exempt Chinese SOEs from the coverage of the AML or, put differently, can

767 Legislation Law (n 24) art 87.

768 ibid art 88: 'The effect of laws is higher than that of administrative regulations, local regulations, and rules.'

769 ibid.

770 Michael Gu and Charles Xiang, 'SAMR Adopts Stricter View on Identification of Competitors In Monopoly Agreement Case' (30 August 2018) <https://www.chinalawvision.com/2018/08/competition-law-anti-monopoly-law/samr-adopts-stricter-view-identification-competitors-monopoly-agreement-case/>; Thomas Jones and others, 'Competition Law in Asia Pacific: Highlights from 2018 and What's Coming Next in 2019' (Bird & Bird Law Firm, April 2019) 9 <https://www.twobirds.com/en/news/articles/2019/global/competition-law-in-asia-pacific-highlights-from-2018-and-2019>.

771 《国家市场监督管理总局行政处罚决定书》 [Administrative Penalty Decision of the State Administration for Market Supervision] SAMR, Guoshijian Jiajian Chufa [2018] No 5 and No 6, 9 July 2018.

the state action defence be used by Chinese SOEs to avoid liability under the AML? Based on the hierarchy of legal norms noted above, it is the position of this research that theoretically industrial policy, like the sectoral regulations, cannot override the legislation, the *AML*.

6.2 Main Issues with the AML Enforcement Against SOEs

6.2.1 Competition Enforcement Authorities of the AML

384. Prior to March 2018, the administrative enforcement structure of the AML derived from two levels of governance.[772] The first level was the Anti-Monopoly Commission Office (AMC) within the State Council, which included 21 government officials[773] and generally is 'comprised of senior officials from 15 ministries.'[774] The second level of the administrative competition enforcement consisted of three competition enforcement authorities, namely the Ministry of Commerce (MOFCOM) in charge of merger control, the State Administration for Industry and Commerce (SAIC) tasked with price-related enforcement, and the National Development and Reform Commission (NDRC) responsible for other non-price related enforcement.[775] The three competition authorities could also, when needed, delegate enforcement functions to their local and regional subdivisions.[776]

Anti-Monopoly Commission

385. The responsibility of the AMC is set out in Article 12 of the AML and includes:

> researching and drafting policies relating to competition; organizing investigations and evaluations of the overall conditions of competition in the market and publishing assessment reports; stipulating and releasing anti-monopoly guidelines; coordinating the administrative anti-monopoly enforcement work; and other duties stipulated by the State Council.[777]

772 Angela Huyue Zhang, 'The Enforcement of the Anti-Monopoly Law in China: An Institutional Design Perspective' (2011) 56(3) Antitrust Bull 631.

773 For more detailed discussion of the Anti-Monopoly Commission, see Ng (n 136) 147–49.

774 Su and Wang (n 71) 200. For the full list of the members of the Anti-monopoly Commission before 2018, see 《国务院办公厅关于国务院反垄断委员会主要职责和组成人员的通知》 [Notice of the General Office of the State Council on the Main Functions and Members of the Anti-Monopoly Commission of the State Council] Guo Ban Fa [2008] No 104, 28 July 2008.

775 For more detailed discussion, see Harris and others (n 567) 216–99; Ng (n 136) 139–47.

776 Zhang (n 771) 634. See also Ng (n 136) 139–47.

777 AML (n 65) art 12.

386. The AMC survived institutional reform in March 2018. The current composition of the AMC includes high-ranking government officials like Wang Yong, the State Councillor, as its chairman and senior officials from 14 ministries.[778] However, the majority of the AMC's members were changed in the 2018 reform.[779]

387. The enforcement activities of the three competition authorities since the enactment of the AML are remarkable. Until October 2018, there were 165 monopoly agreement cases, including 55 cases involving companies abusing their market dominance position handled by the SAIC and NDRC with penalties of more than 11 billion yuan ($1.6 billion) issued.[780] The MOFCOM, on the other hand, had assessed 2,437 merger cases.[781]

State Administration for Market Regulation

388. On 17 March 2018, the First Session of the 13th NPC approved the Institutional Reform Plan of the State Council which merged three competition enforcement authorities into one ministry-level agency directly under the lead of the State Council, the SAMR.[782] Almost four months later, the institutional reform of the SAMR at the central level was completed, now comprised of 27 bureaux and employing 805 people.[783] The SAMR is chaired by Luo Wen[784] and covers a range of functions, including food safety-related inspection, drug-related supervision, product quality and safety inspection and

778 ibid. There are two Vice Chairs in the AMC, namely Zhang Mao, Director of the SAMR, and Meng Yang, Deputy Secretary General of the State Council. There are 13 listed members including: Hu Zhucai, Vice Chairman of the NDRC; Wang Jiangping, Vice Minister of the Ministry of Industry and Information Technology (MIIT); Gan Zangchun, Member of the Ministry of Justice Leading Party Group; Cheng Lihua, Vice Minister of Finance; Dai Dongchang, Vice Minister of Transport; Li Chenggang, Assistant Minister of Commerce; Liu Guoqiang, Assistant Governor of the People's Bank of China; Wen Jieming, Vice Chairman of the SASAC; Gan Lin, Vice Minister of SAMR; Jia Nan, Deputy Commissioner of National Bureau of Statistics; Liang Tao, Vice Chairman of the Chinese Bank and Insurance Regulatory Commission; Yan Qingmin, Vice Chairman of China Securities Regulatory Commission; Qi Chengyuan, Deputy Director of National Energy Administration; He Hua, Deputy Director of the State Intellectual Property Office.

779 《国务院办公厅关于调整国务院反垄断委员会组成人员的通知》 [Notice of the General Office of the State Council on the Adjustment of the Members of the Anti-Monopoly Commission of the State Council] Guo Ban Fa [2018] No 51, 11 July 2018.

780 State Council (n 79). There is overlap in relation to jurisdiction between the SAIC and the NDRC. In practice, whichever agency takes the case first will have the jurisdiction. Peter J Wang, Yizhe Zhang and Qiang Xue, 'Looking Ahead: The Integration of Chinese Anti-Monopoly Enforcement Authority' (2018) 18(1) Antitrust Source 4.

781 Ma Si, 'Antitrust Officials: All Firms Treated Equally', *China Daily* (17 November 2018) <https://www.chinadaily.com.cn/a/201811/17/WS5bef4e89a310eff303289412.html>.

782 State Council (n 170).

783 《国家市场监督管理总局职能配置、内设机构和人员编制规定》 [Provisions on the Functions, Structure and Staffing of the State Administration for Market Regulation] General Office of the Central Committee of the CPC and General Office of the State Council, 30 July 2018, art 5 (Provisions on State Administration for Market Regulation).

784 Luo Wen took this position in 2022 after Zhang Gong, who is now served as a member, standing committee and deputy secretary of the Tianjin Municipal Party Committee. Before Zhang Gong, the SAMR was chaired by Xiao Yaqing, former Chairman and Deputy Secretary of the Party Committee of the SASAC of State Council. For more detailed information, see Zhong Nan, 'New Head of Market Regulator Appointed' *China Daily* (22 May 2019) <https://www.chinadaily.com.cn/a/201905/22/WS5ce49d19a3104842260bcff2.html>; 'China names Zhang Gong as Head of Market Regulator' *Reuters* (12 August 2020) <https://www.reuters.com/article/us-china-minister-samr-idUSKCN25809J>.

enforcement of the AML.[785] The State Anti-Monopoly Bureau (in Chinese *Guo Jia Fan Long Duan Ju;* hereafter SAMB) is formed[786] and will be discussed further below.

State Anti-Monopoly Bureau

389. The SAMB, chaired by Gan Lin, was launched on 18 November 2021 as a deputy ministerial level (in Chinese *Fubuji*) institution affiliated with SAMR, which oversee anti-monopoly matters.[787] This newly established SAMB has taken over the role of the Anti-Monopoly Bureau of SAMR established in 2018, a director-general level (in Chinese *Zhengjuji*) sub-division of SAMR[788] that integrated functions of the Anti-Monopoly Bureau of MOFCOM, the Anti-Monopoly and Price Bureau of NDRC and the Anti-Monopoly and the Anti-Unfair Competition Bureau of SAIC.[789]

390. Unfortunately, the mandate and staffing of the SAMB are not available publicly as the time of writing. However, scholars observed that there are over 60 staff members and three divisions under the SAMB.[790] Given the limited enforcement resources at the SAMB, it is essential for the SAMR to authorise the corresponding governmental agencies at the provincial level (the local branches of the SAMR) to conduct investigations of AML cases within delegated authority.[791]

785 Provisions on State Administration for Market Regulation (n 782) art 3.

786 ibid art 4(7).

787 国家反垄断局 [National Anti-Monopoly Bureau],《中国反垄断执法年度报告（2021）》[Annual Report of China on Anti-Monopoly Law Enforcement (2021)] (Report, 2021) 121 <https://www.samr.gov.cn/xw/zj/202206/P020220608430645470953.pdf>. See also Xiaoye Wang and Yajie Gao, 'China's Antimonopoly Law Enforcement in the Digital Economy' (2022) 67(4) Antitrust Bull, 562, 565.

788 The Anti-Monopoly Bureau of SAMR in Chinese is called 市场监管总局反垄断局 (*Shichang Jianguan Zhongju Fanlongduan Ju)* while National Anti-Monopoly Bureau is called 国家反垄断局 (*Guojia Fanlongduan Ju*). The administrative ranking of NAMB is deputy ministerial level, which is higher than the administrative ranking of the Anti-Monopoly Bureau of SAMR, a director-general level institution. See Annie Xue and He Jing, 'What Was China's National Anti-Monopoly Administration Created For?' CPI Columns Asia (January 2022) <https://www.competitionpolicyinternational.com/wp-content/uploads/2022/01/Asia-Column-January-2022-Full.pdf>.

789 See Wang, Zhang and Xue (n 779) 3. See also Jet (Zhisong) Deng and Ken (jianmin) Dai, 'Everything you must know about China's Antitrust Law revision and authority reshuffle' (14 December 2021) <https://www.dentons.com/en/insights/articles/2021/december/14/everything-you-must-know-about-chinas-antitrust-law-revision-and-authority-reshuffle>.

790 For example, Xiaoye Wang observed that there were about 45 staff members for AMB of SAMR. NAMB is recruiting 18 civil servants in 2022, which brings the total number of staff at NAMB to 63. See Xiaoye Wang, 'Retrospective and prospects of China's Anti-Monopoly Law' in Steven Van Uytsel, Shuya Hayashi and John O Haley (eds), *Research Handbook on Asian Competition Law* (Edward Elgar 2020) 209, 229. See also '《国考招考18名反垄断工作人员！》[National Public Service Exam to recruit 18 civil servants for the National Anti-Monopoly Bureau!]' 北京日报[Beijing Daily] (21 October 2021) <https://news.bjd.com.cn/2021/10/21/201011t100.html>.

791 《市场监管总局关于反垄断执法授权的通知》[Notice of the State Administration for Market Regulation on the Empowerment of Anti-Monopoly Law Enforcement] SAMR, Guoshijian Fandongduan [2018] No 265, 28 December 2018; See also Wang (n 789) 229; 《市场监管总局关于试点委托开展部分经营者集中案件反垄断审查的公告》[Announcement on Piloting the Entrustment of Anti-Monopoly Review in Selected Concentration of Undertakings] SAMR, [2022] No 23, 23 September 2022; Hogan Lovells,'SAMR's Triple Guidance on Antitrust Enforcement' (July 2019) <https://f.datasrvr.com/fr1/219/35628/New_SAMR_rules.pdf>.

391. Three divisions under the SAMB are: Competition Policy Liaison Division, Anti-Monopoly Enforcement Division I and Anti-Monopoly Enforcement Division II. Based on the official website[792], the Competition Policy Liaison Division is mainly responsible for:

392. promoting competition policy and coordinating anti-monopoly enforcement activities; leading the formulation of anti-monopoly measures and guidelines; facilitating the implementation of Fair Competition Review System while supervising the implementation of FCRS at the local level; law enforcement activities in relation to abuse of administrative power by administrative organisations; carrying out the internal review of at-monopoly cases; liaising international cooperation and coordinating the daily work of the AMC of the State Council.

393. The Anti-Monopoly Enforcement Division I is in charge of:

394. Enforcement matters related to monopoly agreements, abuse of market dominance and abuse of intellectual property rights to exclude or restrict competition; enforcement activities regarding to monopoly agreement or abuse of dominant market positions in the field of platform economy; providing guidance or coordinating local branches of the SAMR to conduct investigations related to monopoly agreements or abuse of market dominance.

395. The Anti-Monopoly Enforcement Division II is responsible for:

396. Reviewing the concentration between business operators; investigating the implemented concentration between business operators that reached the notification thresholds but failed to provide notification, or investigating the concentration between business operators that did not reach the notification threshold but there is evidence to prove that such concentration between business operators has or is likely to have the effect of eliminating or restricting competition; reviewing the concentration of business operators in digital economy; supervising the concentration with conditional approval; guiding firms in relation to antitrust litigation abroad and compliance matters.

397. The establishment of the SAMB is viewed as a positive step forward by many scholars, who have been calling for a centralised enforcement model since the adoption of the AML.[793] Particularly, over the past 10 years, the

792 See Competition Policy Liaison Division of SAMR, '司局介绍[Introduction of the Division]' <https://www.samr.gov.cn/jzxts/sjjs/> (in Chinese); The Anti-Monopoly Enforcement Division I of SAMR, '司局介绍[Introduction of the Division]' <https://www.samr.gov.cn/fldys/sjjs/>(in Chinese). See the Anti-Monopoly Enforcement Division II of SAMR, '司局介绍[Introduction of the Division]' <https://www.samr.gov.cn/fldes/sjjs/>(in Chinese).

793 For example, Jessica Su and Wang Xiaoye have advocated a 'truly integrated agency model' which is envisaged as 'a ministry-level commission with concrete enforcement powers … to limit overlaps, duplications and inefficiencies [caused by the decentralised tripartite enforcement model]': Su and Wang (n 71) 231. See also Xiaoye Wang and Yajie Gao (n 786), 565.

parallel enforcement model by three agencies (i.e., the MOFCOM, the SAIC and the NDRC) has been accused of causing overlapping issues. For example, the benchmark used for dividing the enforcement jurisdictions between the NDRC and SAIC (i.e., whether the alleged violation conduct is price related) has caused duplication issues.[794] The newly launched SAMB is expected to optimise the organisation of enforcement resources and to help further promote consistency in the AML's enforcement practice. However, it is too early to provide a detailed analysis of whether the SAMB can provide more effective control over the potential anti-competitive conduct of Chinese SOEs, especially central SOEs. Nevertheless, the section below attempts to examine the challenges faced by competition enforcement agencies when enforcing against Chinese SOEs over the past decade. A brief evaluation of whether the enforcement challenges in relation to SOEs may potentially be solved by the centralised SAMR will be discussed following an introduction to the structure of Chinese competition enforcement.

398. Competition enforcement in China, like most jurisdictions, can be divided into public enforcement, in which public authorities apply public sanctions,[795] and private enforcement, which involves litigation between private parties.[796] Chinese public AML enforcement is carried out by the government authority, the SAMR (the amalgamation of MOFCOM, SAIC, and NDRC). In contrast, private enforcement of the AML is carried out by private parties (who often suffered economic losses because of monopolistic conduct and have the incentive to claim damages) before the Court either through civil or administrative litigation.[797]

399. It is agreed that competition enforcement authorities should be independent from other government departments as competition enforcement 'can have [an] important impact on the market and society more generally.'[798] However, as William Shughart points out, '[a]ntitrust authorities, no less than regulatory authorities, are vulnerable to capture by the collective interests of groups having the most salient stakes in antitrust law enforcement outcomes.'[799] Inspired

794 Zhang (n 771) 640. As Zhang observes, in the field of anti-competitive agreement, the NDRC is mainly responsible for enforcement against price fixing, whereas the SAIC is responsible for the restriction of output or sales, the division of sales on raw material markets, the restriction of the purchase or development of new technologies equipment, and boycotting. For example, from 2015 to 2016, both the NDRC and the SAIC issued a consultation draft for the *Anti-monopoly Guidelines for the Abuse of Intellectual Property Rights*, which sheds further light on the issue of duplication of jurisdictions between the NDRC and the SAIC.

795 Roger J Van den Bergh and Michael Faure, 'Critical Issues in the Enforcement of The Anti-Monopoly Law in China: A Law and Economics Perspective' in Michael Faure and Xinzhu Zhang (eds), *Competition Policy and Regulation: Recent Developments in China, the US and Europe* (Edward Elgar 2011) 54, 56–58.

796 Roger J Van den Bergh, 'Enforcement' in Roger J Van den Bergh (ed), *Comparative Competition Law and Economics* (Edward Elgar 2017) 382, 408.

797 Zhang (n 771) 636.

798 Wang (n 789) 227.

799 William F Shughart II, 'Antitrust, Regulation and the "Chicago School"' (ProMarket, 17 February 2017) <https://promarket.org/antitrust-regulation-chicago-school/?mc_cid=a5b9f818b8&mc_eid=08df55fd49>.

by this view and the state capture theory articulated in Section 1.3.2, the section below argues that when enforcing cases that involve Chinese SOEs (especially political SOEs), it may be challenging for the Chinese competition authorities to remain independent and resist interference from other government departments.

6.2.2 Merger Enforcement and the Concentration of Central SOEs

400. Under the AML, parties to a proposed merger (or 'concentration'), whether SOEs or non-SOEs, should file notifications to the SAMR, provided that they reach the notification thresholds and wait for clearance before officially finalising the proposed merger.[800] Fines may apply if the parties meet the notification thresholds but fail to file notifications according to the AML.[801] Since 2012, the SAMR has actively imposed sanctions against firms for not notifying.[802] In practice, the MOFCOM has sanctioned several companies, including a number of subsidiaries of local SOEs, for not notifying before completion of their transaction and made the penalty decision public.[803] However, the current concentration of central SOEs has not yet been challenged.

401. Central SOEs in particular are expected to be 'stronger, better, and bigger'[804] and currently there is a process of reorganision under the direct or indirect guidance of the SASAC, beginning in 2013.[805] From January 2013 to 8 July 2019, 20 mergers of central SOEs were finalised which involved 38 central SOEs as merging parties. A summary of these transactions is provided in Table 6.1.

800 Zheng (n 199) 158. Below-threshold concentration can be investigated by the SAMR if such concentrations are deemed as 'has or is likely to have the effect of eliminating or restricting competition.' See AML (n 65) art 26. For a more detailed discussion, see Wang Xiaoye and Adrian Emch, 'Procedure and Substance in China's Merger Control Regime' in Deborah Healey, Michael Jacobs and Rhonda L Smith (eds), *Research Handbook on Methods and Models of Competition Law* (Edward Elgar 2020) 436, 438–39.

801 《未依法申报经营者集中调查处理暂行办法》 [Interim Measures for the Investigation and Handling of the Failure to Declare Concentration of Business Operators in Accordance with the Law] MOFCOM, Decree 2011 No 6, 1 February 2012, art 13 (Interim Investigation Measures).

802 Before 2018, the decision of administrative penalty for non-compliance with merger notification requirements was issued by the MOFCOM. After 2018, SAMR is responsible to publish such administrative penalty decisions. See also Ng (n 136) 283; Yuni Yan Sobel, 'Domestic-to-Domestic Transactions (2014–2015): A Narrowing Gap in China's Merger Control Regime' (2016) 15(3) Antitrust Source, 2–3.

803 For example, Huayu Automotive System Co Ltd, a subsidiary of SAIC Motor Co Ltd (a Shanghai state-owned automotive design and manufacturing company), has been fined RMB 200,000 for failing to notify before establishing a joint venture with Continental Automobile Investment (Shanghai) Co Ltd. See 《商务部行政处罚决定书》 [Administrative Decision of Penalty by the Ministry of Commerce] MOFCOM, Shang Fa Han [2016] No 682, 12 April 2017.

804 The slogan '推动国企做强做优做大' has also been translated as 'pushing for stronger, optimized and enlarged Chinese SOEs': Xi Jinping (n 1).

805 For a more detailed discussion of current reform, see Section 3.2.

No.	Year	Central SOEs	Outcome
1	2019	China Poly Group Corporation & China Silk Corporation	China Silk Corp. merged into China Poly Group Corporation and became its subsidiary
2	2018	China National Nuclear Corporation (CNNC) & China Nuclear Engineering Group Corporation (CNEC)	CNEC merged into CNNC and became its subsidiary
3	2017	China Guodian Corporation & Shenhua Group Corporation Limited	Establishing a new company, China Energy Investment Corporation
4	2017	Sinolight Corporation (Sinolight) & China National Arts and Crafts (Group) Corporation (CNACGC) & China Poly Group Corporation	Sinolight and CNACGC merged into China Poly Group Corporation and became its subsidiaries
5	2017	China National Machinery Industry Corporation (Sinomach) & China Hi-Tech Group Corporation Limited (Hi-Tech)	Hi-Tech merged into Sinomach and became its subsidiary
6	2016	China Grain Reserves Corporation (Sinograin) & China National Cotton Reserves Corporation (National Cotton)	National Cotton merged into Sinograin and became its subsidiary
7	2016	Baosteel Group Corporation (Baosteel) & Wuhan Iron and Steel (Group) Corporation (WISCO)	Establishing a new company, China BaoWu Steel Group Corporation Limited
8	2016	China National Building Materials Group Corporation (CNBM) & China National Materials Group Corporation Limited (Sinoma)	Sinoma merged into CNBM and became its subsidiary
9	2016	China National Cereals, Oils and Foodstuffs Corporation (COFCO) & Chinatex Corporation Limited (Chinatex)	Chinatex merged into COFCO and became its subsidiary
10	2016	China Travel Service (HK) Group Corporation (HKCTS) & China International Travel Service Group Corporation (CITS)	CITS merged into HKCTS and became its subsidiary
11	2015	China Merchants Group Company Limited & Sinotrans and CSC Holdings, Corporation Limited (Sinotrans Group)	Sinotrans Group merged into China Merchants Group and became its subsidiary

No.	Year	Central SOEs	Outcome
12	2015	China Ocean Shipping (Group) Company (COSCO) & China Shipping (Group) Company (China Shipping)	Establishing a new company, China COSCO Shipping Corporation Limited (COSCOCS)
13	2015	China Minmetals Corporation (Minmetals) & China Metallurgical Group Corporation (MCC)	MCC merged into Minmetals and became its subsidiary
14	2015	Nam Kwong (Group) Company Limited (Nam Kwong) & Zhuhai Zhen Rong Company (Zhen Rong)	Zhen Rong merged into Nam Kwong and became its subsidiary
15	2015	China CNR Corporation Limited (CNR) & CSR Corporation Limited (CSR)	Establishing a new company, China Railway Rolling Stock Corporation Limited (CRRC)
16	2015	China Power Investment Corporation (CPI) & State Nuclear Power Technology Corporation Limited (SNPTC)	Establishing a new company, State Power Investment Corporation Limited
17	2014	China Huafu Trade and Development Corporation (Huafu) & China National Cereals, Oils and Foodstuffs Corporation (COFCO)	Huafu merged into COFCO and became its subsidiary
18	2013	China National Erzhong Group Corporation (Erzhong) & China National Machinery Industry Corporation (Sinomach)	Erzhong merged into Sinomach and became its subsidiary
19	2013	China Grain and Logistics Corporation (China Grain) & China National Cereals, Oils and Foodstuffs Corporation (COFCO)	China Grain merged into COFCO and became its subsidiary
20	2013	Caihong Group Corporation (Caihong) & China Electronics Technology Group Corporation (CETC)	Caihong merged into CETC and became its subsidiary

Table 6.1 List of Central SOE mergers between January 2013 and 8 July 2019.[806]

402. The impacts of the above noted concentrations on competition in the relevent market are concerning. Both horizontal and vertical mergers can be observed in the Table 6.1, based on the competitive relationship of the central SOEs involved. For example, the merger between the two largest shipping groups – China Ocean Shipping (Group) Company and China Shipping Group (listed as No. 12 in the Table 6.1) – is considered a horizontal merger in the

806 Mergers are reported and updated on the official website of the SASAC (in Chinese) <www.sasac.gov.cn/n2588035/n2641579/n2641660/index.html>.

competition law context. Horizontal mergers are often at the heart of merger enforcement because of the potential effect such mergers may have on the competition in the market. As explained by Roger Van de Bergh, Peter Camesasca and Andrea Giannaccari, horizontal mergers 'reduce the number of competing firms … [and] increase market concentration, as the post-concentration market share is larger than either of the parties' share prior to the concentration.'[807]

403. In a vertical merger, the parties are not directly competing but operate at different levels of the supply chain.[808] For example, the merger between China Guodian Corporation (Guodian), an electricity producer, and Shenhua Group Corporation Limited (Shenhua), a coal producer (listed as No. 3 in the Table 6.1), is a vertical merger. Vertical mergers can be anti-competitive because of their adverse effects 'on the upstream, downstream and neighbouring market.'[809]

404. According to data released by MOFCOM,[810] the majority of concentrations of central SOEs (11 out of 20) received unconditional approval. There are still nine concentrations of SOEs not on the unconditional approval list of the MOFCOM (and the SAMR). These statistics reveal two critical issues of merger enforcement relating to SOEs which will be discussed below.

Cleared Mergers of Central SOEs

405. The 11 cleared central SOE mergers, from a competition law standpoint, sent three important signals. The first is that concentrations between SOEs is subject to merger review, even though both entities are owned by a common owner – the state, or in the current case, the SASAC. This finding implies that central SOEs cannot rely on the single entity defence provided in Article 27(2) of the AML to exempt themselves from the merger notification. Article 27(2) reads as follows:

> Where a concentration between business operators meets any of the following conditions, the business operators need not to file a notification with the Anti-Monopoly Authority under the State Council: …
>
> (2) more than 50% of the voting shares or assets of each business operator involved in the concentration are owned by the same business operator which is not involved in the concentration.[811]

807 Roger J Van den Bergh, Peter Camesasca and Andrea Giannaccari, 'Merger Control' in Roger J Van den Bergh (Ed.), *Comparative Competition Law and Economics* (Edward Elgar 2017) 454–532, 458.

808 ibid 458.

809 Wang, Su and Han (n 745) 52.

810 The unconditionally cleared merger list by the MOFCOM from 2012 to the second quarter of 2018 can be found on the official website: <http://fldj.mofcom.gov.cn/article/zcfb/> (in Chinese).

811 AML (n 65) art 27.

406. Additionally, the statistics of central SOE merger approvals by the MOFCOM also suggest that SOEs need to comply with the AML, even if the concentration received approval from other government agencies (such as the approval from the SASAC in current case). Figure 6.1 compares the publication date of the SASAC and the clearance date of the MOFCOM on the 11 cleared central SOEs' mergers.

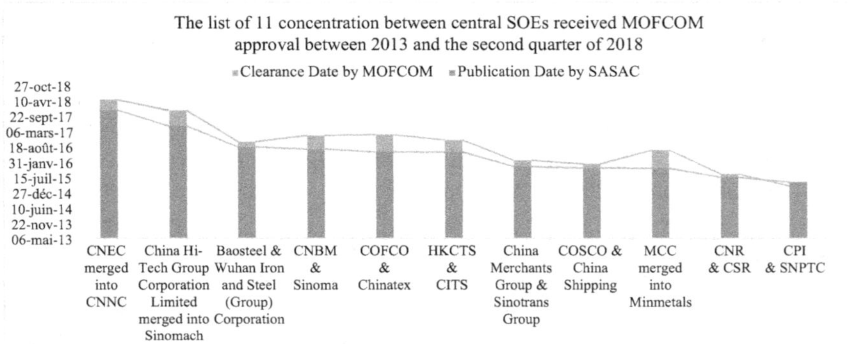

Figure 6.1 List of 11 concentrations of central SOEs approved by MOFCOM between 2013 and the 2nd quarter of 2018.

407. The comparison in Figure 6.1 reveals that 10 (out of 11) concentrations of central SOEs were published by the SASAC at least 30 days before the clearance date of MOFCOM.[812] For example, the transaction of China Hi-Tech Group Corporation Limited and Sinomach was published by the SASAC at least 211 days (almost 7 months) before the clearance date of the MOFCOM. This shows that Chinese competition authority may take the other government departments' decision into account in merger assessments involving the concentration of central SOEs.

408. Finally, the 11 cleared mergers of central SOEs also reveals the significance of non-competition factors in merger assessment of China. Particularly, protecting public interest, as one of the goals pursued by the AML, has been incorporated into merger assessments in an explicit public interest provision, Article 34:

> The Anti-Monopoly Enforcement Authority under the State Council shall take the decision to prohibit the concentration between business operators if the concentration between business operators has or is likely to have the effect of eliminating or restricting competition. However, if the business operators can

812 The only exception case is the merger between China Power Investment Corporation (CPI) and State Nuclear Power Technology Corporation Ltd (SNPTC), which received clearance from the MOFCOM 53 days before it was published by the SASAC. This research argues that it is problematic that the merger review agency in China (now the SAMR, formerly the MOFCOM) takes the other government departments' decision into account in merger assessments involving the concentration of central SOEs because it indicates the competition enforcement is not independent in their investigation and decision-making.

> prove that the positive impact of such concentration clearly outweighs the negative impact or is *in line with the public interest*, the Anti-Monopoly Enforcement Authority under the State Council can take the decision not to prohibit the concentration.[813]

409. It is worth noting that the AML is not the only competition legislation to have a public interest provision in merger assessments. For example, an empirical study conducted by David Reader revealed that 47 (out of a surveyed 75 countries, or 62.6 per cent) afforded direct scope to the public interest in their merger legislation.[814] In China, the public interest test is assessed by the competition authority, the SAMR, who oversees merger control.[815] Nevertheless, one possible explanation for the SAMR to approve mergers between central SOEs is because this type of merger is often associated with national industrial policy considerations and could be considered as 'public interest' provided in Article 34. For example, both the horizontal and vertical integration of central SOEs serve goals like 'optimizing the allocation of resource in upstream and downstream industry chains and promoting the transformation and upgrading of central enterprises … enhancing the overall competitiveness of central enterprises.'[816]

410. Yet it is premature to conclude that industrial policy constitutes 'public interest' in the context of Article 34, based only on the 11 cleared central SOEs' merger cases. This is because the criteria used by the Chinese competition authority to assess matters such as whether the advantages of the merger outweigh the disadvantages, or that a merger in the 'public interest' is not transparent. To date, efforts on clarifying 'public interest test' in Article 34 have not been made, possibly because the SAMR (with limited human and financial resources) is not required to issue written decisions on cleared mergers,[817] and written decisions with reasons are given only to mergers that are refused or allowed with conditions.[818] As observed by Deborah Healey:

> There is no indication of what will constitute 'advantages' and 'disadvantages', whether they are tied to competition, or have a

---

813 AML (n 65) art 34 (emphasis added).

814 David Reader, 'Accommodating Public Interest Considerations in Domestic Merger Control: Empirical Insights' (CCP Working Paper No 16-3, 18 February 2016) <http://dx.doi.org/10.2139/ssrn.2736917>.

815 In Australia, the public interest test is not routinely considered in mergers which are generally assessed under an informal clearance procedure by the competition authority, the ACCC. Public benefit is assessed with a single procedure called 'authorisation. This procedure is generally used only where a merger is likely to result in a substantial lessening of competition but also produces public benefits which might allow it to proceed. Very few of these applications for authorisation of mergers are made. For the summary of the discussion on public interest consideration in merger control, see OECD 'Summary of Discussion of the Roundtable on Public Interest Considerations in Merger Control' (DAF/COMP/WP3/M(2016)1/ANN4/FINAL, 7 February 2017) <https://one.oecd.org/document/DAF/COMP/WP3/M(2016)1/ANN4/FINAL/en/pdf>.

816 《国务院办公厅关于推动中央企业结构调整与重组的指导意见》 [Guiding Opinions of the General Office of the State Council on Promoting the Restructuring and Reorganisation of Central Enterprises] Guo Ban Fa [2016] No 56, 17 July 2016, Preamble s 2 para 2.

817 Article 31 only requires competition authorities to issue reasons for prohibiting the concentration of undertakings in writing. See AML (n 65) art 31, para 1.

818 Healey (n 406) 198.

> wider focus … whether they need to be significant or substantial, to counteract the lessening of competition.[819]

411. Similarly, the public interest factors that have been (or should have been) considered in balancing the benefits of the merger against its anti-competitive effects have been largely unknown during the past 15 years of AML enforcement. The lack of reliable assessment criteria in relation to the 'public interest test' in the Chinese merger control regime opens criticism to the risk of political intervention in the AML enforcement,[820] which could incentives Chinese SOEs to use their government ownership and political connections to influence the AML enforcement outcome correlative with the benefits of SOEs. In particular, the absence of a tangible assessment criteria in relation to the public interest test may lead to speculation that the national industrial policy takes precedence in merger analysis at the expense of a more competitive market. As Massimo Motta argues, 'the willingness of national governments to allow domestic firms to "go bigger" in the belief that this will help them be more successful ...' carries the risk of 'allow[ing] inefficient firms to survive at the expense of more efficient ones.'[821] Likewise, David Reader asserts that affording industrial policy goals in merger control should be cautious of 'sending an inefficient firm into the global marketplace prematurely … as these firms may ultimately struggle to operate on a worldwide scale and are very much prone to failure as a result.'[822]

412. To alleviate the risk of losing credibility over speculation, it is critical for SAMR to provide a guideline document to clarify the meaning of 'public interest test' and the 'advantage/disadvantage analysis' to promote transparent procedures for future merger enforcement (see recommendations presented in Chapter 8).

Uncleared Mergers of Central SOEs

413. There are nine completed concentrations of central SOEs (involving 18 central SOEs, as listed in Table 6.2) that have not been cleared by the SAMR, according to the clearance data published from January 2013 to July 2019.[823]

---

819 Deborah J Healey and Zhang Chenying, 'Bank Mergers in China: What Role for Competition?' (2017) 12 AsJCL 81, 103. A similar opinion is expressed by Xiaoye Wang and Adrian Emch who argue that although the AML incorporates 'public interest' as a factor in the merger review, the concept is very high-level without concrete guidance. See Xiaoye Wang and Adrian Emch, 'Chinese Merger Control Eight Years On' (2017) 38 ECLR 53, 58–59.

820 Antonio Capobianco and Aranka Nagy, 'Public Interest Clauses in Developing Countries' (2016) 7(1) JECL & Pract 46.

821 Motta (n 69) 29–30.

822 David Reader, 'Revisiting the Role of the Public Interest in Merger Control' (PhD thesis, University of East Anglia 2015) 32–34 <https://ueaeprints.uea.ac.uk/id/eprint/68329/>.

823 See MOFCOM (n 809).

No.	Central SOEs	Outcome	SASAC Publication Date
1	China Poly Group Corporation & China Silk Corporation	China Silk Corp. merged into China Poly Group Corporation and became its subsidiary	08-Jul-2019
2	China Guodian Corporation & Shenhua Group Corporation Limited	Established a new company, China Energy Investment Corporation	28-Aug-2017
3	Sinolight Corporation (Sinolight) & China National Arts and Crafts (Group) Corporation (CNACGC) & China Poly Group Corporation	Sinolight and CNACGC merged into China Poly Group Corporation and became its subsidiaries	21-Aug-2017
4	China Grain Reserves Corporation (Sinograin) & China National Cotton Reserves Corporation (National Cotton)	National Cotton merged into Sinograin and became its subsidiary	23-Nov-2016
5	Nam Kwong (Group) Company Limited (Nam Kwong) & Zhuhai Zhen Rong Company (Zhen Rong)	Zhen Rong merged into Nam Kwong and became its subsidiary	1-Dec-2015
6	China Huafu Trade and Development Corporation (Huafu) & China National Cereals, Oils and Foodstuffs Corporation (COFCO)	Huafu merged into COFCO and became its subsidiary	26-Nov-2014
7	China National Erzhong Group Corporation (Erzhong) & China National Machinery Industry Corporation (Sinomach)	Erzhong merged into Sinomach and became its subsidiary	18-July-2013
8	China Grain and Logistics Corporation (China Grain) & China National Cereals, Oils and Foodstuffs Corporation (COFCO)	China Grain merged into COFCO and became its subsidiary	12-Mar-2013
9	Caihong Group Corporation (Caihong) & China Electronics Technology Group Corporation (CETC)	Caihong merged into CETC and became its subsidiary	5-Jan-2013

Table 6.2 List of 9 concentrations of Central SOEs that have not received approval from the MOFCOM.[824]

824 Table adapted by the author from two sources: the list of central SOE mergers between January 2013 and January 2018, and the unconditionally cleared merger list from 2012 to the second quarter of 2018 by the MOFCOM.

414. When the finalised merger is not cleared by the SAMR there are generally two possible explanations. The first explanation for not reporting a merger is that the merger does not need approval from the SAMR because it fails in the first instance to meet the notification thresholds required by the AML. Particularly, the notification thresholds for concentration of business operators in China are:

- the combined worldwide turnover of all undertakings involved in the last fiscal year exceeds RMB 10 billion [approximately USD 1.6 billion], and the China-wide turnover of each of at least two undertakings exceeds RMB 400 million [approximately USD 64 million]; or
- the combined China-wide turnover of all undertakings involved in the last fiscal year exceeds RMB 2 billion, and the China-wide turnover of each of at least two undertakings exceeds RMB 400 million.[825]

415. The nine uncleared concentrations of central SOEs in Table 6.2 are all likely to meet this relatively low filing threshold. For example, China Guodian Co, one of the largest power generators in China, has been on the Global Fortune 500 list since 2010, ranking 397th in 2017 based on its total revenue of approximately USD 27,315 million in the fiscal year of 2016.[826] Shenhua Group Co Ltd, a state-owned coal company, was ranked 276th in 2017 on the Global Fortune 500 based on its total revenue of approximately USD 37,322 million in the 2016 fiscal year. Judging by these statistics, the concentration of China Guodian and Shenhua Group (listed No. 2 in Table 6.2) easily satisfies the notification standards for anti-competitive merger review.

416. The second explanation for not notifying a merger is that the merging SOEs (in Table 6.2) violate their notification obligation under the AML which may result in those SOEs being penalised by the SAMR. However, based on public information available, the SAMR has not challenged these 19 central SOEs in Table 6.2 for not fulfilling their notification obligations.[827] This practice reflects the politically difficult position of Chinese competition authorities when punishing the merger of SOEs approved by other state agencies like the SASAC.[828] Particularly, the government and political ties of SOEs may create pressure and subsequently, directly or indirectly, interfere with the enforcement activities of a competition authority when taking cases against SOEs.[829] For example,

825 《国务院关于经营者集中申报标准的规定(2018修订)》 [Provisions of the State Council on the Thresholds for Declaring Concentration of Business Operators (2018 Revision)] Order No 703, 18 September 2018, art 3; Interim Investigation Measures (n 802).

826 '中国国电集团公司 [China Guodian Corporation]', 财富 [Fortune China] <http://www.fortunechina.com/global500/536/2017>.

827 Nine out of 20 completed mergers have *not* received approval from the competition authority, SAMR. The discussion in this section argues that these nine completed mergers in Table 6.2 are all likely to meet the relatively low filing threshold. Accordingly, this research argues that SAMR should punish them for not fulfilling their notification obligation under the AML. The decision of administration penalty for non-compliance with merger notification requirements issued by the MOFCOM can be found at the official website: < http://tfs.mofcom.gov.cn/article/xzcf/> (in Chinese).

828 Ng (n 136) 285.

829 The pressure faced by the NDRC when investigating the case of China Telecom/China Unicom is a good example of how the government ties and political position of SOEs can create additional difficulty for the

Deborah Healey pointed out that '[a]s a practical matter it is also difficult for a regulator to penalize a merger that has been approved by another government body such as an industry regulator.'[830] From a practical perspective, the merger review agency in China (now the SAMR) may be reluctant to impose administrative sanctions (such as fines) on central SOEs listed in Table 6.2, especially when the merger notification is made after the approval of the State Council and published by the SASAC, as is revealed in Figure 6.1.

6.2.3 Non-Merger Enforcement of SOEs

417. Non-merger enforcement activities prior to March 2018 were shared between the NDRC and SAIC. The enforcement activities against SOEs are commonly observed in China though 'more frequently against local SOEs than central SOEs.'[831] There were unfortunately only a handful of cases brought against central SOEs, like the investigation of potential abuse of dominance by two telecommunication SOEs, China Telecom and China Unicom in 2011,[832] and the investigation of suspected price fixing by the ticketing website of Civil Aviation Administration of China, TravelSky Technology Ltd in 2009.[833] Both of the cases, as observed by competition law experts, reflect the difficulty or at least the tension between competition authorities, such as the NDRC Bureau, when enforcing against SOEs and sectoral regulators who directly manage the SOEs being investigated.[834]

Shanxi Electric Power Association Case

418. In 2017, the NDRC found[835] that the 23 electric generation companies under the Shanxi Electric Power Association (hereafter Association[836]) had agreed to fix the minimum price charged to their consumers at 0.3 yuan kilowatt/hour and not

enforcement of the NDRC. For more detailed analysis, see Ng, 'The Influence of Socialist Principles on the Legal Regulation of Markets in China' (n 754) 368–70.

830 Deborah Healey, 'Competition Law and State-Owned Enterprises: Enforcement' (DAF/COMP/GF(2018)11, 30 November 2018) 9-11 <https://one.oecd.org/document/DAF/COMP/GF(2018)11/en/pdf>.

831 Ng (n 754) 364.

832 Zhang (n 134).

833 王毕强 [Wang Biqiang] and 刘伟勋 [Liu Weixun], '《涉操纵机票涨价 发改委调查中航信》 [Alleged Domestic Airline Ticket Price Fixing by TravelSky Technology Ltd is Under NDRC's Investigation]' 经济观察报 [Economic Observer] (17 May 2009); Hejing Chen and John Whalley, 'The State-Owned Enterprises Issue In China's Prospective Trade Negotiations' (CIGI Papers No 48, October 2014) 3 <https://www.files.ethz.ch/isn/185024/no.48.pdf>.

834 Wendy Ng points out the position and status of the investigated central SOEs outranks competition authorities, such as the NDRC Bureau: Ng (n 754) 366. A similar opinion is shared by Fang Xiaomin, who argues that the application of the AML to SOEs, especially national champions, conflicts fiercely with the privileged position and traditional advantages of SOEs: 'The Application of the Chinese Antimonopoly Law to State-Owned Enterprises' in Fabiana Di Porto and Rupprecht Podszun (eds), *Abusive Practices in Competition Law* (Edward Elgar 2018) 318, 321.

835 '《山西直供电价格垄断协议案被依法查处》 [The NDRC Investigates a Price-Fixing Agreement in Shanxi Province]' 新华社 [Xinhua News] (3 August 2017) <http://www.gov.cn/xinwen/2017-08/03/content_5215766.htm>.

836 The industrial associations in the context of China are often semi-regulatory in nature and can function as forums to facilitate the communication with competitors. As observed by Wentong Zheng, many of these industrial associations are officially 'affiliated' (*Guakao*) with various government agencies: Zheng (n 199) 150.

to apply the discounts lower than 0.02 yuan kilowatt/hour in 2016.[837] Among the 23 electric generation companies, four were found to be the subsidiaries of central SOEs in Shanxi Province – namely China Datang Co, China Guodian Co, China Huaneng Group Co, and China Huadian Co – while four were provincial SOEs of Shanxi. The NDRC announced that the Association, as 'the ringleader', had violated the AML by organising and facilitating a price monopoly agreement among competing companies. The NDRC accordingly imposed the maximum monetary penalty applicable for an industry association of RMB 50 million (approximately USD 72,693). The 23 participating companies were also being fined approximately 1 per cent of their respective sales revenue in the preceding financial year, approximately RMB 72.88 million. Commentators have observed that the Shanxi Electric Power Association case is the first case that, in the NDRC's 10 years of enforcement, the competition authority imposed penalties against central SOEs and perhaps one of the largest AML penalties ever imposed on wholly state-owned companies.[838]

419. The Shanxi Electric Power Association case raises two critical issues in relation to the AML enforcement. The first is the crisis cartel defence raised by the association, in arguing that

> the economy in Shanxi is in a downturn. Particularly, coal-fired power companies located in Shanxi are currently experiencing financial hardship and exacerbate the already-severe overcapacity problems … the reform [industrial capacity reduction reform[839]] in this sector is ongoing … the fixed discount rate in the agreement is thus in line with the exemption provision [in Article 20].[840]

420. The crisis cartel defence provided in Article 20 of the AML reads:

> Any concluded agreement shall be exempted from the application of Articles 17 and 19 if the business operators could prove that the concluded agreement falls into any of the following circumstances: …
>
> (5) alleviating serious decreases in sales volumes or significant production overcapacities during economic recession;

837 Coco Feng, 'Quick Take: China Fines 23 Coal Power Firms for Monopolistic Practices', *Caixin* (4 August 2017) <https://www.caixinglobal.com/2017-08-04/quick-take-china-fines-23-coal-power-firms-for-monopolistic-practices-101126540.html>.

838 '《首例直供电价格垄断协议案被依法查处》 [The NDRC's Penalty Decision Against the Shanxi Power Generator Companies for Price-Fixing]' (3 August 2017) <http://www.gov.cn/xinwen/2017-08/03/content_5215802.htm>; Michael Gu, 'China' in Aidan Synnott (ed), *The Public Competition Enforcement Review* (10th edn, Law Business Research 2019) 78, 80.

839 Industrial Capacity Reduction Reform (*Qu Chan Neng*) is implemented under the wider Supply-Side Structure Reform which aimed to solve the excess capacity in certain industrial sectors, like coal and steel, by reducing production. For a more detailed explanation regarding Industrial Capacity Reduction Reform, see Linxi Chen, Ding Ding and Rui Mano, 'China's Capacity Reduction Reform and Its Impact on Producer Prices' (IMF Working Papers, WP/18/216, September 2018) <https://ssrn.com/abstract=3267240>.

840 林远 [Lin Yuan], '《电力反垄断第一案浮出水面 山西发电企业几乎全部卷入》 [First Case of Direct Power Supply Price Monopoly Agreement has Surfaced in Shanxi Province]' 经济参考报 [Economic Information Daily] (6 June 2017).

421. According to the association, Article 20 should apply and thus SOEs being investigated by the NDRC should not be penalised for price-fixing. The final decision of the NDRC denied this argument, which reflects the cautious position taken by Chinese competition authorities towards the defence of crisis cartel. Moreover, the NDRC dismissed the defence's claim that they had acted pursuant to the capacity reduction policy, which shows that industrial policy cannot override the application of the AML, as discussed in Section 6.2.2. As Shi Jianzhong commented,

> the supply-side structure reform aims to solve the issue of overcapacity. However, such reform is also guided by the rule of market. ... Companies should not mis-interpret the intention of the reform as cooperating [instead of competing] with competitors and exempting them from the coverage of the anti-monopoly law.[841]

422. The second issue raised by this case is whether related entities such as four provincial SOEs of Shanxi (ultimately owned by Shanxi Province SASAC) or four subsidiaries of central SOEs (ultimately owned by the SASAC under the State Council) constitute competitors in the context of cartel arrangement. The final decision of the NDRC to some extent reflects the competition authorities' standpoint in relation to the single entities defence in the context of non-merger enforcement. SOEs that often belong to the same group or share a common owner are generally treated as independent market players in the context of AML enforcement (both merger and non-merger) and thus should not assume that the defence of being a single entity can easily provide immunity from the application of the AML.

6.3 Regulating Chinese SOEs Under the Competition Policy

423. The notion of competition policy is relatively underdeveloped compared to industrial policy in China. As explained in Chapter 2, the concept of Chinese competition policy had for a long time revolved largely around the competition legislation, the AML and the regulative policy issued to support the substantive law provisions in the AML. However, this narrowly-constructed competition policy concept in China has since 2016 broadened to include not only competition legislation and the AML enforcement-related policy but also policies designed to promote competition.

424. Under this competition policy definition, the Fair Competition Review System (FCRS) established in 2016 qualifies as competition policy because

841 ibid.

the purpose of the FCRS is to promote competition in China by preventing unjustified competition restrictions via government regulations. The implementation of the FCRS reflects a growing appreciation of competition policy in the context of China.[842] For example, the recent Amendment of the Anti-Monopoly Law in 2022 has added the fundamental role of competition policy into Article 4 of the AML.[843]

6.3.1 Fair Competition Review System

425. In essence, the FCRS rests on the premise that government authorities[844] should not issue policies that restrict competition unless it is justified on the grounds of 'national security-related circumstances; social security purposes; social and public interests; and any other circumstances prescribed by laws and administrative regulations.'[845] The aim of the FCRS is to

> Standardising relevant government activities, preventing the introduction of policy measures that exclude or restrain competition, and gradually cleaning up and abolishing provisions and practices that hinder fair competition and the development of a unified national markets.[846]

426. The FCRS is a mechanism put in place to provide an *ex-post* competition scrutiny for the existing regulatory policies that have an impact on 'the economic activities of market players',[847] and an *ex-ante* competition analysis for regulatory proposals.[848] The establishment of the FCRS has been viewed as a milestone in the development of competition policy in China. For example, Yang Hongfeng, Deputy Inspector of the Price Supervision and Anti-Unfair Competition Bureau of the SAMR, commented that the FCRS is 'a key step towards China's establishment and reinforcement of the fundamental role of competition policy.'[849]

---

842 Ye Weiping and Mel Marquis, 'Competition Policy and Industrial Policy in China: Toward a New Equilibrium?' in Adrian Emch and Wendy Ng (eds), *Wang Xiaoye Liber Amicorum: The Pioneer of Competition Law in China* (Concurrences 2019) 205, 211.

843 AML (n 65) art 4. See also 《<中华人民共和国反垄断法>修订草案(公开征求意见稿)》 [Draft Amendment to the Anti-Monopoly Law] SAMR, 2 January 2020.

844 Government authorities refer here to administrative organs and organisations that have the functions of public affairs administration as authorised by laws and regulations. Opinions on Establishing FCRS (n 88) art 3(1); 《公平竞争审查制度实施细则》[Detailed Rules for the Implementation of the Fair Competition Review System] (People's Republic of China), State Administration for Market Regulation, National Development and Reform Commission, Ministry of Finance, Ministry of Commerce, Ministry of Justice, Guoshijian Fanlongduan [2021] No 2, 29 June 2021 and effective on the same day, art 2 (FCRS Implementation Rules 2021).

845 Opinions on Establishing FCRS (n 88) art 4.

846 ibid, art 3(1).

847 ibid.

848 Healey and Fox (n 755) 202.

849 Yang Hongfeng, 'Using Fair Competition Reviews to Actively Promote Establishment of the Competitive Neutrality Principle' (Paper delivered at the Opening Up and Competitive Neutrality: The International Experience and Insights for China conference, 24 April 2019) 29 <https://www.imf.org/en/News/Seminars/Conferences/2019/04/19/7th-pbc-imf>.

'Fair' Competition

427. For competition law experts from other jurisdictions it seems odd that competition law and competition policy in China are designed to protect 'fair' competition rather than protect 'competition or competitive process'. Generally, the protection of competition (or the competitive process[850]) is justified on the assumption that competition in the market will lead to greater economic efficiency[851] and ultimately benefit consumer welfare.[852] The virtues of competition are often directly or indirectly linked to improving efficiency and will eventually 'enhance consumer welfare',[853] which is integrated into competition law in most jurisdictions.[854]

428. In the context of China, the notion of 'protection of competition' is replaced by 'protection of *fair* competition'. It is perhaps easy to explain, from a political point of view, that comparing 'competition' to the language of 'fair competition' is likely to gather more political as well as public support in China.[855] However, the notion of 'fair competition' is very vague, especially when considering to what extend the competition is perceived as 'fair' or 'unfair'. As pointed out by Herbert Hovenkamp, 'fairness means nothing without a reference point'.[856] In essence, those with a goal of protecting fair competition need to answer the question of fair to *whom*? The discussion

---

850 Maurice E Stucke, 'Reconsidering Competition' (2011) 81 Miss LJ 107, 114. Competition can be viewed as rivalry, that is, 'the effort of two or more parties acting independently to secure the business of a third party by offering the most favourable terms.' Competition can also be viewed as a dynamic process that 'forces firms to be responsive to consumers' needs with respect to price quality variety, etc.; over time it also acts as a selection mechanism, with more efficient firms replacing less efficient ones.' See Katharine Kemp, *Misuse of Market Power: Rationale and Reform* (CUP 2018) 33.

851 OECD, 'The Objectives of Competition Law and Policy: Note by the Secretariat' (CCNM/GF/COMP(2003)3, 29 Janurary 2003) 9 <http://www.oecd.org/daf/competition/2486329.pdf>; Eleanor M Fox, 'US and EU Competition Law: A Comparison' in Edward M Graham and J David Richardson (eds), *Global Competition Policy* (Institute for International Economics 1997) 339, 340–41. For the definition of efficiency, see the discussion in Chapter 4.

852 Herbert Hovenkamp states that protection of consumer welfare is anti-trust's ultimate purpose. See Herbert Hovenkamp, *The Antitrust Enterprise: Principle and Execution* (HUP 2008) 31. Competition between producers forces them to ensure 'that goods and services are produced in a way that minimises the resources used in that production', thus promoting productive efficiency and drive for innovations; competition between consumers promotes allocation efficiency as it 'tends to result in those buyers who receive a product valuing that product more highly than those buyers who miss out.' See King (n 402) 9.

853 Consumer welfare is often interpreted as consumer surplus, which is the difference between the amount a buyer is willing to pay for a good and the amount they actually pay for it. A total welfare standard is often discussed together with the consumer welfare standards. In short, the consumer welfare standard is narrower as it requires consumers are made better off, or at least not made worse off, and it focuses on efficiency saving that will be passed on to consumers. The total welfare standard reflects the overall economic surplus, which not only takes into account consumer surplus but also the producer surplus. For more detailed discussion, see Roger J Van den Bergh, 'The Goals of Competition Law' in Roger J Van den Bergh (ed), *Comparative Competition Law and Economics* (Edward Elgar 2017) 95–97; Russell V Miller (n 5) 4; Roger D Blair and D Daniel Sokol, 'The Rule of Reason and the Goals of Antitrust: An Economic Approach' (2012) 78(2) ALJ 471, 473.

854 For example, as explained in Chapter 4, the objective stated in the Australian competition law, the CCA, is 'to enhance the welfare of Australians through the promotion of competition': CCA (n 431) s 2. For more detailed discussion on the goals of the competition law, see Deborah Healey, 'The Ambit of Competition Law: Comments on its Goals' in Deborah Healey, Michael Jacobs and Rhonda L Smith (eds), *Research Handbook on Methods and Models of Competition Law* (Edward Elgar 2020) 12.

855 As observed by Deborah Healey, the concept of 'competition' was not part of the political vocabulary in China until after 1979. See Healey (n 569) 126.

856 Herbert Hovenkamp, 'Whatever Did Happen to the Antitrust Movement?' (2019) 94(2) Notre Dame L Rev 583, 587.

of fair competition is thus often associated with the ideology of whether the competition law is enacted to protect certain type of competitors. There are unsurprisingly different ways to interpret the meaning of fair competition; three will be discussed directly below.

429. First, 'fair competition' can mean fair to domestic firms (compared to foreign firms). This view was observed when the AML was first enacted. Particularly, when it first came into effect, scholars suspected that the AML was aimed at targeting foreign companies to protect domestic firms.[857] Wentong Zhou argues that in the nascent WTO era for China in the post-millennium, the sentiment of protecting Chinese firms from multinational corporations may have resolutely contributed to the enactment and promulgation of the AML.[858] However, this view is denied by Wu Zhenguo, then Director of the Anti-Monopoly Bureau of the government officials from the SAMR, who argued that

> firms in China, no matter SOEs or non-SOEs, *domestic or foreign*, are all equally treated and protected in the enforcement of the AML ... take [a] statistic from the SAIC for example, [over the past ten years, 2008–2018] around 41 per cent of investigated cases involved SOEs while only 10.7 per cent [of] cases involve foreign companies.[859]

430. Second, compared to dominant firms, 'fair competition' can mean fair to small and medium sized enterprises (SMEs). In this sense, fair competition is likely to exempt the anti-competitive behaviours of SMEs in the name of 'increasing the efficiency and competitiveness of SMEs.'[860] However, affording protection to SMEs in the application of competition law and policy is not without issue. As argued by Eleanor M Fox, '[i]f fair competition means that efficient firms must pull their punches so as not to harm their higher-cost rivals, fairness to competitors injures consumers.'[861] Herbert Hovenkamp further asks the critical question of whether 'it [is] "fair" that consumers be asked to pay high prices in order to accommodate the shortcomings of some businesses'.[862]

431. Third, 'fair competition' can mean fair to non-SOEs. In this sense, fair competition is likely to address the 'unfair' competitive advantages of SOEs

857 Ng (n 136) 67. Wang and Su (n 71) 384.

858 Zheng (n 199) 160–62. H Stephen Harris shares the similar opinion, arguing Chinese admission into the WTO accelerated the draft of the AML due to a broad consensus that China needed protection from multinational firms: H Stephen Harris, 'The Making of an Antitrust Law: The Pending Anti-Monopoly Law of the People's Republic of China' (2006) 7(1) Chi J Intl L 169, 171.

859 'Information Office Press Conference' (n 79) (emphasis added).

860 AML (n 65) art 15(3).

861 Eleanor M Fox, 'Outsider Antitrust: "Making Markets Work for People" as a Post-Millennium Development Goal' in Tembinkosi Bonakele, Eleanor M Fox and Liberty Mncube (eds), *Competition Policy for the New Era: Insights from the BRICS Countries* (OUP 2017) 22, 32.

862 '[I]s it "fair" that small businesses suffer simply because they are not able to compete with larger firms on price or quality; or "fair" that firms heavily invested in old brick-and-mortar distribution lose out to more technologically entrepreneurial firms?': Hovenkamp (n 855) 587.

to ensure non-SOEs and SOEs can compete on a level playing field. This interpretation is closely linked to the concept of competitive neutrality as discussed in Chapter 2 and will be explored further in Section 6.3.3.

6.3.2 Implementation of the FCRS

432. The FCRS process (see Table 6.3 schematic of the FCRS process) is conducted according to the principle of 'whoever formulates a policy shall be responsible for policy review'.[863] The administrative agencies or authorised bodies (termed 'policy-making organs', *Zhengce Zhiding Jiguan* in Chinese[864]) are required to self-assess each regulatory policy and proposal. Currently, there are two crucial regulatory documents in place to guide the review process, namely, the Opinions of the State Council on Establishing a Fair Competition Review System During the Development of Market-oriented Systems, issued in 2016 (which established the FCRS in 2016), and Detailed Rules of Implementation of the Fair Competition Review System issued in 2021.[865]

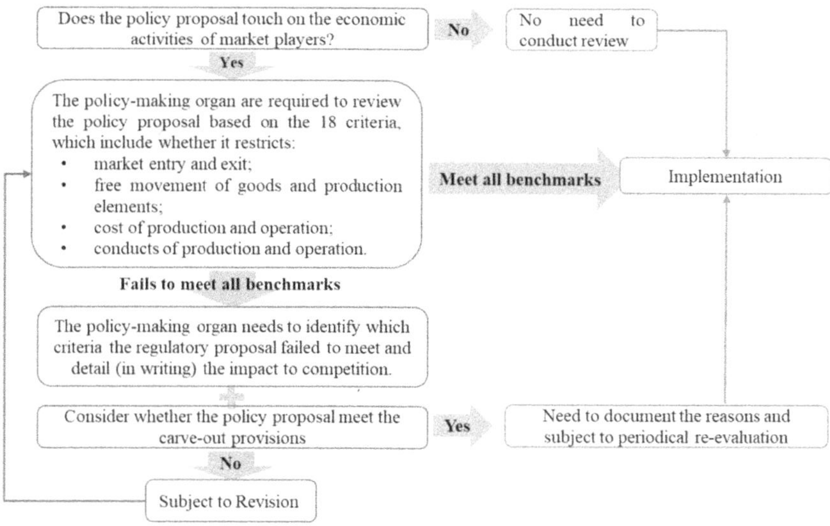

Table 6.3 Schematic of the FCRS process.[866]

433. The review criteria for the FCRS process are more detailed but generally in line with the Chapter V – Abuses of Administrative Powers to Eliminate or Restrict Competition under the AML, which reflects the commonly observed

863 Opinions on Establishing FCRS (n 88) s 4(2).

864 ibid. Art 3(a) defines policy-making organs as administrative organs and organisations that are authorised by law and regulations to perform functions of the public affairs administration.

865 Opinions on Establishing FCRS (n 88); FCRS Implementation Rules 2021(n 843).

866 Chart by the author, based on FCRS Implementation Rules 2021 (n 843).

regulatory restrictions to a unified domestic market and fair competition in China. The assessment factors under the FCRS, especially the impact on production and operating cost assessment, correspond closely to competitive neutrality principle. In particular, when assessing the impact of a policy measures on production and operating cost, it is required to analysis whether the policy in question grants preferential treatment to specific business operators against law.[867] An example of how SOEs have been advantaged by regulations will be provided here to show how the FCRS can help to reduce the regulatory advantages of SOEs as identified in Chapter 5.

434. The Government Office of Shanghai issued a policy proposal noting 'government authorities in the project located area (county area), are responsible for organising *SOEs* to conduct projects of developing rail transit stations.'[868] This provision has shown that SOEs are selectively being advantaged by restricting other market players from entering the market of rail transit stations. After carrying out the FCRS, the Government Office of Shanghai has reformed this provision, which now reads: 'in principle, the government authorities in the project located area (county area), are responsible for organising and developing the rail transit stations.'[869] This case shows that the regulatory advantages afforded to SOEs in regulatory policy, at least in theory, can be remedied by the FCRS.

435. The implementation of the FCRS in China has been remarkable since 2016, with a set of supporting policies and mechanisms established to facilitate the development of the FCRS. For example, an Inter-Ministerial Joint Meeting System (led by the SAMR and including 28 ministries) was approved by the State Council, 'making overall arrangement for work related to fair competition review; strengthening macro guidance to the implementation of the fair competition review system; and coordinat[ing] to resolve major issues in the implementation of the fair competition review system.'[870] Since its establishment, members of the Inter-Ministerial Joint Meeting System have inspected the implementation progress of the FCRS in 29 provinces. The inspection method, according to Li Qing, includes randomly selecting the published regulatory policies to evaluate whether the issuing government authorities have conducted the FCRS before publishing.[871] Until the end of 2018, all departments in the

867 ibid art 15.

868 朱凯 [Zhu Kai], '《中国公平竞争审查制度实施进展》 [Progress on the Implementation of China's Fair Competition Review System]' (Roundtable of EU-China Competition Cooperation presentation, 22 March 2017) <http://www.euchinacomp.org/attachments/article/528/02%20-%20NDRC%20-%20Zhu%20Kai_NDRC%20booklet%20session_I_CN.pdf>.

869 《关于推进本市轨道交通场站及周边土地综合开发利用的实施意见》[Opinions of Shanghai Municipal People's Government on Promoting Comprehensive Development and Utilisation of Shanghai Rail Transit Stations and Surrounding Land] General Office of the Shanghai Municipal People's Government Forwarding Development and Reform Commission of Shanghai and the Municipal Planning and Land Resources Bureau of Shanghai, Hu Fu Ban [2016] No 79, 7 October 2016.

870 《国务院办公厅关于同意建立公平竞争审查工作部际联席会议制度的函》[Letter of the General Office of the State Council on Approval of the Establishment of the Inter-Ministerial Joint Meeting System for Fair Competition Review] Guo Ban Han [2016] No 109, 22 December 2016, s 1.

871 李青 [Li Qing], '《建立公平竞争审查制度情况介绍》[An Introduction of the Implementation of Fair Competition Review System]' (2018) 6中国价格监管与反垄断 [Price Supervision and Anti-Monopoly in China] 78.

State Council,[872] all provinces and 98 per cent of the government agencies in municipalities, and 85 per cent of the county-level government agencies have conducted the FCRS. At the end of 2021, it is estimated that around 244,000 pieces of existing regulatory policies and 442,000 new regulatory policies have been reviewed.[873] However, it will take some time to evaluate whether the implementation of the FCRS fosters a competition culture by fundamentally changing the way the Chinese government regulates the market.

6.3.3 The FCRS and Administrative Monopoly

436. Before the FCRS, anti-competitive regulations promulgated by government bodies were addressed in Article 45 of the AML:

> Administrative authorities[874] and organizations authorised by laws or regulations to perform public functions shall not abuse their administrative power to formulate *regulations* with the contents of eliminating or restricting competition.[875]

437. In practice, the power of Chinese competition authorities is limited when dealing with administrative monopoly.[876] In particular, under the AML competition authorities are responsible for drawing the line between 'abusing' and 'legitimising' the exercise of government power but cannot act against the government body involved directly. The competition authority, however, could notify the relevant higher-level administrative authority of the offending government body, which has the power to make rectification based on recommendations provided by the competition authority.[877] For example, the Public Security Department of the Inner Mongolia Autonomous Region (hereafter the PSD) in 2013 issued a governmental notice (or official document[878]) which contains the following:

> Firstly, direct appointing a local company, Inner Mongolia Kung An JinFeng Network Seal Technology Co Ltd (hereafter 'JinFeng

872 The SASAC, as a member of the Inter-Ministerial Joint Meeting System for the FCRS, had identified and removed almost 30 pieces of regulation that failed to comply with the requirement of the FCRS (to November 2017). See 《国务院国资委关于公布规章规范性文件清理结果的公告》 [Announcement of the State-Owned Assets Supervision and Administration Commission on the Results of the Clean-Up of Certain Regulatory Documents] SASAC [2017] No 1, 29 December 2017.

873 National Anti-Monopoly Bureau, 'Annual Report of China on Anti-Monopoly Law Enforcement (2021)' (n 786), 3.

874 Sometimes the term 'administrative organs' is used to refer to administrative departments and other organisations authorised by laws or regulations to perform the function of administering public affairs.

875 AML (n 65) art 45 (emphasis added).

876 For discussion of the limited power of the competition authority in relation to administrative monopoly in China, see generally Healey and Fox (n 755) 198–201; Zhanjiang Zhang and Baiding Wu, 'Governing China's Administrative Monopolies Under the Anti-Monopoly Law: A Ten-Year Review (2008–2018) and Beyond' (2019) 15(1) JCL & E 718, 725-36; Weiping and Marquis (n 841) 201–02.

877 AML (n 65) art 61.

878 《市场监管总局办公厅关于建议纠正内蒙古自治区公安厅滥用行政权力排除限制竞争有关行为的函》 [Advice Letter of the General Office of the State Administration for Market and Regulation on the Correction of Abuse of Administrative Power that Restricted Competition by the Public Security Department of the Inner Mongolia Autonomous Region] SAMR, Shi Jian Jia Jian Han [2018] No 412, 19 June 2018 (SAMR Advice Letter).

> Company') *to be responsible for developing the anti-counterfeiting seal system within the region*, and;
>
> Secondly, requiring all the public security units within the region to uninstall the software system that was being used (and tested by the Ministry of Public Security), and uniformly *install the system software developed by JinFeng Company.*
>
> Thirdly, requiring all seal-making enterprises within the region to *purchase seal equipment and related materials from JinFeng.*[879]

438. The SAMR found that the PSD abused its administrative powers by prohibiting its subordinate branches and enterprises in the region from purchasing or using the products of any suppliers but the authorised JinFeng Company and by issuing anticompetitive regulations that restricted competition in the regional market.[880] Consequently, in June 2018, the SAMR[881] issued a notification letter and proposed measures to address the identified abuses to the Government Office of the Inner Mongolia Autonomous Region (the higher-level administrative authority of the PSD).[882] The office has not yet responded publicly to the letter and it is not clear whether the PSD has rectified its anticompetitive conduct in practice. It is important to note that the government, under the AML, is not required to accept the recommendations of the SAMR.

439. Competition enforcement against administrative monopolies also illustrates how government regulations in China afford regulatory advantages (as discussed in Section 5.2) to Chinese SOEs. For example, in the investigation of abuse of administrative power by the SASAC of Chengdu, the NDRC and its Sichuan bureau found that, in a meeting summary report,[883] Chengdu's SASAC had required all SOEs under its supervision to prioritise 'the insurance services offered by local SOEs when choosing their insurance service providers.'[884] While Chengdu's SASAC voluntarily rectified its anti-competitive conduct,

---

879 'Government Department Supporting Monopoly is Not Upholding Rule of Law', *China Daily* (25 June 2018) <http://www.chinadaily.com.cn/a/201806/25/WS5b302beba3103349141de778.html>.

880 SAMR determined that the Public Security Department has contravened Articles 10, 39 and 45 (previously known as Articles 8, 32 and 37) of the AML (n 65):

> Article 10 Administrative authorities and organisations authorised by law or regulations to perform public functions shall not abuse their administrative powers to eliminate or restrict competition.
>
> Article 39 Any administrative authorities and organisations empowered by a law or administrative regulation to perform public functions shall not abuse its administrative power to require, expressly or in disguised form, entities or individuals to deal with, to purchase from, or to use the products of, a business operator designed by them.
>
> Article 45 Any administrative authorities and organisations authorised by law or regulations to perform public functions shall not abuse its administrative power to set regulations containing provisions that exclude or restrict competition.

881 Based on Article 61 of AML, the Anti-Monopoly Enforcement Authority can only make a proposal to the relevant superior authorities on the handling in accordance with the law. See AML (n 65) art 61.

882 SAMR Advice Letter (n 877).

883 In the context of China, authoritative government and party bodies can issue seemingly non-binding measures like directions, meetings, instructions, and speeches, which generally must be followed by the market players. See Zhang and Wu (n 875).

884 Angela Huyue Zhang, 'The Antitrust Paradox of China Inc.' (2017) 50 NYUJILP 159–226.

this case shows, from a competitive neutrality perspective, how regulatory advantages are afforded to Chinese SOEs over their private sector counterparts in practice.

6.3.4 The FCRS and Competitive Neutrality

440. The introduction of the FCRS into the regulatory policy-making process is an important step forward to achieving a level playing field in the Chinese market as the FCRS can help to reduce the competitive advantages of SOEs conferred in government regulations (noted in Section 5.2[885]). The FCRS may help Chinese SOEs to thrive on their merits, not regulatory favours. As stated by Deborah Healey and Eleanor M Fox: 'The FCRS provides a substantial blueprint for tackling the impact of the State in the market.'[886]

441. Under the FCRS, the policy-making authorities have a discretion in choosing which regulations are subject to the FCRS and in determining whether to exempt the regulations or proposal that restricts competition.[887] In attempting to prevent the abuse of this discretion, the FCRS imposed the obligation of documenting (in writing) the reasons for granting the exemptions to the policies that restricted competition to policy-making authorities.[888] In addition, competition law experts or competition authorities (like the fair competition review division of the SAMR[889]) and the people whose activities are expected to be affected by regulations are encouraged to participate in the review process.[890] The established third-party assessment for the FCRS[891] and annual

885 For example, regulations that grant 'fiscal subsidies; reduction of the amount of tax; allocating land-use rights (LURs) or favourable land price; special treatment of environment protections terms and special treatment of administration fees, etc.' without justification are considered as favouring SOEs: Opinions on Establishing FCRS (n 88) art 16.

886 Healey and Fox (n 755) 203.

887 Under the FCRS, the regulatory policy or proposal should not restrict competition unless the policy-making authority can demonstrate the concerned policy or proposal can meet the following conditions:

> Safeguarding national economic security, cultural security, or scientific and technological security or are related to national defence construction;
>
> Achieving social security purposes such as poverty alleviation and national development, disaster relief and rescue, or other social security purposes;
>
> Achieving social and public interests, such as conserving energy and resources, protecting the ecological environment or other social and public interests;
>
> Any other exceptions prescribed by laws and administrative regulations.
>
> Opinions on Establishing FCRS (n 88) s 3(4); FCRS Implementation Rules 2021 (n 843) art 17.

888 Opinions on Establishing FCRS (n 88) s 3(4):

> Policy-making organs shall explain that relevant policy measures are indispensable for achieving policy objectives, and that they will not seriously exclude and restrain market competition, and shall specify the implementation period of such policy measures.
>
> Policy-making organs shall assess the implementation effects of relevant policy measures on an annual basis. They shall promptly cease or adjust the implementation of policy measures whose implementation period has expired or that failed to achieve the desired effects.

889 There are currently four staff members in the fair competition review division of the SAMR. '国家发展改革委设立公平竞争审查处进一步强化公平竞争审查工作 [National Development and Reform Commission Establishes a Fair Competition Review Office to Further Strengthen Fair Competition Review Work]' (9 January 2018) <http://www.gov.cn/xinwen/2018-01/09/content_5254755.htm>.

890 FCRS Implementation Rules 2021 (n 843) art 7.

891 《市场监管总局关于发布公平竞争审查第三方评估实施指南的公告》 [Guidelines on the Third-Party Assessment of the Fair Competition Review System] SAMR, No 6, 12 February 2019 (Third-Party Assessment Guidelines).

random inspection from the SAMR[892] can be relied on to tackle regulatory advantages of Chinese SOEs. These obligations under the FCRS undoubtedly increased the transparency of the policy-making process in China and help to discover regulatory policies that favour SOEs over other firms.

442. However, it is essential to recognise the possible limitation of the FCRS in addressing regulatory advantages of SOEs. Firstly, unlike the regulatory neutrality requirement in Australia (noted in Chapter 4), removing the preferential treatment from certain market players (*Teding Jingyingzhe*) in government policies is only one type of many regulatory restrictions on competition targeted by the FRCS.[893] The FCRS also tackles regional blockades that disrupt the free movement of goods and production in the market of China,[894] and other governmental actions that restrict competition without adequate justification, such as organising anti-competitive agreements by means of administrative orders,[895] or setting government-guided prices for goods and services without the pricing authority.[896] It is important to note that, whereas the FCRS applies to the preferential treatments provided to both SOEs and non-SOEs in regulations, the regulatory neutrality requirement under Australia's competitive neutrality policy specifically targets the preferential treatments provided to SOEs. This broad coverage of the FCRS may distract the focus of local authorities (often with limited expertise and staff) in carrying out the FCRS, leading regulatory advantages of SOEs to escape the scrutiny of the FCRS.

443. Additionally, there is a risk that the FCRS can be suppressed by policy-making authorities to accommodate SOE interests based on the state capture theory (discussed in Chapter 1). SOEs (especially local ones) are closely linked with the interests (revenue) of the local government (as Chapter 5 demonstrates). There are cases, like the Government Office of Shanghai noted above, which suggest that government authorities favour their own SOEs over competitors in regulations. Under the FCRS, a government authority that carries out the FCRS is often the part of the machinery of government that owns SOEs. This conflict of interest could thus discourage local policy-making authorities from initiating reviews that could have negative implications for local SOEs, given that policy-making authorities have discretion in choosing which regulations are subject to the FCRS.

892 《市场监管总局等四部门关于进一步推进公平竞争审查工作的通知》[Notice on Advancing Fair Competition Review System by the State Administration for Market Regulation, National Development and Reform Commission, Ministry of Finance, Ministry of Commerce] Guoshijian Anti-Monopoly (2020) No 73, 9 May 2020 (Competition Review Notice).

893 FCRS Implementation Rules 2021 (n 843) art 15 (1). For example, the preferential treatment in granting financial incentives and subsidies; reimbursing taxes; reducing land assets prices or providing land by means of allocation or injection of land assets into operators; granting any special treatment to particular businesses in terms of environmental protection standards and pollution discharge privileges; waiving administration fees, government, and housing funds etc. will be targeted by the FCRS.

894 ibid art 14 (1)-(5).

895 ibid art 16 (1).

896 ibid art 16 (3).

444. Finally, SOEs (as the vested interests) are likely to resist the FCRS and make efforts to retain their regulatory advantages rather than face more competition. Given both the formal oversight mechanism for the review and a feedback mechanism for the FCRS are currently absent in practice, SOEs could use their government ownership and political connections to exert influence on the review process. Additionally, the local authorities' insufficient understanding of competition and lack of experience in determining when it is appropriate to restrict competition may put local authorities that carry out the self-review at high risk of being captured by the SOEs. Encouragingly, the newly introduced third-party oversight for the FCRS[897] and annual random inspection from the SAMR[898] can to some degree alleviate the state capture risk. However, more empirical findings of the FCRS cases are needed in the future to confirm this point view.

6.4 Conclusion

445. The foregoing analysis has shown that the AML and the FCRS can address some of the competitive neutrality concerns caused by Chinese SOEs (identified in Chapter 5). The case studies and examples provided in Sections 6.2.2 and 6.2.3 indicate that the anti-competitive conduct of Chinese SOEs is subject to scrutiny under the AML. However, a closer analysis of the AML reveals that its application to Chinese SOEs is not without problems. Firstly, the uncertainties around Article 8 make its application indeterminate in relation to SOEs. Secondly, sectoral legislation, according to the principle of *lex specialis*, can create exemptions to the AML's application to SOEs in regulated sectors. As argued in Section 6.1.2, granting exemptions based on sectoral legislation is risky because it may incentivise SOEs to lobby legislators to provide exemptions in sectoral legislation in favour of the interests of SOEs. Finally, Chinese competition authorities are facing additional difficulties when dealing with SOEs. As discussed in Section 6.2.2, merger enforcement can be affected by the involvement of SOEs. It is especially problematic that in merger assessments involving the concentration of central SOEs, the merger review agency in China (the SAMR) takes the decisions and views of other government departments into account because it indicates the competition enforcement is not independent in investigation and decision-making.

446. For competitive neutrality concerns that do not amount to a competition law infringement, policy instruments like the FCRS can address only one part of the concerns, the regulatory advantages of Chinese SOEs, which leaves competitive neutrality concerns in relation to land and bank loans unaddressed.

897 Third-Party Assessment Guidelines (n 890).

898 Competition Review Notice (n 891).

Hence, more needs to be done to address the lack of a level playing field between SOEs and non-SOEs in China. Section 6.3 analyses the FCRS in terms of its function, implementation, and impact on the regulatory advantages of Chinese SOEs (identified in Section 5.2). Introducing the FCRS into the policy-making process is an important step towards a level playing field in the market in China. However, the broad discretion enjoyed by policy-making authorities, and the shared interests between SOEs and government owners, present conflicts of interest and the risk of capture, which may undermine the effectiveness of the FCRS when addressing the advantages of SOEs provided by regulation (as discussed in Section 5.2.1). Importantly, the complaints mechanism of the FCRS is still developing. The actual procedural mechanism and how it will be used to rectify breaches in practice is currently unclear and more case studies are needed for a better assessment. In brief, while the FCRS is an important step in achieving a level playing field in the Chinese market by going some way in solving the regulatory advantages enjoyed by SOEs, other competitive neutrality concerns of SOEs (as identified in Chapter 5) escaped the reach of the FCRS.

447. In conclusion, though the application of the AML and the FCRS can alleviate the extent of competitive neutrality advantages of Chinese SOEs, some aspects of competitive neutrality concerns about SOEs cannot be solved through the AML and the FCRS, leaving the issue of lack of a level playing field between SOEs and non-SOEs only partially addressed. For example, the AML prohibits anti-competitive conduct of SOEs, however, the legitimate activities of SOEs, like borrowing from banks with more favourable lending rates, are not within the coverage of the AML. The FCRS cannot remove the preferential interest rates of SOEs because these preferential interest rates are afforded by government guarantee not preferential government regulation. Accordingly, as presented in Chapter 8, this research proposes to reform the AML to achieve better coherence in its coverage, and calls for the introduction into the Chinese legal system of an explicit competitive neutrality policy to improve the competitive environment between SOEs and non-SOEs.

CHAPTER 7

IMPLEMENTATION OF COMPETITIVE NEUTRALITY POLICY IN AUSTRALIA

448. Chapter 4 provided an overview of what the competitive neutrality commitments mean at the conceptual level in the context of Australia. This chapter investigates the operation of competitive neutrality policy in Australia at a procedural level and includes the scope of competitive neutrality policy, the complaint-handing bodies, and the institutional structures that facilitate the implementation of competitive neutrality policy in Australia. The primary purpose of the chapter is to illustrate how the substantive elements of competitive neutrality commitments (explained in Chapter 4) are being enforced in practice. This chapter is also useful for the subsequent discussion in Chapter 8, which discusses the possible ways to introduce the competitive neutrality policy into the Chinese legal system based on the substantive (Chapter 4) and procedural (this chapter) aspects of Australia's competitive neutrality policy. This chapter is in three parts.

449. Section 7.1 clarifies the normative criteria deployed by the Australian government to draw the boundaries of competitive neutrality policy. The analysis in this part explains the threshold test for identifying 'significant business activity' and its implications for the scope of competitive neutrality policy. The rationale for employing the 'significant business activity' test will also be discussed in this section. Further, as a means to align with the public interest, implementing competitive neutrality policy is required only 'to the extent that the benefits to be realised from implementation outweigh the costs', as stated in the CPA.[899] Interpretation of the public interest (or public benefit) and the methodology for a public-interest analysis under the competitive neutrality policy will be discussed in this section. The last part of this section assesses the current public interest model used by the government to weigh the envisaged public interest and the potential competition benefits from the

899 CPA (n 384) cl 3(6).

application of competitive neutrality policy. Section 7.1.2 argues that there are generally two models used by government to apply public interest test in practice, namely the *ex-post* model and the *ex-ante* model.

450. Sections 7.2 explores the procedural tools used for enforcing competitive neutrality policy in practice, which include the complaint-handling body and the relevant complaint-handling procedures. Given Australia is the only country with operational competitive neutrality complaint-handling mechanisms,[900] the role of the current complaint-handling bodies and their effectiveness will be discussed. However, there has been only a small number of cases on the competitive neutrality issues in Australia, making evaluation on the effectiveness of complaint-handling process difficult. One major issue with the current complaint-handling process in Australia is the lack of penalties for the breach of competitive neutrality obligations. While amendments to the compliance of competitive neutrality policy have been discussed and proposed by the *Harper Review*, few substantive changes have been made to complaint-handling procedures. The section ends by briefly identifying the governmental institutions (both current and past) that facilitate the implementation of competitive neutrality policy in Australia.

7.1 Scope of Competitive Neutrality Policy

451. The discussion of Australia's competitive neutrality policy has so far proceeded on the assumption that competitive neutrality policy automatically applies to all SOEs engaged in business activities in Australia. However, this is not the case, as the scope of competitive neutrality policy is narrower in practice, reflecting the delicate balance between competition and other public interests.[901] Two tests are designed to narrow the scope for the application of competitive neutrality in Australia, namely the significant government business activity test and the public interest test (which will be discussed in Section 7.1.2).[902]

7.1.1 Significant Government Business Activity Test

452. For competitive neutrality commitments to apply in the context of Australia, two thresholds need to be satisfied by the government entity. First, the government entity needs to be engaging in 'business activity.' Second, the business activity of the government entity needs to be 'significant' for the purpose of competitive neutrality policy.

900 OECD (n 7) 45.

901 For example, the CPA requires Australian governments to apply competitive neutrality principles to the extent that the benefits of implementation outweigh the costs. See CPA (n 384) cl 3(6).

902 Andrew Trembath, for example, argues that the scope of competitive neutrality has been driven largely by the interpretation of the phrases 'significant business activities' and 'where appropriate' in cl 3 of the CPA. See Trembath (n 719) 8.

Government Business Activity Test

453. While there is no precise definition of 'business activity' in the CPA,[903] the discretion for developing the concept is entrusted to government at all levels in their application of competitive neutrality policy. Regardless of the variance in the thresholds of 'business activity', the intention of identifying government business activity (or applying the business activity test) is to separate commercial government activity from non-commercial government activity, such as the regulatory activities of imposing or collecting taxes, or granting licences. The business activity test thereby excludes the application of competitive neutrality policy to non-commercial activities of the government.

454. In practice, governments have adopted different criteria for the business activity test. For example, in Victoria, an activity that 'do[es] not result in sales of good or provision of service – either directly to a purchaser or through an arms length contract with another party or parties' should not be regarded as a business activity.[904] By contrast, at the Commonwealth level, an activity does not constitute a business activity for the purpose of competitive neutrality policy if such activity: does not involve charging users for goods or services; does not have an actual or potential competitor; and the manager of such activities does not have a degree of independence in relation to the production or supply of the good or service and the price at which it is provided.[905] As Andrew Trembath observed, most governments in Australia use the threshold of 'charg[ing] users and trade in goods or services' to determine the business nature of government activities while others incorporate standards of 'managers have a degree of independence in production or supply, and price decisions' when making such decision.[906]

455. An examination on how the business activity test is applied in practice is considered useful and will be briefly explored below. The two selected cases, involving the Bureau of Meteorology and the Australian Protective Service, show that the criteria of the business activity under the competitive neutrality policy is designed to be very easy to satisfy as it has low evidentiary standards. The low threshold also reflects a preference for the implementation of the policy in practice.

Bureau of Meteorology[907]

456. The Bureau of Meteorology ('the Bureau'), a non-corporate Commonwealth entity funded by the Commonwealth budget (on a cost-recovery basis)

903 For example, the CPA states only that competitive neutrality policy 'only apply to the business activities of publicly owned entities, not to the non-business, non-profit activities of these entities.' It did not provide further explanation of what constitute business activity under the competitive neutrality policy: CPA (n 384) cl 3(1).

904 Victoria Department of Treasury and Finance, 'Competitive Neutrality Guide to Implementation Victoria 2000' (2000) 3 <https://www.vic.gov.au/sites/default/files/2019-06/Competitive-Neutrality-Guide-to-Implementation.pdf>.

905 Commonwealth CN Policy Statement (n 375) 7.

906 See Trembath (n 719) 11–12.

907 *Meteorological Services to Aviation* (n 486).

and supervised by the Civil Aviation Safety Authority (CASA), provides national meteorological services related to weather forecasting and climate etc. In February 2000, Metra Information Ltd (Metra), a subsidiary of the government-owned Meteorological Services of New Zealand Ltd which provided a range of value-added meteorological services to the aviation industry, submitted a complaint to the Commonwealth Competitive Neutrality Complaints Office (CCNCO).[908] Metra alleged that administrative regulation issued by CASA prevented Metra from 'competing in the market for meteorological services to the aviation industry' and thereby conferred a regulatory advantage on the meteorological service of the Bureau.

457. To assess whether competitive neutrality policy applied, the CCNCO first needed to evaluate whether the Bureau's meteorological services provided to the aviation industry satisfied the definition of 'business activity' for the purpose of competitive neutrality policy. According to the Commonwealth CN Policy Statement, three criteria are used to determine when government agencies are engaging a business activity for the purpose of competitive neutrality:

- there must be user-charging for goods or services (the user may be in the private sector or public sector);
- there must be an actual or potential competitor (either in the private or public sector) ie users are not restricted by law or policy from choosing alternative sources of supply; and
- managers of the activity have a degree of independence in relation to the production or supply of the good or service and the price at which it is provided.[909]

458. It was straightforward to argue that the Bureau's meteorological services met the user-charging requirement in the sense that the 'services provided by the Bureau to the aviation industry are negotiated with the users' (there is distinction between the provider and purchaser), and there were 'cost recovery charges in place and collected by Airservices Australia (totalling around $14 million in 1999–2000).'[910] However, it was not straightforward to assess whether there were (actual or potential) competitors of the Bureau's meteorological services. According to the design of business activity test, it is generally assumed that there is an actual or potential competitor in place *unless* it can be demonstrated otherwise. For example, it could be assumed that the Bureau's meteorological services do not have actual or potential competitors if the relevant party can demonstrate that there are laws or specific government policies in place to prohibit the user from choosing alternative

908 ibid.

909 Commonwealth CN Policy Statement (n 375) 7.

910 *Meteorological Services to Aviation* (n 477) 1.

sources of supply.[911] The finding of the CCNCO shows that the restriction (from choosing alternative sources of supply to users) provided by the law and government policies needs to be in the government regulation itself (i.e. in its text) rather than the administration of the law or government policies.[912] Additionally, the management autonomy requirement under the business activity test does not have to be strong. For example, the aviation service of the Bureau satisfied the management autonomy element because it had independence in 'how it delivers its value-added service, the method it uses to allocate costs to those services, and the prices it charged for them (instead of following the mandated prices directed by law or by ministers).[913] Based on the above finding, the CCNCO found that the aviation meteorological services provided by the Bureau were 'business activities' for the purposes of competitive neutrality, and thus the circumstances were within the jurisdiction of CCNCO to further investigate the complaint.

Australian Protective Service

459. Australian Protective Service (APS) was a division within the Commonwealth Attorney-General's Department (1984–2004) that provided Counter Terrorist First Response (CTFR) services at 11 major Australian airports and charged for their CTFR services. In 1998, both the board of Airlines Representatives of Australia (BARA) and the Airline Association of Australia (AAA) submitted a complaint to the CCNCO. The AAA and BARA alleged that competitive neutrality policy should not apply to the APS's CTFR services as it was not a business activity for the purpose of competitive neutrality policy. Mainly, the AAA and BARA both argued that 'there is no actual or potential competitor to the APS for the delivery of those services, and airports cannot choose the level of service they purchase or the provider.'[914]

460. The CCNCO assessed whether the APS's CTFR services satisfied the business activity test and found that the APS was charging its users (airport operators) for its CTFR services on a cost-recovery basis (satisfying the first criterion), and that the management of the APS had a degree of independence for the purpose of competitive neutrality as it could determine the price it charged (satisfying the third criterion). The remaining question was whether there were actual or potential competitors in place in competition with the APS's CTFR services. While private operators for CTFR services were excluded under regulations of the Air Navigation Act 1920, the CCNCO found that individual state or territory police forces and the Australian Federal Police

911 *CN Guidelines for Managers* (n 380) 9.

912 In other words, in the absence of specific text in regulation or government policy prohibiting the choice of alternative supply, it can be concluded that an actual or potential competitor is in place for the purpose of competitive neutrality. *Meteorological Services to Aviation* (n 477) 4.

913 ibid 5.

914 CCNCO, *Competitive Neutrality Investigation into Provision of Counter Terrorist First Response Services by the Australian Protective Service* (Report No 1, December 1998) 2 <https://www.pc.gov.au/__data/assets/pdf_file/0011/158474/report1.pdf>.

(AFP) had recently been allowed to provide CTFR services as a result of government policy review in 1997. The CCNCO found that the APS's CTFR services constituted a business activity in the context of the competitive neutrality policy, and it was thereby within the jurisdiction of CCNCO to further investigate other aspects of the complaint (whether the APS's CTFR services is 'significant' and justified on public benefit ground) which will be discussed directly below.

Significant Government Business Activity Test

461. While the business activity test determines whether the activity of a government entity is relevant to competitive neutrality policy (or within the scope of competitive neutrality), the significant government business activity test determines whether to apply competitive neutrality policy.[915] In other words, for competitive neutrality policy to apply, the government business activity needs to be 'significant' and justified on public benefit grounds. This public interest (or public benefit) test is explained in Section 7.1.2 below. The primary rationale for targeting significant government business activity (instead of all government business activity) is to solve practical difficulties of applying competitive neutrality policy to a plethora of 'small-scale' government business activity, as 'the costs of implementing competitive neutrality are assumed to outweigh the benefits in such cases.'[916] For example, as observed by Rennie and Lindsay, the rationale for excluding small-scale government business activities from the application of competitive neutrality is based on 'the significant costs that will be incurred ... both initial establishment costs and ongoing administrative costs.'[917] This provides an answer to the question of why most of the jurisdictions in Australia tend to employ a business-size or turnover threshold to determine 'significant' business activities for the purpose of competitive neutrality policy. One exception is the ACT government in deciding to apply competitive neutrality policy to all government business activity without reference to 'significant'.[918]

Government Business Activity Deemed to be 'Significant'

462. The business activity of some types of government entity are deemed to be significant because 'they have been specifically structured to operate along commercial lines'[919] and have a predominantly commercial or profit-making orientation. As commented by Deborah Healey and Rhonda L Smith,

---

915 The significant government business activities test answers the question of when government entities need to implement competitive neutrality commitments in practice.

916 CN Review 2017 (n 495) 9.

917 Rennie and Lindsay (n 7) 17.

918 Independent Competition and Regulatory Commission, 'Competitive Neutrality Complaints Guideline' (2015), 3 <https://www.icrc.act.gov.au/__data/assets/pdf_file/0010/1241695/ICRC-Guideline-Competitive-Neutrality-Complaints-August-2015.pdf>.

919 OECD (n 339) 4.

> significant GBEs [Government Business Enterprises] in each jurisdiction classified by the Australian Bureau of Statistics as Public Trading Enterprises and Public Financial Enterprises were made subject to full Commonwealth, state and territory taxes or tax equivalent systems, and debt-guarantee fees directed towards offsetting the competitive advantages which they might have.[920]

463. For example, in Queensland, government business activities are deemed to be significant for the purpose of competitive neutrality policy if they:

1. fall within the Australian Bureau of Statistics' classification of a Public Financial Enterprise (PFE) or Public Trading Enterprise (PTE); and/or
2. (a) trade goods and/or services as their predominant activity; and
   (b) meet a substantial part of their operating costs or earn a substantial part of their operating revenue from user charges; and
   (c) are expected to have a predominantly commercial or profit-making focus.[921]

464. Similarly, at the Commonwealth level, the business activity of the following Commonwealth government entities is deemed to be significant for the purpose of competitive neutrality policy:[922] 'the business activity of all Government Business Enterprises (GBEs) and their subsidiaries;[923] the business activities of other share-limited trading companies,[924] and the business activity of all designated business Units.'[925]

---

920 Healey and Smith (n 6) 241. The primary function of Public Trading Enterprises is to provide goods and services which are mainly market, nonregulatory, and nonfinancial in nature, financed mainly through sales to consumers of these goods and services. Public Financial Enterprises (PFE) refers to agencies which have one or more of the following functions: that of central bank; the acceptance of demand, time or saving deposits; or the authority to incur liabilities and acquire financial assets in the market of their own account. See Queensland Government, 'Competitive Neutrality and Queensland Government Business Activities' (July 1996) 46 <https://s3.treasury.qld.gov.au/files/ncp-competitive-neutrality.pdf> (Queensland CN Policy Statement).

921 Queensland CN Policy Statement (n 919) 25.

922 Commonwealth CN Policy Statement (n 375).

923 The term 'government business enterprise' (GBE) was adopted in the 1980s and is now widely used in Australia. See Brian Galligan and Winsome Roberts, *The Oxford Companion to Australian Politics* (OUP 2007). A GBE is a Commonwealth entity or Commonwealth company that is prescribed by the regulations. For example, NBN Co Ltd (ACN 136 533 741) is wholly owned by the Commonwealth of Australia as a GBE, incorporated under the Corporations Act 2001 and operated in accordance with the Public Governance, Performance and Accountability Act 2013. The Australian government's relationship to its GBEs is similar to the relationship between a holding company and its subsidiaries. See Department of Finance, 'Government Business Enterprises' (updated 14 December 2020) <https://www.finance.gov.au/business/government-business-enterprises>.

924 A Commonwealth Company is legally and financially separate from the Commonwealth and established under the *Corporations Act 2001* wherein the Commonwealth controls

- the composition of the company's board or
- is in a position to cast, or control the casting of, more than one-half of the maximum number of votes at a general meeting of the company or
- holds more than one-half of the issued share capital of the company (excluding any part of that issued share capital that carries no right to participate beyond a specified amount in a distribution of either profits or capital).

Commonwealth companies include wholly-owned Commonwealth companies and GBEs. See Department of Finance, 'Commonwealth company' (updated 3 September 2022) <https://www.finance.gov.au/about-us/glossary/pgpa/term-commonwealth-company>.

925 Designated business units are established through administrative arrangements and are identifiable parts of the *Financial Management and Accountability Act 1997* (Cth). Agency that has the primary objective of

465. Applying competitive neutrality policy to the 'significant' category noted above is 'relatively clear'[926] because government activities are often listed by the relevant government.[927] For example, there are currently nine Commonwealth GBEs[928] that belong to the deemed 'significant' category and thereby automatically required to comply with the competitive neutrality commitments such as tax neutrality, debt neutrality, regulatory neutrality, and commercial rate of return commitments under the competitive neutrality policy.

Government Business Activity Identified as 'Significant'

466. Apart from the deemed 'significant' category, competitive neutrality policy also applies to business activity carried out by government departments and agencies that satisfies the threshold of 'significant'.

467. There are two approaches to assess whether a business activity is 'significant' for the purpose of competitive neutrality policy: the principles-based approach and the threshold-based approach.[929] The principles-based approach requires the relevant government (instead of the government business entity itself) to evaluate whether the business activity is 'significant' based on a set of guiding principles. For example, a set of criteria used by the Western Australia government to guide the assessment of 'significant business activity' includes:

> the extent of competition (or the potential for competition) between the public and private sectors; and the significance of the market in which the government business activity takes

---

trading goods and services in the market for the purpose of earning a commercial return. The management and accounting structures of business units are separate from other parts of the overall organisation. Treasury, 'The Importance of Competition Policy for Australia' 8 <http://archive.treasury.gov.au/documents/1056/HTML/docshell.asp?URL=Ch2_Competitive_Neutrality.htm>. See also OECD (n 339) 4.

926 Healey and Smith (n 6) 241.

927 For example, in Queensland, a list of significant business activities was listed by the Queensland Competition Authority <https://www.qca.org.au/project/competitive-neutrality/>.

928 The nine GBEs identified by the Commonwealth government include: ASC Pty Ltd (ACN 008 605 034), a company wholly owned by the Commonwealth, represented by the Minister for Finance (Shareholder Minister); Australian Postal Corporation, incorporated under the provisions of the Australian Postal Corporation Act 1989 (as amended), and an Australian government owned for-profit entity; Australian Naval Infrastructure Pty Ltd (ACN 051 762 639), a wholly-owned Commonwealth company, bound by the Corporations Act 2001 and the Public Governance, Performance and Accountability Act 2013, which operates at arm's length from government, and prescribed as a GBE with effect from 1 July 2017; Australian Rail Track Corporation Ltd (ACN 081 455 754), a company incorporated under the Corporations Act 2001 and owned by the Commonwealth of Australia, represented by the Minister for Infrastructure and Transport and the Minister for Finance; Defence Housing Australia, an Australian GBE established by the Defence Housing Australia Act 1987; Moorebank Intermodal Co Ltd (ACN 161 635 105), a GBE incorporated under the *Corporations Act 2001*, and operating under the *Public Governance, Performance and Accountability Act 2013*; NBN Co Ltd (ACN 136 533 741), an Australian government-owned corporation established in 2009 to design, build, and operate Australia's wholesale broadband access network; and WSA Co Ltd (ACN 618 989 272) established by the Australian government to develop and operate Western Sydney International (Nancy-Bird Walton) Airport. WSA Co is required to execute its responsibilities in accordance with a Project Deed with the government to open the airport by 2026. Snowy Hydro Limited (ACN 090 574 431). For more information, see Department of Finance (n 922).

929 CN Review 2017 (n 495) 9–10.

> place to the Western Australian economy ... its annual revenue base or turnover is more than $10 million; or it has an asset base with a value in excess of $10 million.[930]

468. In contrast to the principles-based approach, the threshold-based approach does not require the relevant government to evaluate the significance of the business activity. Instead, it is the responsibility of the managers of the government business entity, such as the managers of the SOE, to self-determine whether their business activity is 'significant' based on the threshold criteria (i.e. turnover) provided. At the Commonwealth level the business activity of the government agency or department needs to have a minimum of $10 million commercial turnover to be deemed 'significant'.[931] As the case of the Australian Protective Service discussed in this section shows, the APS's CTFR services were considered as 'significant' by the CCNCO because the total revenue from CTFR was around $18 million. However, it is worth acknowledging that the $10 million commercial turnover developed decades ago is currently under review.[932] Notably, the appropriateness of using the $10 million commercial turnover alone as the threshold to determine the scope of the competitive neutrality policy is under question.

469. On the one hand, as warned by Treasury, judging 'significance' by one factor alone (the commercial turnover) may risk excluding government business activity that earns less revenue but is still significant in its particular market from the application of competitive neutrality.[933] This exclusion may harm competition in the long run. On the other hand, judging 'significant' through a principles-based approach will inevitably increase the cost for the

---

930 Government of Western Australia, 'Policy Statement on Competitive Neutrality' (June 1996) 7–8 <https://www.wa.gov.au/system/files/2020-01/policy-on-competitive-neutrality.pdf>. Similarly, the factors provided by Tasmania government when assessing significant government business include: what is the relevant market for goods and service; the barriers to entry in the market; the degree of concentration in the market, including the criticality of the good or service provided; and the potential impact on other markets (e.g. the loss of efficiency in an upstream or downstream market). See Office of the Tasmanian Economic Regulator, 'Competitive Neutrality Complaints Mechanism Guideline (Version 2)' (July 2015) 12 <https://www.economicregulator.tas.gov.au/Documents/Competitive%20neutrality%20complaints%20guideline%20July%202015%20(683OOS70).pdf>. For the factor used in Victoria to assess significant government business, see Commissioner for Better Regulation, 'Identifying Significant Business Activities for Competitive Neutrality' (Guidance Note, 16 September 2016) <https://www.vic.gov.au/competitive-neutrality#guidance>.

931 *CN Guidelines for Managers* (n 380) 13. Commonwealth significant business activity criteria are set to include:

> baseline costing for activities undertaken for market testing purposes;
> public sector bids over $10 million;
> business activities not in these categories that are undertaken within (non-GBE) Prescribed Agencies; and Commonwealth Authorities or Departments, with a commercial turnover of at least $10 million per annum. (emphasis added)

Put differently, the business activity of other Commonwealth government entities (rather than declared 'significant' category) will be excluded from the application of competitive neutrality policy if they do not have the $10 million commercial turnover. For more detailed discussion, see Healey and Smith (n 6) 242; CN Review 2017 (n 495) 9–10.

932 CN Review 2017 (n 495) 9.

933 ibid.

government to apply and advance competitive neutrality policy and may create uncertainty for the scope of competitive neutrality policy. As Deborah Healey and Rhonda L Smith comment:

> The application of competitive neutrality policy needs to strike a balance between fostering competition in the public interest and overburdening smaller government and local government bodies with regulatory obligations and investigations which are overly costly and time-consuming.[934]

470. The above arguments echo the viewpoint of the *Harper Review* that there is a need for each jurisdiction to reconsider the current threshold for 'significant business activities.'[935]

7.1.2 Public Interest Test

471. The principle of competitive neutrality is designed to promote competition, but at the same time it acknowledges that there are situations where competition does not achieve economic efficiency or conflicts with other social objectives.[936] For example, the *Hilmer Review* stated:

> Competition policy is not about the pursuit of competition for its own sake. Rather, it seeks to facilitate effective competition in the interests of economic efficiency while accommodating situations where competition does not achieve economic efficiency or conflicts with other social objectives.[937]

472. The public interest test[938] incorporated in the implementation of competitive neutrality policy[939] is expected to align the application of such policy with other the public interest (or public benefit) considerations.[940] Debate arose during the 1990s between divergent interest groups over whether to include the public interest test in the context of CPA.[941] Those against the public interest test, often from business and industry groups, argued that its insertion detracted from the emphasis on economic efficiency in

934 Healey and Smith (n 6) 242.

935 *Harper Review* (n 404) 268.

936 Situations where competition does not achieve economic efficiency or conflicts with other social goals are often called 'market failure' by economists. In other words, competitive neutrality policy acknowledges concerns in situations where there is a market failure or where there might be a market failure. For more general discussion, see King (n 402) 12–13.

937 *Hilmer Review* (n 92) 6.

938 Public interest tests are often referred to as public benefit tests. This research uses the terms interchangeably.

939 CPA (n 384) cl 3(6).

940 Morgan, Bai and Bhasker (n 340) 251.

941 Some of the debate is detailed in Michael Paddon and others, *Competition in Whose Interest? Socio-Economic Impacts of National Competition Policy* (Public Sector Research Centre & Public Interest Advocacy Centre 1999); Standing Committee on Financial Institutions and Public Administration (n 718).

competition policy.[942] By contrast, many of its advocates, often from unions and community groups, argued that competition policy (including competitive neutrality policy) should not focus solely on competition and efficiency at the expense of social equity and public welfare.[943] As a result, the public interest test 'was inserted into the CPA after lobbying from trade unions and consumer, environment, and community organisations.'[944] In particular, an illustrative but non-exhaustive list of factors is provided by the CPA, which includes:

> ecologically sustainable development; social welfare and equity considerations, including community service obligations; occupational health and safety, industrial relations and access and equity; employment and investment growth; the interests of consumers generally; competitiveness of Australian businesses; and efficient allocation of resources.[945]

473. The public interest factors noted above are broad (including both economic and non-economic factors) and 'touch on complex areas of social and economic regulation'.[946] Moreover, the public interest noted in the CPA shares some similarity with the public benefits for the purpose of authorisation or notification under the CCA, which includes

> anything of value to the community generally, any contribution to the aims pursued by the society including as one of its principal elements (in the context of trade practices legislation) the achievement of the economic goals of efficiency and progress. Plainly the assessment of efficiency and progress must be from the perspective of society as a whole: the best use of society's resources.[947]

474. However, unlike the public interest under the CCA (which is assessed by the ACCC[948] or on appeal the Australian Competition Tribunal[949]), the public interest

942 Patricia Ranald and Richard Thorowgood, *Review of Competitive Neutrality Policies and Local Government Policies of Government Under National Competition Policy* (Public Sector Research Centre, UNSW 1997) 9.

943 For detailed argument, see Morgan (n 346) 96–97.

944 Ranald and Thorowgood (n 941) 9.

945 CPA (n 384) cls 1(3)(d)-(j).

946 National Competition Council, 'National Competition Policy: Some Impacts on Society and the Economy' (January 1999) <http://ncp.ncc.gov.au/docs/OINcpIm-002.pdf>. Interpreting public interest matters are inherently subjective and political in nature, which additionally contributed to its complexity. For more detailed discussion, see Gary Banks, 'Competition and the Public Interest' (Speech to the NCC Workshop 'Public Interest Test Under National Competition Policy', Melbourne, 12 July 2001) <http://www.pc.gov.au/news-media/speeches/cs20010712>.

947 ACCC, 'Guidelines for Authorisation of conduct (non-merger)' (n 350) 43.

948 For detailed discussion on how the ACCC assesses public interest in Australia, see Rod Sims and Graeme Woodbridge, 'Public Interest in Antitrust Enforcement: An Australian Perspective' (2020) 65(2) Antitrust Bull 282.

949 For detailed discussion on the function of the ACCC and the Australia Competition Tribunal, see Duke (n 414) 180–83.

is mostly dealt by relevant government agencies on a case-by-case basis.[950] The procedure established by the governments to apply the public interest test for the purpose of competitive neutrality policy is administrative in nature and government agencies at each level have discretion to implement the public interest test under its own agenda. Due to various approaches of the public interest test used by individual governments, it is not entirely clear how finding the balance between public interest and potential competition benefits from the application of competitive neutrality policy occurs in practice. For example:

> [Government in] Victoria articulates two separate processes for weighing the public policy dimensions of competitive neutrality: a standard cost-benefit analysis, and a separate process for considering the public benefit issues listed in cl 5 [of the CPA] as well as some additional objectives related to local economic development and local community impacts.[951]

475. As a result, criticism such as lack of 'consistency' and scrutiny from the legislature and public oversight is often associated with the application of the public interest test for the purpose of competitive neutrality policy.[952] An examination on how some of the public interest factors (such as community service obligation, CSO) are examined in the complaint process is considered useful and will be briefly explored below.

Australian Hearing

476. Australian Hearing[953] is a corporate Australian government owned entity which reports and is accountable to the Minister for Human Services.[954] The main functions of Australian Hearing can be divided into two groups: the first function is that it is the sole provider of the government's CSO[955] in hearing services (i.e. it provides subsidised hearing services and assistive hearing technology to eligible hearing patients[956]); the second function is to

---

950 As Deborah Healey and Rhonda L Smith have commented, the public interest test involves an individual consideration of the facts and circumstances of each case. See Healey and Smith (n 6) 243.

951 Morgan, Bai and Bhasker (n 340) 255.

952 Healey and Smith (n 6) 243.

953 For more detailed information on its governance arrangements and executive governance structures, see Australian Hearing, *2018-19 Annual Report*, 24 <https://www.hearing.com.au/HearingAustralia/media/assets/Documents/HA-Annual-Report-2019_1.pdf>

954 ibid; *Australian Hearing* (n 477) 12.

955 The definition of CSOs is not provided by the CPA, which means that it leaved to individual jurisdictions to decide. However, the definition of CSO proposed by the Steering Committee for National Performance Monitoring of Government Trading Enterprises (SCNPMGTE) enjoys wide recognition in Australia. It provides:

> A Community Service Obligation arises when a government specifically requires a public enterprise to carry out activities relating to outputs or inputs which it would not elect to do on a commercial basis, and which the government does not require other businesses in the public or private sectors to generally undertake, or which it would only do commercially at higher prices.

See Steering Committee for National Performance Monitoring of Government Trading Enterprises, *Community Service Obligations: Some Definitional, Costing and Funding Issues* (April 1994) xi <https://www.pc.gov.au/research/supporting/community-service-obligations/cso.pdf>.

956 Eligible patients for Australian Hearing's service include individuals who are under 26 years of age, eligible adults with complex hearing needs, and Aboriginal and Torres Strait Islanders over 50 years of age: *Australian Hearing* (n 477) 11.

provide commercial hearing services under the Voucher Program (a commercial voucher hearing service market where Australian Hearing competes with private hearing services providers).[957] Australian Hearing should comply with the Australian government's competitive neutrality policy and is subject to competitive neutrality complaints.

477. In 2017, two complaints against Australian Hearing were lodged to AGCNCO by an individual hearing care services business and the Hearing Business Alliance (HBA) (representing small to medium, privately-owned businesses that provide hearing care services). One of the concerns raised by the complaints was a CSO-related issue, which is relevant to this section as CSO is one component of public interest factors mentioned in the CPA.

478. Firstly, the complaint questioned whether Australian Hearing should be the sole provider of the government's CSO for hearing services in serving clients under the National Disability Insurance Scheme (NDIS). This issue was found to be a broader government policy decision and outside the realm of the AGCNCO. Secondly, the complaint questioned whether Australian Hearing should be competing with the private sector in the commercial voucher market.[958] The AGCNCO noted that

> competitive neutrality policy is not aimed at inhibiting or prohibiting government businesses from competing with their private sector counterparts. Rather, it aims to promote efficient competition between public and private businesses. ... Indeed, given that the standard of living of all Australians is ultimately dependent on how productively we use our resources, that standard of living is best served by having the most efficient users of those resources supplying goods and services. Whether those most efficient and most productive businesses are private or government owned is irrelevant.[959]

479. Finally, the complaint questioned whether government funding for Australian Hearing's CSO operations had been used to cross-subsidise its commercial voucher business activities.[960] The AGCNCO found that this complaint was not substantiated. In particular, the AGCNCO did a market study and found that there are generally three channels to deliver the hearing services in the Australia market. The first is community service obligations channel,[961] which

957 ibid 12.

958 ibid 14 (emphasis added).

959 ibid 35.

960 ibid; in other words, whether government funding for CSO activities is subsidising Australian Hearing's commercial activities.

961 Community service obligations channel is a component of the Government's Hearing Services Program (administered by the Department of Health) which provides subsidised hearing services and assistive hearing technology to eligible patients, including individuals who are under 26 years of age, eligible adults with complex hearing needs, and Aboriginal and Torres Strait Islanders over 50 years of age.

accounted for about 8 per cent of total market revenue in Australia and where the services were delivered solely by Australian Hearing. The second channel is voucher services,[962] which accounted for about 60 per cent of total market revenue in Australian and where the services were delivered through some 300 approved service providers and 13 device manufacturers. The third channel is the private market, which accounted for about 31 per cent of total market revenue and where the hearing services and assistive hearing technology were delivered to consumers at a market-determined price. Australian Hearing was involved in two channels to deliver the hearing service in the Australia market. However, Australian Hearing did not cross-subsidise its commercial voucher operations with the government funding for its CSOs because it employed an activity-based costing (ABC) method to measure the cost and ensure that only expenses related to a particular commercial or CSO activity are allocated to that activity. Under the ABC approach, all costs associated with Australian Hearing's voucher operations were identified and paid for by the respective revenue or funding associated with that activity. Additionally, the delivery of CSOs by Australian Hearing was subject to regular monitoring. The AGCNCO was 'satisfied that Australian Hearing's cost allocation model and the regular scrutiny of its CSO monitoring reports are sufficient to prevent the cross-subsidisation of its voucher business with CSO funding.'[963]

480. In general, the case study of the Australian Hearing suggests that the application of competitive neutrality policy does not challenge a government's decision on the provision of community service obligations as long as these are funded in a transparent manner and subject to ongoing regulatory monitoring.

Approaches to Applying the Public Interest Test

481. There are generally two approaches to applying the public interest test in Australia: the *ex-ante* approach and *ex-post* approach. The key difference between the two approaches will be examined in the section below.

Ex-Ante Approach of Public Interest Test

482. This approach assumes that the public interest test is designed to be an *ex-ante* requirement for the implementation of competitive neutrality policy. Under this enforcement approach, protecting the public interest is, arguably, maximised when individual governments are obliged in each case to conduct public interest tests *before* applying competitive neutrality to their significant SOEs. Put differently, under the *ex-ante* approach, the public interest test is needed in any government decisions on the implementation of competitive neutrality policy. As noted by Ed Willett and Deborah Cope, the *ex-ante*

962 Voucher services channel is a component of the Hearing Services Program (also administered by the Department of Health) which provides subsidised hearing services and assistive hearing technology to eligible clients who are predominantly pension concession cardholders.

963 *Australian Hearing* (n 477) 26.

approach of the public interest test places the burden of 'demonstat[ing] the implementation of competitive neutrality will benefit … the community'[964] on supporters of competitive neutrality policy. As a result, the *ex-ante* approach to the public interest test may constitute a hurdle for the implementation of competitive neutrality.[965] In particular, the implementation cost under the *ex-ante* approach will inevitably increase because the public interest test often involves matters like documentation and consultation with affected parties. This increased implementation cost for government may lead to less application of competitive neutrality policy in practice as the cost of implementation may outweigh its benefits.

Ex-Post Approach of Public Interest Test

483. This approach assumes that the public interest test is designed to be an *ex-post* review process for the implementation of competitive neutrality. Under the *ex-post* enforcement approach, the application of competitive neutrality policy is maximised in the sense that individual governments are obliged to apply competitive neutrality policy to their significant SOEs *unless* the relevant party (the governments or its SOEs) can establish that the application of that policy will undermine the public interest. Put differently, under the *ex-post* review approach, the public interest test applies only in exceptional circumstances (i.e. when there is a potential conflict between the application of competitive neutrality policy and the government's policy objectives) rather than serving as a standard procedure in the *ex-ante* approach noted above.

484. In contrast to the *ex-ante* public interest test approach, the *ex-post* approach reflects a strong preference on the implementation of competitive neutrality policy because it places the burden of demonstrating that the implementation of such policy will undermine the public interest on parties (governments or their SOEs) who seek to be exempted from competitive neutrality policy. Consequently, the potential implementation cost of competitive neutrality under the *ex-post* approach is less than that of the *ex-ante* approach. This reduced implementation cost could potentially lead to more implementation of competitive neutrality policy in practice. However, it has been argued that the application of the public interest test in an *ex-post* manner may restrict the ability of individual governments to evaluate social and equity issues effectively.[966] The *ex-post* approach may also increase the possibility of social or environmental matters being downplayed, given these are generally difficult to quantify or value.[967] An example is helpful to glimpse what constitutes public interest for the purposes of competitive neutrality policy and how the *ex-post* approach works in practice.

964 Ed Willett and Deborah Cope, 'A New Competitive Neutrality' (2018) 25 CCLJ 280, 297.

965 ibid 298.

966 Quiggin (n 337) 34.

967 Morgan, Bai and Bhasker (n 340) 256.

Pelican Park Recreation Centre in Victoria

485. In the state of Victoria, Pelican Park Recreation Centre ('the Centre') has been owned and operated by the Mornington Peninsula Shire Council ('the Council') since 2003. The Centre provides a range of activities and services including swimming classes, group fitness activities, gym access, occasional childcare services, and sales of merchandise (i.e. Pelican Park merchandise, a small range of swimwear and accessories, and snack foods).[968] A complaint was made in 2007 to the Victorian Competition and Efficiency Commission (VCEC, now the Office of the Commissioner for Better Regulation, OCBR), the Victorian government's competitive neutrality complaint-handling body, alleging that the Centre operated by the Council failed to comply with Victorian government's Competitive Neutrality Policy. Particularly, the complainant, the Mornington Peninsula Ratepayers Association (MPRA), questioned the decision (based on public interest test) made by the Council to not implement competitive neutrality policy to the business activities of the Centre.[969] While the MPRA's complaints touched on a number of issues, the issue regarding the public interest test is important and will be discussed below.

486. The VCEC found that the Centre as a whole was a significant business activity for the purpose of competitive neutrally and within the scope of competitive neutrality policy. However, under the Victorian government's Competitive Neutrality Policy, as summarised by Ed Willett and Deborah Cope:

> government organisations may decide not to implement competitive neutrality principles ... if they conduct a public interest test that includes public consultation and demonstrates that applying competitive neutrality would undermine other government policy objectives.[970]

487. The VCEC noted that the Council's decision to exempt the business activities of the Centre from the implementation of competitive neutrality policy (the full-cost pricing in particular) was documented in a public interest test process conducted in 2006. As a result of the test, the Council argued that the imposition of competitive neutrality policy to the business activities of the Centre would affect other public policy objectives that the Centre wished to achieve, such as 'ensuring access to facilities and services for all sectors of the community'.[971] It had thereby decided to continue to subsidise the services of the Centre to meet its community needs.[972]

---

968 Victorian Competition and Efficiency Commission, *Competitive Neutrality Complaint Investigation Final Report: Pelican Park Recreation Centre Mornington Peninsula Shire Council* (Investigation Report, 13 June 2008) (*Pelican Park Recreation Centre*).

969 Victoria Department of Treasury and Finance, 'Competitive Neutrality Policy' (September 2012), 7–9 <https://www.vic.gov.au/sites/default/files/2019-10/Competitive-Neutrality-Policy-2012.pdf>.

970 Willett and Cope (n 963) 297–98.

971 *Pelican Park Recreation Centre* (n 967) 5.

972 ibid. The Council in 2006 found that during 2004-05 the Centre required a subsidy if it was going to meet its public policy objectives.

488. The VCEC acknowledged that the 2006 public interest test demonstrated that the Council was aware of its competitive neutrality obligations. However, the VCEC found the public interest test conducted by the Council did not fully satisfy the requirements of competitive neutrality policy. In particular, for the public interest test to satisfy the requirement of competitive neutrality policy in Victoria, it should (at the minimum) meet the following three standards:

- clearly identify the policy objective(s) that is to be achieved and ensure that the policy objective(s) has official endorsement (for example, stated by a Minister, a local government body or in an official policy document);
- demonstrate that the achievement of the stated policy objective(s) would be jeopardised if the particular competitive neutrality measure under consideration was implemented; and
- determine the best available means of achieving the overall policy objectives, including an assessment of alternative approaches.[973]

489. The VCEC noted that, while the public interest test of the Council had clearly identified the policy objective and to some extent established that the identified policy objectives would be jeopardised due to the application of competitive neutrality, it did not fully explore any alternative approaches that could be used to achieve the overall policy objectives.[974] As a result, the VCEC found that the Council had breached the competitive neutrality commitments and recommended the Council conduct a revised public interest test regarding the operation of the Centre.

Section Conclusion

490. The inclusion of the public interest test within competitive neutrality policy reflects the desire of the Australian government to 'ensure that all relevant factors were assessed and that the value of economic reforms did not override other valid benefits to the community [as a whole].'[975] For example, the National Competition Council (NCC) explicitly noted that, when assessing the public interest, the social and environmental values carry no more or less weight than financial considerations.[976]

---

973 Victoria Department of Treasury and Finance (n 968) 8–9.

974 *Pelican Park Recreation Centre* (n 967) 17. The VCEC found that the public interest test document failed to include sufficient or relevant data about the preferred option or any alternatives necessary for participants in the public interest test process to provide meaningful feedback.

975 Rennie and Lindsay (n 7) 20. A similar view is shared by Deborah Healey and Ian Hanrahan, who observe that the CPA does not intend competitive neutrality to override the policy obligation of government agencies or the range of social, environmental, economic, and regional responsibilities of government agencies, which are all relevant to determining whether the application of competitive neutrality is in the public interest. See Healey, 'Australia' (n 352) 357; Ian Hanrahan, 'Becoming Competitively Neutral: Removing the Gilded Edge of Government Business' (2004) 12 TPLJ 19, 20.

976 National Competition Council (n 945) 20.

491. However, the discussion in this section shows that the scope of competitive neutrality policy in Australia can to some degree be influenced by the particular public interest test approach adopted by government. Arguably, the *ex-ante* public interest test approach provides maximum protection to public interest by requiring government to prove the application of competitive neutrality policy is in the public interest. By contrast, the *ex-post* approach of the public interest test provides minimal protection to public interest by requiring government (or sometimes SOEs) to prove that the implementation of competitive neutrality policy is not in the public interest. Nevertheless, as Ed Willett and Deborah Cope argue, 'the public interest test should be the sole determinant of appropriate exemptions from competitive neutrality policy.'[977]

7.2 Complaint-Handling Under Competitive Neutrality Policy

492. The aim of having a complaint-handling body in place, according to the NCC, is to 'provide a means for interested parties to pursue concerns regarding government policy insofar as it confers competitive advantages or disadvantages on government-owned businesses.'[978] In other words, the aim of having a complaint mechanism is to double-check the competitive neutrality-related decisions made by government in practice[979] and to provide remedial recommendations for parties who have suffered from a breach of competitive neutrality commitments.

493. Under the CPA, the governments agreed to set up a complaints mechanism to handle allegations of non-compliance with competitive neutrality commitments.[980] However, the method for setting up the complaints body (either within a government department or an independent unit) and the way that relevant complaint-handling bodies should conduct an investigation (i.e. the procedure it must follow) is not specified in the CPA and is decided by each government individually.[981] For example, the Better Regulation Victoria (BRV) operates as the Victorian government's competitive neutrality complaint-handling body, while the Independent Pricing and Regulatory Tribunal (IPART) is the responsible body in New South Wales.[982]

977 Willett and Cope (n 963) 283. The discussion in this section shows that government at each level have the flexibility to adopt a public interest test that suits their jurisdiction. For example, the *ex-post* approach of the public interest test is adopted in Victoria while the *ex-ante* approach of the public interest test is used in Queensland.

978 National Competition Council (n 398) 22.

979 For example, a complaint-handling body can address concerns over whether an SOE has not been exposed to competitive neutrality arrangements, or that it is not complying with the arrangements, or that the arrangements are not effective. Productivity Commission, 'Make a Competitive Neutrality Complaint' <https://www.pc.gov.au/competitive-neutrality/make-a-complaint#lodge>.

980 CPA (n 384) cl 3(8).

981 Healey and Smith (n 6) 229.

982 The Queensland Competition Authority (QCA) oversees competitive neutrality investigations in Qld; see <http://www.qca.org.au/project/our-role-competitive-neutrality/>; the Regulatory Reform Unit of the Department of

7.2.1 Potential Shortcomings of Complaint Mechanisms

494. It is clear that having a complaint mechanism in place is crucial as it provides an outlet for interested parties to express their dissatisfactions regarding competitive neutrality compliance by SOEs. The question as to whether competitive neutrality complaints mechanisms are working effectively in practice warrants further consideration.

495. Under competitive neutrality complaint mechanisms, governments are not obliged to remedy the infringement of competitive neutrality commitments,[983] and the complaint-handling body's recommendations are advocacy (rather than being binding outcomes of investigation). For example, in the ACT, the Independent Competition and Regulatory Commission (ICRC), notes:

> The ACT government is responsible for deciding how to respond to the Commission's [ICRC's] recommendations and is *not required* under the [ICRC] Act to implement any recommendations.[984]

496. Many scholars have been questioning the effectiveness of Australia's complaint-handling bodies for competitive neutrality policy. Alexandra Merrett and Rachel Trindade have accurately noted the issue of unenforceable recommendations of the complaint-handling bodies.[985] Deborah Healey and Rhonda L Smith also highlighted the shortcomings in the current competitive neutrality complaint-handling procedurals, noting that

> there is no need for government action following a successful claim in relation to competitive neutrality. There is no need for the government to formally justify this non-action.[986]

Treasury operates as the WA government's competitive neutrality complaint-handling body; see <https://www.wa.gov.au/organisation/department-of-treasury/regulatory-reform>; the Competition Commissioner operates as the SA government's competitive neutrality complaint-handling body; see <https://dpc.sa.gov.au/resources-and-publications/competitive-neutrality>; the Independent Competition and Regulatory Commission (ICRC) operates as the ACT's competitive neutrality compliant-handling body; see <https://www.icrc.act.gov.au/competition-issues/competitive-neutrality-and-government-regulated-activities>; the Office of the Tasmanian Economic Regulator operates its government's competitive neutrality complaint-handling body; see <https://www.economicregulator.tas.gov.au/other-industries/competitive-neutrality>; the Department of Treasury of the NT government operates as the competitive neutrality complaint-handling body within its jurisdiction; see <https://nt.gov.au/employ/money-and-taxes/economy/competitive-neutrality>; the Australian Government Competitive Neutrality Complaints Office (AGCNCO), a separate unit within the Productivity Commission, operates as the Australian government's competitive neutrality complaints mechanism; see <https://www.pc.gov.au/about/core-functions/competitive-neutrality>.

983 *Harper Review* (n 404) 262. The government or its SOE is not obligated to implement or even respond to any of the recommendations provided by the competitive neutrality complaint-handling body.

984 Independent Competition and Regulatory Commission (n 917) 6 (emphasis added). A similar statement can be observed in Queensland, for example, Queensland Competition Authority noted 'Our report provides advice and recommendations only, and *the Treasurer is not required to accept the advice or to take any action in response to our report,* other than to give us a response to the report as soon as practicable after receiving it.' See Queensland Competition Authority, 'Handbook: Making competitive neutrality complaint to the Queensland Competition Authority: State government' (September 2021) 20 <https://www.qca.org.au/wp-content/uploads/2021/11/handbook-for-competitive-neutrality-complaints-state-government.pdf>.

985 Alexandra Merrett and Rachel Trindade, 'Has Competitive Neutrality Run Its Course?' (September 2013) (13) The State of Competition 1–3 <http://thestateofcompetition.com.au/wp-content/uploads/2013/09/TSoC-Issue-13-competitive-neutrality.pdf>.

986 Healey and Smith (n 6) 239.

497. The lack of enforceable sanctions, both pecuniary and non-pecuniary, to government (and its SOEs) when breach of competitive neutrality obligation presents a major issue in the current competitive neutrality complaint-handling procedures.[987] For example, in 2011, the Queensland government's competitive neutrality complaint-handling body, the Queensland Competition Authority found that the waste and resources management business activity of the Sunshine Coast Regional Council breached competitive neutrality commitments and provided four recommendations in its report to address this breach.[988] The Council rejected 'both the reasoning and conclusions made in the report'[989] and no steps was taken to rectify the breach of competitive neutrality policy. Similarly, at the Commonwealth level, the AGCNCO found that PETNET Australia Pty Ltd (PETNET) breached the competitive neutrality policy (by failing to adhere to the commercial rate of return requirement).[990] PETNET is an SOE that manufactures and sells the most common PET radiopharmaceutical, fluoro-deoxy glucose, and is wholly owned by the Commonwealth government business, the Australian Nuclear Science and Technology Organisation (ANSTO). The AGCNCO's findings, however, did not receive any formal response from ANSTO/PETNET.

498. Secondly, as noted by Deborah Healey and Rhonda L Smith, the ongoing legal costs for competitive neutrality cases often fall on the complainant because there is no compensation available for the firms that have suffered loss as a result of breaches of competitive neutrality policy by government (and its SOEs).[991] In the PETNET case, for example, the complainant Cyclopharm Limited (the competitors of PETNET) received no compensation after the complaint was upheld.[992]

499. It follows that there are no follow-up monitoring procedures to ensure that steps has been taken by government or its SOEs to rectify the identified breaches. As a result, firms (or individuals) may hold back from initiating complaints, which may have contributed to the relatively small number of

---

987 Competition payments, as noted in Section 4.5, are made by the Australian government to state and territory governments under the National Competition Policy on the condition that reform promised by government at each level were satisfactory based on the assessment of National Competition Council (see also discussion in Section 7.2.3). Competition payments are considered a pecuniary sanction by this research because one crucial qualifier to receive the payment was to comply with competitive neutrality obligations. Thus, governments may lose competition payments if they failed to ensure ongoing compliance with competitive neutrality policy. Given the competition payments ceased around 2006, this pecuniary sanction for the breach of competitive neutrality obligation is largely missing.

988 Queensland Competition Authority, 'Final Report: Sunshine Coast Regional Council: Competitive Neutrality Complaint' (June 2012) <https://www.qca.org.au/wp-content/uploads/2023/02/qca-final-report-waste-sunshine-coast-competitive-neutrality-complaint-june-2012.pdf>.

989 Dan Kelley, 'Local Government Competitive Neutrality in Queensland' (Expert Symposium on Competitive Neutrality presentation, 28 October 2015).

990 *PETNET Australia* (n 482). For detailed analyses of the *PETNET* case, see Healey and Smith (n 6) 232–40.

991 Healey and Smith (n 6) 247.

992 ibid.

competitive neutrality complaints in Australia.[993] During 2015–20, only one complaint was investigated by the AGCNCO.[994]

500. Finally, the concern over the potential conflicts of interest when using the government department or agencies (instead of an independent body) to investigate SOEs (or government agencies' business activity) is raised by Alexandra Merrett and Rachel Trindade. For example, a very vivid comment by the authors on this point is that 'the gamekeeper is the very party who has been accused of poaching.'[995] Fortunately, the issue of conflicts of interest is recognised by *Harper Review*, which will be discussed in detail in the next section.

Recommendations of the Harper Review

501. The issue of conflicts of interest (when using a government body to investigate the breach caused by another government body) was addressed in the *Harper Review* recommendation. In particular, the *Harper Review* suggested that each state and territory government should 'assign ... responsibility for investigation of complaints to a body independent of government',[996] as currently some complaints are handled by regulators or departments within the government.[997] The Australian government supported this recommendation and encouraged 'those jurisdictions without independent complaint bodies to consider establishing such a body.'[998] However, this suggestion was only accepted by some governments (not all governments) in Australia. For example, in the Northern Territory, the complaint-handling body is not an independent authority because the Department of Treasury and Finance (DTF) remains the nominated complaint-handling body for competitive neutrality policy. The reason for this arrangement, according to the DTF, is that '[t]here are currently insufficient complaints to justify the establishment of a specialist body to deal solely with complaints.'[999]

502. The *Harper Review* also addressed the issue of the lack of formal responsibility of government (and its SOEs) to address the recommendations about competitive neutrality complaint-handling bodies. It suggested, for example, that governments around Australia should 'respond publicly to the findings of

993 For example, John Kettle seems to believe that the low level of complaints and investigations means it is just not worth the hassle and cost to raise complaints. See John Kettle, 'Competitive Neutrality, State Aid and Australia – Worth Reconsidering?' (2019) 93 CCLJ 545.

994 AGCNCO, 'Competitive Neutrality Investigations' <https://www.pc.gov.au/competitive-neutrality/investigations>.

995 Merrett and Trindade (n 984) 1–3. The Australia Newsagents' Federation Ltd shares similar concerns over the conflict of interest in setting the competitive neutrality complaint bodies within government. See Australia Newsagents' Federation Ltd, Response to Competition Policy Review – Draft Report September 2014 (17 November 2014) 7.

996 *Harper Review* (n 404) 268.

997 OECD (n 339) 16.

998 *Response to Harper Review* (n 445) 15.

999 Northern Territory Government, 'Competitive Neutrality' (18 March 2020) 12 <https://nt.gov.au/__data/assets/pdf_file/0003/469515/Competitive-Neutrality-Policy.pdf>.

the complaint investigation.'[1000] The Australian government in 2015 supported this recommendation, noting that it 'will include a requirement for portfolio ministers to publicly respond to findings of future complaint investigations undertaken by the Australian Government Competitive Neutrality Complaints Office (AGCNCO).'[1001] At the time of writing, only the Commonwealth government has committed to this formalised responsibility. However, the Commonwealth CN Policy Statement has not been updated to reflect this commitment at this stage.

503. The issue of the lack of sanctions when there is a breach of competitive neutrality obligations, and the issue of lack of follow-up monitoring of government's actions to rectify the identified breaches, however, were not addressed by the *Harper Review*. For example, in an attempt to increase the effectiveness of the competitive neutrality complaint-handle process, the *Harper Review* recommended a periodic disclosure obligation (to both government and complaint-handle body). SOEs are required to self-document their compliance with competitive neutrality policy in their annual reports (discussed in Section 4.5.4),[1002] while the complaint-handling bodies are required to report 'the number of complaints received, and investigations undertaken'[1003] on an annual basis to the proposed national competition body, the Australian Council for Competition Policy (ACCP).

504. However, the periodic disclosure obligation proposed by the *Harper Review* may have limited success in improving the effectiveness of enforcement processes. Firstly, as explained in Section 4.5.4, although requiring SOEs to incorporate a compliance statement in their annual report could improve the compliance transparency, it does little to ensure that actions are taken to rectify the identified breaches by the complaint body. Moreover, the proposed ACCP will not be created as the Australian government did not support this recommendation, which will be discussed in detail in Section 7.2.3 below. Without such a body, the complaint bodies in some states are not expected to reveal 'the number of complaints received, and investigations undertaken' on an annual basis. Even if the ACCP was created, the proposed transparency requirement by the *Harper Review* will have limited effect on improving compliance as the complaint bodies in some states are already required to publish the investigation report on the website for disclosure.[1004] The periodic disclosure requirement suggested by the *Harper Review* thus merely duplicates the existing reporting obligations of some complaint-handling bodies.

505. In conclusion, if the Australian government wishes to increase the effectiveness of the competitive neutrality complaint-handling process, it should

1000 *Harper Review* (n 404) 268 Recommendation 16.

1001 *Response to Harper Review* (n 445) 15.

1002 *Harper Review* (n 404) 268 Recommendation 17.

1003 *Harper Review* (n 404) 268.

1004 For example, Queensland Competition Authority requires a written report to be published on the website. See Queensland Competition Authority (n 983), 20.

consider conducting an inquiry to explore ways in which competitive neutrality breaches may be better remedied. The starting point for such an inquiry would be to investigate the possibility of setting up a follow-up monitoring procedure for successful claims. This inquiry should further explore ways of compensating firms that have suffered loss as a result of SOEs failing to adhere to their competitive neutrality obligations.

7.2.2 Complaint-Handling Procedures

506. As noted above, Australia adopts an administrative approach to handling competitive neutrality complaints, which means that the executive branch in each jurisdiction determines the procedure.[1005] The complaint-handling structure in each jurisdiction is broadly similar, but the specific requirements are slightly different. For example, the reason for initiating competitive neutrality complaints in each jurisdiction is largely the same – the alleged non-adherence to competitive neutrality principle by SOEs or its government owner.[1006] However, in some states, competitive neutrality complainants are required to contact SOEs or its government owner before making a formal complaint to complaint-handling body. By contrast, other states do not have this requirement. In addition, the complaint in some jurisdictions needs to be against SOEs that satisfy the significant business activities test[1007] while the complaint in other jurisdictions can be against business activities of all SOEs (regardless of such activities satisfied the significant test or not).[1008]

Initiating Complaints

507. In general, competitive neutrality complaints body do not have rights to launch an investigatation without a complaint. Some jurisdictions in Australia require the competitive neutrality complainant to be a competitor while others do not. In NSW, the complaint 'must be made either by the actual or potential competitor.'[1009] Similarly, Queensland requires the complainant to be *either* a competitor in competition with an SOE in a market *or* a person (or a business) affected by the alleged competitive advantage of the SOEs.[1010] By contrast, at the Commonwealth level, any person or entity can initiate a competitive neutrality complaint. However, the complaint-handling bodies

1005 For a list of complaint-handling bodies in each state, territory, and Commonwealth government, see footnote 981.

1006 Queensland Government Treasury, 'Queensland's Competitive Neutrality Complaints Process' (March 2001) 5 <https://s3.treasury.qld.gov.au/files/ncp-complaints.pdf>; Office of the Tasmanian Economic Regulator (n 929); Independent Competition and Regulatory Commission (n 917).

1007 Queensland Competition Authority (n 983), 12.

1008 For example, at the Commonwealth level, SOEs that fail to satisfy the 'significant business activity' test can still be the subject of competitive neutrality complaints. Commonwealth CN Policy Statement (n 375) 20.

1009 See New South Wales Treasury, 'NSW Government Policy Statement on the Application of Competitive Neutrality' (January 2002) 18 <https://www.treasury.nsw.gov.au/sites/default/files/pdf/TPP02-1_Policy_Statement_on_the_Application_of_Competitive_Neutrality_Policy_and_Guidelines_Paper.pdf>.

1010 Queensland Government Treasury (n 1005) 11; Queensland Productivity Commission (n 1003) 3.

in the Commonwealth can reject an unrelated complaint if the complaints are 'made by someone with an insufficient interest in the matter of the complaint.'[1011]

508. It is straightforward that the person or business that suffers directly from the alleged breach of competitive neutrality will have an incentive to make a complaint. A question worth considering is whether a third (unrelated) party should be able to initiate a competitive neutrality complaint. Based on the current complaint procedures in Queensland, a complaint initiated by the non-related third-party will be rejected.[1012] By contrast, a complaint initiated by a non-related third-party may be accepted in the ACT as long as the costs of investigation are being paid by the complainant.[1013]

509. Complaints initiated by third parties, in my opinion, should be allowed in the current competitive neutrality complaint-handling procedures because it will bring additional oversight to the implementation of competitive neutrality policy by government. In particular, as discussed in Section 7.2.1, there is currently no compensations available for competitive neutrality complainants even when the complaint has been substantiated. If a non-related third party is willing to devote time and money to ensure that government and its SOEs are complying with competitive neutrality policy, there seems little harm for a complaint-handling body to respond to the suspected breaches brought by third parties.

510. Additionally, some jurisdictions, like Tasmania and Queensland, require the complainant to discuss the competitive neutrality concerns with the relevant SOE or its government owner before making a formal complaint (in writing) to the complaint-handling body.[1014] The complaint-handling body could refuse to investigate a competitive neutrality complaint if the complainant failed to do so. For example, in Queensland, one of the reasons that Queensland Competition Authority could refuse to investigate is 'the person making

---

1011 See Productivity Commission (n 978).

1012 Queensland Government Treasury (n 1005) 12. For example, the Queensland Treasury requires a person or business lodging a complaint with the Treasurer against an SOE to demonstrate they compete, or seek to compete, in the same market as the SOEs.

1013 Independent Competition and Regulatory Commission (n 917) 3. For example, in the ACT, anyone can make a complaint by issuing a reference to the Commission. A person who makes the complaint is a 'referring authority'. … A referring authority must pay the reasonable costs of an investigation as determined by the Commission.

1014 In the state of Tasmania, for example: 'A person may make a complaint to the Regulator if that person … has discussed that supposed contravention with the government body against which the complaint is made.' See Office of the Tasmanian Economic Regulator (n 929) 14.

Similarly, in the state of Queensland, a complaint is required to attempt to resolve the matter of complaint with the relevant state or local government agency. See Queensland Competition Authority (n 983), 12.

In NSW, complainants are obligated in the first instance to lodge a compalint with the Government business that is the subject of the complaint. If the complainants are not satisfied with the response, they may then request the Premier to refer their complaint to complaint body for investigation. See New South Wales Treasury, 'NSW Policy Statement on the Application of Competitive Neutrality' (January 2002) 18 <https://www.treasury.nsw.gov.au/sites/default/files/pdf/TPP02-1_Policy_Statement_on_the_Application_of_Competitive_Neutrality_Policy_and_Guidelines_Paper.pdf>.

the complaint has not made a genuine attempt to resolve the issue with the relevant local government before making a formal competitive neutrality complaint.'[1015]

511. Other jurisdictions, like the Commonwealth and ACT, do not have this requirement, but encourage the complainant to do so. In the ACT government, for example, potential complainants are encouraged to discuss their concerns with relevant SOEs (and/or complaint-handling body) as 'it may allow the matters to be resolved without the need for a formal investigation'.[1016]

Investigation of Complaints

512. After a formal complaint is made in writing, the complaint-handling body can decide whether to accept or reject the complaint. In general, complaint deemed as frivolous or vexatious will be rejected. A written decision by the complaint-handling body must be issued to the complainant regardless of whether the complaint is accepted or not. For example, the AGCNCO is required to provide written advice to the complainant outlining the reasons for not investigating.[1017] This disclosure requirement is important to ensure transparency and reduce the suspicion that the complaint-handling bodies within government may be favouring their own SOEs. However, that the level of transparency could be improved by requiring the complaint-handling body to publish and display their administrative decision (and reasoning) on why a complaint will not be investigated.

513. Once a complaint is accepted, the complaint-handling body generally has great flexibility to investigate in terms of methods and time fame. For example, the ICRC can investigate through 'interviews, public hearings, public submissions or simply data gathering and analysis.'[1018] The time frame to finish the investigation is often indicative and will depend on the specific case. For example, it may take up to six months in Queensland to complete a competitive neutrality investigation (from when the notice of investigation is sent).[1019] IPART has 10 weeks to investigate and report on the complaint.[1020]

514. This section revealed the administrative procedures adopted in Australia to resolve competitive neutrality disputes. It covers the basis for initiating complaints, who can participant in the complaint process, and the general

1015 Queensland Competition Authority, 'Handbook: Making competitive neutrality complaint to the Queensland Competition Authority: local government' (September 2021) 21 <https://www.qca.org.au/wp-content/uploads/2021/09/handbook-for-competitive-neutrality-complaints-local-government.pdf>.

1016 Independent Competition and Regulatory Commission (n 917) 4.

1017 Productivity Commission (n 978).

1018 Independent Competition and Regulatory Commission (n 917) 5.

1019 Queensland Productivity Commission, 'Guidance note: Queensland Productivity Commission's Process for Competitive Neutrality Complaints' (2018), 4.

1020 Independent Pricing and Regulatory Tribunal (IPART), 'Competitive Neutrality' <https://www.ipart.nsw.gov.au/Home/About-IPART/competitive-neutrality>.

investigation methods and timeframe used by complaint-handling bodies. Australia's complaint-handling procedures discussed here could provide valuable information about the practical challenges of enforcing competitive neutrality policy. It is useful for China to consider when designing its own Chinese competitive neutrality policy (as discussed in Chapter 8).

7.2.3 Complementary Institutions for the Implementation of Competitive Neutrality Policy

515. The institutions mentioned in this section are regulatory bodies that have played or continue to play a role in facilitating the development of competitive neutrality in the context of Australia.

National Competition Council

516. The National Competition Council (NCC) was established as a national[1021] independent[1022] statutory authority[1023] to conduct competition research and provide recommendations. In its initial years (1995–2005), the NCC played a critical role in assisting governments to implement reforms agreed by all Australian governments under the CPA. As one component of the CPA was the competitive neutrality obligation, the NCC also had a formal role to assess and support the competitive neutrality reforms. For example, the NCC in 1997 published a report that elaborates some issues encountered when implementing competitive neutrality policy.[1024]

517. As part of its monitoring obligations, the NCC provided assessments on whether individual states and territories were eligible for competition payments (from the Commonwealth)[1025] based on their reform progress.[1026] For example, the assessment conducted by NCC in 2004 noted that some government sectors/business in Western Australia were not exposed to competitive neutrality arrangements at that time.[1027] There were seven assessments

1021 Though a national body, the NCC is created by federal legislation. NCC Commissioners are appointed by a vote of all states and territories from a list approved by the (non-voting) federal government, thus presenting a 'national' perspective. See Morgan (n 346) 122.

1022 ibid. The NCC is an independent agency made up of five private sector appointees from business backgrounds supported by 20–30 staff, most of whom are economists, and some lawyers. Many of the inaugural Council members were from academia, law, accounting, mining, and investment banking as well as presence from social welfare sector.

1023 Because of the 1995 Competition Policy Reform Act (Cth), the NCC was established under the TPA 1974 (now the CCA).

1024 National Competition Council (n 398).

1025 For example, according a press release from then Treasurer Peter Costello, competition payments to the states and territories in 2005–06 totalled approximately AUD 834 million: Treasurer, 'National Competition Policy Payments to States and Territories For 2005' (Press Release, No 113, 15 December 2005) <http://ncp.ncc.gov.au/docs/AST7As-%20Treasurers%20press%20release.pdf>.

1026 Sarah Sheppard, 'Privatisations: An Advocacy Role for the Competition Regulator?' (2015) 23 CCLJ 140, 143.

1027 National Competition Council, *Assessment of Governments' Progress in Implementing the National Competition Policy and Related Reforms: Volume One – Overview of the National Competition Policy and Related Reforms* (2003) xix <http://www.ncp.ncc.gov.au/docs/2004%20assessment.pdf>.

conducted by the NCC from 1995 to 2005.[1028] The NCC could recommend that the Commonwealth Treasurer reduce or defer the expected competition payment to a state if its assessment found that the state government failed to make sufficient progress to implement their competitive neutrality commitments.[1029] The monitoring role of the NCC, together with the regular competition payments, provided a strong incentive for jurisdictions to comply with their competitive neutrality commitment under the CPA.[1030]

518. However, the role of the NCC had only a 10-year life span and came to an end in 2006 when the National Competition Policy reforms were 'finalised or put aside unfinished' around 2005.[1031] Since then, the function of the NCC is not relevant to the implementation of competitive neutrality policy and will not be discussed further here.[1032]

The Proposed Australian Council for Competition Policy

519. A new national competition body, the Australian Council for Competition Policy (ACCP), was proposed by the *Harper Review* in 2015. It was designed to be a permanent body to promote the implementation of a competition policy agenda in a nation-wide manner (like the NCC).[1033] The proposed functions of the ACCP were to advocate for competition, recommend reform and report on government progress on reform.[1034] In terms of supporting the competitive neutrality policy, the *Harper Review* envisaged that the ACCP could oversee the government progress on the review of competitive neutrality policy, improve the transparency and effectiveness of the complaints processes through receiving an annual report from complaint mechanisms in each jurisdiction, and report on compliance with competitive neutrality principles in annual reports.[1035]

520. The establishment of proposed ACCP (as the experience of the NCC suggested) relied heavily on the willingness of state and federal governments

---

1028 The NCC's assessment reports for 1997, 1999, 2001, 2002, 2003, 2004 and 2005 are publicly available, and can be found at: <http://ncp.ncc.gov.au/pages/about>.

1029 There were three types of penalties: (1) Permanent deduction, the most serious type as it is irrevocable. (2) Specific suspension, it could be lifted by the NCC if a significant progress is made; otherwise it could be switched to permanent deduction by the NCC. (3) Pool suspensions, it could be lifted by the NCC if a specific progress is made. The NCC could also convert pool suspensions to permanent deduction if progress was unsatisfactory. See National Competition Council (n 1026) xxv.

1030 It is worth noting that the role of the NCC at the Commonwealth level was limited. In particular, the assessment of the NCC had no financial implications for the Commonwealth government because the Commonwealth government was not eligible for competition payments (nor subject to the penalty for non-compliance).

1031 The main function of the NCC is to recommend on the regulation of third-party access to services provided by monopoly infrastructure. See National Competition Council, 'About Us' <http://ncc.gov.au/about/about_us>.

1032 After 2006, the NCC's main function was limited to recommendations on the regulation of third-party access to services impeded by monopoly infrastructures.

1033 *Harper Review* (n 404) 75.

1034 ibid 453–54.

1035 ibid 268.

to set it up. However, the proposal for creating the ACCP was not generally welcomed by Australian governments (Commonwealth, state, and territory).[1036] Deborah Healey and Rhonda L Smith noted, for example, that 'the government ultimately did not adopt the recommendation for an independent jointly funded Australian Council for Competition Policy.'[1037] It is not entirely clear why governments were unwilling to support the establishment of the ACCP. One suspicion is that the state governments did not want more obligations following the establishment of the ACCP without any compensation (such as competition payments). As Stephen King noted,

> the ACCP will oversee government progress on reform. It will be an irritation to the government but, unlike the NCC, it will have no designated pool of funds to distribute to compensate governments for this irritation. … [T]his means that governments may see a potential ACCP as a political liability.[1038]

521. In summary, without the proposed ACCP body, some of the competitive neutrality recommendations proposed by the *Harper Review* (as noted in Section 7.2.2) will not be implemented appropriately or at all. For example, the ACCP was suggested by the *Harper Review* to oversee all Australian governments in their review of competitive neutrality policies.[1039] Without the ACCP's guidance, the progress of that review will be slow (or sometimes may not happen) in some jurisdictions.[1040]

7.3 Conclusion

522. This chapter has shown how Australia's competitive neutrality policy was implemented at a procedural level and has set the standard which China could replicate to some extent. The discussion shows that while Australia is considered to be the only country with operational competitive neutrality complaint-handling mechanisms,[1041] the scope and the effectiveness of those mechanism could be improved in practice.

1036 For example, the Queensland Government supports the ACCP overseeing Australian regulatory review processes on the basis that the ACCP's function will be to develop high-level principles and frameworks and monitor progress, with jurisdictions remaining responsible for detailed implementation: See Queensland Government, 'Queensland Government Response: Competition Policy Review Final Report' 11 <https://www.cabinet.qld.gov.au/documents/2015/jun/comprevresp/Attachments/Response.pdf>.

1037 Healey and Smith (n 6) 240.

1038 Stephen P King, 'Competition Policy and the Competition Policy Review' (2015) 48(4) Australian Economic Review 402, 408.

1039 *Harper Review* (n 404) 268.

1040 For example, Treasury has been responsible for the review of the Commonwealth government's competitive neutrality policy since March 2017. At the time of writing, this review has not been finalised.

1041 OECD, 'Regulating Market Activities by the Public Sector' (n 7) 45.

523. In particular, the application of competitive neutrality policy is narrowed by two tests: the significant government business activity test and the public interest test. The content of each test is dependent on the approach adopted by individual governments. For example, there are two ways to conduct a public interest test for the purpose of competitive neutrality policy: the *ex-ante* approach and the *ex-post* approach. While both public interest tests reflect the desire of the Australian government to align the application of competitive neutrality policy with public interest (or public benefit) considerations, the scope of competitive neutrality policy can be influenced by the public interest test adopted by government to some extent. Arguably, the *ex-ante* public interest test approach provides maximum protection to public interest by requiring government to prove the application of competitive neutrality policy is in the public interest. By contrast, the *ex-post* public interest test approach provides minimal protection to public interest by requiring government (or sometimes SOEs) to prove that the implementation of competitive neutrality policy is not in the public interest.

524. Moreover, although the non-legislative competitive neutrality complaint-handling mechanism is working, its effectiveness has been questioned by scholars on several grounds. Firstly, governments under competitive neutrality complaint mechanisms are not liable to implement recommendations of the complaint-handling body. Even if a government decided to act on a complaint body's recommendation, there is no time frame or follow-up monitoring procedures in place to indicate how long the government should take to rectify its breach of competitive neutrality obligation and whether its actions have rectified the identified breaches successfully. Secondly, the government can ignore the recommendations from the complaint-handing body without justification even when the complaint is upheld. Finally, while firms may decide to initiate a complaint and use the current complaint-handling body as a means to remedy the breaching of competitive neutrality commitments by SOEs, there is no compensation available for firms that have suffered loss as a result of breaches of competitive neutrality. The limitations on the current complaint handling process identified above may have contributed to the relatively low number of complaint cases in practice, and calls for improvement in the whole complaint-handling process in Australia.

525. Finally, the institution that has played or continues to play the role of facilitating the development of competitive neutrality policy in Australia is the NCC, while the competition regulator, the ACCC, continues to have little involvement in competitive neutrality policy. Prior to 2005, the NCC had been the main institution in Australia overseeing competitive neutrality policy compliance though competition payments, in accordance with the CPA. The NCC's role has diminished since 2005 as the competition payments have run out. As a result, an oversight body for competitive neutrality compliance is largely missing in Australia. Efforts of tasking the ACCP, the body proposed by the *Harper Review*, to fulfil the oversight role of the NCC in relation to

competitive neutrality have not been adopted by governments. The issue of the lack of a national body to oversee competitive neutrality policy compliance remains unchanged.

526. Based on the Australia's implementation approach and potential shortcomings identified in this chapter, the following chapter will discuss whether it is possible for China to mirror the administrative approach adopted in Australia to implement competitive neutrality policy while avoiding the potential shortcomings identified in the current complaint-handling mechanism in Australia.

CHAPTER 8

MAKE COMPETITIVE NEUTRALITY HAPPENING IN THE CHINESE LEGAL SYSTEM

The full adoption of competitive neutrality would make a big difference to the acceptability of SOEs (State-Owned Enterprises) internationally.

Allen Fels[1042]

527. This concluding chapter has two aims. The first aim is to highlight the need for China to adopt measures to safeguard a level playing field between SOEs and non-SOEs. The second aim is to lay out reform proposals for the AML and to provide policy recommendations (or issues for policymaker to consider) to ensure a level playing field between SOEs and non-SOEs in mainland China. The proposed reforms and measures, if adopted by the Chinese government, could not only boost the competitiveness of Chinese firms, especially SOEs, in the international market, but could also improve long-term economic efficiency and ultimately bring benefits to consumers.

8.1 Why Competitive Neutrality is Needed in China

528. As argued in Chapter 3, the market presence of Chinese SOEs has increased after several rounds of reforms. The question of whether these Chinese SOEs are competing based on efficiency rather than on their government ownership and their connection with the Party has become a significant one in the

1042 Kirsty Needham, 'China's New Australian Buzzwords to Counter Trump', *The Sydney Morning Herald* (17 October 2018) <https://www.smh.com.au/business/the-economy/china-s-new-australian-buzzwords-to-counter-trump-20181016-p50a1c.html>.

context of China. As argued in Chapter 4, in the absence of a competitively neutral environment, SOEs can reduce allocative efficiency by relying on their government ownership-generated advantages to take business from more efficient firms in the market. The competitive advantages enjoyed by Chinese SOEs due to government ownership and political connections have the potential to undermine allocative efficiency, as discussed throughout Chapter 5. For example, Chinese SOEs with better access to bank loans and lower borrowing costs due to government ownership could price lower than more efficient competitors in the market and undercut these competitors in the competition process. Markets that allow less efficient SOEs to survive by relying on government ownership-generated competitive advantages are unlikely to be economically efficient.[1043]

529. To ensure that competition between SOEs and non-SOEs is based on efficiency (rather than on who can benefit from government ownership and political connections), strong competition law enforcement (which effectively addresses the anti-competitive conduct of SOEs) and carefully crafted competitive neutrality policy should be adopted in China. The rationale for this argument is based on the experience of Australia, as highlighted in Chapters 4 and 7, which effectively enforced competition law and carefully drafted competitive neutrality policy to ensure competition between SOEs and non-SOEs is based on efficiency.

530. By analysing the extent to which Chinese competition law and competition policy applies to Chinese SOEs, this research argues (in Chapter 6) that the Chinese competition law (the AML) and the Fair Competition Review System (FCRS) cannot address all aspects of competitive neutrality concerns caused by SOEs (identified in Chapter 5), leaving the issue of the lack of competitive neutrality between SOEs and non-SOEs unaddressed in the market of China.

531. Adopting tools to ensure SOEs compete based on efficiency will greatly benefit China, a country with a substantial number of SOEs active in the competitive market. Having effective AML enforcement and a Chinese competitive neutrality policy in place will bring increased domestic competition between SOEs and non-SOEs. This strong domestic competitive environment brought by the AML and competitive neutrality policy should put pressure to companies, particularly SOEs, to improve their production efficiency through innovation, and ultimately toughen them for the international market. The protection of SOEs from competition at home, on the other hand, may make them less likely to succeed in the international market. For example, research

1043 As Massimo Motta explains, 'the willingness of national governments to allow domestic firms to "go bigger" in the belief that this will help them be more successful' carries the risk of 'allow[ing] inefficient firms to survive at the expense of more efficient ones.' See Motta (n 69) 29–30. Generally, a competitive market is considered the best possible way to increase economic welfare by ensuring that goods and services are delivered at the lowest possible cost.

conducted by Michael Porter suggests that the competitiveness of a country is associated with

> the capacity of its industry to innovate and upgrade. Companies gain advantage against the world's best competitors because of pressure and challenge. They benefit from having strong domestic rivals, aggressive home-based suppliers, and demanding local customers.[1044]

532. In this sense, embracing competitive neutrality policy in China, in the long term, could help Chinese SOEs to become more successful and achieve the goal of being 'bigger, stronger and more competitive'[1045] in the market.

8.2 How AML can Promote Competitive Neutrality in China

533. The findings in Chapter 5 highlight three limitations within the current competition law regime in relation to safeguarding the level playing field between SOEs and non-SOEs in China. The first limitation is that the different interpretations of Article 8 impede the regulatory certainty of the AML when it comes to Chinese SOEs. The second limitation is that sectoral legislation potentially creates exemptions from the application of the AML to SOEs in regulated sectors. Thirdly, while the AML enforcement cases involving SOEs exist, the competition authority faces more challenges enforcing against SOEs because of their government ownership or political position.

8.2.1 Removing Article 8

534. Although the AML Amendment 2022 did not make any change in relation to Article 8, this research respectfully recommends removing Article 8 from the AML to reduce the confusion that some SOEs are outside its reach, as explained in Chapter 6. Particularly, as Chapter 3 revealed, Chinese SOEs (particularly competitive SOEs) are likely to be more active in the market of China. Chapter 5 reinforced the position that without a competitively neutral environment, Chinese SOEs can be advantaged (or disadvantaged) by their government ownership and sometimes political position, thereby taking business away from more efficient competitors. Chapter 6 identified that one of the reasons that the current AML is perceived to protect Chinese SOEs is because of the different interpretations of Article 8. Applying the AML equally to SOEs and private firms, as argued in Chapter 6, would

1044 Michael Porter, *On Competition* (HBR Press 2008) 171.

1045 Xi Jinping (n 1).

assist with the creation of a level playing field between SOEs and non-SOEs in the market because it would ensure greater neutrality in the regulatory environment, as highlighted by the comparative analysis of Australia's competition law reform experience in Chapter 4. Accordingly, to keep up with the increasingly profit-driven Chinese SOEs (because of current reform, as noted in Chapter 3), it is essential from a competitive neutrality perspective to make a clear stand that SOEs operate under the same AML as other market players.

535. To achieve this aim, this research suggests deleting Article 8 in order to provide greater clarity of the AML. Removing Article 8, rather than changing its wording, would be easily achieved as it would not significantly change the structure of the AML.[1046] Such a reform would also send a strong signal to all SOEs in the market that anti-competitive conduct, regardless of the ownership of the firm or sector in which it operates, will be prosecuted under the AML.

8.2.2 Review Exemptions in Relation to SOEs in the AML

536. The second recommendation in relation to the AML is to re-evaluate the possible exemptions available to SOEs. Based on the principle of the *lex specialis*, as discussed in Chapter 6, sectoral laws that operate at the same level of hierarchy as the AML may permit exemptions from the application of the AML for certain conduct. This is relevant because the government ownership and political position of SOEs allows them to shape the formulation and implementation of the sectoral legislation to their own preference, which could make certain anti-competitive conduct of SOEs lawful under the sectoral legislation and thus escape the application of AML. While further empirical cases on how Chinese SOEs can exert influence over sectoral legislation are needed, the discussion in Chapter 4 has revealed that, in Australia, state and territory SOEs were found to use their links with government owners to take advantage of the exemptions which could be authorised by state and territory statutes. To achieve the universal application of the competition legislation in Australia, the *Hilmer Review* suggested tightening the statutory exemptions by imposing a timeframe on the exemptions and by requiring exemptions to show public interest.

537. In stark contrast to the detailed guidelines in relation to statutory exemptions in Australia, there are currently no guidelines available in China to review the exemptions authorised by sectoral legislation. Granted, sectoral legislation exemptions in China are difficult to discover in a systematic manner, it is

1046 Wang Xiaoye also argues that Article 7 (now known as Article 8) of the AML should be deleted because it has never been applied in practice and is unlikely to be applied in the future; the Article will also be an obstacle to the promotion of competition policy in China, especially the FCRS. See Wang Xiaoye (n 562) 12.

important nonetheless to recognise that the sectoral legislation exemptions represent a substantive limitation to the application of the AML. The risk of sectoral legislation being used to grant exemptions that favour specific interests (i.e. SOEs) should not be underestimated. Stemming from the insights gained from the competition law reform experience in Australia, this research advocates for the SAMR within its authority to issue supplementary guidelines to refine and narrow the scope of immunity which may be afforded by sectoral legislation.

8.2.3 Improve Anti-Monopoly Law Enforcement in Relation to SOEs

538. To advocate neutral enforcement of the AML, one needs to be aware of the pressure that competition authorities face when taking cases against Chinese SOEs compared to non-SOEs. Chapter 6 discussed how the government ownership and privileged political positions of SOEs can pose challenges to investigations. For example, in the case of a merger, challenges can arise when establishing the need for notification of a merger when the merging SOEs are all controlled by SASAC of State Council which has given its permission. Another challenge for the competition authority is whether to fine a merger involves SOEs for not notifying when the merger decision is being approved by another agency. In addition, by their privileged political positions and government ties, SOEs may have the means to interfere AML investigation proceedings through implicit government pressure.

539. While the newly upgraded deputy ministerial level State Anti-Monopoly Bureau (SAMB affiliated with SAMR) has been appraised by many competition law scholars (as explained in Section 6.2.1), it will not become an independent agency (like the ACCC in Australia) and cannot be immune from bureaucratic hierarchy and interference of SOEs. It is thus unrealistic to expect SAMB to completely ignore the additional challenges when taking a case against an SOE. This research argues that when a case is taken against an SOE, the most effective way to minimise potential conflict faced by SAMB is to improve the enforcement transparency and streamline procedures by issuing more detailed implementation rules for the AML. Moreover, transparency can help to increase the predictability of the decision-making of SAMB to reduce interference from other government departments or SOEs. For example, the current merger enforcement transparency process would be significantly improved if a written decision on the cleared merger was routinely published or published on request. In addition, SAMB ought to issue a detailed guideline on how the non-competition factors, such as the public interest provision in Article 34 of the AML, are being considered and balanced in the merger assessments stage. This guideline would to some extent reduce the risk of pressure to accommodate special interests during the investigation stage.

8.2.4 The Question of Introducing Competitive Neutrality via the AML

540. As detailed in Chapter 6, the FCRS has been legislated into the AML in 2022, which reads that the

> State shall establish a fair competition review system. Administrative authorities and organisations authorised by laws or regulations to perform public functions shall conduct a fair competition review when formulating regulations that involve economic activities of market players.[1047]

541. The detailed implement rules of FCRS also specifies the liability for government officials that failed to compliance with the FCRS.[1048] Competition authorities currently do not have a formal role in the FCRS. SAMR, however, become involved in the FCRS by providing staff training programs for the policy-making bodies of the governments[1049] or by providing recommendations to the policy making bodies directly if non-compliance of FCRS has been identified.[1050]

542. Incorporating the FCRS into the AML is an important move that China made in achieving competitive neutrality because the FCRS provides a structured approach to neutralising the regulatory environment between firms, including SOEs and their non-SOE rivals (as discussed in Chapter 6). Legislating the FCRS into the AML also shows a preference for using legalistic approach to promote a competitive environment in China. This preference, as discussed in Chapter 2, reflects China's strong reliance on the AML to promote competition. In contrast to the preference of using competition legislation, Australia prefers to use competition policy to promote competition, as discussed in Chapter 6. Competition policy in China is less understood by both government and the public, and has long been interpreted as equivalent to the AML.

543. The observation above has led this research to consider whether the AML should incorporate competitive neutrality as a provision to address the competitive neutrality concerns caused by the presence of SOEs in the competitive market. The research holds the position that introducing competitive neutrality by way of legislation is challenging at the current stage for the following reasons.

544. Firstly, the AML punishes defendants for breach of its provisions by imposing fines or making rectification suggestions to superior government agencies (in the case of administrative monopoly). Legislating competitive neutrality

1047 AML (n 65842) art 5.

1048 FCRS Implementation Rules 2021 (n 843) art 26.

1049 For example, SAMR designed a national FCRS educational training program (in Chinese公平竞争审查业务培训班), which trained about 100 staff in 2021. See 国家反垄断局 [National Anti-Monopoly Bureau] (n 786) 72.

1050 李青 [Li Qing] (n 870).

in the AML can enhance compliance with such policy because of the deterrence effect of legal sanction of AML. However, one should not overlook the possible concerns about the effectiveness of legal sanction when dealing with Chinese SOEs. Particularly, imposing the financial sanctions (i.e. fines) on SOEs amounts to transferring money from one government agency to another. The administrative correction tool under the AML[1051] (available to administrative monopoly) is not useful when discipline SOEs. Administrative sanction under the AML relies on bureaucratic hierarchy in the administration system (as discussed in Chapter 6). This administrative sanction however may not be directly applicable to SOEs because SOEs are often independent from the government and should not be treated as a part of Chinese government agencies (as Chapter 2 discussed).

545. Secondly, the inclusion of competitive neutrality provisions in the AML may raise enforcement issues. Inclusion of competitive neutrality provisions will extend the reach of the AML and consequently the reach of the competition enforcement agencies towards SOEs. This extending reach of competition authority may conflict with the current jurisdiction of the regulator of SOEs, SASAC, as the merger enforcement records revealed in Chapter 6. Theoretically, SOEs that violate the competitive neutrality obligations under the AML may be directed or approved by SASAC. For example, an SOE may cross-subsidise its public service and commercial activities under the direction of SASAC, but such conduct may prima facie violate the competitive neutrality principle under the AML because it can distort the playing field. Under this scenario, a breach of the competition neutrality obligation is not the result of an SOE's conduct but of a regulation decision by SASAC. To remedy this breach, there is a potential risk that the competition authority may need to intervene with the regulatory action of other government authorities if the competitive neutrality principle is legislated in the AML.

546. Finally, the inclusion of competitive neutrality provisions in the AML means its enforcement authority is responsible for handling competitive neutrality complaints. Given the large number of SOEs in China, it is likely that the competition authority will receive a massive number of competitive neutrality complaints from individuals or firms who have been negatively affected by breaches. The investigation of competitive neutrality complaints will demand human resources from the competition authority, currently already understaffed (as illustrated in Chapter 6). The weight of the regulatory burden imposed on the Chinese competition authority to oversee such complaints is likely to be too heavy and thus make the competition authority the undesirable body to handle the competitive neutrality complaints.

547. This research therefore proposes that a non-legislative (competition policy) approach should be used as the primary means to introduce competitive

1051 AML (n 65) art 51.

neutrality in China rather than a legislative mechanism like the AML. Firstly, as Chapters 4 and 7 demonstrate, the implementation experience of competitive neutrality policy in Australia suggests that the competitive neutrality concerns caused by SOEs can be successfully remedied through competition policy (competitive neutrality policy). Particularly, Chapter 4 showed competitive neutrality policy has been introduced through national competition policy, which is implemented by administrative government in each jurisdiction by focusing on the widespread competitive neutrality advantages enjoyed by SOEs. Chapter 7 revealed that the application of competitive neutrality policy is a gradual process in Australia and relies heavily on the willingness of government.

548. Secondly, the Chinese government has shown a greater readiness to address government restraints on competition through policy means. For example, competition policy, as a fundamental element of China's economic policy, has been acknowledged by the Party and government.[1052] The implementation of the FCRS also shaped government attitude and raised awareness within Chinese government that competition policy can be used to address competitive restrain imposed by Chinese government.[1053]

549. The non-legislative competition policy approach for introducing competitive neutrality is considered preferable as it is less disruptive compared to the legislative means. A detailed proposal on how to incorporate competitive neutrality in China's competition policy system will be discussed directly in the section below.

8.3 Proposal for Competitive Neutrality Principle in Chinese Competition Policy

8.3.1 Rationale to Adopt Competitive Neutrality Principle in China

550. As argued in Section 8.1, the primary rationale for adopting competitive neutrality principles in China is market efficiency. However, the fairness rationale for adopting the competitive neutrality principle is worth discussing,

1052 For example, AML states that 'the State shall adhere to the principles of marketisation and the rule of law, *enhance the fundamental position of competition policy*, formulating and implementing competition rules that are compatible with the socialist market economy, improving macroeconomic regulation and establishing an integrated, open, competitive, and orderly market system' (emphasis added). See AML (n 842) art 4.

1053 As highlighted in Section 6.3.3, government restraint on competition was largely addressed through the application of the AML (via administrative monopoly provisions) until the FCRS. Yang JiaJia, from the Division of Fair Competition Review within SAMR, shares a similar view, noting: 'Fair competition review plays a vital role in competition advocacy, raising awareness in the market and deepening the understanding of fair competition among governments.' See Yang Jiajia, 'Briefing on the Implementation of the Fair Competition Review System' (Presentation to the 18th EU-China Competition Week, 19 March 2019) <https://competitioncooperation.eu/wp-content/uploads/2019/04/Day-2_Session-3_YANG-EN.pdf>.

especially in the context of China. As Chapter 6 explains, fairness is often associated with the question of whether competition policy is designed to protect the competitive process or competitors. Australia's competition policy, as explained in Chapter 4, is centred around market efficiency and is not designed to promote fairness by protecting certain types of competitors (non-SOEs) from being disadvantaged in comparison with SOEs.[1054] The prevailing thought underpinning this view can be observed in the *Harper Review*, which noted:

> The CCA [Competition and Consumer Act] (and competition policy more generally) is not designed to support a particular number of participants in a market or to protect individual competitors.[1055] …
>
> Ordinarily, competition law is not concerned with harm to individual competitors. Indeed, harm to competitors is an expected outcome of vigorous competition. Competition law is concerned with harm to competition itself – that is, the competitive process.[1056]

551. Chinese policymakers, however, argue that the adoption of the principle of competitive neutrality can protect Chinese small and medium-sized enterprises (SMEs). For example, Guiding Opinions on the Promotion of Healthy Development of Small and Medium-Sized Enterprises advocates operating 'according to the principle of competitive neutrality, to create a fair and convenient business environment, and to further spark the vitality of Small and Medium-Sized Enterprises.'[1057]

552. The main purpose of competitive neutrality policy, argued by this research, should not be interpreted to protect SMEs nor to discriminate against SOEs.[1058] The purpose of adopting competitive neutrality policy is to protect competition (or competitive process) by requiring that competition between SOEs and non-SOEs is based on efficiency rather than on who can benefit from government ownership and political connections. It seems the adoption of the competitive neutrality principle can to some degree benefit the development of Chinese SMEs. However, such an outcome is achieved through the increased

1054 Achieving fairness or equity, as argued in Chapter 4, should be understood as an outcome – rather than a goal – of competitive neutrality policy in Australia.

1055 *Harper Review* (n 404) 307.

1056 ibid 339.

1057 Guiding Opinions on SMEs (n 526) s 1.

1058 For example, Peng Huagang, then Deputy Secretary-General of SASAC (now Secretary-General of SASAC), stated in a press conference in 2018 that he advocates 'ownership neutrality' (rather than competitive neutrality) and is against 'discriminatory treatment of SOEs in the formation of international rules.' See 王希 [Wang Xi], '国务院国资委：反对在国际规则制定中给予国有企业歧视性待遇 [SASAC: Against Discriminatory Treatment of SOEs in the Formation of International Rules]' 新华网 [Xinhuanet] (15 Oct 2018) <http://www.xinhuanet.com/politics/2018-10/15/c_129971816.htm>.

competition resulting from the adoption of the competitive neutrality principle. For example, the adoption of debt neutrality can improve the allocation of bank loans in China, resulting in non-SOEs (such as SMEs) having more access to bank loans in practice. Thus, the rationale for adopting competitive neutrality principles in China should be based on market efficiency and it should not be altered to include market fairness (or the promotion of SMEs).

553. Inevitably, the implementation of competitive neutrality in China will require a tacit to accommodate SOE interests. Chinese SOEs, as the beneficiaries of the competitive advantages generated from government ownership and political connections, has incentives and resources to lobbying against the adoption of competitive neutrality policy in China. In particular, SOEs may retaliate against competitive neutrality by emphasising the potential negative impact on their competitiveness international. For example, although promoting debt neutrality will improve the allocation of resources in banking sectors, removing government guarantees (explicitly or implicitly) given to SOEs could affect their profitability, or could lead to bankruptcy and negatively impact employment rates and social stability.[1059] The term 'ownership discrimination' used by the Peng Huagang, the former deputy head of the SASAC, when discussing competitive neutrality signals some degree of resistance. Additionally, Chinese SOEs, like all the firms in the market, would prefer to face less competition than more, and adoption of competitive neutrality policy will expose them to greater competition pressure. However, this research argues that when promoting competition, concerns over the potential negative impact on a particular group of market player (i.e. SOEs) should not be used to downplay the detrimental influence on market efficiency and the cost to society as a whole by allowing inefficient SOEs to survive in the market.

8.3.2 Support from the Party and Government

554. While the FCRS and the AML can help to level the playing field between SOEs and non-SOEs to some extent, competitive neutrality rules are largely absent in China. In contrast to Australia's comprehensive competitive neutrality policy, discussed in Chapter 4 and 7, China currently does not have a functional equivalent to Australia's competitive neutrality policy. There is no instrument specifically established to preserve a level playing field between SOEs and non-SOEs.

555. Given the root cause of the competitive neutrality concerns in China is the government ownership and political ties of SOEs, as identified in Chapter 5, it is essential for both government owners and the Party to demonstrate the willingness to support the application of a competitive neutrality policy. Encouragingly, the Chinese government is considering the adoption of

1059 For example, the introduction of SOE reform from 1993 to 2002 (as noted in Chapter 3) brought on large-scale bankruptcies which led to rising unemployment (*Xiagang*). Workers were impacted by these reforms as most were not compensated.

the principle of competitive neutrality as reiterated in government reports, speeches, and media interviews. For example, in the March 2019 Report on the Work of the Government, Premier Li Keqiang stressed:

> We will follow *the principle of competitive neutrality*, so that when it comes to access to factors of production, market access and licenses, business operations, government procurement, public biddings, and so on, enterprises under all forms of ownership will be treated on an equal footing.[1060]

556. However, the real political will for adopting competitive neutrality is currently missing in China, as demonstrated by the lack of expression of such principle in official documents issued by the Party. The high-level commitment to the principle of competitive neutrality, as highlighted in Chapter 4, has contributed to the successful implementation of policy in Australia. Given the unique political environment, as highlighted in Chapter 2, the expression of willingness of the Party is the foundation for the implementation of any policies in China. For example, in 2013, the Party specifically expressed that 'fair competition'[1061] is one element of a modern market system, and that further reform would involve moves to 'tidy up and annul all sorts of regulations and methods that impede the national unified market and fair competition'.[1062] To help achieve this commitment made by the Party, the State Council in 2015 established the FCRS, which aims to reduce government regulations that restrict competition without justification (as discussed in Chapter 6).

557. Without the willingness of the Party, it is unlikely that China will formulate and adopt a functional competitive neutrality policy, especially since such a policy could potentially undermine the profitability of Chinese SOEs (at least in short term), which are at the heart of socialist market economy of China.

8.3.3 Elements of Competitive Neutrality Policy

558. To draft competitive neutrality policy, the Chinese government needs to develop a broad principle to identify the competitive neutrality advantages or disadvantages of Chinese SOEs. An inventory of competitive neutrality concerns caused by Chinese SOEs can be helpful to identify the main competitive neutrality issues that Chinese competitive neutrality policy should address. To develop this inventory, the Chinese government could set up a discussion program to provide maximum opportunity for all relevant parties to comment on the matter, including but not limited to sector regulators, industrial policy planners, competition authorities, representatives from both local and centra SOEs, competition experts and representatives from non-

1060 Li Keqiang (n 525) (emphasis added).

1061 CCCPC Reforms Decision (n 233) s 3.

1062 ibid s 3(9).

SOEs, foreign firms etc.[1063] However, the Chinese competitive neutrality policy does not need to target all the identified competitive neutrality advantages and disadvantages of Chinese SOEs in the proposed inventory. As Chapter 4 showed, Australia's competitive neutrality policy targeted only four types of advantages which are widespread and relatively easy to correct, such as debt advantages, regulatory advantages, tax advantages, and commercial rate of return advantages (although a list of competitive neutrality advantages, termed as 'net advantages' in Australia, was discovered by the *Hilmer Review*).

559. The Chinese government would need to decide which of the competitive neutrality concerns caused by Chinese SOEs should be addressed in its competitive neutrality policy. In essence, the targeted competitive neutrality concerns of SOEs forms the main content of the Chinese competitive neutrality policy. Chapter 5 mapped several types of competitive advantages enjoyed by Chinese SOEs as a result of government ownership and political connections, which are considered a breach of the competitive neutrality principle. These include regulatory advantages, easier access to land-use rights, better access to bank loans, and favourable bank lending rates.[1064] Based on the competitive neutrality advantages (and disadvantages) of Chinese SOEs identified in Chapter 5, this research proposes that regulators and legislators should consider the following elements for Chinese competitive neutrality policy: regulatory neutrality, debt neutrality, land neutrality, and a public interest test.

Regulatory Neutrality

560. The FCRS, as discussed in Section 6.5, can be considered as the starting point in promoting competitive neutrality in China as it targets the preferential treatment to business (including both SOEs and non-SOEs) in government regulations, which helps to level the regulatory environment between all market players. However, this research argues that the current FRCS cannot adequately address the preferential treatment to SOEs in regulations and a regulatory neutrality requirement in Chinese competitive neutrality policy is recommended to review the prima facie regulatory differences between SOEs and non-SOEs. For example, a regulatory neutrality commitment is proposed as follows:

> Policymakers should ensure, as far as practicable, that SOEs operate in the same regulatory environment as non-SOE competitors. Policymakers that choose to provide different regulatory treatment between SOEs and non-SOEs should demonstrate in writing why this different treatment is necessary.

1063 The EU Chamber of Commerce in China has expressed its position regarding how China can realise competitive neutrality across country. See European Union Chamber of Commerce in China, 'European Business in China Position Paper 2019/2020' (24 September 2019) <https://www.europeanchamber.com.cn/en/publications-archive/756/European_Business_in_China_Position_Paper_2019_2020>.

1064 The competitive neutrality disadvantages identified by this research include less discretion in managing operations because of the Party committee and higher disclosure standards of corporate social responsibility imposed by government regulation.

561. The current FRCS is limited when addressing the regulatory preferential treatment to SOEs for the following reasons. Firstly, the FCRS and regulatory neutrality commitment in Australia share some characteristics insofar as both are mechanisms put in place to level the regulatory environment. However, the focus of the FCRS is broader than the focus of the regulatory neutrality requirement under Australia's competitive neutrality policy. For example, the regulatory neutrality requirement under Australia's competitive neutrality (as noted in Section 4.5) has one specific focus, namely to subject SOEs to the same regulations[1065] to which private firms are normally subject in the same situation.[1066] The FCRS, by contrast, not only focuses on the preferential treatment of firms in regulations but also targets regulatory restrictions on competitive conduct such as setting maximum or minimum price of goods and services in government regulation[1067] and directly specifying 'that non-local business operators may not participate in specific local activities of bidding and bids' in government regulations.[1068] In Australia, the broader issues such as regulatory restriction on competitive conduct are generally addressed by other policies, like regulatory review.[1069]

562. Additionally, the effect of the FCRS in addressing regulatory advantages of SOEs is limited partially because the FCRS is not specifically enacted to ensure that the regulatory environment is neutral between SOEs and non-SOEs. For example, when the issue of regulatory neutrality arises under the competitive neutrality policy in Australia, as noted in Section 4.5.3, SOEs are required to either subject to the regulation or alternatively make a regulatory payment (notional or actual) that reflects its regulatory benefits. For example, Australian Hearing (as noted in Section 7.1.2) is required by the AGCNCO to make a regulatory neutrality payment (of around AUD 100,000 annually) to the Official Public Account to neutralise their regulatory advantage.[1070] The FCRS requires no adjustment payment from SOEs even when the favouring treatment of SOEs are detected in regulation. For example, when government policies that are found to have preferential provisions, as the case of Shanghai Government Office in Section 6.3.2 suggested, it often required the revision or abolition of such policy. Additionally, no provision in the FCRS specifically requires favourable treatment in government policy should not be provided to SOEs, even though the major beneficiaries of regulatory advantages are SOEs (as discussed in Chapter 6).[1071] Thus, it will be difficult

1065 Regulations here include those relating to the protection of the environment, and planning and approval processes.

1066 CPA (n 384) cl 3(4)(b)(iii).

1067 FCRS Implementation Rules 2021 (n 843) art 16 (4).

1068 ibid art 14 (3).

1069 CPA (n 384) cl 5(1). The regulatory review of Australia was the primary inspiration for the OECD Competition Assessment Toolkit (which offers guidance to policymakers on how to assess the competitive impact on new laws, regulations, and polices) adopted in 2006 as a model for other countries. See Duke (n 414) 12.

1070 *Australian Hearing* (n 477) Recommendation 2.1, 21. See also Australian Hearing *2017–18 Annual Report*, 21 <https://www.hearing.com.au/HearingAustralia/files/5c/5ce309ad-b082-4046-ba8d-cf813a66961e.pdf>.

1071 Healey (n 406) 198.

for Chinese governments to break the habit of granting favourable treatment to SOEs in government regulations when there is no specific regulation requiring them to do so.

563. Finally, as noted in Chapters 5 and 6, the shared interests between SOEs and governments often make SOEs (especially local SOEs) the main beneficiaries of government policies. However, this the FCRS cannot adequately address the regulatory advantages of SOEs granted by the local regulations. For example, as identified in Section 5.3, Chinese SOEs have three additional channels[1072] (unavailable to non-SOEs) to acquire land-use rights (LURs) in the primary market, which provides SOEs with better access to LURs. Policies that grant SOEs additional channels to acquire LURs are considered as preferential policies to specific business operators (SOEs in this context)[1073] and thus should be subject to the FCRS. Local government authorities can also issue preferential policies to SOEs, such as converting allocated LURs into shares of SOEs. However, the preferential policies issued by local authorities are not captured by the FCRS as it is deemed 'lawful' in the context of the FCRS. According to the FCRS Implementation Rules 2021:

> Preferential policies shall not be granted to specific business operators in violation of the law, including but not limited to any of the following circumstances: …
>
> Where the policy , *in the absent of laws and regulations or the provisions of the State Council serving as bases*, extends preferential policies to specific business operators in terms of access to elements such as land, labour, capital, technology, data, etc.[1074]

564. Therefore, without repealing the highest authority-issued policies granting SOEs additional channels to acquire LURs, the current FRCS cannot adequately address the competitive advantages of SOEs granted by the government regulations issued by local policy-making authorities.

Debt Neutrality

565. The Chinese government can choose to address the issue of easier access to bank loans and favourable bank lending rates by SOEs (identified in Chapter 5) in Chinese competitive neutrality policy. For example, it can mandate debt neutrality as part of Chinese competitive neutrality policy, which requires either SOEs to access loans on the same terms as the private sector or state-owned banks to provide loans on equal terms to both SOEs and non-SOEs.

1072 The three additional channels for SOEs to acquire LURs in the primary land market are: leasing land use rights (LURs) to SOEs; converting allocated LURs into shares of SOEs; and authorising selected SOEs to manage LURs.

1073 MLR Opinions (n 628).

1074 FCRS Implementation Rules 2021(n 843), art 15(3) (emphasis added).

566. Reform policies that aim to control preferential access to bank loans by SOEs have recently been implemented in China. The China Banking and Insurance Regulatory Commission (CBIRC), for example, announced policy measures in 2019 to require state-owned banks to increase loans to private borrowers by at least 30 per cent.[1075] It will take time to assess whether government control over the allocation of bank loans can effectively create a level playing field between SOEs and non-SOEs in the banking sector. Nevertheless, such policy measures (which aim to improve the allocation of bank loans between SOEs and non-SOEs) should be considered as part of Chinese competitive neutrality policy. Further, policy that aims to address the favourable bank lending rates by SOEs is currently absent in China. As observed in Chapter 5, the explicit and implicit government guarantees of SOEs can translate into preferential or below-market interest rates from state-owned banks,[1076] which lower the borrowing cost of SOEs, thus undercutting its non-SOEs rivals. Finally, existing policies such as those allowing loss-making (or zombie) SOEs to exit the market will need to work with those of debt neutrality to ensure a level playing field between SOEs and non-SOEs in the Chinese banking sector.

567. To make further progress towards a level the playing field in the Chinese banking market, Chinese competitive neutrality should be designed within a more integrated framework to pull all the components of debt neutrality together. This research proposes that debt neutrality policy in China should include the following elements:

568. Firstly, for banks, especially Chinese state-owned banks (as the providers of the bank loans), commitments to debt neutrality should require not only changing the banking system's lending preference to SOEs, but also to disclose the loan interest-rate data according to the ownership type of the borrowers. As Chapter 5 suggests, one of the difficulties in assessing whether and to what extent loan interest rates of SOEs are favoured because of their government ownership is the lack of loan interest data. Mandating banks, especially Chinese state-owned banks, to disclose such data will increase the transparency of lending rates and enable comparative analyses between SOE lenders and non-SOEs lenders. This mandatory disclosure of banks, for example, could be supervised by the People's Bank of China in its annual report.

569. Additionally, for Chinese SOEs (as the receivers of bank loans), complying with debt neutrality mandates should at the very least mean to calculate the difference in the current cost of borrowing (with implicit guarantees from its government owner) and the cost of borrowing without implicit government guarantees (i.e. for a private entity) under the same circumstances. This

---

1075 'China to Increase Bank Loans to Private Firms' *Xinhuanet News* (25 February 2019) <http://www.xinhuanet.com/english/2019-02/25/c_137849420.htm>. Gabriel Wildau, 'China Tells Banks to Increase Lending to Small Businesses' *Financial Times* (13 March 2019) <https://www.ft.com/content/e3a77c2e-4580-11e9-b168-96a37d002cd3>.

1076 OECD (n 30) 22.

requirement will make SOEs more aware of the actual cost of debt. A further step for SOEs to neutralise their preferential debt treatment, as observed in the practice of Australia,[1077] involves either making actual payments to the fiscal budget based on government-generated advantages or to make a notional adjustment to accounts to reflect the cost advantages associated with government ownership. Evidence from Australia indicates that managers of SOEs are responsible for making such debt adjustments in practice.[1078] Compared to Australia, Chinese SOEs are far more pervasive and many of the borrowing advantages enjoyed by SOEs are not only the result of SOEs' lower default risk, but also the better connections with government and the Party (as Chapters 3 and 5 explain).

570. Finally, Chinese SOEs have a strong incentive to resist debt neutrality reform as such reform will increase costs for SOEs. For example, some SOEs may find that its ability to compete is reduced as a result of debt neutrality reform, leading to bankruptcy (and lower employment rates and social stability). However, it is essential for policymakers to bear in mind the positive benefit of debt neutrality reform (such as improvement in loans allocation) to the overall society. It is also important for Chinese policymakers to anticipate the difficulty for SOEs, particularly SOE managers, to accurately calculate the cost of government guarantees afforded to SOEs in practice. Thus, Chinese policymakers should make necessary research efforts to provide some guidelines that could assist SOE managers on the implementation of debt neutrality policy.

Land Neutrality

571. Section 5.2 has shown that Chinese SOEs have competitive advantages in land markets because of government ownership. When land authorities transfer LURs in the primary land market, SOEs can use their government ownership ties and political advantage to either negotiate a cheaper price from land authorities or to leverage their advantaged position in the banking sectors to outbid their competitors in obtaining LURs from land authorities. Moreover, SOEs have three additional channels,[1079] unavailable to non-SOEs, to acquire LURs in the primary market, thus providing better access to LURs.

572. The proposed regulatory neutrality and debt neutrality outlined above can to some extent neutralise SOEs' preferential access to LURs. Particularly, regulatory neutrality requirements could address the preferential policies that grant additional channels for SOEs to acquire LURs. Debt neutrality requirements could tighten the deep pockets of SOEs and to some degree prevent the crowding out of non-SOEs in the LURs bidding process.

1077 For example, as referenced in Chapter 4, to eliminate the government guarantees to SOEs, the Australian government requires SOEs to pay a debt guarantee fee (notionally or actually to government revenue) to offset their cost advantages because of government ownership.

1078 *CN Guidelines for Managers* (n 380) 21–26.

1079 Leasing, converting allocated LURs into shares of enterprise, and authorising selected SOEs to manage LURs.

573. However, as discussed in Chapter 5, all land is owned by the state and the allocation of LURs is solely dependent on land authorities (either through allocation or transfer). Given land resource is scarce and valuable, land authorities are at great risk of being captured by SOEs. For example, although there are rules to ensure the transfer fee charged by land authorities reflects the market value in the LURs transfer process,[1080] land authorities may have broad discretion in determining the means for such transfers. Such discretion potentially allows land authorities to decide whether to grant commercial-purpose LURs by means of auction, bidding, or bilateral negotiations. Arguably, SOEs have a stronger ability to exert influence on land authorities to acquire LURs through means of direct bilateral negotiations (rather than auction or bidding) as the LURs price charged under such transaction is only required to 'not be lower than the lowest price determined in accordance with the regulations of the State.'[1081]

574. To ensure a level playing field among market actors in the land market, Chinese policymakers are encouraged to consider land neutrality when SOEs are involved in the primary land market. On the one hand, land neutrality could subject SOE land users to higher standards of public transparency when acquiring LURs from land authorities. For example, mandatory open access to information related to the LURs transaction could assist public oversight of the granting process. On the other hand, land neutrality could require land authorities to consider differences between commercial SOE and non-SOE land users and ensure non-discriminatory processes when granting LURs in the primary land market. For example, to avoid the risk of granting LURs negotiated at a cheaper price with an SOE land user (as the result of the government ownership and political connections), the Chinese land authority should consider prohibiting SOEs to achieve LURs through the method of negotiation in the primary land market.

Public Interest Test

575. The public interest test[1082] embedded in Australia's competitive neutrality regime (as discussed in Chapter 7) enables its government to align the objectives of competitive neutrality policy (promoting competition for the welfare of consumers) with other public interest objectives when there is a conflict. While the CPA provided some guidance on what factors constitute public interest by listing seven relevant factors for the purposes of competitive neutrality policy,[1083] the Australian government has discretions on the interpretation and application of a public interest test in practice.

1080 MLR Provisions (n 609).

1081 Urban Real Estate Administration Law (n 607) art 13.

1082 The public interest test here refers to the public interest test designed solely to assess whether to implement competitive neutrality arrangements proposed in the above section.

1083 The seven relevant public interest factors provided by the CPA include but are not limited to:

> the interests of consumers generally; ecologically sustainable development; social welfare and equity considerations (such as community service obligations); occupational health and safety; economic and regional development (includes employment and investment growth); the competitiveness of Australian businesses; and the efficient allocation of resources.

See CPA (n 384) cls 1(d)–(j).

576. Similarly, the content of a public interest test for competitive neutrality policy in China should ultimately be decided by Chinese policymakers based on China's economic conditions. For example, the non-commercial objectives assigned to SOEs, like corporate social responsibility (discussed in Chapter 5), should be considered when assessing whether to apply the competitive neutrality policy to Chinese SOEs. The key aspect of the public interest test is to have full transparency around the assessment of the non-commercial objectives. For example, the research on competitive neutrality policy in Australia (in Chapters 4 and 7) reveals that its application does not prevent SOEs from carrying non-commercial obligations (also known as CSOs in Australia) as long as such obligations are compensated in a form that is 'transparent, appropriately costed and directly funded by government.'[1084] In China, SOEs, even commercial SOEs, are expected to pursue goals other than commercial ones; they are currently not required to separate the accounts of non-commercial and commercial activities,[1085] and cross-subsidisation from profit-making to loss-making non-commercial activities are generally permitted in China.[1086] As highlighted in Chapter 5, low transparency and a lack of data on how non-commercial obligations of Chinese SOEs are compensated in practice may make it difficult for the government to assess whether the application of competitive neutrality policy conflicts with the delivery of non-commercial obligations by SOEs. Based on this observation, this research encourages the Chinese government take steps to require Chinese SOEs to separate cost and assets between commercial and non-commercial accounts.[1087]

577. In addition, the Chinese government is encouraged to consider articulating the detailed elements of the public interest test for the purpose of Chinese competitive neutrality policy. It is recommended that the policymaker consider the appropriateness of adopting into the competitive neutrality policy the public interest factors mentioned in the FCRS. For example, under the FCRS, policymakers are encouraged to consider the following factors of public interest when issuing policy that will exclude or restrain competition:

> the interest of national economic security, cultural security or scientific and technological security, or [those] related to national defence construction; social security issues (such as poverty alleviation and national development, disaster relief and rescue, etc); other social and public matters (such as energy

1084 National Competition Council (n 1026) 2.13.

1085 There is no practice of separating the accounts of commercial and non-commercial activities in China. See OECD (n 715) 48.

1086 ibid 49. The public service obligations of the Chinese companies may be compensated through derogations from other obligations. In addition, it is worth acknowledging the possibility that Chinese SOEs are sometimes required to deliver public service objectives (not directly linked to their commercial objectives) without explicit compensation from government. Under this scenario, SOEs are considered disadvantaged as a result of the government ownership.

1087 This suggestion is consistent with the recommendation provided by the OECD *Guidelines on Corporate Governance of State-Owned Enterprises* (n 62) 45–46.

and resource conservation, ecological and environmental protection, etc); and other exceptions under laws and administrative regulations.[1088]

578. This research recommends that the public interest test for the purpose of competitive neutrality could build on the public interest factors listed in the FCRS as it will be more cost-effective.

Approach to Applying the Public Interest Test

579. This research also encourages Chinese policymakers to consider the possible implementation approaches for a public interest test. As explained in Chapter 7, the design of public interest provisions will have an impact on the scope of competitive neutrality policy in practice. For example, the *ex-ante* public interest test approach provides maximum protection to the public interest by requiring government to prove the application of competitive neutrality policy *is* in the public interest. By contrast, the *ex-post* public interest test approach provides minimal protection to public interest by requiring government (or sometimes SOEs) to prove that the application of competitive neutrality policy *is not* in the public interest.

580. It is the recommendation of this research that China adopt the *ex-post* public interest test approach for Chinese competitive neutrality policy. The reason for this recommendation is that the *ex-post* public interest test is designed to favour competition because it assumes the implementation of competitive neutrality policy is in line with public interest factors unless demonstrated otherwise. The public interest test under the FCRS is designed as an *ex-post* public interest test.[1089] For example, the FCRS requires policymakers to not issue policy that will exclude or restrain competition unless they can demonstrate that such a policy is 'indispensable for achieving policy objectives, will not seriously exclude and restrain market competition, and is subject to a specific implementation time.'[1090] Under the *ex-post* public interest test, the onus of proof that implementing the competitive neutrality policy will undermine public interest falls on parties who seek exemptions. Therefore, the *ex-post* public interest test, from a practical perspective, can reduce the cost for government to implement competitive neutrality policy.

581. Finally, to ensure public interest is assessed in an open and objective way, the discretion or 'flexibility' afforded to government needs to be more tightly defined to reduce uncertainties around the application of the public interest test. One way to minimise the likelihood of uncertainties in relation

---

1088 FCRS Implementation Rules 2021 (n 843) art 17.

1089 The design of the public interest test under the FCRS reflects a strong preference for competition because the burden of proving policy that will exclude or restrain competition is in the public interest is placed with the policymaker.

1090 FCRS Implementation Rules 2021 (n 843) art 17.

to a public interest test is to promote transparency and increase disclosure mechanisms over its application. Therefore, it is recommended that public interest provisions should require a written decision which outlines what public interest factors are concerned and explains how the public interest tests are applied and justified when there is a decision to not apply competitive neutrality policy.

8.3.4 Approach to Introducing Competitive Neutrality Policy

Implementation and Complaint-Handling Authority

582. While the content of competitive neutrality policy is relatively straightforward, the discussion in Chapter 7 has established that implementation of such policy is in practice complex. Particularly, Chapter 7 revealed that, in Australia, the government who owns or controls SOEs has responsibility for implementing competitive neutrality arrangements in relation to their SOEs. Similar self-implementation principle is used for implementing the current SOE reform (in Chapter 3) and the FCRS (in Chapter 6). For implementation of competitive neutrality policy, this research suggests that the principle of 'government who owns or controls SOEs shall be responsible for the implementation of competitive neutrality policy' should be adopted, which means the government owner have the responsibility to assist responsible SOEs in implementing competitive neutrality arrangements. Under this approach, SOEs are mainly responsible for the regulatory compliance burden of competitive neutrality. One potential issue with reliance on the self-implementation approach, however, is the lack of supervision and potentially transparency. The design of the complaint-handling process could potentially remedy this shortcoming, which will be discussed below.

583. While FCRS and competitive neutrality in Australia assigned task of complaints-handling to an independent unit within government, the institutional design of complaint-handling authority for the purpose of competitive neutrality in Chinese context will need to keep bureaucratic hierarchy of regulatory agencies in mind, as discussed in the merge control enforcement in Chapter 6. Investigating compliance with competitive neutrality by SOEs may involve different government authorities, such as SASAC, sector regulators, SAMR or local governments. The designated complaint-handling unit within government would not be completely free from interference especially when other regulators interests are at stake.

584. This research therefore encourages the policy makers to consider an inter-ministerial joint conference (in Chinese *Buji Lianxi Huiyi*) for competitive neutrality, which consists multiple government regulators to handle

competitive neutrality complaints.[1091] As the time of writing, State Council has established approximately 100 inter-ministerial joint conferences,[1092] which is working mechanism to 'handle matters involving the responsibilities of multiple government departments'.[1093] The inter-ministerial joint conferences often led by a ministry that acts as the convener while other government agencies serve as members. The matter that inter-ministerial joint conference aims to solve need to be articulated in the work rules of the conference. The inter-ministerial joint meeting system for fair competition review discussed in Chapter 6 is a good example of how a joint conference works in practice.

585. This research suggests State Council create an inter-ministerial joint conference system for competitive neutrality policy, which could guide the implementation of competitive neutrality, evaluate the progress, put forward suggestions on how to handle competitive neutrality complaints. This joint conference system should be led by SASAC, which in author's opinion, maybe best-suited to take the lead on complaint-handling matter as it has years of experience dealing with SOEs, and recommendations provided by SASAC would face less resistance from responsible SOEs (compared with competition authorities). However, when using the SASAC (that manages SOEs) to investigate the alleged non-compliance practices of SOEs may raise the concern over the potential conflicts of interest, which has been observed in Australia (discussed in Chapter 7). Therefore, the research argues that SASAC alone is not well-placed to handle competitive neutrality complaint cases. The joint conference system also includes competition authority, SAMR[1094] and relevant sector regulators such as State Taxation Administration, the China Banking and Insurance Regulatory Commission, the Ministry of Natural Resources and the National Development and Reform Commission etc. For example, the elements of competitive neutrality policy (noted in Section 8.3.3) are heavily related to competition considerations, which SAMR could be consulted on matters such as how to address the breach of competitive neutrality obligations by SOEs.

586. While the complaint-handling procedures are designed to suit Australia's circumstances, the discussion in Chapter 7 has shown that an oversight system that monitors compliance and a follow up process on how non-compliance have been addressed is essential for the effectiveness of competitive neutrality policy. To ensure compliance, any individual or entity should be allowed to

1091 This research acknowledges the possible risk of discrepancy by having multiple government regulators handle competitive neutrality complaints. However, the cooperation between SAMR and SASACs is critical to effective competitive neutrality enforcement, especially when dealing with Chinese SOEs. This proposed arrangement can also help to solve possible disputes between multiple government agencies.

1092 The author calculates the number of inter-ministerial joint conferences based on the official government website. See '中华人民共和国中央人民政府[The State Council of the PRC]' <http://www.gov.cn/>.

1093 《国务院办公厅关于部际联席会议审批程序等有关问题的通知》[Notice of General Office of the State Council on Approval Procedures and Other Related Issues of the Inter-Ministerial Joint Conference] Guo Ban Han [2003] No 49, 18 July 2003.

1094 It is worth noting that Section 8.2.4 have explained in detail why the SAMR alone might not be a desirable institution to handle compliance with competitive neutrality policy.

initiate a competitive neutrality complaint to encourage additional oversight to the implementation of competitive neutrality policy in China. One way to prevent the abuse of such system, the design of complaint-handling procedures in China could provide discretion to complaint-handling authorities to reject a complaint in writing. However, the administrative decision (and reasoning) as to why a complaint is rejected should be published and displayed publicly to avoid ambiguity. As discussed in Chapter 7, the complaint-handling body in Australia (at the Commonwealth level) is required to provide a written decision if a complaint is rejected by such body. Such requirement is the necessary precondition for an effective and transparent complaint-handle process, especially when taking a case against Chinese SOEs.

Narrowing the Scope

587. The policy maker needs to consider the appropriate scope of competitive neutrality policy. Particularly, setting the threshold for competitive neutrality policy would determine whether all Chinese SOEs or just a select group are subject to its application, and is also linked to the ambit of complaint-handling mechanisms. The discussion in Chapter 7, for example, revealed that while the applicability of competitive neutrality policy in Australia is broad, the reach of this policy is largely determined by two thresholds. Firstly, an SOE needs to be engaging in 'business activity' and, secondly, the business activity needs to be 'significant' for the purpose of competitive neutrality policy.

588. Given the large number of Chinese SOEs, this research would encourage policymakers to introduce competitive neutrality policy in a gradual manner by narrowing the scope of application, which would ease the workloads of the complaint-handling institution, as noted above. Bu Lingqiang, for example, suggests (in Section 5.1.2) that the design of Chinese competitive neutrality policy should adapt to the current classification of non-financial SOEs and only require commercial SOEs to be subjected to competitive neutrality policy. However, using the current SOE classification as a benchmark to draw the boundary of competitive neutrality policy requires further consideration. Particularly, the current classification reform, as highlighted in Chapter 3, does not require SOEs assigned in the commercial SOEs group to be prohibited from taking on public welfare functions, and vice versa. As a result, Chinese SOEs listed as public welfare SOEs can still have a commercial focus and compete with non-SOEs in the market. Thus, it makes little sense to exempt public welfare SOEs from the application of competitive neutrality policy.

589. This research further encourages policymakers to consider using the ownership structure of Chinese SOEs as a benchmark for the application of competitive neutrality policy. For example, to introduce competitive neutrality in phases, SOEs that have 100 per cent of government shares (wholly owned SOEs) should be targeted in the first phase because it is relatively straightforward for

this type of SOE to adopt competitive neutrality reforms (such as corporate governance[1095] reforms) without the need to consider the interest of non-SOE shareholders. The boards of directors or managers of wholly owned SOEs would need to be trained to ensure that SOEs comply with the competitive neutrality requirements.

590. Additionally, based on the experiences accumulated from the first phase of implementation, the application of competitive neutrality policy could in the second phase gradually expand to government controlled SOEs[1096]. However, how to incentivise government controlled SOEs to implement competitive neutrality arrangements will require more research from a corporate governance perspective.

1095 Corporate governance in this research refers to 'a set of relationship between a company's management, its board, its shareholders and other stakeholders.' See OECD, *Principles of Corporate Governance* (2004) 11 <http://www.oecd.org/corporate/ca/corporategovernanceprinciples/31557724.pdf>.

1096 Chapter 1 defines government controlled SOEs as enterprises that government hold either more than 50 percent of its shares (absolute majority shareholder) or less than 50 percent of its shares but is still a larger shareholder than others.

CHAPTER 9
CONCLUSION

591. In advocating that a level playing field between SOEs and non-SOEs in China is essential, this research draws on the experience of Australia's adoption of a competitive neutrality policy framework in the 1990s. As the comparative study in Chapter 4 found, government ownership within SOEs can generate competitive advantages (such as lower interest rates on loans), enabling those SOEs who benefit from government ownership-generated competitive advantages to take business from more efficient firms in the market. This outcome is undesirable for several reasons, as Chapter 4 has shown. Firstly, allowing SOEs to compete based on their government ownership-generated advantages sends the wrong signal to market participants, namely that to succeed against rivals, firms need to pursue government ownership rather than focusing on performing activities more efficiently than their competitors. Secondly, allowing SOEs to benefit from their government ownership-generated competitive advantages is likely to lead to sub-optimal use of scarce resources because a market that allows less efficient firms to survive is unlikely to ensure their goods and services are delivered at the lowest possible cost. To ensure that SOEs compete based on efficiency, the Australian government adopted two comprehensive tools: competition law and competitive neutrality policy. In particular, as Chapter 4 highlighted, the universal application of competition law to all firms (regardless of their ownership status) provides solutions to the anti-competitive conduct of SOEs that infringe competition law. A principles-based competitive neutrality policy, working in conjunction with competition law, can provide a forward-looking solution to neutralise government ownership-generated competitive advantages of SOEs.

592. In China, as shown in Chapter 3, the different stages of reform have altered the relationship between government and Chinese SOEs. However, the connection between SOEs and government, and the close proximity of Chinese SOEs to the political authorities, still exists. Additionally, by analysing the current reform of SOEs implemented since 2013, this research found that these connections within SOEs will continue to be strong in the future. Given that the presence of Chinese SOEs in the market is growing, it is an opportune

time for China to reconsider how to level the playing field between SOEs and non-SOEs.

593. In an attempt to investigate how level the playing field is between SOEs and non-SOEs currently in China, Chapter 5 analysed the extent of competitive neutrality concerns caused by Chinese SOEs in the regulatory environment, land market, and banking sector. The findings indicated a lack of a level playing field between SOEs and non-SOEs in various markets of China. Particularly, the close proximity of Chinese SOEs to regulators and the political authorities provides Chinese SOEs with greater opportunities to shape the legal environment to their own advantage. In the banking sector, the overwhelming literature suggests that Chinese SOEs have benefited from more favourable lending conditions (i.e. access to loans and lending rates) than their non-SOE rivals by virtue of their government ownership. In the primary land market, government ownership and the politically privileged position conferred on Chinese SOEs suggest they can either negotiate a cheaper price for LURs from land authorities or leverage their favourable position (advantages generated by their inherent government ownership and political connections) in the banking sector to outbid their competitors in obtaining LURs from land authorities. Additionally, for historical reasons, SOEs have three channels (unavailable to non-SOEs) to acquire LURs in the primary market: leasing, converting allocated LURs into shares of the enterprise, and authorising selected SOEs to manage LURs. Chapter 5 also noted that government ownership and political connections can in some circumstances limit the ability of Chinese SOEs to compete with non-SOEs. For example, the involvement of the Party committee in the decision-making process of SOEs is more intensive than for non-SOEs, which could reduce the operational autonomy (especially that of management) of SOEs. Additionally, while all firms in China are encouraged to carry out corporate social responsibility activities voluntarily, Chinese SOEs are required by regulation to maintain higher disclosure standards over their social responsibility activities, which could impose disadvantages to SOEs when competing with non-SOEs.

594. The comparative study in Chapter 4 illustrated that the presence of SOEs in the market does not necessarily cause competitive neutrality concerns if the anti-competitive conduct of SOEs is successfully scrutinised by the competition law and there are competitive neutrality rules in place to maintain a level playing field between SOEs and non-SOEs. Encouraged by this observation, Chapter 6 evaluated the ability of current Chinese competition law, the AML, and competition policy to maintain a level playing field between SOEs and non-SOEs, and found that the AML alone is not sufficient, and that functionally equivalent rules to Australia's competitive neutrality policy are largely missing in China. Particularly, Chapter 6 found that, although the application of the AML and the introduction of the FCRS can alleviate the extent of competitive neutrality concerns of Chinese SOEs, some aspects of competitive neutrality advantages and disadvantages of SOEs identified in Chapter 5 cannot be addressed through the AML and the FCRS. For example, the AML

prohibits anti-competitive conduct of SOEs, but legitimate activities of SOEs, such as borrowing from banks with more favourable lending rates, are not in the coverage of the AML. The FCRS, also, cannot remove the SOEs' preferential interest rates as these are the result of government guarantee, not preferential government regulations. Additionally, there are no specific Chinese rules functionally equivalent to Australia's competitive neutrality policy, which specifies that SOEs should not enjoy any competitive advantages simply as a result of government ownership.

595. To propose sound recommendations on how China can adopt tools to ensure Chinese SOEs compete based on efficiency advantages (rather than on government ownership-generated advantages), Chapter 7 investigated the operation of competitive neutrality policy in Australia at a procedural level, covering the scope of competitive neutrality policy, the complaint-handling process, and the institutional structures that facilitate its implementation. Chapter 7 found that the application of competitive neutrality policy in Australia is largely narrowed by two tests: the significant government business activity test and the public interest test. However, the content of each test is largely dependent on the approach adopted by individual governments. Additionally, Chapter 7 found that though the non-legislative competitive neutrality complaint-handling mechanism is working in Australia, its effectiveness has been questioned by scholars on several grounds. Firstly, governments under competitive neutrality complaint mechanisms are not liable to implement recommendations of the complaint-handling body. Even if a government decided to act on a complaint body's recommendation, there are no time frames or follow-up monitoring procedures in place to indicate how long the government should take to rectify a breach or whether its actions have successfully rectified an identified breach. Secondly, the government can ignore the recommendations from the complaint-handing body without justification even when the complaint is upheld. Finally, while firms may decide to initiate a complaint and use the current complaint-handling mechanism as a means to remedy a breach, no compensation is available for firms that have suffered loss as a result of a breach of competitive neutrality. While Australia's non-legislative competitive neutrality complaint-handling mechanism reflects its domestic political features (noted in Chapter 4), it serves as a useful reference when considering which elements should be included in the process and how to avoid the identified shortcomings when introducing competitive neutrality policy in China. Finally, Chapter 7 found that while the competition regulator, the ACCC, had little involvement in the context of competitive neutrality policy, the NCC played an essential role in facilitating the implementation of the competitive neutrality policy through competition payments until 2005. The newly proposed government body, the ACCP, was expected to help with the compliance of the competitive neutrality policy. However, based on public evidence, the ACCP has not been adopted by governments, leaving no national body in Australia to oversee the compliance of competitive neutrality policy.

596. Building on the findings from Chapters 1 to 7, Chapter 8 outlined the reform proposals for the AML, arguing that, in order for the AML to address SOEs

more effectively, Article 8 should be deleted and the possible exemptions available to SOEs in the AML should be re-evaluated in a systematic manner. For example, this research encourages the Chinese competition authority, the SAMR, to issue supplementary guidelines to refine and narrow the scope of immunity which may be afforded by sectoral legislation. The legal reform proposal suggested here, if adopted, could put an end to the lack of clarity regarding issues noted in Chapter 6. Chapter 8 further considered the appropriateness of introducing competitive neutrality through the AML. This research maintains that introducing competitive neutrality by way of legislation is challenging, and proposes that a non-legislative (competition policy) approach would be a more appropriate way to introduce competitive neutrality in China.

597. Chapter 8 found that the Chinese government has shown a greater acceptance of the competitive neutrality principle by advocating its adoption in order to protect Chinese small and medium-sized enterprises (SMEs). This research argues that the rationale for adopting competitive neutrality principles in China should not be altered to protect certain market participants but should rather focus more on protecting competition (or the competitive process) by requiring that competition between SOEs and non-SOEs is based on efficiency. In addition, Chapter 8 found that in contrast to the willingness shown by the Chinese government, political support for competitive neutrality policy is currently missing in China. For competitive neutrality policy to be fully effective in China, the expression of willingness from the Party is fundamental.

598. Chapter 8 further described the importance and the potential benefits to China in adopting measures to safeguard a level playing field between SOEs and non-SOEs. For example, improved domestic competition brought by the introduction of a competitive neutrality policy would pressure Chinese SOEs to be more competitive to survive in the competitive process. It would also help Chinese SOEs to achieve the goal set by the current reform which urges them to be 'bigger, stronger and more competitive'[1097] as the increased domestic competition could ultimately increase SOEs' chances of survival in international markets. However, it is useful to bear in mind that Chinese SOEs, as the beneficiaries of the competitive advantages generated from government ownership and political connections, will have incentives and resources to resist the adoption of competitive neutrality policy, and the potential benefits brought by a more competitive market should not be downplayed by vested interests.

599. While Chinese policymakers will form the main content of the Chinese competitive neutrality policy, this research has outlined several elements for regulators and legislators to consider when drafting such policy based on the findings in Chapter 5. Importantly, Chinese competitive neutrality

1097 Xi Jinping (n 1).

policy should include regulatory neutrality, debt neutrality, land neutrality, and a public interest test. For example, the regulatory neutrality commitment should require Chinese policymakers to ensure, as far as practicable, that SOEs operate in the same regulatory environment as non-SOE competitors. Policymakers choosing to provide a different regulatory treatment for SOEs and non-SOEs should demonstrate (in writing) why this different treatment is necessary for the purpose of the competitive neutrality policy. For the design of a complaint-handling authority in China, this research encourages government to consider create an inter-ministerial joint conference for competitive neutrality, which should help guide the implementation of such policy, evaluate the progress and handle the competitive neutrality complaints. Additionally, this research suggested that China should gradually introduce competitive neutrality policy by narrowing its application scope. For example, the competitive neutrality policy could apply first to SOEs that have 100 per cent of government shares (wholly owned SOEs). The measures proposed in this research, if adopted, would provide stronger domestic competition and help China to build a more dynamic economy.

BIBLIOGRAPHY

Books and Book Sections

In English

Ang YY, *China's Gilded Age: The Paradox of Economic Boom and Vast Corruption* (CUP 2020)

Bai C-E and Li DD and Wang Y, 'Thriving on a Tilted Playing Field: China's Non-State Enterprises in the Reform Era' in Nicholas Hope, Dennis Yang and Mu Li (eds), *How Far Across the River? Chinese Policy Reform at the Millennium* (SUP 2003)

Cheng CB, 'Land' in Michael J Moser and Fu Yu (eds), *Doing Business in China* (Juris Publishing)

Chow GC, *China's Economic Transformation* (3rd edn, John Wiley & Sons 2015)

Clarke PH, *Competition Law and Policy: Cases and Materials* (3rd edn, OUP 2011)

Corones SG, *Competition Law in Australia* (6th edn, Thomson Reuters 2014)

Dabbah MM, *International and Comparative Competition Law* (CUP 2010)

Duke A, *Corones' Competition Law in Australia* (7th edn, Thomson Reuters 2019)

Elliott FJ and Yan K, *The Chinese Financial System: An Introduction and Overview* (China Center Series No 6, July 2013)

Fels A, 'Australia: A Regulator's Perspective' in Mark Williams (ed), *The Political Economy of Competition Law in Asia* (Edward Elgar 2013)

Feng D, 'Indigenous Evolution of SOE Regulation' in Benjamin L Liebman and Curtis J Milhaupt (eds), *Regulating the Visible Hand? The Institutional Implications of Chinese State Capitalism* (OUP 2016)

Fox EM, 'US and EU Competition Law: A Comparison' in Edward M Graham and J David Richardson (eds), *Global Competition Policy* (Institute for International Economics 1997)

Fox EM, 'State Action in Comparative Context: What if Parker V Brown Were Italian?' in Barry E Hawk (ed), *International Antitrust Law & Policy: Fordham Corporate Law 2003* (Juris Publishing 2004)

Fox EM, 'Outsider Antitrust: 'Making Markets Work for People' as a Post-Millennium Development Goal' in Tembinkosi Bonakele, Eleanor M Fox and Liberty Mncube (eds), *Competition Policy for the New Era: Insights from the BRICS Countries* (OUP 2017)

Galligan B and Roberts W, *The Oxford Companion to Australian Politics* (OUP 2007)

Gerber DJ, 'Asia and Global Competition Law Convergence' in Michael W Dowdle, John Gillespie and Imelda Maher (eds), *Asian Capitalism and the Regulation of Competition: Towards a Regulatory Geography of Global Competition Law* (CUP 2013)

Graells AS, *Public Procurement and the EU Competition Rules* (2nd edn, Hart Publishing 2011)

Gretton P, 'National Economic Reform in a Federal System: The Case of the Australian National Competition Policy and Related Reforms' in Stephen Howes and M Govinda Rao (eds), *Federal Reform Strategies: Lessons from Asia and Australia* (OUP 2013)

Gu M, 'China' in Aidan Synnott (ed), *The Public Competition Enforcement Review* (10th edn, Law Business Research 2019)

Harris HS and others, *Anti-Monopoly Law and Practice in China* (OUP 2016)

Healey D, 'A Comparative Look at the Competition Law Control of State-Owned Enterprises and Government in China' in Josef Drexl and others (eds), *More Common Ground for International Competition Law?* (Edward Elgar 2011)

——'Australia' in Mark Williams (ed), *The Political Economy of Competition Law in Asia* (Edward Elgar 2013)

——'Australian Experience with Competition Law: The State as a Market Actor' in Thomas Cheng, Ioannis Lianos and D Daniel Sokol (eds), *Competition and the State* (SUP 2014)

——'Competitive Neutrality: Addressing Government Advantage in Australian Markets' in Josef Drexl and Vicente Bagnoli (eds), *State-Initiated Restraints of Competition* (Edward Elgar 2015)

——'Competitive Neutrality and the Role of Competition Authorities: A Glance at Experiences in Europe and Asia-Pacific' in Paulo Burnier Da Silveira and William Evan Kovacic (eds), *Global Competition Enforcement: New Players, New Challenges* (Wolters Kluwer 2019)

——'The Ambit of Competition Law: Comments on Its Goals' in Deborah Healey, Michael Jacobs and Rhonda L Smith (eds), *Research Handbook on Methods and Models of Competition Law* (Edward Elgar 2020)

——and Fox EM, 'State Restraints in China: A Different Case?' in Adrian Emch and Wendy Ng (eds), *Wang Xiaoye Liber Amicorum: The Pioneer of Competition Law in China* (Concurrences 2019)

Hong S and Nong Z, *China's State-Owned Enterprises: Nature, Performance and Reform* (World Scientific 2012)

——and Nong Z and Junfeng Y, *Administrative Monopoly in China: Causes, Behaviors and Termination* (World Scientific 2015)

——and Pu Q, *Opening Up China's Markets of Crude Oil and Petroleum Products: Theoretical Research and Reform Solutions* (World Scientific 2015)

Hovenkamp H, *The Antitrust Enterprise: Principle and Execution* (HUP 2008)

Hsueh R, *China's Regulatory State: A New Strategy for Globalization* (Cornell University Press 2011)

Hu A and others, *The Modernization of China's State Governance* (Springer 2017)

Hu R, 'Understanding Chinese Real Estate: The property boom in perspective' in John Garrick (ed), *Law and Policy for China's Market Socialism* (Routledge, Taylor & Francis 2012)

Huang Y, *Capitalism with Chinese Characteristics: Entrepreneurship and the State* (CUP 2008)

Huang Y, 'State-Owned Enterprises Reform' in Ron Duncan and Yiping Huang (eds), *Reform of State-Owned Enterprises in China: Autonomy, Incentive and Competition* (Asia Pacific Press 1988)

——and Xun Wang, '"Strong on Quantity, Weak on Quality": China's Financial Reform Between 1978 and 2018' in Ross Garnaut, Ligang Song and Cai Fang (eds), *China's 40 Years of Reform and Development: 1978–2018* (ANU Press 2018)

Jinglian W and Guochuan M, *Whither China? Restarting the Reform Agenda* (Xiaofeng Hua and Nancy Hearst trs, OUP 2016)

Jun Z, 'China's Price Liberalisation and Market Reform: A Historical Perspective' in Ross Garnaut, Ligang Song and Cai Fang (eds), *China's 40 Years of Reform and Development: 1978–2018* (ANU Press 2018)

Kemp K, *Misuse of Market Power: Rationale and Reform* (CUP 2018)

King SP, 'The Economics of National Competition Policy' in Christopher Arup and David Wishart (eds), *Competition Policy with Legal Form: Reviewing Australian and Overseas Experience* (Federation Press 2002)

Kroeber AR, *China's Economy What Everyone Needs to Know* (OUP 2016)

Lardy N, *Markets Over Mao: The Rise of Private Business in China* (PIIE 2014)

——'The Changing Role of the Private Sector in China' in Iris Day and John Simon (eds), *Structural Change in China: Implications for Australia World* (RBA 2016)

——'Private Sector Development' in Ross Garnaut, Ligang Song and Cai Fang (eds), *China's 40 Years of Reform and Development 1978–2018* (ANU Press 2018)

——*The State Strikes Back: The End of Economic Reform in China?* (PIIE 2019)

Lei Z and Liebman BL and Milhaupt CJ, 'SOEs and State Governance: How State-Owned Enterprises Influence China's Legal System' in Benjamin L Liebman and Curtis J Milhaupt (eds), *Regulating the Visible Hand? The Institutional Implications of Chinese State Capitalism* (OUP 2015)

Lin L-W, 'Balancing Closure and Openness: The Challenge of Leadership Reform in China's State-Owned Enterprises' in Benjamin L Liebman and Curtis J Milhaupt (eds), *Regulating the Visible Hand? The Institutional Implications of Chinese State Capitalism* (OUP 2015)

Lin P and Qiao Y, 'Understanding the Economic Factors that Have Affected China's Anti-Monopoly Law' in Michal S Gal and others (eds), *The Economic Characteristics of Developing Jurisdictions: Their Implications for Competition Law* (Edward Elgar 2015)

Liu S, 'The Structure of and Changes to China's Land System' in Ross Garnaut, Ligang Song and Cai Fang (eds), *China's 40 Years of Reform and Development: 1978–2018* (ANU Press 2018)

Michaels R, 'The Functional Method of Comparative Law' in Mathias Reimann and Reinhard Zimmerman (eds), *The Oxford Handbook of Comparative Law* (OUP 2006)

Milhaupt CJ and Zheng W, 'Reforming China's State-Owned Enterprises: Institutions, Not Ownership' in Benjamin L Liebman and Curtis J Milhaupt (eds), *Regulating the Visible Hand? The Institutional Implications of Chinese State Capitalism* (OUP 2015)

Miller RV, *Miller's Australian Competition Law and Policy* (Thomson Reuters 2018)

Morgan B, *Social Citizenship in the Shadow of Competition: The Bureaucratic Politics of Regulatory Justification* (Ashgate 2003)

Motta M, *Competition Policy Theory and Practice* (CUP 2004)

Naughton B, *The Chinese Economy: Transitions and Growth* (MIT Press 2006)

——'The Transformation of the State Sector: SASAC, the Market Economy, and the New National Champions' in Barry Naughton and Kellee S. Tsai (eds), *State Capitalism, Institutional Adaptation, and the Chinese Miracle* (CUP 2015)

——*The Chinese Economy: Adaptation and Growth* (2nd edn, MIT Press 2018)

Ng W, 'The Influence of Socialist Principles on the Legal Regulation of Markets in China' in Hualing Fu and others (eds), *Socialist Law in Socialist East Asia* (CUP 2018)

——*The Political Economy of Competition Law in China* (CUP 2018)

Ning S and Peng K and Gao S, 'China' in Ilene Knable Gotts (ed), *The Private Competition Enforcement Review* (12th edn, Law Business Research 2019)

OECD, *Economic Surveys: China 2005* (16 September 2005)

——*State-Owned Enterprises as Global Competitors: A Challenge or an Opportunity?* (2016)

——*Economic Surveys: China 2017* (21 March 2017)

Paddon M and others, *Competition in Whose Interest? Socio-Economic Impacts of National Competition Policy* (Public Sector Research Centre & Public Interest Advocacy Centre 1999)

Peart S, 'Australia and New Zealand: Their Competition Law Systems and the Countries' Norms' in Eleanor M Fox and Trebilcock MJ (eds), *The Design of Competition Law Institutions: Global Norms, Local Choices* (OUP 2013)

Peerenboom R, 'Judicial Independence in China: Common Myths and Unfounded Assumptions' in Randall Peerenboom (ed), *Judicial Independence in China Lessons for Global Rule of Law Promotion* (CUP 2010)

Porter ME, *The Competitive Advantage of Nations* (Free Press 1998)

——*On Competition* (HBR Press 2008)

Pozsar Z and others, 'Shadow Banking' (Staff Report No 458, NY Federal Reserve Bank February 2012) <https://www.newyorkfed.org/medialibrary/media/research/staff_reports/sr458.pdf>

Qian Y and Wu J, 'China's Transition to a Market Economy: How Far Across the River?' in Nicholas Hope, Dennis Yang and Mu Li (eds), *How Far Across the River? Chinese Policy Reform at the Millennium* (SUP 2003)

Quiggin J, 'Governance of Public Corporations: Profits and the Public Benefit' in Michael J Whincop (ed), *From Bureaucracy to Business Enterprise: Legal and Policy Issues in the Transformation of Government Services* (Ashgate 2003)

Ranald P and Thorowgood R, *Review of Competitive Neutrality Policies and Local Government Policies of Government Under National Competition Policy* (Public Sector Research Centre, UNSW 1997)

Rithmire ME, *Land Bargains and Chinese Capitalism: The Politics of Property Rights under Reform* (CUP 2015)

Rodger B and Macculloch A, *Competition Law and Policy in the EU and UK* (5th edn, Routledge 2014)

Round K and Shanahan M, *From Protection to Competition: The Politics of Trade Practices Reform in Australia* (Federation Press 2015)

Sauvant KP and others, 'Trends in FDI, Home Country Measures and Competitive Neutrality' in Andrea K Bjorklund (ed), *Yearbook on International Investment Law and Policy 2012-2013* (OUP 2014)

Shaoming Z, *Chinese Conflicts of Laws: A Restatement and Legisprudence Proposal* (Wildy, Simmonds & Hill 2018)

Shen W, *Shadow Banking in China: Risk, Regulation and Policy* (Edward Elgar 2016)

Sturgess G, *A Fair Field and No Favours: Competitive Neutrality in UK Public Service Markets* (Confederation of British Industry 2006)

Su J and Wang X, 'China the Competition Law System and the Country's Norms' in Eleanor M Fox and MJ Trebilcock (eds), *The Design of Competition Law Institutions: Global Norms, Local Choices* (OUP 2013)

Taggart M, *Corporatisation, Privatisation and Public Law* (Legal Research Foundation, UoA 1990)

Van den Bergh RJ, 'Enforcement' in Roger J Van den Bergh (ed), *Comparative Competition Law and Economics* (Edward Elgar 2017)

——and Camesasca P and Giannaccari A, 'Merger Control' in Roger J Van den Bergh (ed), *Comparative Competition Law and Economics* (Edward Elgar 2017)

——and Michael Faure, 'Critical Issues in the Enforcement of The Anti-Monopoly Law in China: A Law and Economics Perspective' in Michael Faure and Xinzhu Zhang (eds), *Competition Policy and Regulation: Recent Developments in China, the US and Europe* (Edward Elgar 2011)

Wang X, 'China's Macroeconomics in the 40 Years of Reform' in Ross Garnaut, Ligang Song and Cai Fang (eds), *China's 40 Years of Reform and Development 1978–2018* (ANU Press 2018)

——'Retrospective and prospects of China's Anti-Monopoly Law' in Steven Van Uytsel, Shuya Hayashi and John O Haley (eds), *Research Handbook on Asian Competition Law* (Edward Elgar 2020)

——and Emch A, 'Procedure and Substance in China's Merger Control Regime' in Deborah Healey, Michael Jacobs and Rhonda L Smith (eds), *Research Handbook on Methods and Models of Competition Law* (Edward Elgar 2020)

——and Su J, 'China's Anti-Monopoly Law: Agent of Competition Enhancement or Engine of Industrial Policy?' in Daniel Zimmer (ed), *The Goals of Competition Law* (Edward Elgar 2012)

——and Su J and Han W, *Competition Law in China* (3rd edn, Wolters Kluwer 2018)

Wang Y, *Tying the Autocrat's Hands: The Rise of the Rule of Law in China* (CUP 2014)

Wank DL, *Commodifying Communism: Business, Trust, and Politics in a Chinese City* (CUP 1999)

Weiping Y and Marquis M, 'Competition Policy and Industrial Policy in China: Toward a New Equilibrium?' in Adrian Emch and Wendy Ng (eds), *Wang Xiaoye Liber Amicorum: The Pioneer of Competition Law in China* (Concurrences 2019)

Wilks S, 'Competition Policy' in David Coen, Wyn Grant and Graham K Wilson (eds), *The Oxford Handbook of Business and Government* (OUP 2010)

Williams M, *Competition Policy and Law in China, Hong Kong and Taiwan* (CUP 2005)

——'China' in Mark Williams (ed), *The Political Economy of Competition Law in Asia* (Edward Elgar 2013)

World Bank and Development Research Centre of the State Council (DRC), *China 2030: Building a Modern, Harmonious, and Creative Society* (World Bank 2013)

Xianlin W, 'Some Key Issues Concerning Further Development of China's Anti-Monopoly Law' in Tembinkosi Bonakele, Eleanor M Fox and Liberty Mncube (eds), *Competition Policy for the New Era: Insights from the BRICS Countries* (OUP 2018)

Xiaomin F, 'The Application of the Chinese Antimonopoly Law to State-Owned Enterprises' in Fabiana Di Porto and Rupprecht Podszun (eds), *Abusive Practices in Competition Law* (Edward Elgar 2018)

Xu T, *The Revival of Private Property and Its Limits in Post-Mao China* (Wildy, Simmonds & Hill 2014)

Zhang AH, 'Antitrust Regulation of Chinese State-Owned Enterprises' in Benjamin L Liebman and Curtis J Milhaupt (eds), *Regulating the Visible Hand? The Institutional Implications of Chinese State Capitalism* (OUP 2015)

——Chinese Antitrust Exceptionalism: How The Rise of China Challenges Global Regulation (OUP 2021)

Zheng W, 'State Capitalism and the Regulation of Competition in China' in Michael W Dowdle, John Gillespie and Imelda Maher (eds), *Asian Capitalism and the Regulation of Competition: Towards a Regulatory Geography of Global Competition Law* (CUP 2013)

——'Competition law in China' in John Duns, Arlen Duke and Brendan J Sweeney (eds), *Comparative Competition Law* (Edward Elgar 2015)

Zweigert K and Kötz H, *An Introduction to Comparative Law* (Tony Weir tr, 3rd edn, OUP 1998)

In Chinese

季晓楠 [Ji Xiaonan], 《坚持和完善基本经济制度十论》[Ten Essays on Adhering to and Improving the Basic Economic System] (社会科学文献出版社 [Social Science Academic Press] 2014)

徐士英 [Xu Shiying], 《竞争政策研究—国际比较与中国选择》[Study on Competition Policy: International comparison and China's Choice] (法律出版社 [Law Press] 2013)

吴敬琏 [Wu Jinglian], 《当代中国经济改革教程》[Understanding and Interpreting China's Economic Reform] (2nd edn, 上海远东出版社 [Shanghai Far East Publishers] 2016)

SASAC《中国国有资产监督管理年鉴》[China's State-Owned Assets Supervision and Administration Yearbook] (中国经济出版社 [China Economic Publishing House] 2016)

Journal Articles, Reports, and Papers

In English

Agricultural Bank of China, *Joint Dedication to Build a Beautiful China: 2017 Annual Report* (2017) <http://www.abchina.com/en/investor-relations/performance-reports/annual-reports/201803/P020180428379127252057.pdf>

Bank of Communications, *Hello 2018: 2017 Annual Report* (2017) <https://vpr.hkma.gov.hk/statics/assets/doc/100023/ar_17/ar_17_eng.pdf>

Banks G, 'Competition and the Public Interest' (Speech to the NCC Workshop 'Public Interest Test Under National Competition Policy', Melbourne, 12 July 2001) <http://www.pc.gov.au/news-media/speeches/cs20010712>

——'Public Inquiries in Policy Formulation: Australia's Productivity Commission' (Address to the International Workshop 'Australia's Public Inquiry Experience and Economic System Reform in China', China-Australia Governance Program, Beijing, 3 September 2007) <https://www.pc.gov.au/news-media/speeches/cs20070903/cs20070903.pdf>

Batson A, 'The State of the State Sector' (Gavekal Dragonomics 21 March 2017)

Biau C and others, *Governments as Competitors in the Global Marketplace: Options for Ensuring a Level Playing Field* (E15Initiative, ICTSD and WEF 2016) <http://e15initiative.org/wp-content/uploads/2015/09/E15-Investment-OECD-FINAL.pdf>

Blair RD and Sokol DD, 'The Rule of Reason and the Goals of Antitrust: An Economic Approach' (2012) 78(2) ALJ 471

Cao X and others, 'Political Promotion, CEO Incentives, and the Relationship Between Pay and Performance' (2018) 65(7) Management Science

Capobianco A and Christiansen H, 'Competitive Neutrality and State-Owned Enterprises: Challenges and Policy Options' (OECD Corporate Governance Working Papers No 1, 1 May 2011) <http://dx.doi.org/10.1787/5kg9xfgjdhg6-en>

Capobianco A and Nagy A, 'Public Interest Clauses in Developing Countries' (2016) 7(1) JECL & Pract

Chen H and Whalley J, 'The State-Owned Enterprises Issue in China's Prospective Trade Negotiations' (Paper No 48, Centre for International Governance Innovation, October 2014) <https://www.files.ethz.ch/isn/185024/no.48.pdf>

Chen L and Ding D and Mano R, 'China's Capacity Reduction Reform and Its Impact on Producer Prices' (IMF Working Papers, WP/18/216, September 2018) <https://ssrn.com/abstract=3267240>

Chen T and Kung JK-S, 'Busting the "Princelings": The Campaign Against Corruption in China's Primary Land Market' (2019) 134(1) The Quarterly Journal of Economics

Chen T and others, 'Political Connections and Rent-Seeking: Evidence from China's Land Market' (14 June 2015) <https://editorialexpress.com/cgi-bin/conference/download.cgi?db_name=NEUDC2015&paper_id=355>

Cheng T, 'Competitive Neutrality from an Asian Perspective' (DAF/COMP/WD(2015)49, 11 June 2015) <http://www.oecd.org/officialdocuments/publicdisplaydocumentpdf/?cote=DAF/COMP/WD(2015)49&docLanguage=En>

Cheng W and Wu Y, 'Bank Finance for Private Firms in China: Does Political Capital Still Pay off?' (Discussion Paper, December 2015) <https://www.monash.edu/business/economics/research/publications/publications2/0716bankfinancechengwu.pdf>

China Construction Bank Corporation, *Annual Report 2017*: *Exploring the Blue Ocean* (2017) <http://www.ccb.com/en/newinvestor/upload/20180817_1534487897/20180817143224827527.pdf>

Christiansen H, 'Balancing Commercial and Non-Commercial Priorities of State-Owned Enterprises' (Corporate Governance Working Papers No 6, OECD 2013) <https://www.oecd.org/corporate/OECDCorporateGovernanceWorkingPaper6.pdf>

CITIC Industrial Bank, *2017 Annual Report* (2017) <http://iis.quamnet.com/media/IRAnnouncement/998/EN_US/003128598-0.PDF>

Cull R and others, 'Government Connections and Financial Constraints: Evidence from a Large Representative Sample of Chinese Firms' (2015) 32 Journal of Corporate Finance

Deitz A, 'Competitive Neutrality in Australia' (Presentation to the OECD 11th Global Forum on Competition: Session III – OECD Project on State Owned Enterprises and Competitive Neutrality, 17 February 2012) <https://www.oecd.org/competition/globalforum/49771663.pdf>

Doueihi J, 'The Effectiveness of the National Tax Equivalent Regime (NTER) in Encouraging Competitive Neutrality' (PhD thesis, Curtin University 2019) <https://espace.curtin.edu.au/bitstream/handle/20.500.11937/75706/Doueihi%20J.%202019.pdf?sequence=1&isAllowed=y>

Du F and Tang G and S Young M, 'Influence Activities and Favoritism in Subjective Performance Evaluation: Evidence from Chinese State-Owned Enterprises' (2012) 87(5) Accounting Review

Du M, 'China's State Capitalism and World Trade Law' (2014) 63(2) ICLQ

Eaton S and Kostka G, 'Central Protectionism in China: The "Central SOE Problem" in Environmental Governance' (2017) 231 The China Quarterly

Editorial, 'Competitive Neutrality: At the Crossroads of Reform' (2018) 25 CCLJ

European Commission, 'On Significant Distortions in the Economy of The People's Republic of China for the Purposes of Trade Defence Investigations' (SWD [2017] 483 final/2, 20 December 2017) <https://trade.ec.europa.eu/doclib/docs/2017/december/tradoc_156474.pdf>.

European Union Chamber of Commerce in China, 'European Business in China Position Paper 2019/2020' (24 September 2019) <https://www.europeanchamber.com.cn/en/publications-archive/756/European_Business_in_China_Position_Paper_2019_2020>

Evrard SJ, 'Civil Antitrust Litigation in China' (2016) 12(1) CLI

Fels A, 'China's Antimonopoly Law 2008: An Overview' (2012) 41(1) Review of Industrial Organization

Forsyth PJ, 'Microeconomic Policies and Structural Change', *The Australian Economy in the 1990s* (RBA 2000)

Fox EM, 'An Anti-Monopoly Law for China: Scaling the Walls of Government Restraints' (2008) 75(1) ALJ 173

——'Against Goals' (2013) 81(5) Fordham L Rev 2157

——and Healey D, 'When the State Harms Competition: The Role for Competition Law' (2014) 79(3) ALJ

——and Healey D, 'Competition Law and the State: Volume 1: Summary of Answers to Questionnaire' (UNCTAD/DITC/CLP/2015/3, 2015) <https://unctad.org/en/PublicationsLibrary/ditcclp2015d3_en.pdf>

Gray A, 'Options for the Doctrine of Crown Immunity in 21st Century Australia' (2009) 16(4) AJ Admin L

Garnaut R and Song L and Yao Y, 'Impact and Significance of State-Owned Enterprise Restructuring in China' (2006) 55 The China Journal

Gatley T, 'Softening Up on SOE Deleveraging' (Gavekal Dragonomics 9 August 2018)

——'More Loans for the Private Sector' (Gavekal Dragonomics 18 October 2018)

Griffiths J, 'Application of the Australian Consumer Law to Government Commercial Activities' (Paper delivered at Commercial Law and Government Conference, NSW State Library, 16 September 2016) <https://www.fedcourt.gov.au/digital-law-library/judges-speeches/justice-griffiths/griffiths-j-20160916>

Hanrahan I, 'Becoming Competitively Neutral: Removing the Gilded Edge of Government Business' (2004) 12 TPLJ

Harris HS, 'The Making of an Antitrust Law: The Pending Anti-Monopoly Law of the People's Republic of China' (2006) 7(1) Chi J Intl L

Healey D, 'Competitive Neutrality: The Concept' in *Competitive Neutrality and its Application in Selected Developing Countries* (UNCTAD RPP, 2014) 12 <https://unctad.org/system/files/official-document/ditcclpmisc2014d1_en.pdf>

——'Competition Law and State-Owned Enterprises: Enforcement' (DAF/COMP/GF(2018)11, 30 November 2018) <https://one.oecd.org/document/DAF/COMP/GF(2018)11/en/pdf>

——and Chenying Z, 'Bank Mergers in China: What Role for Competition?' (2017) 12 AsJCL

——and Coles J, 'From "Carries on Business" to "In Trade or Commerce": Efficiency in Government or Semantic Endeavour?' (2018) 26 CCLJ

——and Smith RL, 'Competitive Neutrality in Australia: Opportunity for Policy Development' (2018) 25 CCLJ

Hellman JS and Jones G and Kaufmann D, '"Seize the State, Seize the Day": State Capture, Corruption, and Influence in Transition' (Policy Research Working Paper No 2444, World Bank Group 2000) <http://documents.worldbank.org/curated/en/537461468766474836/Seize-the-state-seize-the-day-state-capture-corruption-and-influence-in-transition>

——'Seize the State, Seize the Day: State Capture and Influence in Transition Economies' (2003) 31(4) Journal of Comparative Economics

Hilmer FG, 'The Bases and Impact of Competition Policy' (1995) 25(1) Economic Analysis and Policy

Ho D and Young A, 'China's Experience in Reforming Its State-Owned Enterprises: Something new, Something old and Something Chinese?' (2013) 2(4) Int J Econ Manag Soc Sci

Ho SPS and Lin GCS, 'Emerging Land Markets in Rural and Urban China: Policies and Practices' (2003) 175 The China Quarterly

Hogan Lovells, 'SAMR's Triple Guidance on Antitrust Enforcement' (July 2019) <https://f.datasrvr.com/fr1/219/35628/New_SAMR_rules.pdf>.

Hongfeng Y, 'Using Fair Competition Reviews to Actively Promote Establishment of the Competitive Neutrality Principle' (Paper delivered at the Opening Up and Competitive Neutrality: The International Experience and Insights for China conference, 24 April 2019) <https://www.imf.org/en/News/Seminars/Conferences/2019/04/19/7th-pbc-imf>

Hovenkamp H, 'Whatever Did Happen to the Antitrust Movement?' (2019) 94(2) Notre Dame L Rev 583

Hu R, 'China's Paradoxical Reforms on Land and Real Estate Property Markets' (2013) 8(3) Global Built Environment Review

Huang Q, 'How "New SOEs" Come of Age: Four Decades of China's SOE Reform' (2018) 13(1) China Economist

Huang Q and Yang R, 'A Study on Conflict and Coordination Between Industrial Policy and Competition Policy' in Minli Dai (ed), *Innovative Computing and Information: International Conference, ICCIC 2011, Wuhan, China, September 2011, Proceedings, Part 2* (CCIS 232, Springer 2011)

Huiqin J, 'Does Australia's Foreign Investment Review System Discriminate against Chinese Government Investors? A Doctrinal, Comparative and Empirical Review' (PhD thesis, UNSW 2017)

IMF, *The People's Republic of China: Selected Issues* (IMF Country Report No 16/271, August 2016) <https://www.imf.org/external/pubs/ft/scr/2016/cr16271.pdf>

——*People's Republic of China: Selected Issues* (IMF Country Report No 19/274, 23 August 2019) <https://www.imf.org/en/Publications/CR/Issues/2019/08/15/Peoples-Republic-of-China-Selected-Issues-48593>

Industrial and Commercial Bank of China, *Annual Report 2017* (2017) <http://v.icbc.com.cn/userfiles/Resources/ICBCLTD/download/2018/720180423.pdf>

Jiajia Y, 'Briefing on the Implementation of the Fair Competition Review System' (Presentation to the 18th EU-China Competition Week, 19 March 2019) <https://competitioncooperation.eu/wp-content/uploads/2019/04/Day-2_Session-3_YANG-EN.pdf>

Jijian F, 'The Value of Political Connections in China: Government Officials on the Board of Directors' (2016) SSRN Electronic Journal

Junyeop L, 'State Owned Enterprises in China: Reviewing the Evidence' (OECD Working Group on Privatisation and Corporate Governance of State Owned Assets, 26 January 2009) <http://www.oecd.org/corporate/ca/corporategovernanceofstate-ownedenterprises/42095493.pdf>

Kamber G and Mohanty M, 'Do Interest Rates Play a Major Role in Monetary Policy Transmission in China?' (BIS Working Paper No 714, Bank for International Settlements, April 2018) <https://www.bis.org/publ/work714.pdf>

Kelley D, 'Local Government Competitive Neutrality in Queensland' (Expert Symposium on Competitive Neutrality presentation, 28 October 2015)

Kettle J, 'Competitive Neutrality, State Aid and Australia – Worth Reconsidering?' (2019) 93 CCLJ

Khemani RS, 'Application of Competition Law: Exemptions and Exceptions' (UNCTAD/DITC/CLP/Misc.25, 2002)

King SP, 'National Competition Policy' (1997) 73(222) Economic Record

——'Competition Policy and the Competition Policy Review' (2015) 48(4) Australian Economic Review

Kroeber A, 'Role of the State Sector: Still in Retreat, But Getting Bigger' (2012) 16(4) China Economic Quarterly <http://research.gavekal.com/content.php/7837-DG-CEQ-Q4-2012-Role-Of-The-State-Sector-Still-In-Retreat-But-Getting-Bigger>

Leutert W, 'Challenges Ahead in China's Reform of State-Owned Enterprises' (2016) (21) Asia Policy

——'Firm Control: Governing the State-Owned Economy Under Xi Jinping' (2018/1–2) China Perspectives

——'The Political Mobility of China's Central State-Owned Enterprise Leaders' (2018) 233 The China Quarterly

Lawrence SV, 'China's Political Institutions and Leaders in Charts' (Congressional Research Service Reports R43303, 12 November 2013) <http://china.usc.edu/sites/default/files/legacy/AppImages/crs-2013-china-political-leaders-institutions.pdf>

——and Martin MF, 'Understanding China's Political System' (Congressional Research Service Reports R41007, 31 January 2013) <https://www.everycrsreport.com/files/20130131_R41007_ecff2aa5a98d681d66f423fa3afe63b6e8e3faa7.pdf>

Li L, 'The Chinese Communist Party and People's Courts: Judicial Dependence in China' (2016) 64(1) AJCL

Lin L-W, 'Corporate Social Responsibility in China: Window Dressing or Structural Change?' (2010) 28(1) BJIL

——'State Ownership and Corporate Governance in China: An Executive Career Approach' [2013] 3 Colum Bus L Rev

——'China's National Champions: Governance Change Through Globalization?' (2015) 11(1) U Pa Asian L Rev

——'A Network Anatomy of Chinese State-Owned Enterprises' (2017) 16(4) WTR

——and Curtis J Milhaupt, 'We are the (National) Champions: Understanding the Mechanisms of State Capitalism in China' (2013) 65(4) Stan L Rev

Liu Q and Pan X and Tian GG, 'To What Extent Did the Economic Stimulus Package Influence Bank Lending and Corporate Investment Decisions? Evidence from China' (2018) 86 Journal of Banking and Finance

Liu Z and Wang P and Xu Z, 'Interest-Rate Liberalization and Capital Misallocations' (Working Paper 2017–15, SF Federal Reserve Bank, January 2020) <https://doi.org/10.24148/wp2017-15>

Lua Y and others, 'Shadow Banking and Firm Financing in China' (2015) 36 Intl Rev of Economics and Finance

Mattlin M, 'Chinese Strategic State-Owned Enterprises and Ownership Control' (2009) 4(6) BICCS Asia Paper

Merrett D and Corones S and Round D, 'The Introduction of Competition Policy in Australia: The Role of Ron Bannerman' (2007) 47(2) AEHR

Michaels R and Pauwelyn J, 'Conflict of Norms or Conflict of Laws? Different Techniques in the Fragmentation of Public International Law' (2012) 22 Duke J Comp & Intl L

Milhaupt CJ and Zheng W, 'Beyond Ownership: State Capitalism and the Chinese Firm' (2015) 103(3) Geo LJ

Minwoo K, 'Regulating the Visible Hands: Development of Rules on State-Owned Enterprises in Trade Agreements' (2017) 58(1) Harv Intl LJ

Morgan B and Bai S and Bhasker J, 'Competitive Neutrality and the Challenge of Social Enterprise' (2018) 25(3) CCLJ

Morrison WM, 'China's Economic Rise: History, Trends, Challenges, and Implications for the United States' (CRS Report for Congress, 25 June 2019) <https://fas.org/sgp/crs/row/RL33534.pdf>

Naughton B, 'Top-Down Control: SASAC and the Persistence of State Ownership in China' (China and the World Economy conference paper, 23 June 2006)

——'Restructuring and Reform: China 2016' in Iris Day and John Simon (eds), *Structural Change in China: Implications for Australia and the World* (RBA Annual Conference Volume 2016) <www.rba.gov.au/publications/confs/2016/pdf/rba-conference-volume-2016-naughton.pdf>.

——'The Current Wave of State Enterprise Reform in China: A Preliminary Appraisal' (2017) 12(2) Asian Economic Policy Review

——'Economic Policy under Trade War Conditions: Can China Move Beyond Tit for Tat?' (2018) (57) China Leadership Monitor

OECD, 'The Objectives of Competition Law and Policy: Note by the Secretariat' (CCNM/GF/COMP(2003)3, 29 Janurary 2003) <http://www.oecd.org/daf/competition/2486329.pdf>

——'Competition Policy Roundtable: Regulating Market Activities by the Public Sector' (DAF/COMP(2004)36, February 2005) <http://www.oecd.org/daf/competition/sectors/34305974.pdf>

——'Non-Commercial Services Obligations and Liberalisation' (2006) 7(1) OECD J Competition L & Pol

——'OECD Reviews of Regulatory Reform: China 2009: Defining the Boundary between the Market and the State' (2009) <http://dx.doi.org/10.1787/9789264059429-en>

——'Competition Policy Roundtables: State Owned Enterprises and the Principle of Competitive Neutrality' (DAF/COMP (2009)37, 20 September 2010) <http://www.oecd.org/daf/competition/46734249.pdf>

——'Land Use Restrictions as Barriers to Entry' (2010) 10(3) OECD J Competition L & Pol

——*OECD Reviews of Regulatory Reform: Australia 2010 Towards a Seamless National Economy* (OECD 2010)

——*OECD Reviews of Regulatory Reform: Competition Policy in Australia* (2010) <http://www.oecd.org/gov/regulatory-policy/44529918.pdf>

——*Competitive Neutrality: Maintaining a Level Playing Field Between Public and Private Business* (30 August 2012) <https://www.oecd.org/competition/competitive-neutralitymaintainingalevelplayingfieldbetweenpublicandprivatebusiness.htm>

——'Competitive Neutrality: A Compendium of OECD Recommendations, Guidelines and Best Practices' (2012) <http://www.oecd.org/daf/ca/50250955.pdf>

——'Competitive Neutrality: National Practices' (2012) <http://www.oecd.org/daf/ca/50250966.pdf>

——'Competitive Neutrality in Competition Policy: Issues Paper by the Secretariat' (DAF/COMP (2015)5, 12 June 2015) <http://www.oecd.org/officialdocuments/publicdisplaydocumentpdf/?cote=DAF/COMP(2015)5&docLanguage=En>

——'Discussion on Competitive Neutrality: Note by the Secretariat' (DAF/COMP (2015)8/FINAL, 13 April 2016) <https://one.oecd.org/document/DAF/COMP(2015)8/FINAL/en/pdf>

——*OECD Guidelines on Corporate Governance of State-Owned Enterprises* (2015)

——'Roundtable on Competitive Neutrality in Competition Enforcement: Note by Australia' (DAF/COMP/WD (2015)19, 29 May 2015) <http://www.oecd.org/officialdocuments/publicdisplaydocumentpdf/?cote=DAF/COMP/WD(2015)19&docLanguage=En>

——'Roundtable on Competitive Neutrality in Competition Enforcement: Note by the United States' (DAF/COMP/WD(2015)42, 9 June 2015) <http://www.oecd.org/officialdocuments/publicdisplaydocumentpdf/?cote=DAF/COMP/WD(2015)42&docLanguage=En>

——'Summary of Discussion of the Roundtable on Public Interest Considerations in Merger Control' (DAF/COMP/WP3/M(2016)1/ANN4/FINAL, 7 February 2017) <https://one.oecd.org/document/DAF/COMP/WP3/M(2016)1/ANN4/FINAL/en/pdf>

——'Ownership and Governance of State-Owned Enterprises: A Compendium of National Practices' (2018) <https://www.oecd.org/corporate/ca/Ownership-and-Governance-of-State-Owned-Enterprises-A-Compendium-of-National-Practices.pdf>

——'Scoping Note on Competitive Neutrality as a long-term theme for 2019-2020' No DAF/COMP/WD(2018)5, 23 April 2018) <http://www.oecd.org/officialdocuments/publicdisplaydocumentpdf/?cote=DAF/COMP/WD(2018)5&docLanguage=En>

Orbach BY, 'The Antitrust Consumer Welfare Paradox' (2011) 7(1) JCL & E

Owen BM and Sun S and Zheng W, 'Antitrust in China: The Problem of Incentive Compatibility' (2005) 1(1) JCL & E

PBOC, *The People's Bank of China Annual Report 2017* (2017) <https://pic.bankofchina.com/bocappd/report/201803/P020180329593657417394.pdf>

PetroChina Co Ltd, *2017 Annual Report* (2017) <http://www.petrochina.com.cn/ptr/rdxx/201804/7170580a02094cac9afb02f79e891c9d/files/e74108c533964ce190fb01a9d-67cfe0c.pdf>

Poncet S and Steingress W and Vandenbussche H, 'Financial Constraints in China: Firm-level Evidence' (2010) 21 China Economic Review

Reader D, 'Revisiting the Role of the Public Interest in Merger Control' (PhD thesis, University of East Anglia 2015) <https://ueaeprints.uea.ac.uk/id/eprint/68329/>

——'Accommodating Public Interest Considerations in Domestic Merger Control: Empirical Insights' (CCP Working Paper No 16–3, 18 February 2016) <http://dx.doi.org/10.2139/ssrn.2736917>

Rennie M and Lindsay F, 'Competitive Neutrality and State-Owned Enterprises in Australia: Review of Practices and their Relevance for Other Countries' (OECD Corporate Governance Working Papers No 4, 1 August 2011) <http://dx.doi.org/10.1787/5kg54cxkmx36-en>

Riley A, 'Nuking Misconceptions: Hinkley Point, Chinese SOEs and EU Merger Law' (2016) 37(8) ECLR

Rithmire ME, 'Land Institutions and Chinese Political Economy: Institutional Complementarities and Macroeconomic Management' (2017) 45(1) Politics and Society

Rosen DH and Leutert W and Guo S, 'Missing Link: Corporate Governance in China's State Sector' (Asia Society 5 November 2018) <https://rhg.com/research/missing-link-corporate-governance-in-chinas-state-sector/>

Seddon N, 'Holes in Hilmer Re-visited: Government Exemption from Australian Competition and Consumer Law' (Pt 4) (2012) 20 AJCCL

Shen W, 'Market-Based Regulatory Responses to Private Lending in China: Beyond a Law and Society Paradigm' (2017) 4(1) AsianJLS

Sheppard S, 'Privatisations: An Advocacy Role for the Competition Regulator?' (2015) 23 CCLJ

Shiying X, 'Competitive Neutrality of SOEs in China' in *Competitive Neutrality and its Application in Selected Developing Countries* (UNCTAD RPP 2014)

Sims R and Woodbridge G, 'Public Interest in Antitrust Enforcement: An Australian Perspective' (2020) 65(2) Antitrust Bull

Smith RL and Duke A, 'Agreements and Competition Law in Australia' (2014) 54(22) CCLJ

Sobel YY, 'Domestic-to-Domestic Transactions (2014–2015): A Narrowing Gap in China's Merger Control Regime' (2016) 15(3) Antitrust Source

Sokol DD, 'Tensions between Antitrust and Industrial Policy' (2015) 22(5) Geo Mason L Rev

Stucke ME, 'Reconsidering Competition' (2011) 81 Miss LJ

Sun CC and Xu J and Zhang Y, 'Anti-corruption and Bank Lending' (March 2018) <http://pubdocs.worldbank.org/en/277631528721196341/SXZ-Anticorruption0415.pdf>

Sweeney B, 'Globalisation of Competition Law and Policy: Some Aspects of the Interface Between Trade and Competition' (2004) 5(2) MJIL

Szamosszegi A and Kyle C, 'An Analysis of State-Owned Enterprises and State Capitalism in China' (US-China Economic and Security Review Commission 26 October 2011) <http://sites.utexas.edu/chinaecon/files/2015/06/US-China-Commission_State-Owned-Enterprises-and-State-Capitalism.pdf>

Trembath A, 'Competitive Neutrality: Scope for Enhancement' (NCC Discussion Paper, June 2002) <http://ncp.ncc.gov.au/docs/PIReCn-001.pdf>

Tuan Z, 'Land Use Rights in China' (2004) 3 Cornell Real Estate Review

UNCTAD, 'The Role of Competition Policy in Promoting Economic Development: The Appropriate Design and Effectiveness of Competition Law and Policy' (TD/RBP/CONF.7/3, November 2010) <http://unctad.org/en/Docs/tdrbpconf7d3_en.pdf>

——'The Importance of Coherence Between Competition Policies and Government Policies' (TD/B/C.I/CLP/9, July 2011) <https://unctad.org/en/Docs/ciclpd9_en.pdf>

US Chamber of Commerce, 'Competing Interests in China's Competition Law Enforcement: China's Anti-monopoly Law Application and the Role of Industrial Policy' (9 September 2014) <https://www.uschamber.com/report/competing-interests-chinas-competition-law-enforcement-chinas-anti-monopoly-law-application>

US Department of Commerce, 'China's Status as a Non-Market Economy' (26 October 2017) <https://enforcement.trade.gov/download/prc-nme-status/prc-nme-review-final-103017.pdf>

——'Review of China's Financial System for Countervailing Duty (CVD) Benchmarking Purposes' (Memorandum, 21 July 2017)

USCBC, 'China 2015 Regulatory Transparency Scorecard' (March 2015) <https://www.uschina.org/sites/default/files/USCBC%202015%20Regulatory%20Transparency%20Scorecard.pdf>

——'US-China Business Council Comments on Antimonopoly Law Amendment Questionnaire' (18 December 2015) <https://www.uschina.org/advocacy/regulatory-comments-on-china/uscbc-comments-antimonopoly-law-amendment-questionnaire>

——'2017 US-China Business Council Member Survey' (6 December 2017) <https://www.uschina.org/sites/default/files/2017_uscbc_member_survey.pdf>

US-China Economic and Security Review Commission, *2016 Annual Report to Congress* (16 November 2016) <https://www.uscc.gov/Annual_Reports/2016-annual-report-congress>

Virtanen M and Valkama P, 'Competitive Neutrality and Distortion of Competition: A Conceptual View' (2009) 32(3) World Competition

Wang L and Yang Y, 'Political Connections in the Land Market: Evidence from China's State-Owned Enterprises' (2018) SSRN Electronic Journal

Wang PJ and Zhang Y and Xue Q, 'Looking Ahead: The Integration of Chinese Anti-Monopoly Enforcement Authority' (2018) 18(1) Antitrust Source

Wang X and Emch A, 'Chinese Merger Control Eight Years On' (2017) 38 ECLR

Wang Y and Biddulph S and Godwin A, 'A Brief Introduction to the Chinese Judicial System and Court Hierarchy' (ALC Briefing Paper 6) <https://law.unimelb.edu.au/__data/assets/pdf_file/0004/2380684/ALC-Briefing-Paper-6-Wang,-Biddulph,-Godwin_5.pdf>

Wang Y, 'Beyond Local Protectionism: China's State–Business Relations in the Last Two Decades' (2016) 226 The China Quarterly

——'Relative Capture: Quasi-Experimental Evidence from the Chinese Judiciary' (2018) 21(8) Comparative Political Studies

Willett E and Cope D, 'A New Competitive Neutrality' (2018) 25 CCLJ

Williams M, 'Foreign Investment in China: Will the Anti-Monopoly Law Be a Barrier or a Facilitator?' (2009) 45(1) Tex Intl LJ

Wright R, 'The Future of Derivative Crown Immunity: With a Competition Law Perspective' (2007) 14(3) CCLJ

——'Derivative Governmental Immunity: Lessons from Baxter and the Trade Practices Act' (2008) 16(1) CCLJ

Xiaoye W and Yajie G, 'China's Antimonopoly Law Enforcement in the Digital Economy' (2022) 67(4) Antitrust Bull

Ying P, 'Competitive Neutrality and SOEs Reform: Recent Development and China's Practice' (Paper delivered to ARTNeT conference 'Trade in the Asian Country: Delivering on the promise of economic prosperity', 22–23 September 2014) <http://www.unescap.org/sites/default/files/Competitive%20Neutrality%20and%20SOEs%20Reform%20Recent%20Development%20and%20China's%20Practice.pdf>

Yong H, 'Pursuing the Second Best: The History, Momentum, and Remaining Issues of China's Anti-Monopoly Law' 75(1) Antitrust LJ

Yu H, 'The Ascendency of State-Owned Enterprises in China: Development, Controversy and Problems' (2014) 23(85) Journal of Contemporary China

Yu W and Zheng Y, 'Government stakeholder and CSR reports: Evidence from China' (2017) 19(2) China Accounting and Finance Review

Zhang AH, 'The Enforcement of the Anti-Monopoly Law in China: An Institutional Design Perspective' (2011) 56(3) Antitrust Bull

——'Bureaucratic Politics and China's Anti-Monopoly Law' (2014) 47(3) Cornell Intl LJ

——'The Antitrust Paradox of China Inc.' (2017) 50 NYUJILP

Zhang D and Freestone O, 'China's Unfinished State-Owned Enterprise Reforms' (2013) (2) Economic Roundup

Zhang L and Xu X, 'Land Policy and Urbanization in the People's Republic of China' (ADBI Working Paper Series No 614, November 2016) <https://www.adb.org/publications/land-policy-and-urbanization-prc>

Zhang M, 'From Public to Private: The Newly Enacted Chinese Property Law and the Protection of Property Rights in China' (2008) 5(2) Berkeley Bus LJ

Zhang Z and Wu B, 'Governing China's Administrative Monopolies Under the Anti-Monopoly Law: A Ten-Year Review (2008–2018) and Beyond' (2019) 15(1) JCL & E

Zheng W, 'Transplanting Antitrust in China: Economic Transition, Market Structure, and State Control' (2010) 32(2) U Pa J Intl L

——'The Revolving Door' (2015) 90(3) Notre Dame L Rev

Zhou W and Gao H and Bai X, 'Building a Market Economy Through WTO-Inspired Reform of State-Owned Enterprises in China' (2019) 68(4) ICLQ

In Chinese

卜令强 [Bu Lingqiang], '《竞争中立规则与中国国有企业改革初论》[A Preliminary Appraisal on Competition Neutrality Rules and the Reform of China's State-Owned Enterprises]' (2017) (2) 经济法论丛 [Economic Law Review]

邓峰 [Deng Feng], '《中国法上董事会的角色、职能及思想渊源: 实证法的考察》[The Role, Function, and Origins of Ideas in the Chinese Corporate Board Legal Institution: From a Positive Perspective]' (2013) 3 中国法学 [China Legal Science]

丁茂中 [Ding Maozhong], '《我国竞争中立政策的引入和实施》[On China's Adoption of Competitive Neutrality Policy]' (2015) 9 法学 [Law Science]

东艳 [Dong Yan] and 张琳 [Zhang Lin], '《美国区域贸易投资协定框架下的竞争中立原则分析》[An Analysis of the Competitive Neutrality Principle in the Framework of U.S. Regional Trade and Investment Agreements]' (2014) (6) 当代亚太 [Journal of Contemporary Asia-Pacific Studies]

胡改蓉 [Hu Gairong], '《竞争中立对我国国有企业的影响及法制应对》[The Impact of Competitive Neutrality on China's State-Owned Enterprises and Legal Response]' (2014) 6 法律科学 (西北政法大学学报) [Science of Law (Journal of Northwest University of Political Science and Law)]

黄志瑾 [Huang Zhijin], '《国际造法过程中的竞争中立规则——兼论中国的对策》[Competitive Neutrality in the Law-Making Process: A New Challenge for China]' (2013) 3 国际商务研究 [International Business Studies]

贾尽裴 [Jia Jinpei], '《国有企业分类改革实践与展望》[Practice and Prospect of State-Owned Enterprises Reform]' CNKI <http://gb.oversea.cnki.net/KCMS/detail/detail.aspx?filename=JJDK201810012&dbcode=CJFD&dbname=CJFD2018>

蒋大兴 [Jiang Daxing], '《走向"政治性公司法"——党组织如何参与公司治理》[Political Company Law: How Party Organisation Participates in Corporate Governance]' (2017) 23(3) Journal of Central South University (Social Science)

雷爱先 [Lei Aixian], '《关于国有土地使用权授权经营问题的探讨》[A Discussion on the issue of the Authorization Management of the State-Owned Land-Use Rights]' (2001) (1) 中国土地科学 [China Land Science]

——'《国有企业改制土地资产处置政策略论》[A Brief Discussion on the Disposal of Land Assets in the SOEs Reform]' (2006) (11) 中国地产市场 [China Real Estate Market]

李青 [Li Qing], '《建立公平竞争审查制度情况介绍》[An Introduction of the Implementation of Fair Competition Review System] (2018) 6中国价格监管与反垄断 [Price Supervision and Anti-Monopoly in China]

——'《中国竞争政策的回顾与展望》[Retrospect and Prospect of China's Competition Policy]' (2018) 7 中国价格监管与反垄断 [Price Supervision and Anti-Monopoly in China]

刘青山 [Liu Qingshan], '《特别策划 下篇: 那些已经"消失"的地方国资委》[Special Focus Sequel: Those Already 'Disappeared' Local State-Owned Assets Supervision and Administration Commission]' (2016) (8) 国资报告 [State-Owned Assets Report]

——'《攻坚克难 浴火重生——国企国资5年改革掠影》[Conquer the Challenges, Rise from the Ashes: A Glimpse of the Five Years Reform of State-Owned Enterprises]' (2017) (9) 《国资报告》 [State-Owned Assets Report]

卢昌崇 [Lu Changchong], '《公司治理机构及新、老三会关系论》[On the Discussion of Relationship between the New Corporate Governance Organs and the Old Ones]' (1994) 11 经济研究 [Economic Research Journal]

马其家 [Ma Qijia] and 樊富强 [Fan Fuqiang], '《论国际竞争中立规则适用范围的扩张》[On the Extended Scope of International Competitive Neutrality Rules]' (2017) (6) 法律适用(司法案例) [Journal of Law Application (Judicial Case)]

国家反垄断局 [National Anti-Monopoly Bureau], 《中国反垄断执法年度报告（2021）》[Annual Report of China on Anti-Monopoly Law Enforcement (2021)] (Report, 2021)

汤婧 [Tang Jing], '《"竞争中立" 规则: 国有企业的新挑战》[Rule of "Competitive Neutrality": A New Challenge for State-Owned Enterprises]' (2014) (3) 国际经济合作 [Journal of International Economic Cooperation]

屠新泉 [Tu Xinquan] and 徐林鹏 [Xu Linpeng] and 杨幸幸 [Yang Xingxing], '《国有企业相关国际规则的新发展及中国对策》[New Development of International Rules

Concerning State-Owned Enterprises and Its Impacts on China]' (2015) 2 亚太经济 [Asia- Pacific Economic Review]

徐士英 [Xu Shiying], '《中国竞争政策的实施与展望——兼论我国基本经济政策定位》[The Implementation and Prospect of China's Competition Policy—On the Basic Position on China's Economic Policy]' (2017) (1) 经济法论丛 [Economic Law Review]

原诗萌 [Yuan Shimeng], '《共性与差异 地方国企分类改革分析报告》[Similarities and Differences An Analysis Report on the Classification of Local State-Owned Enterprises]' (2016) (12) 国资报告 [State-Owned Assets Report]

王婷 [Wang Ting], '《竞争中立: 国际贸易与投资规则的新焦点》[Competitive Neutrality: The New Focus in the International Trade and Investment Regime]' (2012)(9) 国际经济合作 [World Economy and Trade]

王晓晔 [Wang Xiaoye], '《我国<反垄断法>修订的几点思考>》[Some Reflections on the Amendment of Anti-Monopoly Law in China]' (2020) 2 法学评论 [Law Review]

赵学清 [Zhao Xueqing] and 温寒 [Wen Han], '《欧美竞争中立政策对我国国有企业影响研究》[The Influence of the Competitive Neutrality Policy on China's State-Owned Enterprises]' (2013) 31(1) 河北法学 [Heibei Law Science]

Legislative Materials and Policy Documents

In English

ACCC, 'Merger Authorisation Guidelines' (24 October 2018) <https://www.accc.gov.au/system/files/Merger%20Authorisation%20Guidelines%20-%20October%202018.pdf>

——'Guidelines for Authorisation of Conduct (Non-Merger)' (5 March 2019) <https://www.accc.gov.au/system/files/Guidelines%20for%20Authorisation%20of%20conduct%20%28non-merger%29.pdf>

AGCNCO, *NBN Co* (Investigation No 14, 8 December 2011) <https://www.pc.gov.au/inquiries/completed/nbnco/report14-nbnco.pdf>

——*PETNET Australia* (Investigation No 15, 4 April 2012) <https://www.pc.gov.au/inquiries/completed/petnet/report15-petnet.pdf>

——*Australian Hearing* (Investigation No 16, 23 May 2018) <https://www.pc.gov.au/inquiries/completed/australian-hearing/australian-hearing.pdf>

Australia Industry Commission, 'Community Service Obligations: Policies and Practices of Australian Governments' (February 1997) <https://www.pc.gov.au/research/supporting/community-service-obligation-policy/cso.pdf>

Australian Government, *2015-16 Heads of Treasuries Competitive Neutrality Matrix* (February 2017) <http://www.federalfinancialrelations.gov.au/content/performance_reporting/CNMR_2015-16.pdf>

CCNCO, *Competitive Neutrality Investigation into Provision of Counter Terrorist First Response Services by the Australian Protective Service* (Report No 1, December 1998) <https://www.pc.gov.au/__data/assets/pdf_file/0011/158474/report1.pdf>

——'Rate of Return Issues' (Research Paper, December 1998) <https://www.pc.gov.au/research/supporting/rate-of-return/cnror.pdf>

——*Australian Institute of Sport Swim School* (Investigation No 2, 3 November 1999) <https://www.pc.gov.au/inquiries/completed/ais-swim-school/report2.pdf>

——*Customs Treatment of Australian Post* (Investigation No 5, 7 July 2000) <https://www.pc.gov.au/inquiries/completed/customs-australia-post/report5.pdf>

——*ARRB Transport Research Limited* (Investigation No 6, 14 September 2001) <https://www.pc.gov.au/inquiries/completed/arrb-transport-research/report6.pdf>

——*Docimage Business Services* (Investigation No 9, 20 December 2001) <https://www.pc.gov.au/inquiries/completed/docimage/report9.pdf>

——*Meteorological Services to Aviation* (Investigation No 7, 20 December 2001) <https://www.pc.gov.au/inquiries/completed/aviation-meterological-services/report7.pdf>

——*Sydney and Camden Airports* (Investigation No 8, 20 December 2001) <https://www.pc.gov.au/inquiries/completed/sydney-camden-airports/report8.pdf>

COAG, Agreement to Implement the National Competition Policy and Related Reforms, 11 April 1995

——Competition Principles Agreement, 11 April 1995 (as amended to 13 April 2007)

——Conduct Code Agreement, 11 April 1995

——Competition and Infrastructure Reform Agreement (February 2016)

——Intergovernmental Agreement on Competition and Productivity: Enhancing Reforms (9December2016)<https://www.coag.gov.au/sites/default/files/agreements/IGA-productivity-reforms.pdf>

Commissioner for Better Regulation, 'Identifying Significant Business Activities for Competitive Neutrality' (Guidance Note, 16 September 2016) <https://www.vic.gov.au/competitive-neutrality#guidance>

Commission Implementing Regulation (EU) 2017/969 of 8 June 2017 imposing definitive countervailing duties on imports of certain hot-rolled flat products of iron, non-alloy or other alloy steel originating in the People's Republic of China and amending Commission Implementing Regulation (EU) 2017/649 imposing a definitive anti-dumping duty on imports of certain hot-rolled flat products of iron, non-alloy or other alloy steel originating in the People's Republic of China (OJ L 146/32)

Commonwealth of Australia, *Parliamentary Debates*, House of Representatives, 12 March 1991, 1761 (Bob Hawke, Prime Minister).

——Commonwealth Competitive Neutrality Policy Statement (June 1996) <https://treasury.gov.au/sites/default/files/2019-03/cnps.pdf>

——*Australian Government National Competition Policy Report: 2005-07* (6 September 2007) <https://treasury.gov.au/sites/default/files/2019-03/NCP_Report_2005_07.pdf>

——*Australian Government Response to the Competition Policy Review* (2015) <https://treasury.gov.au/sites/default/files/2019-03/Govt_response_CPR.pdf>

Competition and Consumer Act 2010 (Cth)

Competition Policy Reform (New South Wales) Act 1995 No 8

Competition Policy Reform Act 1995 (Cth)

Corporations Act 2001 (Cth)

Financial Management and Accountability Act 1997 (Cth)

Government of Western Australia, 'Policy Statement on Competitive Neutrality' (June 1996) <https://www.wa.gov.au/sites/default/files/2020-01/policy-on-competitive-neutrality.pdf>

Harper I and others, *Competition Policy Review: Final Report* (March 2015 <https://treasury.gov.au/publication/p2015-cpr-final-report>

Hirson M, 'State Capitalism and the Evolution of "China, Inc.": Key Policy Issues for the United States Testimony before the US-China Economic and Security Review Commission on "China's Internal and External Challenges"' (2019) <https://www.uscc.gov/sites/default/files/Hirson_USCC%20Testimony_FINAL.pdf>

Independent Committee of Inquiry, *National Competition Policy* (AGPS 25 August 1993)

Independent Competition and Regulatory Commission, 'Competitive Neutrality Complaints Guideline' (August 2015) <https://www.icrc.act.gov.au/__data/assets/pdf_file/0010/1241695/ICRC-Guideline-Competitive-Neutrality-Complaints-August-2015.pdf>

National Competition Council, 'Considering the Public Interest Under the National Competition Policy' (November 1996) <http://ncp.ncc.gov.au/docs/PIRePu-001.pdf>

——*Competitive Neutrality Reform: Issues in Implementing Clause 3 of the Competition Principles Agreement* (January 1997) <http://ncp.ncc.gov.au/docs/PICo-001.pdf>

——'National Competition Policy: Some Impacts on Society and the Economy' (January 1999) <http://ncp.ncc.gov.au/docs/OINcpIm-002.pdf>

——*Assessment of Governments' Progress in Implementing the National Competition Policy and Related Reforms: Volume One—Overview of the National Competition Policy and Related Reforms* (2003) <http://ncp.ncc.gov.au/docs/2003%20assessment.pdf>

New South Wales Steering Committee on Government Trading Enterprises, *A Policy Framework for Improving the Performance of Government Trading Enterprises: A Report* (NSW Government 1988)

Northern Territory Government, 'Competitive Neutrality' (18 March 2020) <https://nt.gov.au/employ/money-and-taxes/economy/competitive-neutrality>

Office of the Tasmanian Economic Regulator, 'Competitive Neutrality Complaints Mechanism Guideline (Version 2)' (July 2015) <https://www.economicregulator.tas.gov.au/Documents/Competitive%20neutrality%20complaints%20guideline%20July%202015%20(683OOS70).pdf>

Productivity Commission, *Review of National Competition Policy Reforms* (Inquiry Report No 33, 28 February 2005) <http://www.pc.gov.au/inquiries/completed/national-competition-policy/report/ncp.pdf>

——'Submission to the Competition Policy Review' (June 2014) <https://www.pc.gov.au/research/supporting/competition-policy-review/competition-policy-review-submission.pdf>

Public Governance, Performance and Accountability Act 2013 (Cth)

Queensland Government Treasury, 'Queensland's Competitive Neutrality Complaints Process' (March 2001) <https://s3.treasury.qld.gov.au/files/ncp-complaints.pdf>

Queensland Productivity Commission, 'Queensland Productivity Commission's Process for Competitive Neutrality Complaints' <https://qpc.blob.core.windows.net/wordpress/2019/02/Competitive-Neutrality-Guidance-note-.pdf>

Standing Committee on Financial Institutions and Public Administration (Commonwealth), House of Representatives *Cultivating Competition: Report of the Inquiry into Aspects of the National Competition Policy Reform Package* (Committee Report, June 1997)

State Council of the PRC, '"Made in China 2025" Plan Issued' (19 May 2015) <http://english.www.gov.cn/policies/latest_releases/2015/05/19/content_281475110703534.htm>

Trade Practices Act Review Committee, *Report to The Minister for Business and Consumer Affairs* (August 1976) <https://www.australiancompetitionlaw.org/reports/pdf/swanson1976.pdf>

Treasurer, 'National Competition Policy Payments to States and Territories For 2005' (Press Release, No 113, 15 December 2005) <http://ncp.ncc.gov.au/docs/AST7As-%20Treasurers%20press%20release.pdf>

Treasury, 'The Importance of Competition Policy for Australia' <http://archive.treasury.gov.au/documents/1056/HTML/docshell.asp?URL=Ch2_Competitive_Neutrality.htm>

——'*Australian Government Competitive Neutrality Guidelines for Managers*' (February 2004) <https://consult.treasury.gov.au/market-and-competition-policy-division/competitive-neutrality-review/supporting_documents/2004%20Competitive%20Neutrality%20Guidelines%20for%20Managers%20AGCN_guide_v4.pdf>

——'Review of the Commonwealth Government's Competitive Neutrality Policy' (March 2017)<https://consult.treasury.gov.au/market-and-competition-policy-division/competitive-neutrality-review/supporting_documents/CN%20Review%20Consultation%20Paper.pdf>

Treaty Establishing the European Economic Community, Signed 25 March 1957 (Entered into Force 1 January 1958)

Victoria Department of Treasury and Finance, 'Competitive Neutrality Policy' (2012)

Victorian Competition and Efficiency Commission, *Competitive Neutrality Complaint Investigation Final Report: Pelican Park Recreation Centre Mornington Peninsula Shire Council* (Investigation Report, 13 June 2008)

In Chinese

《商务部行政处罚决定书》[Administrative Decision of Penalty by the Ministry of Commerce] MOFCOM, Shang Fa Han [2016] No 682, 12 April 2017

《国家市场监督管理总局行政处罚决定书》[Administrative Penalty Decision of the State Administration for Market Supervision] SAMR, Guoshijian Jiajian Chufa [2018] No 5 and No 6, 9 July 2018

《市场监管总局办公厅关于建议纠正内蒙古自治区公安厅滥用行政权力排除限制竞争有关行为的函》[Advice Letter of the General Office of the State Administration for Market and Regulation on the Correction of Abuse of Administrative Power that Restricted Competition by the Public Security Department of the Inner Mongolia Autonomous Region] SAMR, Shi Jian Jia Jian Han [2018] No 412, 19 June 2018

《中华人民共和国宪法修正案（1988年)》[Amendment to the Constitution of the People's Republic of China 1988] (12 April 1988)

《中华人民共和国反垄断法》[Anti-Monopoly Law of the People's Republic of China] Standing Committee of the NPC, Order No 68, 1 August 2008

《中华人民共和国反垄断法(2022修正)》[Anti-Monopoly Law of the People's Republic of China (2022 Amendment)] Standing Committee, Order No 116 of the President of the PRC, 1 August 2022

《中华人民共和国公司法》[Company Law of the People's Republic of China] Standing Committee of the NPC, Order No 8, promulgated at the 5th Session of the 8th NPC on 29 December 1993; amended 25 December 1999, 28 August 2004, 27 October 2005, and 28 December 2013; effective 1 March 2014

《中国共产党章程》[Constitution of the Communist Party of China] (24 October 2017)

《中华人民共和国宪法》[Constitution of the People's Republic of China] (11 March 2018)

《中共中央关于深化党和国家机构改革的决定》[Decision of the Central Committee of the Communist Party of China on Deepening the Reform of the Party and State Institutions] CPC Central Committee, 28 February 2018

《中共中央关于建立社会主义市场经济体制若干问题的决定》[Decision of the Central Committee of the Communist Party of China on Matters Concerning the Creation of A Socialist Market Economic System] 3rd Plenum of the 14th Party Congress, 17 November 1993

《中共中央关于全面深化改革若干重大问题的决定》[Decision of the Central Committee of the Communist Party of China on Several Major Issues on Comprehensively Deepening Reforms] CPC Central Committee, Adopted at the 3rd Plenary Session of the 18th Central Committee of the CPC on 12 November 2013

《自然资源部关于第一批废止和修改的部门规章的决定》 [Decision of the Ministry of Natural Resources on the First Group of Repealed and Amended Departmental Rules] Ministry of Natural Resources, Order No 5, 24 July 2019

《公平竞争审查制度实施细则》[Detailed Rules for the Implementation of the Fair Competition Review System] (People's Republic of China), State Administration for Market Regulation, National Development and Reform Commission, Ministry of Finance, Ministry of Commerce, Ministry of Justice, Guoshijian Fanlongduan [2021] No 2, 29 June 2021 and effective on the same day

《<中华人民共和国反垄断法>修订草案(公开征求意见稿)》[Draft Amendment to the Anti-Monopoly Law] State Administration for Market Regulation, 2 January 2020

《划拨用地目录》[Directory of Allocated Land] Ministry of Land and Resources (dissolved), Order No 9, 22 October 2001

《中国银保监会办公厅关于进一步做好信贷工作提升服务实体经济质效的通知》[General Office of the China Banking and Insurance Regulatory Commission on Further Doing a Good Job in Credit Work: Notice to Improve the Quality and Efficiency of Serving the Real Economy] China Banking Regulatory Commission Release, No 76, Prudential Regulation Bureau, 17 August 2017 <http://www.cbrc.gov.cn/chinese/newShouDoc/78EB4C12EEF94CCBABF28E8D807388F9.html>

《中共中央、国务院关于深化国有企业改革的指导意见》[Guiding Opinions of the Central Committee of the Communist Party of China and the State Council on Deepening the Reform of State-Owned Enterprises] Zhong Fa [2015] No 22, 24 August 2015

《国务院办公厅关于进一步完善国有企业法人治理结构的指导意见》[Guiding Opinions of the General Office of the State Council on Further Improving the Corporate Governance Structure of State-Owned Enterprises] Guo Ban Fa [2017] No 36, 24 April 2017

《国务院办公厅关于推动中央企业结构调整与重组的指导意见》[Guiding Opinions of the General Office of the State Council on Promoting the Restructuring and Reorganisation of Central Enterprises] Guo Ban Fa [2016] No 56, 17 July 2016

《关于促进中小企业健康发展的指导意见》[Guiding Opinions on Promoting the Healthy Development of Small and Medium-Sized Enterprises] General Office of CPC Central Committee and General Office of the State Council, 4 July 2019

《关于国有企业功能界定与分类的指导意见》[Guiding Opinions on the Functional Definition and Classification of State-Owned Enterprises] SASAC of the State Council; MOF; National Development and Reform Commission, Guo Zi Fa Yan Jiu [2015] No 170, 30 December 2015

《市场监管总局关于发布公平竞争审查第三方评估实施指南的公告》[Guidelines on the Third-Party Assessment of the Fair Competition Review System] SAMR, No 6, 12 February 2019

《未依法申报经营者集中调查处理暂行办法》[Interim Measures for the Investigation and Handling of the Failure to Declare Concentration of Business Operators in Accordance with the Law] MOFCOM, Decree 2011 No 6, 1 February 2012

《国务院关于推进国有资本投资、运营公司改革试点的实施意见》[Implementation Opinions of the State Council on Promoting the Pilot Reform of State-Owned Capital Investment and Operation Companies] Guo Fa [2018] No 23, 14 July 2018

《国务院国有资产监督管理委员会国有资产监督管理信息公开实施办法》[Implementing Measures of the State-Owned Assets Supervision and Administration Commission of the State Council for the Disclosure of Information on State-Owned Asset Supervision and Administration] Guo Zi Fa [2009] No 18, 5 February 2009

《中央金融企业负责人职务消费管理暂行办法》[Interim Measures for the Administration of Position-related Consumption of Persons in Charge of Central Financial Enterprises] MOF; Ministry of Supervision and National Auditing Office, Cai Jin [2012] No 125, 10 October 2012 [Non-effective]

《国有企业改革中划拨土地使用权管理暂行规定》[Interim Provisions on the Allocated Land-Use Rights Transferred in the State-Owned Enterprises Reform] National Land Resource Management Bureau, Order No 8, 1 March 1998 [Non-effective]

《国有重点金融机构监事会暂行条例》[Interim Regulations on the Board of Supervisors of Important State-Owned Financial Institutions] State Council, 15 March 2000

《中华人民共和国全民所有制工业企业法》[Law of People's Republic of China on Industrial Enterprises Owned by the Whole People] NPC, Order No 3 of the President, promulgated 13 April 1988, revised and effective 27 August 2009

《中华人民共和国企业国有资产法》[Law of the People's Republic of China on State-Owned Assets of Enterprises] Standing Committee of the NPC, promulgated 28 October 2008, effective 1 May 2009

《中华人民共和国立法法》[Legislation Law of the People's Republic of China] NPC, Order No 20 of the President, 15 March 2015

《国务院办公厅关于同意建立公平竞争审查工作部际联席会议制度的函》[Letter of the General Office of the State Council on Approval of the Establishment of the Inter-Ministerial Joint Meeting System for Fair Competition Review] Guo Ban Han [2016] No 109, 22 December 2016

《企业国有资产交易监督管理办法》[Measures for the Supervision and Administration of the Trading of State-Owned Assets of Enterprises] SASAC of the State Council; MOF, Order No 32, 24 June 2016

《国务院办公厅关于调整国务院反垄断委员会组成人员的通知》[Notice of the General Office of the State Council on the Adjustment of the Members of the Anti-Monopoly Commission of the State Council] Guo Ban Fa [2018] No 51, 11 July 2018

《国务院办公厅关于部际联席会议审批程序等有关问题的通知》[Notice of General Office of the State Council on Approval Procedures and Other Related Issues of the Inter-Ministerial Joint Conference] Guo Ban Han [2003] No 49, 18 July 2003

《国务院办公厅关于国务院反垄断委员会主要职责和组成人员的通知》[Notice of the General Office of the State Council on the Main Functions and Members of the Anti-Monopoly Commission of the State Counci] Guo Ban Fa [2008] No 104, 28 July 2008

《国务院办公厅关于印发中央企业公司制改制工作实施方案的通知》[Notice of the General Office of the State Council on Printing and Distributing the Implementing Plan for Corporate-style Restructuring of Central Enterprises] Guo Ban Fa [2017] No 69, 18 July 2017

《市场监管总局等四部门关于进一步推进公平竞争审查工作的通知》[Notice on Advancing Fair Competition Review System by the State Administration for Market Regulation, National Development and Reform Commission, Ministry of Finance, Ministry of Commerce] Guoshijian Anti-Monopoly (2020) No 73, 9 May 2020

'关于成立国资委中央企业社会责任指导委员会的通知 [Notice on the Establishment of the Central Corporate Social Responsibility Steering Committee of the SASAC]' (国资厅发研究 [2012]49号 [SASAC (2012) No 49]) <http://www.sasac.gov.cn/n2588030/n2588939/c4297362/content.html>

'《关于印发<关于中央企业履行社会责任的指导意见>的通知》 [Notice on Issuing the "Guiding Opinions on the Performance of Social Responsibilities of Central Enterprises"]' SASAC (国资发研究 [2008]1号 [Development Research [2008] No 1], 29 December 2007) <http://www.sasac.gov.cn/n2588030/n2588939/c4297490/content.html>

《国务院国资委关于印发<国务院国资委授权放权清单(2019年版)>的通知》 [Notice on Issuing the List of Powers Granted and Delegated by the State-Owned Assets Supervision and Administration Commission of the State Council (2019 Edition)] Guo Zi Fa Gai Ge (2019) No 52, 3 June 2019

《关于加快推进中央企业党建工作总体要求纳入公司章程有关事项的通知》[Notice on Matters Regarding Speeding Up and Advancing the Inclusion of Overall Requirements for Central State-Owned Enterprises' Party-Building Work in Articles of Association] Guozi Dangwei Dangjian [2017] No 1, 3 January 2017

《国土资源部关于印发<规范国有土地租赁若干意见>的通知》[Notice of the Ministry of Land and Resources on Issuing the Opinions on Regulating the Lease of State-Owned Land] Ministry of Land and Resources (dissolved), Guo Tu Zi Fa [1999] No 222, 27 July 1999

《关于印发<关于省属企业功能界定与分类监管的指导意见（试行）>的通知》[Notice on the Printing and Distributing the Guiding Opinions on the Classifications of Provincial SOEs (Trial Implementation)] Sichuan SASAC, Chuan Guoziwei [2016] No 115, 7 June 2016

《市场监管总局关于反垄断执法授权的通知》[Notice of the State Administration for Market Regulation on the Empowerment of Anti-monopoly Law Enforcement] SAMR, Guoshijian Fandongduan [2018] No 265, 28 December 2018

《市场监管总局关于试点委托开展部分经营者集中案件反垄断审查的公告》[Announcement on Piloting the Entrustment of Anti-Monopoly Review in Selected Concentration of Undertakings] SAMR, [2022] No 23, 23 September 2022

《国务院关于印发改革国有资本授权经营体制方案的通知》[Notice of the State Council on Printing and Distribution of the Plan for Reforming the System of Authorised Operation of the State-Owned Capital] Guo Fa [2019] No 9, 19 April 2019

《国务院关于部委管理的国家局设置的通知》[Notice of the State Council on the Setup of National Bureaus Administrated by Ministries and Commissions] Guo Fa [2018] No 7, 22 March 2018

《国务院国有资产监督管理委员会、财政部关于印发<关于完善中央企业功能分类考核的实施方案>的通知》[Notice of the State-Owned Assets Supervision and Administration Commission of the State Council and the Ministry of Finance on Printing and Distributing the 'Implementation Plan for Improving the Functional Classification and Assessment of Central Enterprises'] Guozifa Zonghe [2016] No 252, 24 August 2016

《关于王明辉等三名同志免职的通知》[Notice to Remove the Government Positions of Wang Huiming] Government of Yunnan Province, Yunzhengren [2017] No 22, 22 April 2017

《陕西省国资委关于省属企业实施分类管理的意见》[Opinion of the State-Owned Assets Supervision and Administration Commission of the Shanxi Province on the Classification of Provincial-Owned Enterprises] Shanzhengbanfa [2014] No 112, 30 May 2016

《国务院关于国有企业发展混合所有制经济的意见》[Opinions of the State Council on the Development of Mixed Ownership Economy by State-Owned Enterprises] (Guo Fa [2015] No 54, 23 September 2015

《关于推进本市轨道交通场站及周边土地综合开发利用的实施意见》[Opinions of Shanghai Municipal People's Government on Promoting Comprehensive Development and Utilisation of Shanghai Rail Transit Stations and Surrounding Land] General Office of the Shanghai Municipal People's Government Forwarding Development and Reform Commission of Shanghai and the Municipal Planning and Land Resources Bureau of Shanghai, Hu Fu Ban [2016] No 79, 7 October 2016

《国务院关于在市场体系建设中建立公平竞争审查制度的意见》[Opinions of the State Council on Establishing a Fair Competition Review System During the Development of Market-oriented Systems] Guo Fa [2016] No 34, 1 June 2016

《中华人民共和国物权法》[Property Law of the People's Republic of China] NPC, Order No 62, 1 October 2007

《关于扩大国有土地有偿使用范围的意见》[Opinions on Expanding the Scope of Payable Use of State-Owned Land] Guo Tu Zi Gui [2016] No 20, 31 December 2016

《中央企业领导班子和领导人员综合考核评价办法（试行)》 [Provisional Measures on Comprehensive Evaluation of Corporate Leadership Teams and Leaders of Central SOEs (Trial Implementation)] General Office of the CPC Central Committee and SASAC of the State Council, Zhong Zhu Fa [2009] No 17, 2009

《中央企业领导人员管理暂行规定》[Provisional Rules on Managing Corporate Leaders of Central SOEs] General Office of the CPC Central Committee and General Office of the State Council, 6 November 2009

《国家市场监督管理总局职能配置、内设机构和人员编制规定》[Provisions on the Functions, Structure and Staffing of the State Administration for Market Regulation] General Office of the Central Committee of the Communist Party of China and General Office of the State Council, 30 July 2018

《国务院关于经营者集中申报标准的规定(2018修订)》[Provisions of the State Council on the Thresholds for Declaring Concentration of Business Operators (2018 Revision)] Order No 703, 18 September 2018

《最高人民法院关于审理因垄断行为引发的民事纠纷案件应用法律若干问题的规定》[Provisions of the Supreme People's Court on Certain Issues Relating to the Application of Law in Hearing Cases Involving Civil Disputes Arising out of Monopolistic Acts] Supreme People's Court, Fa Shi [2012] No 5, 1 June 2012

《招标拍卖挂牌出让国有建设用地使用权规定》[Provisions on Transfer of the Right to Use State-Owned Construction Land through Tendering, Auction and Listing] Ministry of Land and Resources (dissolved), Order No 39, 1 November 2007

《行政法规制定程序条例》[Regulations on Procedures for the Formulation of Administrative Regulations] State Council, Decree No 694, 1 May 2018

《规章制定程序条例》[Regulations on Procedures for the Formulation of Rules] State Council, Decree No 695, 1 May 2018

《关于重庆渝富控股集团深化国有资本运营公司改革试点方案的批复》[Reply to the Pilot Plan proposed by the Chongqing Yufu Holding Group on Deepening Reform of State-Owned Capital Operation Companies] Yufu [2020] No 12, 19 March 2020

《中共中央、国务院关于推进价格机制改革的若干意见》[Several Opinions of the Central Committee of the Communist Party of China and the State Council on Advancing the Pricing Mechanism Reform] Zhong Fa [2015] No 28, 12 October 2015

《国土资源部关于加强土地资产管理促进国有企业改革和发展的若干意见》[Several Opinions of the Ministry of Land and Resources on Strengthening Land Asset Management and Promoting the Reform and Development of State-Owned Enterprises] Ministry of Land and Resources (dissolved), Guo Tu Zi Fa [1999] No 433, 25 November 1999

《国务院关于改革和完善国有资产管理体制的若干意见》[Several Opinions of the State Council on Reforming and Improving the State-Owned Asset Management System] Guo Fa [2015] No 63, 25 October 2015

《国务院机构改革方案》[The Institutional Reform Plan of the State Council] NPC, 17 March 2018

《中华人民共和国城市房地产管理法》[Urban Real Estate Administration Law of the People's Republic of China] Standing Committee of the NPC, Order No 72, 30 August 2007

Newspaper Articles and Government Releases

In English

Bo X, 'Former Official Demoted for Disciplinary Violations' *Xinhuanet News* (3 July 2017) <http://news.xinhuanet.com/english/2017-07/03/c_136413333.htm>

'China establishes SOE Structural Adjustment Fund' (27 September 2016) <https://www.scio.gov.cn/32618/Document/1492508/1492508.htm>

'China to Increase Bank Loans to Private Firms' *Xinhuanet News* (25 February 2019) <http://www.xinhuanet.com/english/2019-02/25/c_137849420.htm>

'Economic Watch: China's Monetary Policy Unchanged Despite Reserve Requirement Cut' *Xinhua News* (19 April 2018) <http://www.xinhuanet.com/english/2018-04/19/c_137121802.htm>

'Former China Telecom Boss Chang Xiaobing Sentenced to Six Years for Corruption' *South China Morning Post* (31 May 2017) <http://cdn4.i-scmp.com/tech/enterprises/article/2096382/former-china-telecom-boss-chang-xiaobing-sentenced-six-years>

Hormats RD, 'Ensuring a Sound Basis for Global Competition: Competitive Neutrality' (US State Department, 5 May 2011) <https://2009-2017.state.gov/e/rls/rmk/20092013/2011/163472.htm>

Hornby L, 'China's Top Judge Denounces Idea of Judicial Independence: Civil Rights' *Financial Times* (18 January 2017)

——'Communist Party Asserts Control over China Inc' *Financial Times* (3 October 2017)

Hughes J, 'Communist Party Control Written into Law at China's Big Companies' *Financial Times* (15 August 2017)

Hui L, '440 senior officials investigated for corruption' *Xinhuanet News* (19 October 2017) <http://news.xinhuanet.com/english/2017-10/19/c_136691587.htm>

Li K, 'Report on the Work of the Government' (2nd Session of the 13th National People's Congress of the PRC, 5 March 2019) <http://english.www.gov.cn/premier/speeches/2019/03/16/content_281476565265580.htm>

Needham K, 'China's New Australian Buzzwords to Counter Trump' *The Sydney Morning Herald* (17 October 2018) <https://www.smh.com.au/business/the-economy/china-s-new-australian-buzzwords-to-counter-trump-20181016-p50a1c.html>

Shih G, 'China Mobile Names MIIT Vice Minister Shang Bing New Chairman', *Reuters* (24 August 2015) <https://www.reuters.com/article/china-mobile-managementchanges/china-mobile-names-miit-vice-minister-shang-bing-new-chairman-idUSB9N10E00U20150824>

Si M, 'Antitrust Officials: All Firms Treated Equally', *China Daily* (17 November 2018) <https://www.chinadaily.com.cn/a/201811/17/WS5bef4e89a310eff303289412.html>

Wildau G, 'China Tells Banks to Increase Lending to Small Businesses' (13 March 2019) <https://www.ft.com/content/e3a77c2e-4580-11e9-b168-96a37d002cd3>

In Chinese

'《关于控股股东完成工商变更登记的公告》 [Announcement on Changing the Controlling Shareholders of Business Registration]', *云南白药集团股份有限公司 Yunnan Baiyao Group Co Ltd*, 28 June 2017) <http://pdf.dfcfw.com/pdf/H2_AN201706280674602279_1.pdf>

'中国联合网络通信股份有限公司第五届董事会第十四次会议决议公告' [Announcement on the 5th Meeting of the Board of Directors, No 14 Conference Resolutions of China United Network Communications Limited] 3 <http://www.chinaunicom-a.com/wcm/1/attachments/2018/1/23/1283/1516710056512.pdf>

车玉明 [Che Yuming] and 张旭东 [Zhang Xudong], '《我国财政和货币政策同时调整 4万亿资金力撬内需》 [Fiscal and monetary policies are simultaneously adjusted by 4 trillion yuan to leverage domestic demand]' *China News* (19 November 2008) <http://www.gov.cn/jrzg/2008-11/10/content_1143810.htm>

'经济日报：结构调整基金成国企改革重要推手 [Economic Daily: The China Structural Reform Fund becomes Important Promoter of State-Owned Enterprise Reform]' (21 September 2017) <http://www.sasac.gov.cn/n2588025/n2588139/c7895224/content.html>

‘新闻办就中国《反垄断法》实施十周年有关情况及展望举行新闻发布会 [Information Office Press Conference on the Progress and Prospect of 10th Anniversary of the Enforcement of the “Anti-Monopoly Law” in China]’ (16 November 2018) <http://www.gov.cn/xinwen/2018-11/16/content_5341034.htm#1>

‘刘鹤主持国务院金融稳定发展委员会专题会议 [Liu He presides over the special meeting of the State Council Financial Stability and Development Committee]’ (国务院 [State Council], 20 October 2018) <http://www.gov.cn/guowuyuan/2018-10/21/content_5333237.htm>

刘娜 [Liu Na], ‘马国强任武汉市委书记（图/简历）[Ma Guoqiang Appointed Secretary of Wuhan Municipal Party Committee (Photo/Resume)]’ 新华网 [Xinhuanet] (20 July 2018) <http://www.xinhuanet.com/politics/2018-07/20/c_1123156034.htm>

林远 [Lin Yuan], ‘《电力反垄断第一案浮出水面 山西发电企业几乎全部卷入》 [First Case of Direct Power Supply Price Monopoly Agreement has Surfaced in Shanxi Province]’, 经济参考报 [Economic Information Daily] (6 June 2017) <http://www.xinhuanet.com//2017-06/06/c_1121092318.htm>

李自良 [Li Ziliang] and 吉哲鹏 [Ji Zhepeng], ‘《老字号云南白药的创新路:“均衡股权”探索混改路径》 [Traditional Brand Yunnan Baiyao’s Innovation: Exploring “Balanced Equity” for Mixed-Ownership Reform]’ 新华网 [Xinhuanet] (31 January 2019) <http://www.xinhuanet.com/local/2019-01/31/c_1124067844.htm>

‘明报：肖亚庆指出上市国企设党委 股东利益更受保护 [Ming Pao: Xiao Yaqing Pointed Out That Set Up Party Commitee at Listed Company Will Increase the Protection of Shareholders Interests]’ (23 October 2017) <http://www.sasac.gov.cn/n2588025/n2588139/c8089518/content.html>

‘国家发展改革委设立公平竞争审查处进一步强化公平竞争审查工作 [National Development and Reform Commission Establishes a Fair Competition Review Office to Further Strengthen Fair Competition Review Work]’ (9 January 2018) <http://www.gov.cn/xinwen/2018-01/09/content_5254755.htm>

彭华岗 [Peng Huagang], ‘《国新办举行2018年前三季度央企经济运行情况发布会》 [The State Council Information Office Held a Press Conference on the Economic Performance of Central SOEs in the First Three Quarters of 2018]’ (15 October 2018) <http://www.scio.gov.cn/xwfbh/xwbfbh/wqfbh/37601/39092/index.htm>

‘《以混合所有制改革试点作为深化国企改革的突破口 实现完善治理强化激励突出主业提高效率的改革试点目标——国家发展改革委召开国有企业混合所有制改革试点专题会》 [Pilot Programs of Mixed-Ownership Reform of SOEs]’ (Press Conference, National Development and Reform Commission, 28 September 2016) <http://webcache.googleusercontent.com/search?q=cache:SuaLdLZ9u-YJ:zys.ndrc.gov.cn/xwfb/201609/t20160930_821880.html&hl=en&gl=au&strip=1&vwsrc=0>

‘《新增7个自贸区和深化上海自贸区改革开放方案政策解读》 [Policy Briefing on Seven New Free Trade Zones and Plans for Deepening Reform of the Shanghai Free Trade Zone]’ (State Council Information Office, 1 April 2017) <http://www.scio.gov.cn/34473/34515/Document/1546919/1546919.htm>

'国资委举行新闻发布会通报2017年中央企业经济运行情况 [Press Conference on Central SOE Economic Operating Conditions in 2017]' (17 January 2018) <http://www.sasac.gov.cn/n2588025/n2588119/c8494483/content.html>

任芳 [Ren Fang] and刘兵 [Liu Bing], '国资委：国有经济应保持对七个行业的绝对控制力 [SASAC of State Council: the state should keep absolute control over seven industries]' *Xinhua News* (18 December 2006) <http://www.gov.cn/jrzg/2006-12/18/content_472256.htm>

国资报告：国企改革取得重要阶段性成果 [State-Owned Assets Reports: State-Owned Enterprise Reform Achieved Important Milestones]' (Press release, 12 June 2017) <http://www.sasac.gov.cn/n2588025/n2588139/c4528554/content.html>

'央企公司制改制基本完成"历史性突破"打开改革新空间 [The Corporatisation Reform of the State-Owned Enterprises is Basically Complete]' (25 April 2019) <http://www.gov.cn/xinwen/2018-04/25/content_5285657.htm>

'《山西直供电价格垄断协议案被依法查处》 [The NDRC investigates a price-fixing agreement in Shanxi Province]' 新华社 [Xinhua News] (3 August 2017) <http://www.gov.cn/xinwen/2017-08/03/content_5215766.htm>

'《首例直供电价格垄断协议案被依法查处》 [The NDRC's Penalty Decision Against the Shanxi Power Generator Companies for Price-Fixing]' (3 August 2017) <http://www.gov.cn/xinwen/2017-08/03/content_5215802.htm>

王毕强 [Wang Biqiang] and 刘伟勋 [Liu Weixun], '《涉操纵机票涨价 发改委调查中航信》[Alleged Domestic Airline Ticket Price Fixing by TravelSky Technology Ltd is Under NDRC's Investigation] ', 经济观察报 [The Economic Observer] (17 May 2009) <http://www.eeo.com.cn/finance/other/2009/05/16/137823.shtml>

王希 [Wang Xi], 国务院国资委：反对在国际规则制定中给予国有企业歧视性待遇[SASAC: Against Discriminatory Treatment of SOEs' in the Formation of International Rules] 新华网 [Xinhuanet] (15 Oct 2018) <http://www.xinhuanet.com/politics/2018-10/15/c_129971816.htm>.

习近平 [Xi Jinping], '决胜全面建成小康社会 夺取新时代中国特色社会主义伟大胜利 [Secure a Decisive Victory in Building a Moderately Prosperous Society in All Respects and Strive for the Great Success of Socialism with Chinese Characteristics for a New Era]' (Speech delivered at the 19th National Congress of the CPC, 18 October 2017) <http://www.gov.cn/zhuanti/2017-10/27/content_5234876.htm>

Internet Materials

'十三届全国两会代表委员中的50名央企老总 [50 SOE CEOs in the 13th National Congress]' 新浪财经 [Finance Sina] (12 Feburary 2018) <http://finance.sina.com.cn/china/2018-02-13/doc-ifyrmfmc2232055.shtml>

'《反垄断局》 [Anti-Monopoly Bureau]', 国家市场监督管理总局反垄断局 [Anti-Monopoly Bureau of the State Administration for Market Regulation] <http://www.samr.gov.cn/fldj/sjjs/>

Baker McKenzie FenXun, 'China's New Antitrust Regulator Finalises its Agency Integration' (Client Alert, September 2018) <http://bakerxchange.com/rv/ff0040513e-06fa9d57796b9cb241be848d3bec47>

Cai P, Understanding China's Belt and Road Initiative (Lowy Institute, 22 March 2017) <https://www.lowyinstitute.org/publications/understanding-belt-and-road-initiative>

Central Huijin Investment Ltd, 'Company Profile' (2019) <http://www.huijin-inv.cn/huijineng/About_Us/index.shtml>

China Arts and Entertainment Group Ltd, 'Profile' (11 June 2019) <http://en.caeg.cn/caeg/jtjj/201802/d8066827394c42caa914edb56441fbdd.shtml>

'China Competition Bulletin', Competition Law and Economics Network (Bulletin 47, June 2017) <https://law.unimelb.edu.au/__data/assets/pdf_file/0007/2459185/China-Competition-Bulletin-June-2017.pdf>

'中国国电集团公司 [China Guodian Corporation]', 财富 [Fortune China] <http://www.fortunechina.com/global500/536/2017>

'中国石油集团完成整体改制并更名 [China National Petroleum Corporation Completes its Overall Restructuring and Changes its Name]' (21 December 2017) <http://www.sasac.gov.cn/n2588030/n2588924/c8374019/content.html>

China Structural Reform Fund Co Ltd, 'Company Profile' (2017) <http://www.cctfund.cn/index.php?c=content&a=list&catid=39#page1>

China Unicom, *Annual Report of China Unicom (Hong Kong) Ltd* (2016) <https://www.chinaunicom.com.hk/en/ir/reports/2016_20f.pdf>

China United Network Communications Ltd, '中国联通关于混合所有制改革有关情况的专项公告 [The special announcement by China Unicom regarding proposal of mixed ownership reform]' (2017) <http://pg.jrj.com.cn/acc/CN_DISC/STOCK_NT/2017/08/21/600050_ls_1203829685.PDF>

Datang International Power Generation Co Ltd, 'Proposed Amendments to Articles of Association and Notice of EGM' (30 June 2017) <https://www1.hkexnews.hk/listedco/listconews/sehk/2017/0630/ltn201706301016.pdf>

Department of Finance, 'Commonwealth Company' (updated 25 October 2019)

——'Government Business Enterprises' (updated 14 December 2020) <https://www.finance.gov.au/business/government-business-enterprises>

'《强根铸魂抓党建 踏石留印见实效——国务院国资委党委推进中央企业党建工作纪实》 [Enhancing the Party Building to Strengthen the Roots: The State-Owned Assets Supervision and Administration Commission of the State Council to Promote the Party building in Central State-Owned Enterprises]' (10 October 2017) <http://www.sasac.gov.cn/n2588030/n2588919/c7979758/content.html>

Feng C, 'Quick Take: China Fines 23 Coal Power Firms for Monopolistic Practices', *Caixin* (4 August 2017) <https://www.caixinglobal.com/2017-08-04/quick-take-china-fines-23-coal-power-firms-for-monopolistic-practices-101126540.html>

募资300亿 投资170亿 撬动1700亿 央企扶贫基金全力决战脱贫攻坚 [Fund-Raising 30 Billion Investment of 17 Billion Leveraging 170 Billion Central Enterprises Fully Decisive in Tackling Poverty Alleviation Fund] (17 October 2019) <http://www.sasac.gov.cn/n2588030/n2588939/c12367152/content.html>

'Government Department Supporting Monopoly Is Not Upholding Rule of Law', *China Daily* (25 June 2018) <http://www.chinadaily.com.cn/a/201806/25/WS5b302beba3103349141de778.html>

Gu M and Xiang C, 'SAMR Adopts Stricter View on Identification of Competitors in Monopoly Agreement Case' (30 August 2018) <https://www.chinalawvision.com/2018/08/competition-law-anti-monopoly-law/samr-adopts-stricter-view-identification-competitors-monopoly-agreement-case/>

Hubbard P, '"Fragmented Authoritarianism" and State Ownership' (East Asia Forum, 23 January 2017) <http://www.eastasiaforum.org/2017/01/23/fragmented-authoritarian-ism-and-state-ownership/>

Jones T and others, 'Competition Law in Asia Pacific: Highlights from 2018 and What's Coming Next in 2019' (Bird & Bird Law Firm, April 2019) <https://www.twobirds.com/en/news/articles/2019/global/competition-law-in-asia-pacific-highlights-from-2018-and-2019>

Keohane D, 'SOE You Think You Can Reform? Mixed-Ownership Edition', *Financial Times* (28 September) <https://ftalphaville.ft.com/2015/09/28/2140985/soe-you-think-you-can-reform-mixed-ownership-edition/>

Kroeber A, 'Summertime, and the Jailin' is Easy' (Gavekal Dragonomics, 1 September 2014) <http://research.gavekal.com/content.php/10394-China-CEQ-Q3-2014-Summer-time-And-The-Jailin-Is-Easy>

Li C and Xu L, 'The Rise of State-Owned Enterprise Executives in China's Provincial Leadership' (China-US Focus, 21 Feburary 2017) <https://www.chinausfocus.com/political-social-development/the-rise-of-state-owned-enterprise-executives-in-chinas-provincial-leadership>

Merrett A and Trindade R, 'Has Competitive Neutrality Run Its Course?' (September 2013) (13) The State of Competition <http://thestateofcompetition.com.au/wp-content/uploads/2013/09/TSoC-Issue-13-competitive-neutrality.pdf>

Milhaupt CJ and Zheng W, 'Why Mixed-Ownership Reforms Cannot Fix China's State Sector' (Paulson Policy Memorandum, January 2016) <http://www.paulsoninstitute.org/wp-content/uploads/2017/01/PPM_SOE-Ownership_Milhaupt-and-Zheng_English_R.pdf>

MOF, '中央金融企业名录 [Central State-Owned Financial Enterprises List]' <http://jrs.mof.gov.cn/jinrongleiqiyeguoyouzichanguanli/201501/t20150123_1183782.html>

Nan Z, 'New Head of Market Regulator Appointed', *China Daily* (22 May 2019) <https://www.chinadaily.com.cn/a/201905/22/WS5ce49d19a3104842260bcff2.html>

National Competition Council, 'About the National Competition Policy' <http://ncp.ncc.gov.au/pages/about>

——'About Us', National Competition Council (Web Page) <http://ncc.gov.au/about/about_us>

——'Corporate Plan 2018–19' (August 2018) <http://ncc.gov.au/images/uploads/Corporate_Plan_2018-19,_August_2018_(PDF,_734_KB).pdf>

National People's Congress of the PRC, 'National People's Congress' <http://www.npc.gov.cn/englishnpc/c2846/column2.shtml>

Productivity Commission, 'Making a Complaint' <https://www.pc.gov.au/about/core-functions/competitive-neutrality/complaint>

SAMR, '《国家市场监督管理总局》 [State Administration for Market Regulation]' <http://www.samr.gov.cn/>

SASAC, '地方国资委 [Local SASACs]' (4 January 2016) <http://www.sasac.gov.cn/n2588035/n2641584/index.html>

SASAC, 'What We Do' (17 July 2018) <http://en.sasac.gov.cn/2018/07/17/c_7.htm>

Shughart WF, 'Antitrust, Regulation and the "Chicago School"' (ProMarket, 17 February 2017) <https://promarket.org/antitrust-regulation-chicago-school/?mc_cid=a5b9f818b8&mc_eid=08df55fd49>

Sinopec, 'Company Reports and Publications' <http://www.sinopecgroup.com/group/en/companyprofile/Companyreportsandpublications>

'Yunnan Baiyao Group', *Forbes* (12 May 2020) <https://www.forbes.com/companies/yunnan-baiyao-group/#71deea1a7287>

Yunnan Baiyao Group, 《云南白药集团股份有限公司2016年年度报告》 [Yunnan Baiyao Group Co Ltd Annual Report 2016] (2016) <http://www.yunnanbaiyao.com.cn/upload/files/1704/%E4%BA%91%E5%8D%97%E7%99%BD%E8%8D%AF%EF%BC%9A2016%E5%B9%B4%E5%B9%B4%E5%BA%A6%E6%8A%A5%E5%91%8A.PDF>

Yunnan Baiyao Group, 《云南白药集团股份有限公司 2017 年半年度报告摘要》 [Yunnan Baiyao Group Co Ltd First Half-Year 2017 Report Summary] (2017) <http://www.yunnanbaiyao.com.cn/upload/files/1708/%E4%BA%91%E5%8D%97%E7%99%

BD%E8%8D%AF%EF%BC%9A2017%E5%B9%B4%E5%8D%8A%E5%B9%B4%E5%BA%A6%E6%8A%A5%E5%91%8A%E6%91%98%E8%A6%81.PDF>

张锐 [Zhang Rui], ‘《国有资本投资运营公司将在改革中获更多赋能》[More Power Will Be Given to State-Owned Capital Investment or Operation Companies During the Reform]’ 证券时报网[Securities Times] (8 March 2018) <http://www.stcn.com/2018/0308/14011770.shtml>

朱凯 [Zhu Kai], ‘《中国公平竞争审查制度实施进展》 [Progress on the Implementation of China's Fair Competition Review System]’ (Roundtable of EU-China Competition Cooperation presentation, 22 March 2017) <http://www.euchinacomp.org/attachments/article/528/02%20-%20NDRC%20-%20Zhu%20Kai_NDRC%20booklet%20session_I_CN.pdf>

庄冠蓉 [Zhuang Guanrong], ‘重庆国企改革：抓住管资本“牛鼻子 [Chongqing's Reform of SOEs: Regulating Capital by "Capturing the Nose"]’, 中国经济时报 [China Economic Times] (15 August 2016) A07 <http://jjsb.cet.com.cn/show_477248.html>

INSTITUTE of
Competition Law
Antitrust databases and resources

The Institute of Competition Law

The Institute of Competition Law is a publishing company, founded in 2004 by Dr. Nicolas Charbit, based in Paris, London and NewYork. The Institute cultivates scholarship and discussion about antitrust issues though publications and conferences. Each publication and event is supervised by editorial boards and scientific or steering committees to ensure independence, objectivity, and academic rigor. Thanks to this management, the Institute has become one of the few think tanks in Europe to have significant influence on antitrust policies.

Aim

The Institute focuses government, business and academic attention on a broad range of subjects which concern competition laws, regulations and related economics.

Boards

To maintain its unique focus, the Institute relies upon highly distinguished editors, all leading experts in national or international antitrust: Bill Kovacic, Mario Monti, Eleanor Fox, Laurence Idot, Frédéric Jenny, Ioannis Lianos, Richard Whish, etc.

Authors

4,000 authors, from 85 jurisdictions.

Partners

- Universities: University College London, King's College London, Queen Mary University, Paris Sorbonne Panthéon-Assas, etc.
- Law firms: Allen & Overy, Cleary Gottlieb Steen & Hamilton, Baker McKenzie, Hogan Lovells, Jones Day, Norton Rose Fulbright, Skadden Arps, White & Case, etc.

Events

Brussels, Dusseldorf, Hong Kong, London, Milan, New York, Paris, Singapore, Warsaw and Washington, DC.

Online version

Concurrences website provides all articles published since its inception.

Publications

The Institute publishes Concurrences Review, a print and online quarterly peer-reviewed journal dedicated to EU and national competitions laws. e-Competitions is a bi-monthly antitrust news bulletin covering 85 countries. The e-Competitions database contains over 23,000 case summaries from 4,000 authors.

Concurrences
Competition Laws Review

Concurrences Review

Concurrences is a print and online quarterly peer reviewed journal dedicated to EU and national competitions laws. It has been launched in 2004 as the flagship of the Institute of Competition Law in order to provide a forum for academics, practitioners and enforcers. Concurrences' influence and expertise has garnered contributions or interviews with such figures as Christine Lagarde, Bill Kovacic, Emmanuel Macron, Antonin Scalia and Magrethe Vestager.

Contents

More than 14,000 articles, print and/or online. Quarterly issues provide current coverage with contributions from the EU or national or foreign countries thanks to more than 2,500 authors in Europe and abroad.

Format

In order to balance academic contributions with opinions or legal practice notes, Concurrences provides its insight and analysis in a number of formats:

- Forewords: Opinions by leading academics or enforcers
- Interviews: Interviews of antitrust experts
- On-Topics: 4 to 6 short papers on hot issues
- Law & Economics: Short papers written by economists for a legal audience
- Articles: Long academic papers
- Case Summaries: Case commentary on EU and French case law
- Legal Practice: Short papers for in-house counsels
- International: Medium size papers on international policies
- Books Review: Summaries of recent antitrust books
- Articles Review: Summaries of leading articles published in 45 antitrust journals

Boards

The Scientific Committee is headed by Laurence Idot, Professor at Panthéon Assas University. The International Committee is headed by Frederic Jenny, OECD Competition Comitteee Chairman. Boards members include Douglas Ginsburg, Bruno Lasserre, Howard Shelanski, Richard Whish, Wouter Wils, Joshua Wright, etc.

Online version

Concurrences website provides all articles published since its inception, in addition to selected articles published online only in the electronic supplement.

Write for Concurrences

Concurrences welcome spontaneous contributions. Except in rare circumstances, the journal accepts only unpublished articles, whatever the form and nature of the contribution. The Editorial Board checks the form of the proposals, and then submits these to the Scientific Committee. Selection of the papers is conditional to a peer review by at least two members of the Committee. Within a month, the Committee assesses whether the draft article can be published and notifies the author.

www.ingramcontent.com/pod-product-compliance
Lightning Source LLC
LaVergne TN
LVHW052252200926
848481LV00002B/349

* 9 7 8 1 9 5 4 7 5 0 1 3 5 *